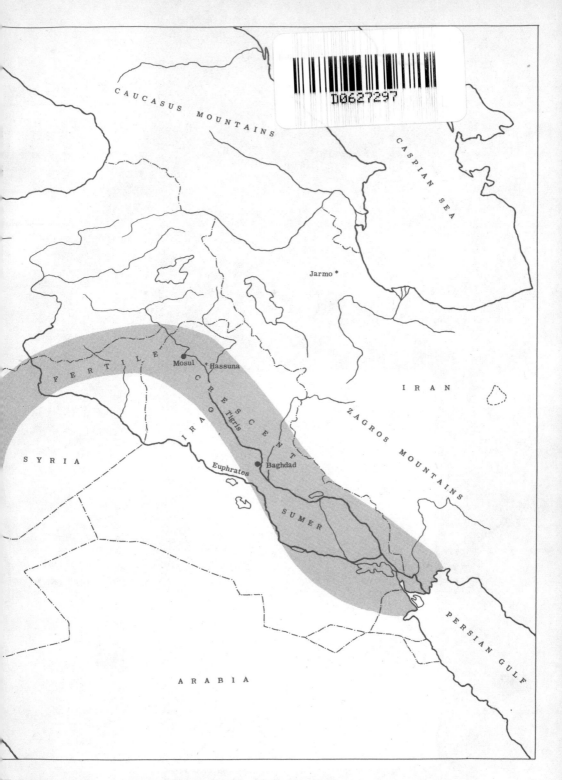

ZONE IN THE NEOLITHIC AGE

OF THE EARLIEST KNOWN NEOLITHIC CULTURES.

INTRODUCTION TO

CULTURAL ANTHROPOLOGY

MISCHA TITIEV

UNIVERSITY OF MICHIGAN

HENRY HOLT AND COMPANY, NEW YORK

28468-0219

Printed in the United States of America

This book is most affectionately dedicated to my sister and brothers, together with their spouses and families.

PREFACE

This book may be regarded, in some ways, as a companion volume to *The Science of Man*. Like the earlier work, it is addressed primarily to college students and other readers who have had no previous experience with anthropology; and it draws very heavily on the writings and ideas of American anthropologists.[1] Unlike its predecessor, it does not attempt to give equal weight to all branches of the subject, but, as the title indicates, it aims to provide an introduction to the vast and important field of cultural anthropology. Once again there has been no attempt to prepare an exhaustive encyclopedia or all-inclusive reference work, and every effort has been made to make this text useful and meaningful to unspecialized readers. No technical term is used without adequate definition, and a certain amount of repetition has been deliberately introduced to provide emphasis for important points. Once again, too, many topics are only lightly touched upon, in order to allow teachers to elaborate whatever they will. For the benefit of those who may wish to delve more deeply into some particular subject, a number of selected references have been appended to each chapter.

Anyone who takes the trouble to compare the present work with *The Science of Man* will find a few passages and illustrations the same, but *Introduction to Cultural Anthropology* contains a great

---

[1] America will often be used in this textbook to signify the United States of America.

deal of fresh material, some of which has never before been published. Only the central viewpoints remain unchanged. Encouraged by the success of his previous book, the author has tried to show once more that much of human behavior is a consequence of the perpetual blending of biological and cultural forces; and he has again attempted to demonstrate that all branches of anthropology form a coherent whole, with each subdivision making a vital contribution toward the total understanding of man. In keeping with these convictions the book offers brief synopses of human evolution and of man's attainments in the past before it turns to a full consideration of cultural anthropology.

Many persons have made direct or indirect contributions to this volume, but the writer alone is responsible for any faults or errors that it may contain. Preliminary outlines of the table of contents were sent to several of my fellow anthropologists: Professors Cora Dubois, Ward Goodenough, Robert Murphy, Hortense Powdermaker, Leslie Spier, and Julian Steward. Their comments were exceedingly valuable, and were gratefully received. Several of my colleagues, particularly Professor James N. Spuhler, as well as Professors James B. Griffin and Kenneth L. Pike, have been especially helpful, and I am deeply indebted to them for their full cooperation at all times. My thanks are also due to Mrs. Marie E. Braden, Mrs. A. June Crockett, Mr. Ralph E. Drischell, and Miss Cynthia Ellenport, who cheerfully typed and retyped various portions of the manuscript. Mrs. Braden and Miss Gaye L. La Guire prepared some of the line drawings for the book, and Mr. Robert E. Oyer was kind enough to proofread carefully most of the final typescript.

As always, I am everlastingly indebted to my wife for her critical comments and suggestions, as well as for her patient assistance in the arduous task of preparing the manuscript for publication.

M. T.

Ann Arbor, Michigan
August 29, 1958

CONTENTS

Contents

LIST OF ILLUSTRATIONS

Figure

Figure

Figure

Figure

Whenever I have studied human affairs, I have carefully labored not to mock, lament, nor condemn, but only to understand.
                                        —Spinoza
1676

CHAPTER 1

MAN: AN ANIMAL WITH CULTURE

A. THE SETTING

Anthropology, or the science of man, is used in this country as a single term that covers a number of related but highly distinctive subdisciplines. Each of the divisions has devised a specialized set of techniques, and each aims at a different target. All the divisions are held together, however, by a common interest in man, regardless of when, where, or in what form he happens to appear on earth. Thanks to this common interest, all anthropologists pursue the same over-all goal, for each of them hopes to make a significant contribution toward a better understanding of man's body or behavior.

At present it seems best to regard anthropology as a social science in the sense that its subject matter concerns aggregates of people who generally occupy a single region and share a common mode of life. Science, as most workers in the field have come to realize, implies not only techniques involving precision, control, objectivity, or reproducible experimentation, but also a search for universals that are repeated wherever identical conditions prevail. Once these universals are recognized, they provide the basis for accurate predictions; and it is the quest for universal forms of human structure or conduct that makes scientists of all anthropologists. Obviously, the more accurately one can predict a future course of events, the better can one plan ahead and establish controls. At the moment, social scientists can make more reliable predictions in general fields than in specific instances. To illustrate this point, let us take the question of **incest.** We may be sure, on the basis of what is already known, that even a hitherto undescribed society will be found to have some sort of **incest regulations** whereby certain relatives are forbidden to wed, but no one can know in advance exactly which relatives will be prohibited from mating.

Subject matter to a greater extent than differences of viewpoint or method separates the social scientist from other scientists. Even those anthropologists who deal with the physical attributes of the human body are more interested in the characteristics that prevail in such clusters of persons as make up a species, stock, or race, than they are in the details of a single individual's anatomy. The same is true of those who specialize in the study of human behavior. As a group, they are far less concerned with learning how and why one particular person acts as he does than they are in discovering and analyzing the repetitive or patterned ways in which numbers of people interact whenever they live together in societies. Students of man firmly believe that no member of *Homo sapiens* can develop into a properly functioning, normal human being unless he is given the opportunity of growing up among others of his kind. This clearly implies that to an individual who is destined to become a fully rounded person a society does not play a secondary role, but is just as fundamental as are limbs or eyes.

It was under the stimulus of Charles Darwin's writings on evolution that anthropology entered its modern phase. Before his time there had been a number of efforts to understand how man's body came into being, how it was constructed, and how it functioned, but on the whole so few facts were available and sacred dogmas were so thoroughly accepted that an objective and scientific study of man was almost impossible. In the light of what has happened since, it may seem hard to believe that Charles Darwin was a shy and religious man, who had little taste for stirring up a world-shaking controversy. Indeed, it is said that only after a good deal of persuasion on the part of his friends and colleagues did he decide to publish *The Origin of Species* in 1859. This book was followed in 1871 by *The Descent of Man.* Together, these works aroused an undying interest in man's origins and past history, and Darwin's unparalleled use of examples, coupled with his straightforward writing and calm reasoning from facts, resulted in a detached view of man's bodily construction and his evolution from earlier members of the animal kingdom. At the same time, Darwin's concepts of natural and sexual selection provided the first effective clues toward an understanding of the mechanisms by which the process of evolution worked.

In 1885, within the short span of 14 years following the appearance of *The Descent of Man,* anthropology was introduced into the curriculum of Harvard College. Soon after, Franz Boas began to teach the new subject at Clark University in Worcester, Massachusetts; and in 1892 that institution awarded the first American doctorate in anthropology to A. F. Chamberlin. By the turn of the present century many students who were destined to become outstanding American anthropologists studied for higher degrees, often under Boas, and a number of them are still active. The bulk of today's mature students of man belong only to the third or fourth generation since Darwin.

B. DEFINITIONS AND OBJECTIVES

Nowadays, large numbers of men and women in college are being trained to become professional anthropologists. As is to be expected, they respond to the pressure for specialization by concentrating on one or another of the many branches of the broad discipline. Such diversity is not a matter of whim but stems directly from a sophisticated awareness of the scope and complexity of the subject. Even a novice promptly discovers that *Homo sapiens,* in matters of biology, is clearly an animal whose physical body closely resembles that of many other animals. In other respects, such as in his development of clothing, houses, tools, language, religion, ethics, and esthetics, man differs from all other animals. He alone seems to have the ability and desire to practice those extrabiological forms of behavior that anthropologists call cultural.

On the basis of the fundamental distinction between human biology and human culture, at least three broad lines of investigation are currently being followed. All who specialize in problems pertaining to the evolution, shape, structure, appearance, functioning, and variations of the human body or any of its parts are grouped together under the heading of **physical anthropologists.** They frequently work as natural scientists, in conjunction with anatomists, physicians, dentists, primatologists, geneticists, and the whole range of investigators who may be called biologists. The principal objectives of physical anthropologists differ from those of their colleagues who are chiefly concerned with the various manifestations of culture. In turn, students of culture are divided into two broad categories. Those who deal with the remains of human handiwork in times past are known as **archeologists**; whereas those who are primarily interested in the behavior of groups of living men and women are variously described as **ethnographers, ethnologists, social anthropologists,** or **cultural anthropologists.**

By a sort of informal convention that has grown up gradually, archeologists are expected to deal with human affairs in any area of the world prior to the emergence of written documents at the spot under investigation. As specialists, they start with the first recognizable remains of human workmanship, known as **artifacts,** and carry forward the story of man's activities until writing appears. In practice, of course, many archeologists continue their studies well beyond the appearance of writing; but on the whole writing represents the point at which historians, linguists, humanists, and various other social scientists step in. To the extent that most of their efforts are devoted to the study of preliterate peoples and cultures, archeologists may properly be called prehistorians. At the same time, it must be realized that archeologists usually delve so far into the past that there are no representatives alive of the cultures they are investigating. Hence, it is also proper to refer to them as students of extinct cultures. The lack of perishable and nonmaterial items, as well as the absence of living informants, confronts archeologists with many severe obstacles that prevent them from presenting completely rounded accounts of ancient or extinct cultures; but were it not for their efforts, we would have no reliable information about the origins of culture and its subsequent developments in times prior to the emergence of written records.

There was a day, not so long ago, when some students of living mankind felt that their principal purpose was to provide full and accurate descriptions of particular cultures. They were known as ethnographers and used to be distinguished from ethnologists, whose main concern was to deal with processes, laws, and theories of culture in general. Today it is recognized that no large-scale theorizing about culture is likely to be valid unless it is based on familiarity with the details of many particular ways of life. As a result, the old division has practically disappeared, and to all intents and purposes modern ethnographers and ethnologists are one and the same. Then again, social anthropologists may emphasize the conduct of the various persons who comprise a society, and are sometimes set apart from cultural anthropologists, who may stress the patterns of behavior that people follow when they live together. The two factors are closely interrelated, but they are not necessarily identical. For example, an individual's social relationships are bound to change markedly at marriage, but his general way of life, including his place of residence, language, religion, and line of work, may remain relatively unchanged. On the other hand, a married man who has shifted his occupation from teaching to farming, let us say, would greatly alter his pattern of culture, but his social relationships might remain comparatively unchanged. Such cases make it altogether likely that something of value might be gained by classifying these approaches separately; but, since no human society exists without a patterned way of life or culture, and since no pattern of culture can exist without a society of men and women, the distinction between social and cultural anthropologists is sometimes impossible to maintain. For this reason, "culture" and "society" are occasionally used interchangeably, and ethnographers, ethnologists, and social anthropologists are treated together in this textbook under the heading of cultural anthropologists. All of them are students of the standardized forms of behavior that prevail wherever living groups of *Homo sapiens* dwell in societies.

At the present time, there is much concern in the profession about the proper placement of **linguists.** There are some who regard students of language as workers in a field that is as distinctive as physical anthropology and just as vital for an understanding of the totality of human behavior. Without denying the validity of such an assumption, others feel that **linguistics** should not be regarded as a separate discipline, but should be integrated with studies of culture and should be part of the equipment of every cultural anthropologist. It is toward this view that the writer inclines. In the last analysis, it is far less important to be able to delineate exact subdivisions of anthropology than it is to remember that the joint aim of all students of man is to acquire an understanding of the full range of body types and forms of behavior that are to be found among the members of *Homo sapiens*. Moreover, the growing realization that much of man's culture is intertwined with human biology (Fig. 1.1) serves to unite all specialists in the manifold aspects of physical and cultural anthropology as co-workers in one vast field.

An interesting sidelight helps to reveal the all-inclusive nature of anthropology. In the United States there are, among numerous others, three national foundations that have traditionally given financial support to investigators in particular fields. The American

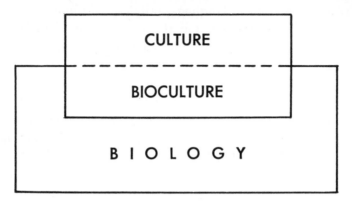

Fig. 1.1. Culture, bioculture, and biology. Although they operate according to different principles, human culture may be said to rest on a foundation of biology. There is also an area of man's behavior, designated as bioculture, in which the forces of culture interplay with the forces of biology.

Council of Learned Societies usually has underwritten projects that fall within the broad area of the humanities, including studies of language and history. The Social Science Research Council, as its name implies, has given assistance, for the most part, to students of human relations and behavior; and the National Research Council ordinarily has helped to further work in the natural and biological sciences. Anthropology is the only discipline that is represented on the boards of all three of these foundations.

C. HUMAN BIOLOGY: POSSIBILITIES AND LIMITATIONS

It has already been said that Man is unique in the development of extrabiological ways of acting and that he is the only animal to have devised and maintained systems of culture. Before we discuss the implications of this twofold manner of behaving, it may be worth-while to explain somewhat more precisely what is meant by the term, **human biology.** Without attempting to go into technical details, human biology may be said to comprise the entire corpus of what a newly conceived infant does or develops solely on the basis of whatever materials he gets from his parents through genetic inheritance. This refers to all the chemical and physical ingredients that enable a child to live, grow, and ultimately reproduce his kind. It includes all the initiating substances, in their proper arrangement and environment, that make up his gross anatomical structure, his entire cerebro-neuro-muscular system, and the complete range of his physiological organs, as well as their manner of working and interacting.

All of the nuclei for these body, or somatic, components are received by each child-to-be at the exact moment of conception, and at no other time, directly as the result of sexual intercourse on the part of the male and female who are becoming its parents. No other individual can, at this instant, introduce anything whatsoever for the about-to-be-formed embryo to acquire. At this stage, too, the ripe egg cell of the prospective mother can exercise nothing but some unknown biophysicochemical [1] choice in the selection of the genetic materials it is receiving from the sperm cell contributed by the father.

When a newly born child, or **neonate,** emerges from its mother's womb, it has no resources of its own for coping with life except for those things arising from the nuclear ingredients it has inherited. Taken by themselves, these are not enough to guarantee the successful formation of a human body. Interaction with a suitable physical environment is equally vital. Realistically speaking, insofar as human beings are concerned, neither the fertilization of an egg cell nor gestation can occur unless there is a suitable environment within a female's reproductive system. Moreover, a fertilized human egg is never self-sufficient and cannot possibly mature unless it can draw what it needs from its immediate setting. Inherited biological factors determine what elements a developing embryo will take from its intra-uterine environment and how this shall be done. Inherited biological factors will also delimit, at the very outset of postnatal life, what interactions a babe is going to establish with its new, external environment.

There is very little in the realm of sheer biological behavior to differentiate a member of *Homo sapiens* from an individual belong-

---

[1] For the sake of convenience, the single word, biology, will frequently be used interchangeably with the compound term, biophysicochemical.

ing to many other species of **mammals,** particularly to the large
Primates such as **orangutans, chimpanzees,** and **gorillas.** Given a
favorable environment, human beings can carry on a wide range
of activities with nothing but their inherited, genetically determined, biological equipment, inadequate though it may be in some
regards. By way of illustration, we have but to consider the life
habits of the earliest **hominids.** No one alive knows exactly how
the very first manlike creatures, presumably lacking all cultural
devices, actually lived, but assuming that their bodies were constituted much like ours, it may be instructive to try to imagine what
they did.

As a guess, it may be supposed that their lives were adjusted to
meet the needs, exclusively, of the biological world. Involuntarily,
their lungs took in oxygen, their hearts pumped blood, and their
body temperatures normally remained at a constantly high level.
Whenever they exerted themselves, they breathed harder than usual
and felt tired; when they were cold, their teeth chattered and their
bodies shivered; when they were hot, they sweated; and whenever
they grew sufficiently weary, they rested or slept. If their stomachs
contracted, they felt hunger pangs and sought to put food into their
mouths, where it was moistened, chewed, and swallowed into the
digestive tract. When there was pressure on the bladder, they
urinated, and when their bowels were full, they defecated.

Male bodies were organized to form sperm cells in the testes and
female bodies to produce egg cells in the ovaries. From time to time
their genital organs were stimulated and they engaged in copulation. If fertilization followed, the female's menstrual periods were
suspended and an embryo formed within her body, where it was
nourished through a gestation of about nine months by means of a
placental arrangement. After giving birth to her child, the female
discharged the placental mechanism from her body as the afterbirth, suckled the baby, and aided it in many ways until it reached
a stage where it could shift for itself. As years passed, the bodies of
males and females became subject to some fatal accident or disease,
or else grew old and deteriorated. Then death came to terminate
the biological aspects of their behavior, and the corpses decom-
posed in response to fixed laws of chemistry and physics.

This is essentially the behavior of any placental, or **eutherian,**
mammal, even when it applies to hominids. Within the limits mentioned, **e**very mechanism for action is biogenetically inherited and

developed, and every response is biologically directed and controlled. Had man continued to live in such fashion, his way of life
would have been virtually indistinguishable from that of other large
Primates.

For all that human beings can do in a favorable environment
with no other resources than those genetically inherited from their
parents, man's biology, as it has presumably functioned for thousands of years, is woefully inadequate, under unfavorable conditions, even for such fundamental purposes as keeping people alive
and giving them a chance to reproduce their kind. Human infants
are notoriously helpless at birth and have no biological means of
getting nourishment unaided; nor are they equipped with any
means of distinguishing palatable from unpalatable or even poisonous substances. Left to themselves, human babies would soon die
of starvation or poisoning. Once again we see how essential other
people are to the very existence of a newly born child.

Even adults are unfit to cope with such things as winter weather.
We speak of ourselves as being **warm-blooded,** and we sometimes
dwell on our possession of various mammalian devices, such as
shivering and the contraction of blood vessels, that help us to resist
cold. But the sad truth is that all of us would quickly freeze to
death in very cold weather if we had nothing to rely on but biologically inherited mechanisms for remaining warm.

Here, then, human beings and other animals come to a parting
of the ways. Other creatures, when faced with a problem that their
inherited biology cannot solve, must somehow change their biological mechanisms before they become extinct. Man, and man
only, when he finds his biology inadequate, escapes extinction not
by readjusting his biology but by turning to an entirely different
kind of behavior. This is what underlies the nonbiologic or extrasomatic form of activity that anthropologists call cultural. Only on
the rarest of occasions, within the past thousands of years, have
human beings changed their biologies when challenged by drastic
changes of environment or other factors that seriously threatened
their abilities to survive. Instead, they have again and again met
challenges by altering their cultures. It has been the diversity of
his cultural mechanisms that has enabled *Homo sapiens,* as a single
species, to dwell in any environment on earth and to outlive many
other animal groups that once seemed more capable of survival.

Man's unique ability to act nonbiologically makes the task of the cultural anthropologist all the harder in at least one fundamental respect. Students of nonhuman animals can make reasonably sound predictions of behavior from a close study of body form. Tooth structures reveal a great deal about eating habits to informed zoologists, fins and gills imply life in the water, and wings suggest flight. In the case of man, however, essentially the same anatomical parts are found throughout the whole range of *Homo sapiens,* but they give no clue whatsoever to those aspects of behavior that are culturally prescribed. Everyone knows that it is not differences of biological construction which determine if an individual is going to eat with spoon and fork or with chopsticks (see Fig. 1.2). To find the repetitive universals of cultural behavior that underlie such variations of detail is no easy matter. One does not have to be a genius to foretell, even with respect to a society that he has never seen, that each normal adult will have two eyes, a nose, and so forth, or that only females will bear and suckle offspring; but not even a genius can tell ahead of time whether the men in an unknown society will be hunters, fishermen, or farmers. The biologic

A   B

Fig. 1.2. Culture and biology. The distinctions of eating techniques between the Korean girl (A), who is using chopsticks, and the Fijian boy (B), who is using a spoon, are due to cultural rather than biological differences. (A. From Arthur Goodfriend, *Something Is Missing.* Farrar, Straus, and Young (Cudahy), New York, 1955. B. Courtesy of British Information Services.)

features of human conduct are much less variable than the cultural ones, and that is why sounder predictions can be made in the realm of man's biology than in the field of his culture.

D. SOME ESSENTIAL ATTRIBUTES OF CULTURE

The term culture can be used in at least two different senses. It may refer to the nonbiological aspects of mankind as a whole, or it may pertain only to the way of life of one particular group of men and women. In either case anthropologists use it to describe the entire range of man's nongenetically acquired implements, as well as all facets of his postnatally learned behavior. There is not a single respect in which culture fails to differ from human biology. Culture is not composed only of biophysicochemical ingredients; it is not passed along by sexual intercourse; it is not transmitted at a single moment of time; it is not received only from the two people who are becoming one's parents; and, in theory, it does not have to be retained for life but can be modified or dropped at the will of an individual. For practical reasons, human beings seldom volunteer to make radical changes in the cultures they learn from their mentors, but surely it cannot be denied that theoretically it is easier to change one's language or religion than the shape of one's head or the color of one's eyes.

Because man's culture and biology differ in every essential regard, and because they operate according to totally different principles, it is not surprising that they should sometimes have different aims or standards of values. Thus, it can be said with assurance that when *Homo sapiens* began to develop cultural behavior, he began to abide by some new and nonbiologic concepts of values. Now, human beings no longer considered it proper to breathe, eat, drink, excrete, or reproduce simply in conformity to the requirements and dictates of biology. Instead, each society differentiated culturally right from wrong ways of fulfilling these functions, and so laid the basis for a moral or ethical code. Breathing is everywhere a biological necessity for man, but in our culture it is considered improper to rush into a room for an important interview while one is gasping for breath. Among us, too, biological pangs of hunger do not justify the theft of food, nor does a compelling sexual urge excuse rape. An indefinite number of teachers contribute to a neonate's education along the lines of cultural values, and it takes a long while for a child to learn all of the approved and disapproved ways of conduct that prevail in his society. Moreover, the process of **enculturation** [2] is by no means easy, for it compels each infant to adjust his innate, biologically determined ways of behaving to the established cultural practices of his group. There are good grounds for believing that the length and difficulty of the process of adjustment are the basic factors that prevent all but the most persevering from readily changing whatever forms of culture were learned in youth.

Human societies are the only groups in the entire animal kingdom to have devised forms of culture that exert powerful modifying influences on the inherited mechanisms of their individual members. Sometimes the biologic and cultural elements coincide or reinforce each other in seeking the same objective; sometimes they have no effect on one another; and sometimes they actually clash or oppose each other. So it is that if a pattern of culture calls for the wearing of a sweater in cold weather, the culture trait is "logical" in so far as it helps the wearer to conserve his body heat as a biological necessity. On the other hand, if a wearer feels that a dark color is preferable to a light color in an otherwise identical sweater, the cultural preference for the dark sweater is "nonlogical," since it neither helps nor retards the workings of biology. But, should a way of life forbid the wearing of sweaters or similar covers in cold weather, the refusal to wear a sweater, where one was available, would be "illogical" because it opposed the biological welfare of the potential wearer.[3]

The possibility of such "illogical" behavior makes it no easy matter to live like a human being. Yet, mankind everywhere takes pride in the cultural structures that it has reared, and wherever the values of biology and culture clash, man is likely to give preference to the cultural, just short of the point where it may cause the extinction of individuals or societies. In fact, the English-speaking

---

[2] The anthropological meaning and use of this term may be found in M. J. Herskovits, *Man and His Works*, New York, 1948, pp. 40-41. In general, it refers to the process whereby a neonate is taught the cultural ways that his society expects him to follow.

[3] Words like "logic" can have a host of meanings in English. Moreover, a comparative analysis of various cultures reveals an amazing variety of "logical" systems. To an American Christian, the wearing of shoes may have no "logical" connection with Christianity. To a group of barefooted, pagan natives, however, among whom a Christian missionary family was the only one to wear shoes, it might appear perfectly "logical" to connect Christianity with the wearing of shoes.

world often expresses contempt by making slighting references to cultureless creatures. How often, when we want to insult someone, do we resort to the names of animals. A list like "Louse!" "Crab!" "Skunk!" "Rat!" and "Pig!" can be extended indefinitely, and seems to express a feeling that beasts which lack culture are somehow objects of contempt. Denizens of the primitive world also show their distaste for nonhuman creatures in numerous ways. Sometimes they knock out teeth to make themselves look different from other members of the animal kingdom; sometimes they pluck face and body hair to emphasize their unique humanity; and occasionally they blacken teeth because "white teeth are no better than a dog's." [4]

At this point we are led to seek the reasons for man's universal willingness to run the danger of glorifying culture at the possible risk of clashing with biology. "Why," it may well be asked, "is *Homo sapiens* unwilling to live according to the dictates of biology, as do most other species of animals?"

It would be a mistake to think that man has developed culture out of sheer whimsey. He has gained many real advantages from his extrabiological devices. Of these, none is more important than flexibility in coping with his external environment. While all mammals have some biological means of keeping warm, only human beings can fashion houses, heating devices, or clothing that provide a great variety of cultural ways of keeping warm. Furthermore, should a cold climate turn hot, as has occasionally happened in times past, or should a society of human beings happen to migrate from the Arctic to the Equator, men and women have it within their control to shut off their heating devices or to give up the wearing of heavy garments. Other creatures, which might have made biological adjustments to cold, lack man's flexibility and face extinction whenever their environments are radically altered.

Another important advantage of culture is the manner in which it can bolster biological weakness or, to a limited extent, do the work of biology. Before culture had achieved much efficiency, man had no way of making palatable foods that were unfit to eat in their natural state; if he wished to get to a distant spot in a hurry, he had no recourse but to run or be carried by others; if he wanted to shatter something, he had to depend primarily on his muscular

---

[4] W. H. Furness III, *The Home-Life of Borneo Head-hunters*, Philadelphia, 1902, p. 157.

strength; if his eyes began to fail, he had to become reconciled to dim vision or blindness; and if a woman could not be delivered normally of a baby she was practically doomed to die in childbirth. Today, each of these matters can be handled differently. Cooking and other methods of preparing food make many things fit to eat that were previously unsuited for human consumption; people who are in a hurry to get to distant places employ all kinds of vehicles, instead of running or being carried by other humans; many power-driven contrivances or explosives are used for shattering hard substances; corrective glasses give excellent vision to people whose eyesight is biologically poor; and modern obstetricians, with the aid of instruments and surgery, regularly deliver women who would otherwise die.

On the other hand, there are situations wherein culture retards the workings of sound biology. This is the case whenever religious regulations forbid hungry people to eat specific nutritious foods or whenever cultural conventions prohibit individuals from eating some of the edible substances to be found in their environment. Man is thus the only creature in the animal kingdom who can go hungry in the midst of biological plenty. Cultural factors usually strike some sort of balance with biological necessities, but it is dangerous to overlook the fact that biology can exist without culture, whereas culture cannot exist without biology. A social scientist should never allow himself to forget that no cultural device has yet been perfected that can completely take the place of biology. Not even the best of eyeglasses can give sight to a person lacking an optic nerve; nor can the finest of iron lungs make a corpse breathe. True enough, there have been times in the history of mankind when it was the fashion to belittle things of the body and to pretend that man was not bound to observe the laws of biology, but deep down we know that such conventions did not express the truth, for men and women could not have lived and maintained societies had they refused to breathe, eat, drink, digest, excrete, and reproduce according to biological principles.

E. BIOCULTURAL BEHAVIOR: THE PRODUCT OF BIOLOGIC AND CULTURAL FORCES

Few words in English are harder to define precisely than "force." Yet, an effort at definition must be made if we are to proceed fruitfully. As it will be used in this book, a "force" may be understood to be anything that impels an action which produces an important change. All animals respond to the forces of chemistry, physics, and biology; but mankind has the additional responsibility of responding to cultural forces. In the present state of our knowledge, all of these forces seem to fall into two divisions: those that originate in the biophysicochemical realm, and those that are of cultural origin.

On this basis there are four possible combinations of stimuli and responses. Sometimes (a) both the stimulus and the response fall within the field of inherited biological factors. One example might be that of an itch which develops within the body and is alleviated by scratching with one's own fingernails. Even here culture may play an important, if secondary part, by stipulating the conditions under which it is proper or improper to scratch oneself. Sometimes (b) the stimulus to action may originate in culture but induce a biological response, as when an individual gets so angry because he has been called a vile name that his adrenalin output is increased. Into this category, too, fall such matters as eating schedules. Anthropologists well know that these are generally determined by one's culture. In popular dining rooms in the United States it is usually easy to find a seat at a quarter before noon, but it is virtually impossible to find an empty place at a quarter past noon. Surely one would have to be very naive to believe that all the diners felt biologically hungry at the same time, except as secondary responses to cultural conditioning.

By way of contrast, (c) some stimuli arise in man's biology but express themselves in culturally determined ways. Thus, a person may feel sexually desirous as a result of biophysicochemical activities within his body, but he may suppress these desires out of deference to cultural values; or else, he may limit all his sexual activities to marital relationships with a legal, socially sanctioned mate. Similarly, biological signals might indicate to an individual that his bladder was full and that he ought to urinate, but in our society a person would wait for culturally approved conditions before relieving himself.

There is also a fourth kind of human behavior (d) in which both the initiating impulse and the response are determined by culture. For example, American males tip their hats when they meet a female acquaintance. In such cases, be it noted, even where the initia-

A

Fig. 1.3. Biocultural behavior. With practically the same anatomical equipment, a young Australian woman wields a digging stick (A) and a concert pianist plays the piano (B). In each case biogenetically inherited mechanisms are being used in ways dictated by culture, to produce biocultural behavior. (A. From H. Basedow, *The Australian Aboriginal.* Adelaide, 1925. Courtesy F. W. Preece. B. Courtesy Eck Stanger, *The Ann Arbor News.*)

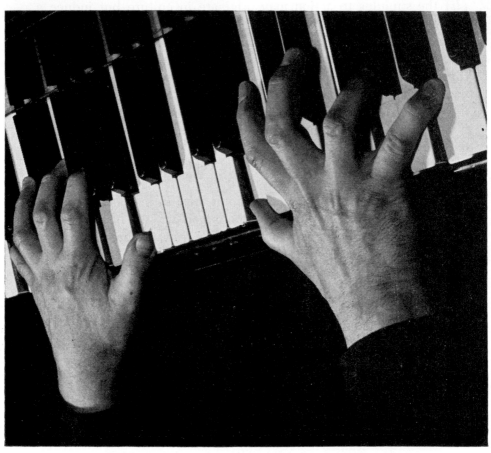

B

tion of an action and the response take place entirely within a cultural circuit, body mechanisms are brought into play, for without their help no man could possibly tip his hat.

In each of the four types of activity just listed, we find that some aspects of culture intertwine with some features of biology. This accords with anthropological observations, made in all sectors of the globe, that the vast majority of voluntary actions [5] performed by human beings are the blended products of two different forces that operate simultaneously to produce a single activity. Whenever an individual manufactures a stone tool, digs edible roots with a pointed stick, plays the piano (Fig. 1.3), makes a speech, knots a necktie, hits a tennis ball, milks a cow, or drives an automobile, he employs some genetically inherited body parts in certain ways and for particular purposes that are determined by the culture of his society. For this entire category of human activity I propose to use the phrase "**biocultural behavior.**"

To some extent the dichotomy between biology and culture has long been recognized, as the old arguments over nature or nurture imply, but today it is more than ever necessary to define each of these factors as accurately as possible, particularly if one is interested in trying to solve pressing social problems. If one is concerned about a sterile couple, for instance, biological correctives will have to be applied if the failure to have offspring arises from biological causes. If, however, to cite a far-fetched, hypothetical situation, the failure to have children results from a cultural convention that prevents a married couple from having sexual intercourse, then the remedy will have to involve a change of culture.

Along these lines, all residents of the United States of America are aware of the existence of certain difficulties that are lumped together under the heading of "race problems." Here again do we find a practical need for distinguishing accurately between biology and culture. Should the failure of diverse races to live together harmoniously prove, on close study, to stem from biology, the solution would have to be attempted by biological techniques. But if the difficulties turn out to be cultural, their solution will have to be found in the field of culture. On this particular score, enough is

---

[5] As it is used here, "voluntary" refers to any aspect of human behavior that calls for a measure of conscious control. It is used in contrast to such involuntary actions as breathing or the beating of the heart, which may be carried on without any conscious control at all.

already known to make it a virtual certainty that race problems are cultural in nature and can never, accordingly, be solved by recourse to biological correctives.

At least as important as the accurate definition of the two basic ingredients that make up practically the entire range of human activity is the clear recognition of the fact that, where mankind is concerned, biology and culture seldom operate separately and independently, but are much more likely to interact (see, once more, Fig. 1.1). To acquire an understanding of how these forces interplay is part of the province of the cultural anthropologist.

F. WHEREIN CULTURAL ANTHROPOLOGY DIFFERS FROM OTHER SOCIAL SCIENCES

Human behavior is so complicated and variable that it may be studied in a great number of ways, depending on which elements are selected for emphasis and which are played down. Underlying the various approaches is the basic fact that we could not behave as human beings unless we interacted, at least on occasion, with other members of our species. One sometimes hears of prisoners in solitary confinement or of hermits who refuse to have contact with their fellows but it must be admitted that such individuals constitute only a tiny minority of our total number, and that even they had dealings with other men and women before they were imprisoned or withdrew.

Although all cultural anthropologists are social scientists, their preliminary training in general anthropology serves to mark them apart from their colleagues in related disciplines. The field of anthropology has grown so vast and diversified that no one can truthfully claim to know all the details of its manifold subdivisions. Nevertheless, students are expected to master the broad principles of anthropology before they begin to specialize. There is an analogy in this regard with the study of medicine. No one is permitted to become a specialist in one aspect of medical practice until after he has received a thorough grounding in general medicine. So it is with the cultural anthropologist. Not until he has demonstrated some grasp of the entire field is he permitted to concentrate on the specialty of his choice.

As a result of such a program, a cultural anthropologist acquires a distinctive viewpoint. This does not mean that other social scientists ignore the matters that concern him. Sometimes the only real distinction is a matter of emphasis or of degree, rather than of kind. While there are subtle differences between cultural anthropologists and other students of human behavior, it is best to regard all social scientists as engaged in a cooperative effort to acquire an ever greater understanding of man and his conduct.

One of the attributes that serves to distinguish the cultural anthropologist is his knowledge of archeology. Not only should he have a detailed grasp of man's activities from the time of the first appearance of hominids on the face of the earth, but he should also gain an idea of the sequence in which various traits of culture were developed and of the varieties which patterns of culture exhibit in different areas of the world. Above all, he should devote his thoughts to the discernment of whatever universal processes may underlie the evolutionary progress of all human culture as one stage grows out of another.

Equally distinctive is the cultural anthropologist's concern with all the manifestations of behavior shown by members of *Homo sapiens,* regardless of race, place of residence, or degree of development when compared to the customs of Western societies. To the cultural anthropologist, primitive peoples are not second-class citizens of mankind, and their activities are as much grist for his mill as are the activities of nonprimitive societies. It is not at all an exaggeration to say that the behavior of all human beings is the object of his studies. In every conceivable way the cultural anthropologist strives to overcome the outlooks that he learned in his own culture, and to call him **ethnocentric,** or unable to see things except in terms of his own particular culture, is to hurt him to the quick. His principal aim is to understand the customs of primitive men and women, not to judge or change them.

Up to now the universities that train cultural anthropologists have generally insisted that each student should make at least one field trip before he is granted the doctorate. As a rule, this means that an advanced student must go to live among a people, usually a primitive group, whose ways of life are quite different from his own. Such an experience has a profound effect on everyone who has gone through it.

A modern cultural anthropologist is trained to view a pattern of culture as a composite of mutually interacting and interrelated parts. He does not look upon economic activities, for example, as entirely

separate from social conventions or religious practices. Anthropologists have learned that even the introduction to a society of a new
and helpful technological device may have tremendous repercus-
sions on every aspect of a group's way of life. Cultural anthropologists do not pretend to know the fine details of political science,
economics, and all the other disciplines that deal with human affairs;
and they cannot always demonstrate just how the various parts of
culture patterns affect each other; but the constant search for relationships gives their work a distinctive quality.

Worthy of the most careful consideration in this connection are
the words of Professor Lauriston Sharp of Cornell regarding the
Yir Yoront, a primitive tribe of Australian aborigines. Professor
Sharp was making an extensive field trip among the Yir Yoront
when steel axes were replacing axes of stone. According to him, the
most disturbing effect of the steel ax was felt not in the field of
technology but in the realm of traditional ideas and values.[6]

Regardless of his own special interests, every cultural anthropologist must learn never to disregard the biological forces that play so
fundamental a part in shaping much of man's conduct. So little of
his basic biology is truly unique to *Homo sapiens* and so much, apparently, was bequeathed to him by animal forerunners that it
behooves each anthropologist to know as well as he can the story
of organic evolution.

Most of the data on which the framework of the evolutionary
hypothesis rests are currently studied by **geologists,** who investigate the earth's history, and by **paleontologists,** who concentrate on
the remains of ancient forms of life, practically all of which are now
extinct, which are popularly termed **fossils.** These two groups of
men work together because remnants of ancient organisms are frequently found embedded in the mud and ooze which formed many
old rocks and layers of earth. These scientists have furnished us with
a chronological scale that serves as an approximate timetable of the
events in which students of man's beginnings are keenly interested
(see Fig. 1.4). Since the soil layers containing remains that come
ever closer to human configurations are, in many cases, piled above
those which hold relics far removed from *Homo sapiens,* students
have fallen into the habit of using phrases like "higher evolution" to
apply to those creatures that most resemble man.

---

[6] The case of the Yir Yoront is discussed by Professor Sharp in *Human Problems
in Technological Change,* E. H. Spicer, ed., New York, 1952, pp. 85-86.

ERA	EPOCH	APPROXIMATE BEGINNING DATE	MAJOR ANIMAL GROUP
Azoic		2,000,000,000 B.C.	None
Archeozoic		1,500,000,000 B.C.	Protozoa
Proterozoic		1,000,000,000 B.C.	Metazoan Invertebrates
Paleozoic		500,000,000 B.C.	Fishes and
	Devonian	350,000,000 B.C.	Amphibians
Mesozoic		200,000,000 B.C.	Reptiles
	Paleocene	70,000,000 B.C.	Insectivora
	Eocene	60,000,000 B.C.	Lemurs and Tarsiers
	Oligocene	40,000,000 B.C.	Monkeys
Cenozoic	Miocene	30,000,000 B.C.	Apes
	Pliocene	13,000,000 B.C.	Man-apes?
	Pleistocene	1,000,000 B.C.	Extinct Hominids
	Holocene	20,000 B.C.	*Homo sapiens*

Fig. 1.4. Geological time-table of organic evolution. A complete list of epochs is given for the Cenozoic era only.

The very earliest rocks known on earth, dating back some two billion years or more before our time, are called **Azoic,** which means that they are literally "without life." Thereafter, successively higher layers of rock are named in the order in which they are supposed to have appeared: **Archeozoic** ("ancient life"), **Proterozoic** ("former life"), **Paleozoic** ("old life"), **Mesozoic** ("middle life"), and **Cenozoic** ("recent life"). These six great eras, and the fossils which the later five contain, yield the evidence on which the theory of evolution is based.

There can be no denying the fact that biology must precede culture in every instance. It is earlier with respect to the beginnings of all hominid life, whether we are dealing with the entire species or with single individuals. Where the species is concerned, scientists can trace the biological predecessors of *Homo sapiens* for about one and one-half billion years before the first recognizable signs of culture appear; and as far as individuals go, no shred of culture can reach them until postnatal life has begun, unless the cultural factor has first been transmuted into biologic form within a mother's body (see (*b*) on p. 15). Because of its priority, we shall turn next to a consideration of human biology as its development is revealed in the story of evolution. Inasmuch as our principal concern is with *Homo sapiens*, we shall move incompletely and irregularly over much of the material, spending more time on the organisms closest to man and omitting entirely such important but collateral groups as plants, insects, and birds.

SELECTED REFERENCES

Boas, F., *et al.*, *General Anthropology*, "Introduction." Boston, 1938.
Daniel, G. E., *A Hundred Years of Archaeology*. London, 1950.
Haddon, A. C., *History of Anthropology*, rev. ed. London, 1934.
Kluckhohn, C., "Cultural Anthropology," in *Frontiers of Knowledge in the Study of Man*, L. White, Jr., ed. New York, 1956, pp. 33-47.
Linton, R., "The Scope and Aims of Anthropology," in *The Science of Man in the World Crisis*, R. Linton, ed. New York, 1945.
Lowie, R. H., *The History of Ethnological Theory*. New York, 1937.
Mitra, P., *A History of American Anthropology*. Calcutta, 1933.
Montagu, M. F. Ashley, *An Introduction to Physical Anthropology*, rev. ed. "Introduction." Springfield, Mass., 1951.
Penniman, T. K., *A Hundred Years of Anthropology*. New York, 1935.
Sears, P. B., *Charles Darwin: The Naturalist as a Cultural Force*. New York, 1950.
Spencer, R. F., ed., *Method and Perspective in Anthropology*. St. Paul, Minn., 1954.
Titiev, M., *The Science of Man*, "Preface" and "Introduction." New York, 1954.
Voegelin, E. W., "Anthropology in American Universities," *American Anthropologist*, Vol. 52, No. 3, 1950.

CHAPTER 2

MAN'S FORERUNNERS,
FROM SEA TO TREE

A. THE EMERGENCE OF LIFE

In the beginning there were chemical elements. No one knows where they came from nor how they came to have their distinctive properties, but once formed they were endowed with particular ways of acting and reacting that were changeless and have so continued for all time. Chemical substances have no choice but to act in fixed ways, and these activities remain the same whether the elements are found in the ground, in the atmosphere, in water, in bottles on drugstore or laboratory shelves, or in·human bodies.

In the beginning, too, there was space in which the chemical elements were distributed. Some were higher than others, in front, or to the right or left. Physical forces such as gravity, attraction, and repulsion also seem to have been active at the outset, for the chemical elements were not fixed permanently in space. Instead, some moved in the direction of others, and once in a while they came so close together that they touched. Whenever this happened, each of the elements reacted in some way and changes of internal composition were sometimes brought about. In due time a great number of chemical elements were drawn into close proximity and found themselves comprising the sun, and that is where the story of the earth may be said to begin.

There are still many unsolved problems pertaining to our globe's formation, but astronomers, geologists, physicists, biochemists, and other scientists have pooled their knowledge to provide us with a plausible starting point. All clues lead back to the sun as the parent of the world we inhabit. About four billion years ago, by one means or another, a stupendous mass of solar material, containing great quantities of superheated chemical elements in gaseous form, became detached from the sun. When this vast cloud had cooled somewhat, it became the planet that we call "Earth."

For an incredibly long time, perhaps as long as two or three billion years, the solar ingredients of which the earth was formed remained lifeless. But this is not to say that they were motionless. Quite the contrary! Whenever temperatures fluctuated, or moisture came and went, or winds blew, or waters flowed, or whenever altitudes differed because hills and mountains were uplifted, numerous chemical elements underwent many changes. Subjected to the shifting pressures of various physical forces, a great number of chemicals changed position, shape, or internal structure, and some new combinations, with previously unknown properties, came into being. Of these new substances, the most important for our purposes was **protein,** a complex material consisting mainly of certain forms of carbon, hydrogen, oxygen, and nitrogen, together with small amounts of other substances.

With the formation of protein the stage was set for the emergence of living matter, but up to this point, it must be emphasized, the highest level of structure was physical or chemical and all responses were dictated exclusively by physicochemical laws. That is to say, the basic chemical elements on earth made changes and adjustments only when influenced by factors like heat, light, humidity, magnetism, atmospheric and other pressures, gravity, radioactivity, natural electricity, and wind or water action.

At the level of physicochemical behavior there is no emotion, no volition, and no sharp distinction between life and death. Whatever may be thought to correspond to processes of growth and reproduction must be understood to represent nothing more than mechanical responses or physicochemical interactions. These are so fixed and standardized that a scientist thoroughly familiar with the laws of chemistry and physics can predict with mathematical accuracy how a particular element will respond under given conditions. That is why scholars who deal only with this realm are able to achieve a degree of certainty and exactness which gradually diminishes as the capacity for voluntary action increases.

About one and one-half billion years ago, certain chemical elements, including minute quantities of potassium, sodium, iron, copper, chlorine, bromine, and other ingredients, somehow combined with protein to form **protoplasm,** which is the key material out of which the bodies of all plants and animals are made. Protoplasm is a highly variable substance, but it exhibits without fail certain characteristics that set it apart from any known combination of nonliving elements. Under one set of conditions protoplasm acts alive, but under another it becomes dead, which signifies that it has reverted to the ingredients of which it is composed and is once more responsive only to physiochemical laws.

From the time of its initial formation to the present, man's body has been made up of protoplasm. Furthermore, man's body has also been an exceedingly subtle and complex manufacturer of chemical substances. Products made by the ductless glandular system, generally known as **hormones,** unquestionably play a great part in man's physical development as well as in the formation of his temperament or personality. Yet, there is some question of the value, even if it could be done, of trying to interpret all of human behavior in terms of chemical and physical laws. One must always face the possibility that even if this were adequately done, it might have little more worth than reducing a Beethoven symphony to its component sound waves or analyzing an Ibsen play in terms of the chemical composition of his manuscripts.

B. OBEY OR DIE

All living things can remain alive only so long as they are able satisfactorily to observe a set of regulations that may conveniently be labeled **biological imperatives.** As a minimum, these require the regular replenishment of some of the component chemical ingredients that every living thing exhausts while maintaining the life process. Chief of these are oxygen, minerals, and vitamins, all of which can be obtained from air, water, or food. As it happens, protoplasm is never self-sufficient in supplying its own requirements for maintaining life, nor can it store enough to supply its wants for the entire range of its normal existence.[1] Hence, all plants and animals must, from time to time, get what they need from their external setting or physical environment. In order to accomplish this, they have to have at least a tiny potential, much more evident in most animals than in plants, for self-initiated or voluntary movement, a potential that is entirely lacking in lifeless chemicals. One of the most important aspects of any animal's capacity for self-initiated motion is its ability to move away from a stimulus that irritates or endangers it and to move toward anything that it somehow interprets as favorable. This points to the existence of a nervous system which, in the earliest forms of life, is thought to have been diffused throughout the entire organism.

After the emergence of protoplasm, it becomes possible to speak of a higher level of organization than had existed in the lifeless world. For the new substance had to continue to observe the laws of physics and chemistry, in addition to satisfying the requirements of the biological imperatives. We are thus brought into a realm that may be designated as biophysicochemical. Workers in this field cannot achieve the mathematical accuracy of knowledge and prediction that is possible for chemists and physicists, because even the smallest exercise of self-initiated activity cannot, at present, be mechanically anticipated. The merest fleck of animal protoplasm occasionally thrusts a bit of itself away from the main body as it reacts to a stimulus or seeks nourishment, and there is no way of foretelling exactly when it will act or whether its thrust will be to the left or right.

All living things, including human beings, are subject to the regulations of biophysicochemical laws. Men, it is true, have everywhere developed cultural systems that greatly affect their responses to the biological imperatives. Thus, the bodies of all healthy human beings of the same sex, age, height, and weight require just about identical amounts of protein to be consumed at intervals. But culture may dictate whether the protein shall be in the form of beef or fish, as well as all the details concerning how and when it should be prepared and eaten. Regardless of differences in culture patterns,

---

[1] In some scientific circles, "normal" is used to describe an expected or recognized occurrence of something in 90 to 95 percent of the cases under study. However, since adequate figures are often lacking, "normal" is frequently used to mean average, ordinarily expected, or customary.

though, man can completely disobey biological imperatives only at the price of death.

In the case of *Homo sapiens,* disregard of the various biological imperatives does not inevitably carry the same degree of weight. A human being deprived of fresh oxygen will faint or die in a matter of minutes, but he may live for several days without water and for many weeks without solid foods. As for reproduction, cases are known where an adult lives out a full life without engaging in any form of sexual activity whatsoever. It is quite another thing, however, to abstain from the consumption of oxygen, food, or drink.

C. ANIMAL LIFE IN THE SEA

From the outset, protoplasm seems to have been organized into tiny units known as cells. Biologists believe that a single cell once sufficed to constitute an entire little animal known as a **protozoan.** In such an animal all the activities of breathing, eating, digesting, excreting, moving, and reproducing had to be performed by the one cell of which it was composed—a cell that must have been a marvelous jack-of-all-biological-trades. Not all scientists are agreed on the environmental setting in which **protozoan** creatures first appeared, but a clear majority favors areas of slightly salty water, not too far from a shore line. They point out that in the shallow part of a sea or ocean a microscopic one-celled animal, most of whose body consists of water, would avoid the dangers of being either dehydrated or crushed by excessive pressure. Basins of salt-water formations are also in less danger of running dry than are bodies of fresh water, are less subject to extremes of temperature, have a greater buoyancy, and contain all the elements needed for building and maintaining protoplasm. Oceans and seas are constantly in motion, so that they continually waft sources of food and oxygen to their protozoan inhabitants and carry away whatever wastes are excreted. Those who favor the hypothesis of salt-water origin add to these facts the observation that body fluids, including the famous trilogy of blood, sweat, and tears, are saline. Some scholars have even gone so far as to say that man's blood plasma is identical with archaic sea water.

When it is studied under a microscope, each cell that makes up a protozoan can be seen to consist of several different parts, of which the most distinctive is called the **nucleus.** Within the nucleus are minute grains of solid matter that can be dyed and are therefore known as **chromatin.** Chromatin is arranged in a fixed number of elongated bodies, or **chromosomes.** When a protozoan reaches a particular stage of growth, its chromosomes cluster in its exact center and are split evenly in two as the cell divides, with one full portion going to make up the nucleus of a daughter cell and the corresponding other half remaining with the parent.

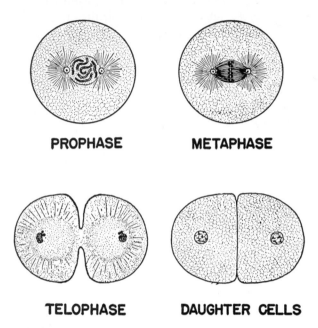

Fig. 2.1. Principal stages of cell division (after Marsland). The steps shown sum up the main stages of the reproductive process in Protozoa. Biologically, cell division is much alike in all living things.

A little disagreement still persists on the question of whether each chromosome is a single object or, as most experts hold, an aggregate of very tiny biochemical particles called **genes.** In either event there is universal agreement that the chromosomes or their constituent genes have always conveyed the ingredients of biological inheritance from parent to child, and that the process of transmission has remained much the same in all animals since the very beginnings of protoplasmic creatures (see Fig. 2.1).

In the case of protozoans, reproduction does not have any sexual connotation, and the whole process appears to be entirely devoid of the subjective and emotional factors that human beings associate with the choice of a mate and the begetting of children.

Somehow, even where there is only a single one-celled parent and offspring presumably get exact duplicates of the ancestral chromo-

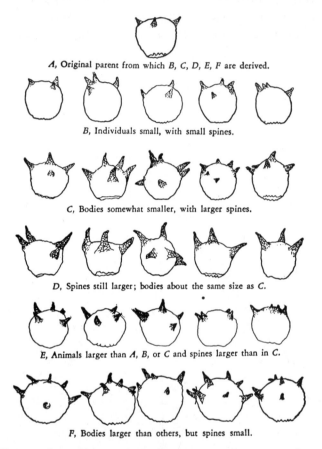

A, Original parent from which B, C, D, E, F are derived.

B, Individuals small, with small spines.

C, Bodies somewhat smaller, with larger spines.

D, Spines still larger; bodies about the same size as C.

E, Animals larger than A, B, or C and spines larger than in C.

F, Bodies larger than others, but spines small.

Fig. 2.2. Creation by evolution. A single parent, in the course of asexual reproduction, may give rise to greatly varied offspring. When two parents join in sexual reproduction, each one's body comprising millions of cells and countless genes, the chances of creating new forms by evolutionary changes which utilize variation are infinitely greater. (From F. B. Mason, *Creation by Evolution*. New York, 1928. Courtesy The Macmillan Co.)

somes and genes, descendants do not always grow into the identical shape and size of their parent (see Fig. 2.2). This variability, which becomes more noteworthy among many-celled animals with bisexual parenthood, provides one of the major keys of an understanding of biological evolution. As a rule, the totality of offspring may be shown to follow a three-branched path. Starting with a common ancestor, one branch is a path of extinction, which some descendants inevitably take in the course of time; a second represents the line followed by successive generations who never wander far from the parental condition; and the third marks the road taken by some offspring who, in later generations, come to differ so much from the original ancestor as to form a different species (see Fig. 2.3).

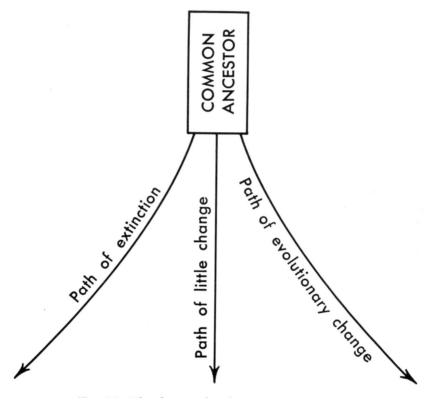

Fig. 2.3. The three paths of evolutionary descent.

Needless to say, although man is faced with the same biological imperatives as are the protozoans and although he resembles them in some details of reproduction, he is so vastly different in physical size and complexity that we must seek his immediate forebears among animals who traveled far on the path of divergence from some ancestral protozoan.

The next major step on the road toward the evolution of man

seems to have been taken when offspring cells adhered to their parent instead of severing all ties and going free. This stage is known as **colonialism** and leads presumably to the evolution of **Metazoa.** These are multicellular organisms which are characterized by the fact that each of their adhering cells is no longer capable of answering to all of the biological imperatives. Instead, some cells become specialized for breathing, others for locomotion, digesting, reproducing, and so on. The result is a single creature made up of a large number of interdependent, specialized cells. Gone is the jack-of-all-biological-trades cell that independently and alone makes up the body of a protozoan.

As we come a bit closer to the ultimate emergence of human beings, we are led to consider the marine Metazoa, none of which possesses a real backbone. All of them are classed as **invertebrates,** but various groups show a tremendous diversity of forms. Taken together, the invertebrates contributed little to the later organization of man's body, except that some of them had well-developed specialized organs associated with full-fledged circulatory, respiratory, digestive, excretory, reproductive, locomotor, muscular, and nervous systems. Furthermore, there are clear indications that, by a series of evolutionary steps, the first **vertebrates** descended from invertebrate ancestors.

Far more important from the standpoint of human ancestry than any of the characteristic invertebrates are a group of aquatic forms that include true fishes. They are the first to set the vertebrate theme which has persisted, with numerous changes, into the formation of the human body. There is much point to the jesting remark that man is nothing but a made-over fish. In addition to an internal, bony, segmented, spinal column that makes possible bending movements of the trunk, practically all vertebrates exhibit the phenomenon of **bilateral symmetry,** which means that each side of the body is a mirror image of the other. Thus, in man, we find right and left nostrils, eyes, ears, arms, breasts, ribs, lungs, kidneys, testes or ovaries, legs, and so forth. From the torso there also extend right and left fins or limbs, one set placed forward near the head or neck, and the other located at the hind end, close by the pelvis. Our own marked tendency toward bilateral symmetry cannot be denied, even though a few vital organs like the heart and liver are not duplicated on each side of the body.

Today, no one knows for what purpose or by what means the

earliest of the true vertebrates developed. bilateral symmetry, but once formed this type of structure provided animals with a form of insurance. Many a creature sustains life with only a single organ of a pair, located either on the left or right side. In the case of *Homo sapiens,* some vision is possible even to those who have only one functioning eye; it is not at all impossible to take in air with a single nostril; people live for years with one or the other lung or kidney removed; and reproduction may take place if only one testicle or ovary is working normally. As to the single heart, it is intriguing to speculate on the length of life man might have achieved had he been provided with two hearts.

Fish are equipped with well-developed, powerful muscles that show a high degree of nervous coordination. In addition, organs corresponding to human nostrils, eyes, and ears permit a number of keen sense perceptions. These organs are lodged in cartilaginous or bony heads that cover and protect a multipart brain. Hereafter, the head leads the way in movements that the brain directs. The head is readily distinguishable from the rest of the body, and comes to be associated with a movable mouth and lower jaw (**mandible**). From this stage of development on, all food enters at the mouth, passes into a digestive system within the main body cavity, and waste matter is excreted at the tail end. Also present is a combined respiratory and circulatory system, by means of which oxygen is taken into the body for the use of the blood stream. A multichambered heart, through a network of enclosed vessels, pumps oxygenated blood to all parts of the organism. Fish blood is "cold," but each cell contains **hemoglobin,** which is the red coloring matter of the blood corpuscles that carry oxygen.

Lastly, there is the matter of reproduction. From fish to man, the excretory system is always linked to the organs of reproduction. Thousands of millennia after this arrangement had become systematized, at the turn of the twentieth century, the great **Sigmund Freud** made it the basis of one of his most brilliant hypotheses. He postulated that the excretory practices of children, especially during their toilet training, might well influence some of their adult attitudes toward sex, and that these factors often play an important role in personality formation.

Among fishes the two sexes can usually be identified, and they retain feminine egg-laying or masculine sperm-producing functions permanently. While it is true that male and female individuals can sometimes be recognized among earlier invertebrates, and while it is also true that egg and sperm cells can generally be distinguished, it must not be forgotten that even animals as highly evolved as oysters are indistinguishable by sex, and may produce egg cells at one time and sperm at another. Such indefinite sexuality comes to be an abnormal phenomenon in those vertebrates that evolved after fishes.

Granted that the main outlines of the forthcoming human body were foreshadowed in fishes, the biological distinctions that set man apart from water dwellers must still be considered. Strange as it may seem, some of these factors were begun, not without a degree of success, by certain fishes.

D. ALL ASHORE THAT'S GOING ASHORE!

So many varieties of fish were in evidence during the Devonian period, about halfway through the Paleozoic era (see Fig. 1.4), that it is often termed the Age of Fishes. But the climate in Devonian times was not always well suited to fish life, for there were violent alternations of rainy and dry seasons. Many bodies of water probably dried out during stages of drought, leading to overcongestion of fish populations in those pools or streams that remained. As a consequence, the supply of available oxygen would have tended to become exhausted, a contingency that would have put the highest of biological premiums on an ability to gulp atmospheric oxygen from the air.

Close to the direct line of man's ancestry were the lobe-finned **crossopterygian** fishes, which combined a capacity to take atmospheric oxygen into air sacs with the possession of strong, muscular, paired fins whose firm flesh rested on a bony framework (Fig. 2.4A). These fins were strong enough to serve as rudimentary limbs whenever the animal found itself forced to progress on dry ground. Without much question, crossopterygian fish may be considered to be ancestral to the earliest **amphibians,** who, in turn, became the ancestors of the first **tetrapods,** four-legged, air-breathing vertebrates that completely forsook water for land.

At first the amphibians were practically indistinguishable from the crossopterygians, but gradually their limbs became better suited for movements on dry soil; their air sacs came to function more and

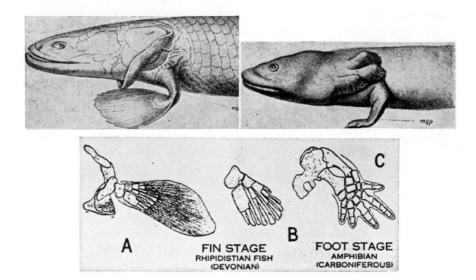

FIN STAGE
RHIPIDISTIAN FISH
(DEVONIAN)

FOOT STAGE
AMPHIBIAN
(CARBONIFEROUS)

Fig. 2.4. A *(above)*. Part of the evolution of land legs. (Upper series.) Students should note the very close resemblance between a crossopterygian fish (left) and an early amphibian (right). (Courtesy Buffalo Museum of Science.) (Lower series.) The postulated evolution of land legs from the powerful fins of crossopterygian fishes is worthy of careful study. Particular attention should be given to the five-digit skeletal arrangement of the amphibian foot. (Courtesy American Museum of Natural History.) B *(below)*. An amphibian life-cycle. Each amphibian begins life in water but matures into a land dweller. (From A. S. Romer, *Man and the Vertebrates,* 2d. ed. Chicago, 1937. Courtesy University of Chicago Press.)

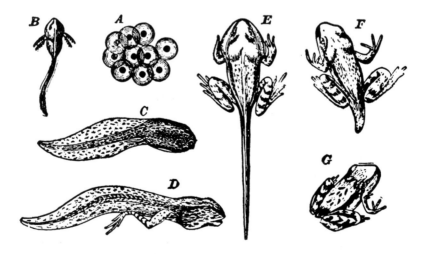

more as true lungs, rather than as mere baglike containers; their senses became adjusted in maturity to receiving impressions on land, rather than through water; and they are thought to have been the first to show **auditory** responses, based on a true sense of **hearing.** Nevertheless, the amphibian life cycle remained partly dependent on a watery environment. At each spawning season, the females laid a mass of small, gelatinous, fishlike eggs in water; and these were externally fertilized by male sperm. Immature amphibians are really little fishes, but as they grow to adulthood a **metamorphosis** takes place which leads to loss of the long tail, the development of limbs from fins, and a change of breathing mechanism from gills to lungs (see Fig. 2.4B).

Reptiles are the first creatures in the evolutionary sequence leading to man to have become complete land dwellers. Among their greatest contributions are those concerned with changes in the manner of reproduction. The key to the new system is to be found in the development of a new kind of egg—large, covered with a hard but porous shell, and containing an assortment of membranes and liquids which protect and nourish a developing embryo without cutting off its supply of atmospheric oxygen. Not until reptilian females acquired the biological mechanism for laying this type of egg on dry land could the ties with water have been completely severed.

If a female is to deposit a hard-shelled egg that contains an embryo, the egg must of necessity be fertilized before its final formation and discharge from her body. To achieve this, the reptiles inaugurated **copulation,** the method of sexual reproduction by which the male genital member must be capable of penetrating a pocketlike female organ, in order to intromit spermatozoa. The basic reptilian mode of reproduction has been retained, albeit with important modifications, by man and almost all other mammals. It is scarcely necessary to call attention to the great mass of cultural values and meanings that human beings have come to associate with the essential bio-physico-chemical activity of copulation.

Among reptiles, likewise, are to be found the first traces of a new organ in the brain. This is known as the **cerebral cortex (neopallium)** and consists of multitudinous cells lodged in the gray matter that overlies the **cerebrum,** which is the front hemisphere of the brain. Judging by what is usually accepted to be the manner in which the brain operates, the cerebral cortex was fated to become the seat of the so-called higher mental functions in later vertebrates.[2]

All reptiles are **cold-blooded,** which really means that they reflect whatever temperature prevails in their immediate surroundings. When winter weather comes, they tend to freeze so literally that they become sluggish in their movements or else they generally resort to the inactivity of hibernation. It is tempting to think that some **warm-blooded mammals,** because of their ability to regulate internal heat and energy, were able to survive changes of landscape and climate that are thought to have carried off vast numbers of their cold-blooded contemporaries.

Even during the centuries when the big, hulking reptiles known as **dinosaurs** (Fig. 2.5) were the most prominent animals on earth,

Fig. 2.5. Huge Mesozoic reptiles. Triceratops (left) was a monstrous dinosaur, approximately 25 feet long. It moved on all fours and ate only vegetal foods. As a contrast, Tyrannosaurus was a meat eater, which moved on its hind legs. It weighed around 10 tons and stood about 18 feet high. Many other varieties of reptiles abounded in Mesozoic times. (Courtesy Chicago Natural History Museum.)

some of their less conspicuous relatives were already beginning to acquire mammalian traits. These devised a new technique for the mastication of food. Most reptiles are provided with peg-shaped teeth that are alike from front to back (**homodont**), continuously replaceable if lost, and utilized primarily for seizing prey and tearing food. Unlike the more orthodox members of their class, the promammalian reptiles evolved a varied assortment of teeth (**heterodont**) including, from the front center of the mouth to the back

---

[2] Very recent experiments have begun to question whether some of the functions hitherto ascribed to the cerebral cortex may not be lodged in the parts of the brain that lie under the cerebral cortex.

along each side, sharp-edged incisors for biting and shearing, pointed canines for piercing, and comparatively broad and flat premolars and molars for crushing and grinding. This is the dental arrangement that is still to be found in man, whose "milk" teeth are shed and replaced by a permanent set that is not regenerating.

Because of the anatomical features inherited from some of their reptilian ancestors, in addition to many contributions of their own, the mammals were well prepared to play a leading role in the animal kingdom. Thanks to their hard, bony, but flexible backbones, and their ribs, shoulders, and pelvic girdles, their skeletal structures were sturdy and well knit, and their muscular systems were powerful and efficiently controlled. Their limbs were strong and properly placed to elevate their bodies above the ground, and a number of mammals were capable of rapid locomotion on land. The lungs, no longer feeble or rudimentary, were activated by movements of the ribs and, aided by a muscular **diaphragm** that separates the chest from the abdomen, they were capable of pulling in great quantities of air. A thick, four-chambered heart, through the agency of an intricate network of arteries, veins, and capillaries, systematically pumped blood to the lungs for oxygenation and out again to every part of the body. Each blood cell contained an adequate amount of hemoglobin, and the blood stream was kept at a consistently high temperature that was not readily affected by climatic conditions. This phenomenon was controlled with the aid of a thermostatic device probably located in the hypothalamus region of the brain. Retention of body heat in mammals was aided by insulation provided by skin covers of fur or hair. Heat and energy production were closely integrated, and together they kept mammalian animals active and energetic in all seasons.

Smelling, seeing, tasting, and hearing abilities continued to improve as mammals became more fully evolved, and a new sensory device—a sensitive skin—sent innumerable contact impressions to the brain, where judgments based on the sense of touch grew highly exact and discriminating. The neopallium expanded with an upward and backward growth of the cerebral hemisphere that it overlay, until together they made up over 80 percent of the weight of the entire brain. Coupled with its increase in size among the higher mammals was the brain's development as an extraordinary sense combiner. Blended impressions sent in from various sources were formed and stored, thereby providing a basis for the association of ideas and imagination, memory and judgment, foresight and planning. All of these various higher mental faculties, which reach their greatest peak in *Homo sapiens,* often depend on the recall and recombination of remembered or stored items. That is what gives meaning to such phrases as "the past is prologue." In other words, we utilize knowledge of what has occurred in the past (experience) for anticipating or planning to deal with whatever is still to come.

Mammals that may most properly be regarded as ancestral to man first appeared in the Cenozoic era. The fullest expression of mammalian development occurs in the subclass of eutherian or placental mammals. Reproduction in this group involves the internal fertilization of a microscopic egg and its retention within a female's body for an extended length of time. Soon after fertilization takes place, some of the embryonic membranes combine with part of the mother's uterine lining to form the **placenta.** Thereafter, this organ brings close together maternal and embryonic blood, although the two blood streams never merge into one. This is the manner in which the embryo is supplied with food and oxygen and gets rid of its waste products (see Fig. 2.6). Among the Eutheria, the placenta is discharged as the afterbirth soon after a child has been born, and a new placenta originates with each succeeding pregnancy. Shortly after her delivery, the mother's breasts fill with milk with which a baby can be fed for many months.

The material presented so far in this chapter is not the major

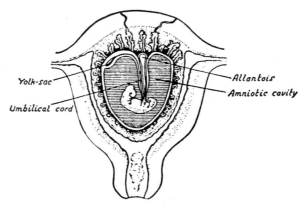

Fig. 2.6. A human placenta. The manner in which an embryo is nurtured and sheltered during its mother's pregnancy is very similar for all placental mammals. (From E. A. Hooton, *Up from the Ape,* rev. ed. New York, 1946. Courtesy The Macmillan Co.)

field within which any anthropologist works. Some physical anthropologists begin to make direct contributions at about this stage of evolution by studying the Primates in detail; and every anthropologist, even if he emphasizes culture, is expected to know all that he can about the ancestral animals whose bodies most nearly approximate those of *Homo sapiens.*

E. PRIMATES IN THE TREES

Although the human body is undeniably that of a placental mammal, it is obviously distinctive in various respects. Some of man's physical specialities are to be found among no other animals, but several of his most typical anatomical parts are duplicated, sometimes with startling exactness, in creatures belonging to the Primate order, a subdivision of eutherian mammals that consists of **lemurs, tarsiers, monkeys, apes,** and **men.**

Among the most important of man's Primate characteristics is the **prehensile grip,** which permits an animal to grasp an object tightly by wrapping its fingers around it. In order to grip a thing firmly, the thumb must be capable of going around it in the opposite direction from the other digits. Technically, this mechanism, found only among Primates, is made possible by the possession of an **opposable thumb,** which is usually taken to mean that the ball of the thumb can be touched (**opposed**) to the inner tips of the other four fingers (see Fig. 2.7). A prehensile grip is particularly valuable to an animal

Fig. 2.7. The opposable thumb of a Primate. The way in which a chimpanzee's hand is holding a cigarette illustrates one use of the Primate anatomical mechanism known as the opposable thumb. (From J. A. Gavan, arranger, *The Non-Human Primates and Human Evolution,* Detroit, 1955. Courtesy Wayne University Press.)

that must grab on to successive branches as it moves among tree-tops. Flat nails rather than claws, features also typical of Primates alone, have likewise been associated with grasping functions, in the belief that they are less likely to get in the way of tree dwellers; and some writers have gone so far as to attribute the ridges on the insides of the fingers to the firmness that they are supposed to provide for gripping the limbs of trees and picking up or holding things.

Then, again, violent movements of the upper body call for the firm attachment of fingers, hands, wrists, and arms to the shoulders. This implies the need of a sturdy shoulder girdle, in which the collarbone (**clavicle**) must play an important part. Without a strong and firmly knit clavicle, such as most Primates possess, strenuous motions of the arms to the sides and rear would be next to impossible.

Another distinctive similarity in human and Primate behavior is made possible by the two long bones of the forearm which can be rotated so that the outer one (**radius**) moves over the inner (**ulna**) (see Fig. 2.8). This makes it a simple matter for the hand and arm below the elbow to be turned so that the palm may face up, down, or to either side. Firm, mobile, opposable digits, a flexible wrist, and a rotating forearm attached to a strong shoulder girdle, together

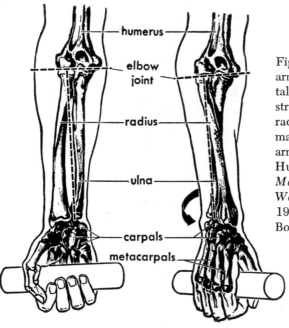

Fig. 2.8. Man's rotating forearm. The anatomical (skeletal) structure shown demonstrates the way in which the radius slides over the ulna to make possible a rotating forearm. (From J. S. Rogers, T. Hubbell, and C. F. Byers, *Man and the Biological World,* 2d ed. New York, 1952. Courtesy McGraw-Hill Book Co.)

Fig. 2.9. It's a pass! In order to throw a forward pass a football player uses a rotating forearm as well as a strong prehensile grip, a sturdy clavicle, and a powerful shoulder girdle. (Courtesy Eck Stanger, *The Ann Arbor News.*)

with their attendant muscles, ligaments, tendons, and nerves, provide the biological potential for many divergent activities (see Fig. 2.9).

Other anatomical features commonly regarded as typical of Primates include a large, greatly convoluted brain, covered with a deeply wrinkled cortex; a highly intensified increase in the sense of sight, with an attendant decline of smell; a bony wall, penetrated by the optic nerve, that shuts off the eye socket at the sides and rear; a tendency for females to bear but one young at a time; and possession, normally, of only two breasts, situated on the chest. During the course of Primate evolution, too, the biological restriction of sexual intercourse to a particular breeding or rutting season tended to disappear. By the time the higher Primates came into being, relations between the sexes could take place at any time of the year. *Homo sapiens* has retained this condition, and the potential for continuous sexuality has played an important part in his development of family life.

1. Lemurs [3]

Although some scientists refuse to classify lemurs (Fig. 2.10) as Primates, most admit these creatures to the ranks but assign them to the separate suborder, **Lemuroidea.** Several kinds of lemurs are still to be found in Madagascar and the vicinity, but during the Eocene epoch they were widely spread through other parts of the world, including the Western Hemisphere. They are, in general, small ani-

---

[3] Some physical anthropologists separate from lemurs a closely related animal called loris. See M. F. A. Montagu, *An Introduction to Physical Anthropology*, rev. ed., Springfield, Mass., 1951, pp. 30-39.

mals about two feet long, with fur-covered bodies and long tails.
Most varieties have pointed projecting snouts and big round eyes
that peer to the sides and fail to provide overlapping, or stereoscopic, binocular vision, such as is typical of higher Primates. They

Fig. 2.10. Ring-tailed
lemur. Lowly though
this Primate may be, it
has strong and flexible
fingers and wrists, ro-
tating forearms, pre-
hensile hands and feet,
opposable thumbs and
great toes, and flat nails
on the digits. The front
and hind limbs are
clearly distinguished.
(Courtesy New York
Zoological Society.)

live in trees and are most active at night. Their brains are poorly
developed and are devoted mostly to the sense of smell. This is
regarded as a backward condition because tree dwellers require
agility and co-ordination that would better be served by increased
visual, tactile, kinesthetic, and motor areas in the brain.

2. Tarsiers

Somewhat more progressive in various biological respects, but
unique and overspecialized in others, is the Primate suborder of
Tarsioidea, generally found in the Indonesian archipelago and the
Philippines. Tarsiers (Fig. 2.11) are so named because of a greatly

Fig. 2.11. A tarsier. Far removed from the structure and appearance of *Homo sapiens* is this lowly Primate, which is specialized for rapid hopping. Yet, its eyes are in a frontal position, and it has prehensile hands and rotating forearms. The front and hind limbs are differentiated in form and function. (Courtesy McGraw-Hill Publishing Co.)

enlarged tarsus bone that helps form the arch of the foot in all Primates. This speciality, coupled with the retention of very flexible toes, seems to enable these animals to make prodigious hops at lightning speed. When they employ this mode of progression in the trees where they habitually reside, they are aided by still another speciality, for the balls of all the digits are extended into roughened, disklike pads that are thought to prevent slipping when a fresh hold is obtained.

Despite their strange appearance, tarsiers show a number of advanced anatomical features. They carry further a fundamental differentiation of front and hind limbs, first noticeable in Primates among the Lemuroidea; their teeth closely resemble those of higher Primates; their brains show an increase of space devoted to sight, and the olfactory (smelling) area is correspondingly reduced. In brain development, the forward hemisphere or cerebrum extends up and back to overlie the cerebellum at the rear. Only one offspring is normally born at a time, and female tarsiers, unlike lemurs, have monthly discharges of blood at the vagina somewhat like menstrual periods. These are probably associated, as they are in human females, with the sloughing off of unfertilized egg cells.

3. Platyrrhini

Within the forests of the more tropical parts of Central and South America there live a great many varieties of monkeys. Together they are known as **Platyrrhini** (Fig. 2.12A), a term that refers to their

Fig. 2.12. New and Old World monkeys. A. Howler monkey. This is an American platyrrhine type with widely spaced, laterally directed nostrils. Its swollen appearance is caused by its prodigious sound mechanism, from which it gets its name. B. A catarrhine (Macaque) monkey from the Old World. It has narrowly spaced nostrils that open downward. This configuration approaches man's much more nearly than does the platyrrhine nasal structure. (Courtesy A. H. Schultz, "Man as a Primate," and *The Scientific Monthly*, 1931.)

broad, fleshy noses which have widely separated nostrils, located at the sides so that they open outward to left and right, instead of downward. These monkeys, together with those of the Old World, apes, and men, comprise the Primate suborder of **Anthropoidea.** Platyrrhini have been in existence in the Western Hemisphere since Oligocene days; they approximate the human body more nearly than tarsiers because they have bigger and more convoluted brains, with considerable space devoted to sight, and overlapping, stereoscopic vision capable of discerning the third dimension (depth), as well as height and width. In addition, the Platyrrhini have flat-nailed digits, unencumbered with disklike pads, and legs and feet well suited for climbing and jumping but not specialized for hopping. When moving along the boughs of trees, American monkeys sometimes go on all fours, but occasionally they swing from branch to branch, using their hands, arms, and shoulder girdles in the manner of gymnasts performing on rings or trapezes. This method of progression is termed **brachiating** and is best developed in America in the spider monkeys.

Besides their broad noses and laterally directed nostrils, the Platyrrhini show two additional features that must serve to put them off the main line of man's evolution. They have teeth that almost resemble those of human beings in structure and numbers, except that they have one additional premolar on each side of the upper and lower jaws. More striking is the specialty of a **prehensile tail,** capable of grasping a branch and holding the body securely suspended while the limbs are left free for other purposes (Fig. 2.13).

All in all, the Platyrrhini are the highest forms of Primates to have evolved in the Western Hemisphere. It is commonly believed that they had become separated from the main anthropoid stem by Eocene times. They are much further advanced than the tarsiers in the direction of hominids, yet they are far removed from apes and men. For reasons that are not yet known, evolution failed to proceed beyond the Platyrrhini in the New World.

4. Catarrhini

Somewhat more highly evolved than the platyrrhine monkeys of the New World are their Old World relatives who, together with apes and humans, may be called the **Catarrhini** (Fig. 2.12B). This term refers to a narrow nose in which the nostrils are close together, centrally located, and pointed downward. Specialists distinguish many varieties, among the best known of which are baboons, mandrills, and macacques or rhesus monkeys, which are widely used in medical laboratories. Members of this group are the first to have the identical dental formula of man. The Catarrhini also anticipate human characteristics in that they are active by day and sleep at night and in that they have relatively large brains, completely stereoscopic vision, thoroughly differentiated front and hind limbs, flat nails on all the digits, and a breeding system that very

Fig. 2.13. American spider monkey. Use of the long, powerful, prehensile tail as an extra limb and hand is well illustrated. Spider monkeys belong to the platyrrhine subdivision. (Courtesy New York Zoological Society.)

nearly approaches man's. They differ from man in that nearly all of them are arboreal. Most of them also have cheek pouches for the temporary storage of food, calloused areas on their bottoms, and tails that may be short or long but are never prehensile. Some species, too, have on the buttocks patches of sexual skin that may become vividly colored, particularly during the menstrual cycles of females.

F. LIVING APES

Laymen regularly confuse monkeys and apes, but students of anthropology must learn to distinguish between them. None of the extant apes has any kind of tail whatsoever; none has ever been found, under natural conditions, in any part of the Americas; none is known to have been in existence before Miocene times, about 30 million years ago; and all have larger and more complex brains than monkeys, as well as dental formulas and nasal configurations that are like those of man. There are only four living varieties of apes: **gibbons, orangutans, chimpanzees,** and **gorillas.** Whereas the gibbons and orangutans inhabit the southeastern portion of the Asiatic mainland and a few of the nearby islands, the chimpanzees and gorillas live in a zone that runs approximately across central Africa.

1. Gibbon

Of the four groups, the gibbons, because of their small body size and brachiating mechanism, are thought to be furthest removed from man. Rarely do they exceed 3 feet in height, and adults of either sex commonly weigh only 12 to 15 pounds. Their heads show low foreheads and large oval eye sockets with thick rims of bone, and their jaws protrude and contain jutting canine teeth that interlock—instead of meeting edge to edge—at the corners of the mouth. The cranial capacity, a term that denotes the size of the skull chamber in which the brain is lodged,[4] is limited to 90 cc, a figure greatly below that of the higher Primates but far in excess of the average for most monkeys.

Nothing is more characteristic of gibbons than their enormous and exceedingly elongated arms (Fig. 2.14). Figuratively speaking, a gibbon can pick up a dime from the floor without stooping. A light, slender body, coupled with powerful arms that culminate in long-fingered hands with short thumbs, seems to be especially well suited for brachiation. With the greatest of ease and nonchalance,

---

[4] To get an approximate measure of the amount of brain that any vertebrate has, anthropologists fill the hollow cranial vault of a skull with a free-flowing material, usually mustard seed, and pour the contents of the vault into a measuring glass or graduate. The resultant reading, expressed in cubic centimeters, is known as the cranial capacity and provides a convenient measure of gross brain size.

a gibbon moves among the trees with a free-swinging, pendulum motion, rapidly shifting its hold from one hand to another. Mothers with infants clinging to them regularly make 15-foot leaps, and the members of a whole troop will occasionally jump 30 or more feet through the air. Such skill in brachiating and hurtling through space implies that gibbons must have excellent eyesight, acute

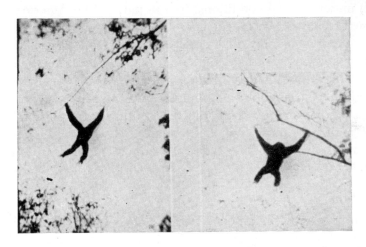

Fig. 2.14. Gibbons. A wild gibbon brachiating in the tree-tops shows its easy, swinging motion, its prehensile hands and feet, and its exceedingly long and powerful arms. (Courtesy Comparative Psychological Monographs.)

judgment of distance, accurate and instantaneous perceptions of depth and size, extraordinary co-ordination of hand and eye, splendid motor controls, and exceedingly fast reaction speeds. All this requires adequate representation in the brain.

2. Orangutan

Orangutans, often close neighbors of the gibbons, stand nearly 5 feet high. Adult males weigh from 165 to 200 pounds (Fig. 2.15), and their cranial capacities may reach up to 400 cc. Big and bulky though they are, the orangutans are still arboreal, but they are by no means such expert and graceful brachiators as gibbons. They move cautiously and ponderously through the trees, and while they sometimes swing by the hands and arms from one stout bough to another, they never attempt to leap across wide stretches of open space.

Fig. 2.15. Orangutan mother and child. Although possessed of long and powerful arms, the adult orangutan is too bulky to leap across wide stretches of open space. As the illustration shows, it has a strong, prehensile grip and rotating forearms, and uses its feet in the same manner as the hands. (Courtesy Zoological Society of Philadelphia.)

In one particular or another, the Asiatic apes may make a very close approximation to man, but on the whole, the differences far outweigh the resemblances. They are not nearly so close to *Homo sapiens* as are the living apes of Africa.

3. Chimpanzee

Under natural conditions, chimpanzees reside only in those parts of equatorial Africa that are drained by the Congo and Niger rivers. Bodily proportions are much like those of man (Fig. 2.16), with full-grown males standing just over 5 feet high and weighing about 110 pounds. Most species have round, low-vaulted heads, and their cranial capacities average about 400 cc. With the approach of adolescence, a male develops a solid, transverse bar of bone over the sockets of the eyes (**supraorbital torus**), and his big chinless jaws bulge forward. Lips are thin but unusually flexible or mobile, and while the front teeth are big and strong, with interlocking canines, the back teeth are apt to look quite human. Fruits and tender vege-

Fig. 2.16. Chimpanzee in walking posture. This animal's hind limbs and feet are poorly adapted for walking upright or for supporting the body in an orthograde position. The great toe is opposable, the arch of the foot is low, and the heel is rudimentary. Much weight, when the animal walks, is placed on the elongated front limbs, which rest on their knuckles. The opposable thumb is high on the hand. Compare Fig. 2.17B. (Courtesy Peabody Museum, Harvard University.)

tal growths of many sorts make up the bulk of their diet, but they probably eat eggs, small birds, and rodents as well. Food is most often plucked or grasped by hand and then brought to the mouth, and while feeding in a tree a chimpanzee may sit, stand, recline, or squat.

Chimpanzees are fine climbers and expert brachiators. They swing easily from one limb to another, but observers have noticed that they never travel for long distances without resorting to the ground for part of the way. This is somewhat unexpected because they have long, narrow, prehensile feet, with massive but opposable great toes, rudimentary heels, and partially webbed outer toes. Ordinarily, a grounded chimpanzee uses a crutchlike stance and has an ungainly waddling, sidewise gait (Fig. 2.16); but under special conditions, as when the ground is wet or cold, a chimpanzee may walk erect for a few paces.

A. Gorilla in sitting position. The huge supraorbital torus and low forehead are plainly revealed. Although the feet can be differentiated from the hands, their prehensile structure is noteworthy. (Courtesy New York Zoological Society.)

B. A grounded gorilla. The quadrupedal stance of a walking gorilla resembles that of a chimpanzee. (Courtesy Newton W. Hartman and Zoological Society of Philadelphia.)

Fig. 2.17.
Two gorillas.

4. Gorilla

Largest by far of all the Primates is the gorilla (Fig. 2.17). These beasts may grow to prodigious sizes, with adult males standing up to 70 inches high and weighing from 350 to as much as 600 pounds. Particularly noteworthy among full-grown males is a massive skull, with great bony crests on top running from front to back, and an enormus supraorbital torus of solid bone that goes from left to right above the eye openings. Cranial capacities average 500 cc, but may run a little higher in exceptional cases. This is the greatest amount reported for any of the living apes, but is surprisingly little in relation to the over-all size of the skull. Most of the big cranium consists of solid bone, and there is comparatively little hollow space to contain a brain. Truly may the gorilla be described as a big bonehead!

Heavy though they are, gorillas spend much time in trees and are good swingers and climbers. When they come to the ground, as they apparently do more frequently than other apes, they have a tendency to stand erect from time to time. They have even been observed to take a few strides forward, placing the feet flat on the ground and moving in a fairly straight line.

Among the least humanoid of gorilla features are the face and jaws (Fig. 2.18). The latter are particularly massive in adult males, forward protruding, and devoid of chin. The huge jaws contain formidable incisors, great tusklike, projecting, and interlocking

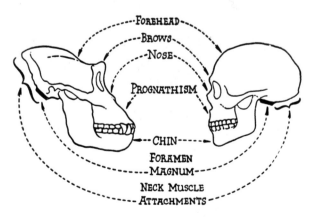

Fig. 2.18. Comparison of gorilla's and human skull. Many essential distinctions are plainly indicated. (From W. W. Howells, *Mankind So Far*, New York, 1944. Courtesy Doubleday & Co.)

canines, and molars that are large but manlike in shape. The lips are elongated and thin, and the ears surprisingly small. The nose is long, narrow at the root but broad at the nostrils. It is not elevated much above the rest of the facial plane, and the nasal bones that underlie the fleshy parts are flat and low. Only hominids have prominent, uplifted nasal bones.

G. GENERAL CONCLUSIONS

The kinship of living apes to humans is still far from being understood. About thirty years ago, it used to be fairly well agreed that the gibbons were too specialized to be close to man's ancestry, but that the larger apes were quite near. Nowadays it is almost the universal consensus that the living big apes represent recent specialties of the Primate form and are far to the side of the path leading to human beings. In the older hypothesis, much was made of the fact that apes and man share a great many traits of the bony skeleton, body organs, nervous and muscular systems, and physiological processes. These resemblances were thought to be explained by the fact that man was descended from an ancestor directly common to the ape and human lines, and that this ancestral creature was a big, arboreal **simian** who forsook brachiating tree life for the ground, began to walk upright on his hind legs, and started to use his forelimbs in the manner of human hands and arms. As the supposed ancestor became better adjusted to the requirements of upright posture on the ground, ran the old argument, modifications took place in the feet, legs, pelvis, spinal column, and head, which provide most of the bodily differences that set modern men apart from their apish cousins who failed to come to earth.

Today a different viewpoint is beginning to make headway. Now it is being argued that the human and simian lines began to follow separate evolutionary paths far back in late Oligocene or early Miocene times, and that the ancestors of man may have been monkeylike quadrupeds who never passed through a brachiating ape stage.[5] According to this view, the differences of ape and human anatomy are stressed and the resemblances somewhat underemphasized.

---

[5] Some of the principal arguments on both sides of the controversy are conveniently summarized in E. A. Hooton, *Up From the Ape*, rev. ed., New York, 1946, pp. 130-133.

Proponents of neither theory have presented an entirely satisfactory case. The riddle of man's ancestry remains a riddle. Each side is caught on the horns of a dilemma. If it is assumed that a large, brachiating simian was the common ancestor of apes and men, an impressive list of distinctively human traits remains to be explained. But if one argues that the large apes are only far distant cousins of man, whose ancestors never went through a brachiating stage, a host of anatomical similarities demand explanation.

Although scientists disagree on many details concerning man's immediate ancestry, they hold firmly to the belief that there is some kind of relationship between hominids and other Primates. If the ideas expressed on p. 30 approximate the truth, they indicate that two related but different paths may become more and more widely divergent as time passes. The figure of a caret, ∧, gives an approximation of the basic notion in simple fashion. The top represents the start of divergence, and the bottom shows separation at a much later date. As we trace the two lines backward in time (upward), the less far apart they are. Such is the case with the living simians and modern man. Today they seem very far apart, but we can discover their common ancestry by tracing their evolutionary lines back in time.

Not many decades ago, the quest for predecessors of modern man used to be spoken of as a "search for missing links." Such a description has fallen into disuse because it gives the impression that there once existed crosswise connections between other Primate and human branches, that is, between the two lines of the caret. Anthropologists do not believe in the existence of such fanciful cross ties, but they do believe that, if man's line is followed back, it will lead to creatures less humanoid than living men and women.

H. PRIMATE EVOLUTION IN REVIEW

To a student of anthropology, it is of the utmost importance to be thoroughly conversant with the story of Primate evolution in order to understand better when, and perhaps how, various aspects of man's body structure and biological activities were first developed.

About one and one-half billion years ago, a number of earthly chemicals combined to form living matter or protoplasm. At the same time a set of biological imperatives was superimposed on the older physico-chemical laws and had to be obeyed as long as life was to be maintained. Identical biological imperatives continue to apply to man until death occurs.

From the beginning, protoplasm, like the human body, was organized into cells. At first, in the Protozoa, a single cell sufficed to carry out all the rules of life, but, in the multicelled Metazoa, specialized cells were grouped into tissues, organs, and systems, each of which was charged with the responsibility of satisfying only one or another of the biological imperatives. Even the most casual observers know that man's body also contains systems of cells that are specialized for breathing, digesting, excreting, reproducing, and so forth. Associated with the organs that make up these systems are sets of muscles which require nerve mechanisms to regulate and direct their activities. Among the early invertebrates, the nerve cells were probably dispersed in scattered units throughout the body, every unit acting almost independently to control muscular activity in its own area. Later, as may be seen in such invertebrates as **jellyfish,** the disparate nerve units were merged into a co-ordinated nervous system that functioned as a central receiving and dispatching center for the entire organism. This scheme was improved upon by various Paleozoic invertebrates, many of which came to have well-developed senses—especially of smell.

With the formation of elongated bodies among truly vertebrate fishes, a pattern was devised that showed clearly marked head, body, and tail divisions; bilateral symmetry; paired appendages; and permanent distinctions of sex. Among vertebrates, all of the sense organs and their associated nerve cells were connected with a brain which was lodged in a hard head that thereafter led the way while it directed the movements of an animal. Fish bodies are so specialized for speedy motions that their responses to external impressions are very quick and in the nature of automatic or **reflex actions.** Thoughtful behavior is something that lies beyond the capacity of fishes, and they are apparently incapable of any activity (such as first-degree murder) that requires premeditation. Above all, they lack a good sense combiner for merging sense impressions received from various sources into a composite whole. Without such an arrangement, a creature cannot store up old impressions to form a backlog of experience from which to draw when confronted with a new or difficult situation.

Following in the footsteps, as it were, of some Devonian fishes that could crawl a bit on dry soil while they gulped free air, came the ambitious amphibians who led the way to partially terrestrial life by contributing adult lungs and limbs to the vertebrate theme composed by fishes. Once their paired fins were metamorphosed to legs, the amphibians required improvements in those parts of the brain and nervous system devoted to locomotor controls. After the necessary changes had been made, adult amphibians could use their legs either to walk or to swim. The senses of sight and smell likewise became adapted to air or water. In addition, amphibians were the earliest in the line of mammalian evolution to develop a genuine sense of hearing.

Pioneer reptiles were the first tetrapods, and they made suitable adjustments for carrying out the vertebrate theme entirely on land. Total emancipation from life in water called for numerous changes of body, limbs, and lungs, but even more vital was a need for a different mode of reproduction. This was achieved with the development of a new kind of egg and internal fertilization by copulation. Most reptiles contributed little else to the progress of evolution, with the exception of starting the cerebral cortex, a new element in the brain that was destined to play a major part in the life of man. A few reptiles converted their teeth from homodont to heterodont, and some may conceivably have begun the internal system of regulating body temperature that is conventionally termed warm-bloodedness, but these features are much better represented in the mammals.

Although mammalian evolution doubtless started over 70 million years ago, it did not reach a climax until the Cenozoic era had begun. Completely mammalian body forms and behavior are restricted to the Eutheria. The females of these warm-blooded, air-breathing, hair- or fur-covered animals give birth to relatively mature living offspring. These are first nourished within the mother's body during a prolonged pregnancy by means of a deciduous placenta, and after birth they are fed on milk from the mother's breasts. As far as their anatomical structures go, the eutherian mammals quite certainly provide the prototype for man, but there are many features of the human body that can be understood only by investigating the order of Primates.

As far back as 1758, the great Swedish naturalist, Linnaeus, gave the name Primate to that order of eutherian mammals which includes lemurs, tarsiers, monkeys, apes, and men. Only a few positive traits of anatomy characterize the Primates, but as a rule they have prehensile hands and feet, opposable thumbs and great toes, flat nails on the digits, one pair of breasts located on the chest, bony eye sockets, large and wrinkled brains, keen and stereoscopic vision, differentiated front and hind limbs, and excellent coordination between hands and eyes. By nearly every test of biology man is a Primate, yet he is sufficiently different to make it evident that he belongs to a separate category.

For the Primates that have survived to the present, the tree shrew seems to fulfill the requirements of an ancestral type, although in itself it does not have the status of a Primate. The lowliest creatures generally admitted to this order are the lemur and the tarsier. Neither of these comes as close to approximating man's bodily form as do the monkeys. These are divided into two varieties, those of the New World (Platyrrhini) and those of the Old World (Catarrhini), the latter being the more highly evolved in the sense that they are biologically nearer to the structure of humans.

Closer still are the apes (**Simiidae**), of whom the least humanoid are the small, lightweight, brachiating gibbons. All of the extant apes are arboreal to some extent, but all of them occasionally resort to the ground. They are not well equipped for walking and they seldom assume an upright posture for more than a few moments at a time. In numerous respects, the large apes show so many biological resemblances to man as to hint that they may share a common ancestry with him, but in other regards man has so many distinctive anatomical features that his relations to the great simians are far from clear. The most that can be said conclusively is that man is a distant relative of the other Primates, but is certainly not descended from any of the living varieties.

People who seek to discredit the science of man sometimes declare that anthropologists teach that human beings have descended from monkeys or apes. As a careful reading of this chapter shows, it would be more accurate to say that anthropologists teach that man's course of evolution has been diverging from that of all other Primates for well over 30 million years.

SELECTED REFERENCES

Bates, M., and Humphrey, P. S., *The Darwin Reader*. New York, 1957.

Blum, H. F., *Time's Arrow and Evolution*. Princeton, 1951.

Carlson, A. J., and Johnson, V., *The Machinery of the Body*, rev. ed. Chicago, 1941.

Carter, G. S., "The Theory of Evolution and the Evolution of Man," in *Anthropology Today*, A. L. Kroeber, ed. Chicago, 1953, pp. 327-342.

Dobzhansky, T., *Genetics and the Origin of Species*, rev. ed. New York, 1951.

Gavan, J. A., arranger, *The Non-Human Primates and Human Evolution.* Detroit, 1955.

Goldschmidt, R. B., *Understanding Heredity.* New York and London, 1952.

Hooton, E. A., *Man's Poor Relations.* New York, 1942.

Raymond, P. E., *Prehistoric Life.* Cambridge, Mass., 1939.

Romer, A. S., "The Evolution of the Vertebrates," in *The Nature of the World and Man*, H. H. Newman, ed. Chicago, 1926.

Simpson, G. G., *The Meaning of Evolution.* New Haven, Conn., 1949.

Strandskov, H. H., "Genetics and the Origin and Evolution of Man," in *Readings in Anthropology*, E. A. Hoebel *et al.*, eds. New York, 1955, pp. 67-77.

CHAPTER 3

THE EMERGENCE OF
HOMO SAPIENS

A. MAN-APES FROM SOUTH AFRICA

Within the last few decades South Africa has become the focus of a vexing evolutionary problem of world-wide significance. It stems from the rapid-fire discovery of a great number of man-ape fossils, collectively called the **Australopithecinae** ("southern apes"). Since 1936 several investigators have brought to light a surprising number of highly diversified Australopithecine specimens, with greatly varying combinations of human and simian characteristics. The finding of so many different kinds of man-apes in South Africa has posed numerous baffling problems for students of human origins. It will take years of hard work before experts will be in a position to make reasonably acceptable hypotheses regarding the proper placement in the animal kingdom of these assorted fossils. (See Fig. 3.1.)

The dates during which the Australopithecinae flourished will also have to be established before their place with reference to man's emergence can be ascertained. If they prove to be of fairly recent date, as many scholars at present believe, it will have to be acknowledged that they cannot be regarded as ancestors of modern humans. Unfortunately, there is no general agreement on this point. Some physical anthropologists think that the diversity of the man-apes, found in a comparatively restricted portion of one

59

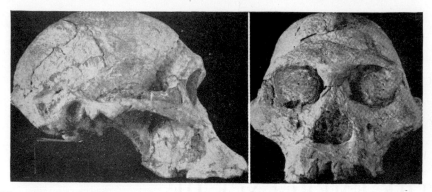

Fig. 3.1. South African man-ape. This specimen of the Australopithecines is called Plesianthropus. It has a big torus, a very projecting jaw, lowlying nasal bones, and a gap in the upper jaw, technically known as a **diastema**, into which an interlocking canine tooth is presumed to have fitted. (From M. F. A. Montagu, *Introduction to Physical Anthropology*, 2d ed. Springfield, Ill., 1951. Courtesy Charles E. Thomas.)

continent, in itself furnishes a presumption of time depth. On this basis, they stand ready to accept a date as early as the borderline between the Pliocene and Pleistocene periods.

By way of a general summary, it has been shown that there once existed in South Africa over a period of many thousands of years a family of higher Primates that were practically human.[1] Although they had relatively small brains which reached an upper limit of 900 cc, it is likely that they walked upright on their hind feet since they had straight femurs and their hands were too delicate to have been used for walking on the ground. They may have utilized crude tools, and it is even possible that they knew the use of fire. This raises a difficult question. Everyone is willing to concede that the Australopithecines had erect posture, but many doubt their ability to have used tools because of their limited cranial capacities. What cannot be settled at present is whether Primate tool usage automatically goes with the assumption of upright posture, or whether it also requires a very big brain. The opinion is currently gaining headway that tool usage might have started before the Primates began to develop large brains, and that the Australopithecinae did use tools.

As for the problem of human origins, it is no longer necessary,

---

[1] R. Broom, "The Ape-Men," *Scientific American*, Vol. 181, 1949, pp. 20-24.

in the light of the South African material, to rely entirely on the older notion that man has derived his distinctive body from some arboreal simian who grew too heavy for tree life and began walking erect on earth. Instead, the South African man-apes, who stood only 4 feet high and weighed an average of some 80 pounds, give additional support to the hypothesis that the human line, long before their day, may have been veering far away from the simian direction.[2] At the moment it seems best to look upon the Australopithecinae as representatives of an early humanoid branch that was moving slowly and incompletely in the direction of man in South Africa, while elsewhere in the Old World some of their more highly evolved contemporaries were approaching and perhaps crossing the threshold of humanity.

B. MAN ON EARTH

For all that has been written on the subject, no one knows exactly how or when the direct forebears of *Homo sapiens* acquired their most distinctive body traits. Despite the South African material, it is still most widely believed that the process was somehow connected with the acquisition of upright posture on solid earth. This process can be most meaningfully discussed at present if it is tentatively assumed to have taken place while large, arboreal, basically quadrupedal Primates were changing to terrestrial bipeds.

Starting from the ground up, it is apparent that if such assumed prehominids were to have gotten into the habit of successfully walking upright, their feet would have had to be changed from flexible, prehensile organs to stabilized, supporting members, capable of bearing the weight of the body. As man's ancestors came to walk habitually upright on their hind legs, the ankle-to-knee bones (**tibia** and **fibula**) became longer and stronger than in other Primates, and the calf muscles (**gastrocnemius**), which some men delight to observe in females, were enlarged and utilized to help raise the legs and feet when in motion or to hold them steady while standing still. Similarly, the thigh bone (**femur**) became elongated and straight of contour, and the muscles attached to it (**gluteus**

---

[2] J. T. Robinson, "The Evolutionary Significance of the Australopithecines," *Yearbook of Physical Anthropology*, G. W. Lasker and J. L. Angel, eds. New York, 1950, pp. 38-41.

maximus just below the hips, and **biceps femoralis** lower down) became larger and more powerful in order to extend the leg fully and to give it strength for walking (see Fig. 3.2). With the attainment of these modifications in the lower limbs, the body was given firm support or flexibility as needed, and the distinction of forelimbs from hindlimbs, first foreshadowed among the lowliest of Primates, received its greatest emphasis.

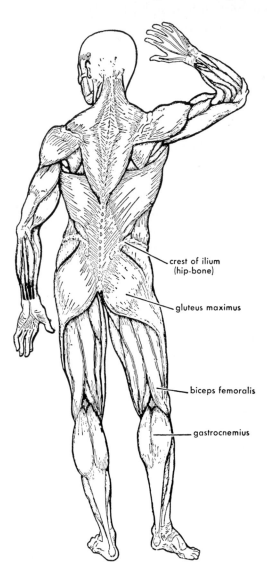

crest of ilium
(hip-bone)

gluteus maximus

biceps femoralis

gastrocnemius

Fig. 3.2. Major leg muscles in man (after Clendening and Rogers, Hubbell, and Byers). These are the muscles primarily concerned with upright posture and bipedal walking. (L. Clendening, *The Human Body.* New York, 1945. Courtesy Alfred A. Knopf.)

In terms of the hypothesis being developed in this section, changes of pelvis, trunk, and backbone also took place, and other significant modifications occurred in the chest, rib cage, shoulders, arms and hands. Of extreme significance, too, is the fact that a human carries his spine vertically with the backbone entering a **foramen magnum** that is centrally situated at the base of the skull. Thus, the head is neatly balanced and poised on top of the vertebral column, and neither the rear (**occipital**) portion of the skull nor the cervical vertebrae are particularly rugged, for only a slight **nuchal musculature** (muscles at the back of the neck) is needed to bind the head securely in place. As a consequence, man has a good deal of free space between the shoulders and head, so that his neck appears long and slender when compared with an ape's. Possibly, this arrangement may also have something to do with one of man's most important and most distinctive anatomical features—his greatly enlarged braincase.

In most species of apes, but best exemplified by the gorilla, the eye sockets are crowned by a thick supraorbital torus. Such an ape, it has just been explained, is also fairly certain to have a great deal of rugged bone at the back of the skull. Compressed between the front and rear areas of solid bone, the cranial vault has only a small chamber left hollow to accommodate the brain. This arrangement seems to be what limits the cranial capacity of so massive a Primate as a gorilla, to an average of about 500 cc. Among modern men and women, on the contrary, the heavy bars of bone over the eye orbits have diminished almost to the vanishing point; and with the attainment of an evenly poised head on the upper end of the spine, the nuchal muscles and ligaments have become so delicate that they do not require massive areas of bone for attachment. The cranial vault gives the appearance of having expanded upward, backward, and from side to side, increasing threefold or so the size of the hollow chamber which holds the brain (see Fig. 2.18). These conditions make possible an average cranial capacity of about 1350 cc for modern man, and the upper limit may even run over 1600 cc.

Some of the cultural consequences of man's expanded brain will be discussed later, but, from any point of view, the swollen cranial vault is one of the most outstanding features of man's physical evolution.

C. EXTINCT HOMINIDS [3]

Remains of so many partially manlike forms that lived and died on earth prior to the appearance of *Homo sapiens* have been discovered that anthropologists find themselves embarrassed with riches. Out of the mass of early hominids already found, they do not know which ones belong in the direct path leading to modern man and which represent side branches that culminated only in dead ends. They do not know with certainty where each of these hominids originated, and they cannot recite the entire cast in the order of its appearance. Moreover, they are forced to deal with the vagaries of asymmetrical evolution.[4] According to this concept, the course of evolution proceeds irregularly, with some body parts evolving more rapidly than others. Only with such a concept in mind can we understand why some specimens of early hominids have human thighbones but apish skulls, or simian jaws containing humanoid teeth. When confronted with such assortments, who is to say whether a particular example should be classed with man or with some other Primate?

From the welter of puzzling details, several facts may be selected as valid. Before man had achieved his present body form, there had lived many kinds of less completely evolved hominids. No one of them is as old as one million years, which marks the start of the Pleistocene period, and the great majority go back only to mid-Pleistocene times, about 500,000 years ago, or less. Some of the early humanoids are probably in the main line of man's descent, but most of them died without known issue, and not one has survived to our day in his original form. Because the extinct hominids help mark the path that man followed after leaving the simian line, anthropologists pay much attention to their study.

So far the most comprehensive classification of extinct hominids has been proposed by the late Dr. Franz Weidenreich. He was of the opinion that even before the middle of the Pleistocene, *Homo* had become separated into at least three major divisions, each of which contained several different types. Weidenreich named the large divisions, in the supposed order of their resemblance to modern man, Archanthropinae ("ancient hominids"), Paleoanthropinae

---

[3] In other anthropological textbooks, the phrase "fossil men" is used in place of "extinct hominids." Since the remains discussed are neither invariably fossilized nor completely human, "extinct hominids" seems to give a more precise description of what is meant.

[4] E. A. Hooton, "The Asymmetrical Character of Human Evolution," *American Journal of Physical Anthropology*, Vol. 8, 1925, pp. 125-141.

("old hominids"), and Neoanthropinae ("new hominids").[5] Weidenreich believed, on rather fragmentary evidence, that the first mannish forms ever to have appeared were as big as giants, although later forms had the proportions of living men and women. Since his death, new materials have been found that tend to support his view.[6]

1. Archanthropinae

In 1891, less than ten years after the death of Charles Darwin, a young and energetic Dutch surgeon named Dr. Eugene Dubois was searching for old bones along the banks of an ancient channel that had been cut in Pleistocene days by the Solo river near Trinil in central Java. He picked up an unusual kind of tooth. Three feet away he came across the upper part of a skull, and nearly 50 feet further off he located a left thighbone. Before he had finished, two more teeth and a piece of a lower jaw, found at a more distant spot, were added to his collection (Fig. 3.3A).

From his knowledge of comparative anatomy, Dubois became convinced that all the skeletal fragments pertained to an intermediate sort of hominid whom he designated as **Pithecanthropus erectus** ("ape-man erect").[7] What was this creature really like? Judged by the skull cap, he was markedly apish. His cranial vault was thick and heavy; a solid torus of bone protruded above the eye cavities; the forehead was exceedingly low and narrowly constricted just beyond the eye sockets; and the nuchal area was so extensive and ran so high up the occiput that the head must have been poorly poised on the spine. Several competent specialists have reconstructed the entire skull on the basis of the portion of the cranium that was actually found, and have measured the cranial capacity. Their results vary somewhat but an average in the neighborhood of 900 cc is fairly representative of all the estimates. This

---

[5] F. Weidenreich, *Apes, Giants, and Man*, Chicago, 1946, pp. 29-31.

[6] The method used by Weidenreich is known as morphological dating, and is not free of scientific objections. See T. D. Stewart, "The Development of the Concept of Morphological Dating . . . in America," *Southwestern Journal of Anthropology*, Vol. 5, 1949, especially pp. 15-16.

As to the presence of giants, P. Wen-chung, "Giant Ape's Jaw Bone Discovered in China," *American Anthropologist*, Vol. 59, No. 5, 1957, pps. 834-838, has reported the presence of huge Primates, possibly apes, in ancient deposits located within the borders of what is now China.

[7] Subsequent discoveries made in Java, particularly by Dr. G. H. R. Von Koenigswald, have done much to confirm and amplify the observations made by Dubois. Particulars may be found in G. H. R. Von Koenigswald, *Meeting Prehistoric Man*, New York, 1956.

figure is nearly twice that of an adult gorilla, but only about two thirds that of an average modern man.

Markedly different from the other fragments is the femur, which is quite modern in every way. The shaft has a straight contour, a sign of upright posture, and its size indicates that its owner stood about 5 feet, 7 inches high, and weighed about 150 pounds. When all the evidence is put together, it gives the impression that *Pithecanthropus erectus* had an apelike head mounted on an essentially human body.

About 30 years or so after Dubois had made his original discoveries in Java, a number of persons began to suspect the presence of extinct hominids in a limestone quarry situated at Chou Kou Tien, 40 miles southwest of Peking. Until 1927, the evidence was extremely meager, but in later years more and more skeletal material came to light from Chou Kou Tien, all of which pertained to the same kind of hominid, now known as **Sinanthropus pekinensis** ("Chinese man from Peking").

Unlike the Pithecanthropoid relics, the *Sinanthropus* specimens were found in rapid succession, and were so firmly embedded in middle Pleistocene stone as to leave no doubt of their relationship. The remains are slightly variable in character, but it is not impossible to group them into one composite picture.

Sinanthropus skulls (Fig. 3.3B) are provided with heavy, bony brow ridges; the foreheads are low and retreating; the jaws massive, protruding, and relatively chinless; and the nuchal areas are as rugged and extensive as in *Pithecanthropus*. The teeth are far from uniform, but they approach the human rather than the ape condition. Estimates of cranial capacity vary, but an average of slightly over 1000 cc is indicated; and the thighbones show that the Chinese men from Peking walked fully upright. Most writers on the subject accept as reliable cultural objects found associated with *Sinanthropus,* which suggest that he lived in caves, may have been a good hunter, was capable of fabricating stone tools and kindling fires, and that he might possibly have been addicted to cannibalism.

2. *Paleoanthropinae*

Not many years ago there was a tendency to use the term Neandertal man more or less interchangeably with Paleoanthropinae, but recent research has demonstrated that this usage is unsatisfactory. More than one kind of Neandertal man is now distinguished, and

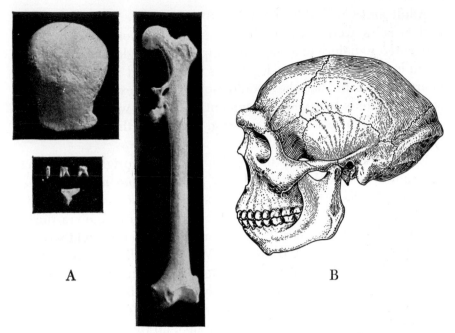

A   B

Fig. 3.3. Two of the best-known Archanthropinae. A. *Pithecanthropus erectus*. The parts recovered which are shown here include fragments of a skull cap, femur, jaw, and teeth. The whole assemblage is intermediate between apish and hominid forms. (Courtesy Peabody Museum, Harvard University.) B. *Sinanthropus pekinensis*. Reconstruction of a female *Sinanthropus* skull (after Montagu, following Weidenreich). There is a surprisingly heavy supraorbital torus for a female, the forehead is retreating, the arch of the skull vault is low, prognathism is pronounced, and there is no forward projection of the chin. (From Montagu, *op. cit.* Courtesy Charles E. Thomas.)

together they make up the major division of Paleoanthropinae, but it is best not to regard Neandertal man and Paleoanthropinae as one and the same thing.[8]

Between 1848 and the present, the remains of nearly a hundred Neandertal men, women, and children have been discovered in the Old World. They lived over a time span that covers more than 100,000 years, from the later stages of the Early Pleistocene well into the late Pleistocene. When their spread in time and space is considered, it is small wonder that they should be greatly diversified.

[8] Some of the distinctions are ably discussed in F. Clark Howell, "The Place of Neanderthal Man in Human Evolution," *American Journal of Physical Anthropology*, new series, Vol. IX, No. 4, 1951, pp. 379-416. Howell's analysis is based on studies of crania only.

Adult males probably stood 2 or 3 inches more than 5 feet high, and females were slightly shorter. This relatively low stature is attributed to failure to achieve a completely upright posture. Classic Neandertal man has short leg bones with bowed shafts, which appear to indicate that they could not be fully extended when he stood up. He is believed, consequently, to have walked with a dip at the knees, a mode of progression known as the **bent-knee gait** (see Fig. 3.4).

Except for his inability to stand completely upright, which may have interfered with his speed and agility, *Homo neandertalensis* was not significantly inferior in physical fitness or gross brain size to human beings now living. Furthermore, much of the era during which he lived in Western Europe was subject to the frigid weather conditions of a protracted Ice Age. With this difficult environment he managed to cope not by adjusting biologically, but by developing cultural aids in the form of cave homes, fireplaces, possibly clothing, and well-made tools and weapons. We shall meet the classic Neandertaloids again when we take up the Mousterian phase of culture in Western Europe.

3. Neoanthropinae

Those hominids that lived prior to the end of the Pleistocene period yet show a near approximation to the structure of contemporary man are ordinarily classified as Neoanthropinae.[9] Two theories have prevailed concerning their relationships to Neandertal man. One group of writers favors the notion that the Neandertalers became completely extinct and are to be regarded only as collateral relatives who contributed nothing to the formation of modern man. The other group avers that some Neandertaloids are directly ancestral to some forms of living man. An up-to-date but conservative statement would declare that Neandertal man as such did become extinct during the Pleistocene, but not before some Neandertaloid

---

[9] Until a few years ago Piltdown man or *Eoanthropus dawsoni* ("Dawson's dawn man") was often placed in this category. Its relics were discovered between the years 1911 and 1915, and always constituted something of a puzzle, because an apish jaw was found associated with a modern, human type of upper skull. Recent investigations, using the most up-to-date of modern techniques, have plainly demonstrated that this combination had deliberately been put together as a hoax, and serious references to Piltdown man are gradually disappearing from anthropological literature. For details, see J. S. Weiner, *The Piltdown Forgery*, New York, 1955.

genes had been contributed through evolution or interbreeding to the basic stock that has produced the present human population.

Anthropological opinion has also undergone a change with respect to the dating of Neoanthropic remains. At first, it was com-

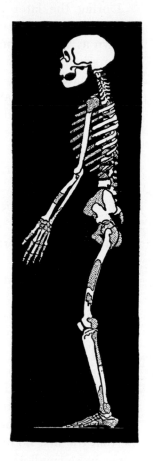

Fig. 3.4. *Homo neandertalensis.* Restoration of a Neandertal skeleton from La Chapelle-aux-Saints (after MacCurdy, following Boule). Particularly noteworthy are the poorly poised skull, slightly developed spinal curves, rounded rib cage, and bowed femur. A recent re-examination indicates that the bowed femur may have resulted from disease and may not be typical of Neandertal anatomy. (From G. G. MacCurdy, *Human Origins,* New York, 1926. Courtesy Appleton-Century-Crofts.)

monly held that the more modern-looking forms of Pleistocene man could not possibly have appeared as early as Neandertal man. Next, the consensus favored the opposite view. Today there is reason to believe that some Neoanthropinae are at least of the same age as Neandertal man, and that a few specimens may even be older.[10] Luckily, the problems that vex specialists deal primarily with the early and the middle phases of the Pleistocene. By the time

10 Fontéchevade man, recently discovered in a cave in southern France, is currently regarded by some anthropologists as a modern type that lived in Western Europe before Neandertal man arrived.

that that period had drawn to a close, the Archanthropinae and Paleoanthropinae had disappeared from the scene throughout the Old World, and Neoanthropic forms predominated and led directly to the varieties of men who now inhabit our globe.

During the later phases of the Pleistocene, there appeared in steadily increasing numbers in Western Europe types of individuals known as **Cro-Magnon.** They were a highly evolved group of Neo-anthropinae who, by absorption, displacement, or elimination, came to dominate the areas where they settled. As a whole, the Cro-Magnon people were characterized by tall and robust bodies, with long arms and shins, and total statures that go as high in males as 5 feet, 10 or 11 inches. Their heads were large and high vaulted, with moderate brow ridges, elevated foreheads, well-formed chins, and capacious brain cases that may have accommodated as many as 1600 cc (see Fig. 3.5). Apart from some unimportant facial and bodily features, which are not unknown among living human beings, there is really nothing to differentiate the Cro-Magnon men from tall and powerfully built people of our day. Many students are convinced that a fraction of Europe's population is directly derived from Cro-Magnon ancestry. It thus becomes a matter of personal preference whether one calls the Cro-Magnons the last of the extinct hominids or the first examples of modern man.

Even if the uncertainties that go with each step in the story of man's origins are frankly admitted, the main episodes in the divergence of the human and simian stocks stand out fairly well. Apparently, by early Pleistocene times the separation had progressed far enough to produce those manlike forms known as Archanthropinae who once inhabited parts of Java and China. It may be that the first hominids were of giant proportions, but later specimens were smaller and had the dimensions of *Pithecanthropus* and *Sinanthropus,* which approximate those of living mankind. About the time that the mid-Pleistocene horizons were being reached, the Archanthropinae seem to have given rise, in the more southerly latitudes of the Old World, to late Archanthropic or early Paleoanthropic forms. These, in turn, may possibly have been ancestral to one or more varieties of the fully developed Paleoanthropinae typified by the Neandertaloids. Contemporaneously, different sorts of hominids, the Neoanthropinae, who closely resemble modern men, began to show up in Europe in growing numbers, especially during the middle and later stages of the Pleistocene. Some of these give no evidence of mixture with Neandertalers but others suggest a degree of contact.

Before the Pleistocene drew to a close, about 20,000 years ago, very highly evolved Neoanthropinae, including the Cro-Magnon group, penetrated into Western Europe from some place further east or south where they are presumed to have originated. They became widespread and dominant in their new environment, and there gave rise to some of the varieties of modern man that still exist.

Fig. 3.5. Restorations of Neandertal and Cro-Magnon man (after McGregor). A, C. Neandertal man. B, D. Cro-Magnon man. Cro-Magnon man's head is higher, his neck is longer, his head and jaws are less out-thrust, his brow ridges are more delicate, and his chin is well developed. In short, he is a modern human being in all respects. (F. Boas, ed., *General Anthropology*. Boston, 1938. Courtesy D. C. Heath.)

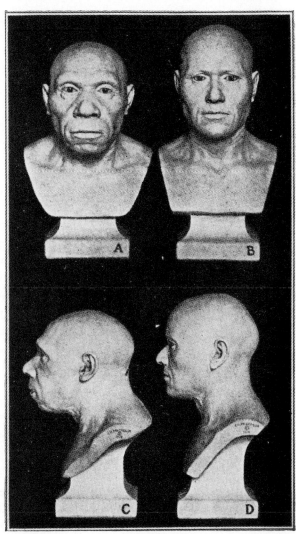

D. THE LIVING VARIETIES OF MAN

By every estimate that has yet been made, the number of human beings now alive is set at about two and one-half billion. Faced with the overwhelming problem of trying to deal with so huge a number of subjects, the anthropologist is forced to classify mankind into large groups. Customarily, attempts at gross classification are based on procedures that have long been practiced by students of all forms of living things. To summarize what any skillful classifier would decide, the biological classification of modern man runs as follows:

Kingdom	Animal
Subkingdom	Metazoa
Phylum	Chordata
Subphylum	Vertebrata
Class	Mammalia
Subclass	Eutheria
Order	Primate
Suborder	Anthropoidea
Family	Hominidae
Genus	Homo
Species	Sapiens

There is no reason to believe that the forces of evolution which served to bring about the emergence of modern man stopped operating as soon as he had arrived. When the physical anthropologist studies *Homo sapiens,* therefore, he must deal with two and one-half billion diversified members of a single species. A student of living man may decide to pay no attention to the differences, or else he may decide to investigate the distinctions in the hope of determining just how extensive they are, how they originated, and what they signify. Invariably, anthropologists have chosen to take the latter course.

An overwhelming majority of scholars takes the position that all the living varieties of mankind stem from a common background, but that they long ago acquired distinctive traits as they settled in variegated environments. As a starting point for such a hypothesis, let us postulate that considerably more than 20,000 years ago there appeared in the Eastern Hemisphere a generalized kind of *Homo sapiens,* whose descendants gradually spread throughout the Old World. Professor Wilton M. Krogman has suggested that a type of man similar to the one we are postulating may have carried genes for skin colors that ranged from white to very dark brown, head shapes that ran from narrow to broad, hair forms that varied from straight to curly, and so on.[11]

Since it is known that the first humans lived by hunting, fishing, and gathering wild foods, it is reasonable to assume that they moved about in small units that could readily have become isolated from one another. Under these circumstances, the conditions for forming distinct physical varieties were practically ideal. Each of the separate bands would, of necessity, become an inbreeding community. Within the inbreeding population, environmental, social, and sexual selection would operate to perpetuate some types at the expense of others. This means that in the course of time its original genetic variability would have been greatly reduced. Furthermore, mutations taking place in the reproductive cells of one of the isolated groups would not have been likely to be duplicated in any of the others. Thus, after many generations of geographical and biological separation, all of the inbreeding units, despite their originally common genetic background, would differ from each other **genotypically** (in the actual composition of their genes), as well as **phenotypically** (in outward form or appearance). Then, as means of communication and travel improved, the once-isolated, varied bands of *Homo sapiens* would be enabled to establish contacts with each other, thus paving the way for the high degree of intermixture that is an outstanding phenomenon of our day. No one denies that there might once have been a stage when the various subdivisions of mankind were genetically "pure"; but the existence of so-called "pure races" nowadays is entirely mythical.

Even a superficial examination of the variations among human beings makes apparent two orders of magnitude. Major distinctions set apart from one another the universally recognized divisions of white, yellow, and black; and lesser differences separate groups of individuals contained within each of the big units. We must not forget that both the major and minor sets of distinctions pertain to members of a single species; hence, whatever subdivisions are made must be recognized to apply to something less than a species. A suggestion has been put forth, and will be followed here, to call the main units by the term **stock**, with the im-

[11] W. M. Krogman, "The Concept of Race," *The Science of Man in the World Crisis*, R. Linton, ed. New York, 1945, p. 46.

plication that each of them corresponds to a subspecies.[12] Then the smaller groups within a stock may be called **races,** with the understanding that they correspond to sub-subspecies. It is a matter of record that biologists find it increasingly difficult to establish clear-cut categories as these become smaller than a species. Anthropologists have exactly the same trouble. There is relatively little disagreement about stocks,[13] but races are hard to distinguish satisfactorily, and a degree of confusion prevails on this score.

Absence of great and outstanding biological differences among the various subgroups of *Homo sapiens* has forced the classifiers of living man to deal with anatomical minutiae. As a rule, they have gone about their task by using a combination of three techniques. Wherever possible, on skeletal material or live bodies, they try to make careful **measurements** between recognizable points (Fig. 3.6).

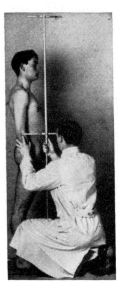

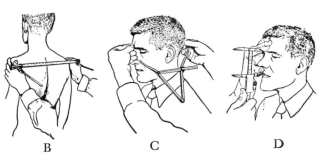

B   C   D

Fig. 3.6. Taking measurements on the human body (after Martin and Hooton). A and B show how an anthropometer is used for taking, respectively, upper arm length and the width of the shoulders. C illustrates how a spreading caliper measures the length of the head, and D pictures the measurement of upper face height with a sliding caliper. (From Hooton, *op. cit.*)

A

Where this is impossible, as in dealing with color differences, they depend on detailed **observations** based on generally accepted standards (Fig. 3.7). For computing averages or establishing pro-

---

[12] For further details, see Krogman, *op. cit.,* p. 48.

[13] The white, black, and yellow stocks are universally accepted. Almost in the same category are Australoid and American Indian. Beyond these there is nothing like universal agreement.
Not all anthropologists use stock in the sense of a subspecies, as it is used here.

portions between one body part and another, they resort to a number of **statistical devices.**

Until the current generation of physical anthropologists began to work, the traditional techniques were universally employed and seldom questioned. It was believed that they would yield an accurate

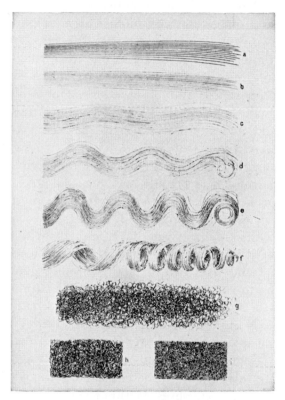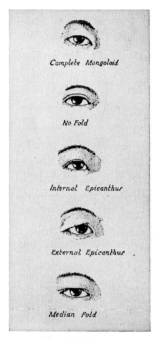

Fig. 3.7. Aids to observations. A. Varieties of human head hair. Mongoloids have types a and b, and, occasionally, c. Caucasoids have some c, but are usually d, e, or f. Negroids generally have the spiral forms lettered g, h, and i. B. Eye folds. Although eye folds are most characteristic of the Mongoloids, they may sometimes be noted in individuals of other stocks. (After Martin and Hooton, *op. cit.*)

knowledge of the nature, range, and meaning of the variations among mankind; throw light on the evolutionary processes that produced man and divided him into stocks and races; afford a sound point of departure for studies of the relationship of race to health and disease, longevity, fertility, alcoholic tolerance, or intelligence; and help to elucidate the biological consequences of such practices as inbreeding or race mixture. Not all of these goals have been achieved, and a large number of contemporary specialists are impatiently objecting to the continued use of old procedures. Their criticisms chiefly center on the neglect of the science of genetics, the exaggerated emphasis on bony structures rather than softer tissues or fluids, and an unsophisticated use of statistics.

Without deviating too far from established biological principles it is possible to divide *Homo sapiens* into stocks or subspecies by grouping in each division those people who live in one area, function as an interbreeding unit, and have bodies that are similar in terms of measurements, proportions, and observations. Only the three best-known stocks will be described.[14] Their boundaries are by no means rigidly fixed, and alternative systems of classification are perfectly possible.

One of the generalized ancestral hominids from whom all living humans may possibly be descended, the **white** or **Caucasoid** stock, was differentiated quite early. It is the least specialized and most variable of the three subspecies to be treated. Within this division may be found individuals with skin colors ranging from clear white through pink or ruddy to light brown or ripe olive. Hair color runs from platinum blond to red and dark brown; and eye color goes from pale gray-blue or green to various shades of brown. Hair form on the head is usually wavy or lightly curled, and the face and body show considerable hairiness. Noses are predominantly high bridged with profiles that vary from straight to concave or convex. Head shapes fluctuate all the way from the very longheaded to the broad-headed, and body builds are too variable to be classified, although pelves are proportionately wide in both sexes. Within the Caucasoid stock are included such races as an **Archaic White,** which appears most prominently among the Ainu, and which may have played a part in the formation of Veddoids and Australoids; the brunet **Mediterraneans** and **Alpines;** the lightly-pigmented **Nordics;** and the darker **Armenoids** and **Dinarics.** (See Fig. 3.8.)

Our second subspecies comprises the **black** or **Negroid** stock. Its members are characterized by dark brown to black skins and eye colors, and by black head hair that tends to loop into narrow or intertwined spirals. Beard and body hair is generally black and less abundant than in the Caucasoid stock. Most Negroids are long-

---

[14] Stock and race descriptions customarily take the adult male as a standard.

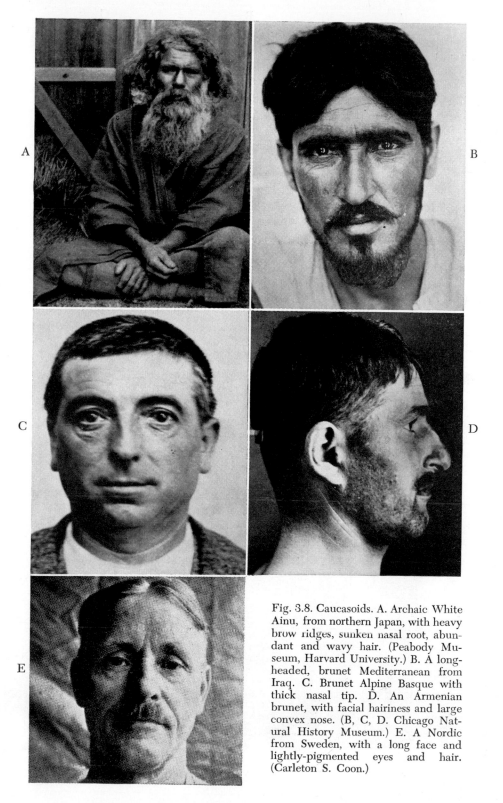

Fig. 3.8. Caucasoids. A. Archaic White Ainu, from northern Japan, with heavy brow ridges, sunken nasal root, abundant and wavy hair. (Peabody Museum, Harvard University.) B. A longheaded, brunet Mediterranean from Iraq. C. Brunet Alpine Basque with thick nasal tip. D. An Armenian brunet, with facial hairiness and large convex nose. (B, C, D. Chicago Natural History Museum.) E. A Nordic from Sweden, with a long face and lightly-pigmented eyes and hair. (Carleton S. Coon.)

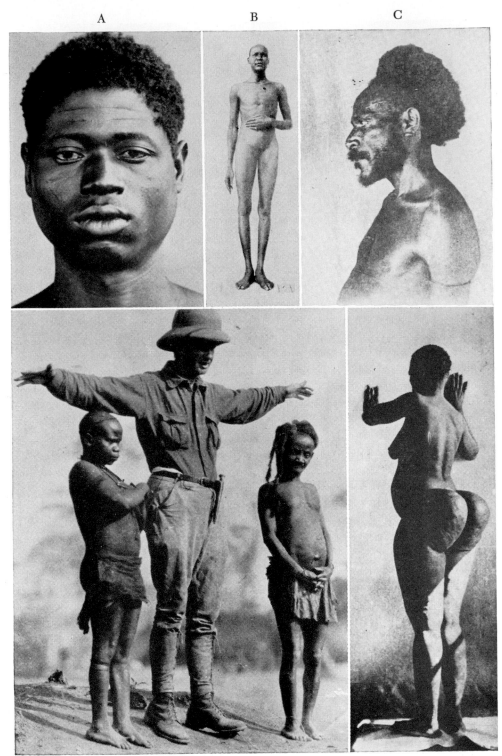

A   B   C

D   E

headed, with considerable jaw protrusion (**prognathism**), broad noses, thick and greatly everted lips, and somewhat receding chins. Body sizes and proportions vary, but the pelves are relatively narrow, calf muscles may be poorly developed, and the arch of the foot is often low. Negroid races include **Forest, Nilotic,** and **Oceanic Negroes, Pygmy Negroes, Bushmen,** and **Hottentots** (Fig. 3.9). Despite the best efforts of numerous physical anthropologists, it must be admitted that the various Negroid groups are so greatly diversified that they are exceedingly difficult to classify satisfactorily.

Although adequate proof is lacking, and there are ample grounds for skepticism, some claim that the **Mongoloid** stock (Fig. 3.10), was the last subspecies of *Homo sapiens* to make its appearance. On the whole, members of the Mongoloid division may be described as broad-headed, broad-faced, and broad-shouldered. Skin colors generally show a yellowish tint but may vary from a lemon color to reddish brown. As a rule, eyes are dark brown. Head hair is long, coarse of texture, straight, and black. On the face and body, Mongoloids are distinctively devoid of hair (**glabrous**). Several special characteristics are found in the facial area. The eyes have narrow openings, give a slanted appearance, and are heavy-lidded, with extra folds of skin (**Mongoloid** or **epicanthic folds**) stretched across the upper lids from the eyebrows to the lashes and from the outer corners to the nose. Nasal bridges tend to be of medium breadth but very low, and cheek bones are padded with fat and prominent, jutting out from back to front as well as from side to side. Prognathism, chin, and lip development are all medium, but the incisor teeth frequently have an unusual concavity that gives them a "**shovel-shaped**" appearance. Infants are sometimes born with

---

Fig. 3.9. Negroids. A. Forest Negro. A man from Dahomey, with all the main features of his stock, including dark pigmentation, spiral-shaped head hair, low, broad nose, and thick, everted lips. B. Nilotic Negro. A tall, thin, Dinka male, from East Africa. He is less dark than a Forest Negro, and his Negroid traits are sufficiently modified to suggest the possibility of ancient race mixture with Caucasoids. C. Oceanic Negro from New Guinea. A Papuan tribesman whose hair form and abundance, as well as whose nasal configuration, differ from those of African Negroes. D. Pygmy Negro adults from the Ituri forest of Africa, shown with a Caucasoid man to contrast their statures. E. A Hottentot woman, with a pronounced degree of steatopygy. (A, C, D, E. Chicago Natural History Museum. B. Museum of Anthropology, University of Michigan.)

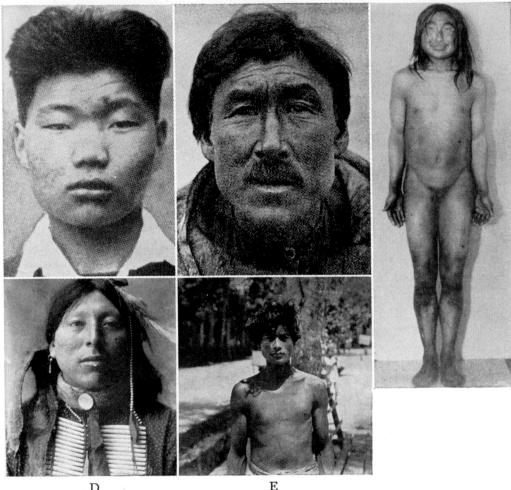

Fig. 3.10. Mongoloids. A. East Asiatic (Classic) Mongoloid. He is a speaker of the Tungus
language, which is widespread in Northeastern Asia, and exhibits all the diagnostic features
of his stock and race, including full Mongoloid eye-folds. (C. S. Coon, S. M. Garn, J. B.
Birdsell, *Races*. Springfield, Ill., 1950. Courtesy Charles E. Thomas.) B. Arctic Mongoloid.
Except for his head hair and a partial epicanthic fold, this Koryak man does not look particularly Mongoloid. (American Museum of Natural History.) C and D. American Indians
(Amerinds): C. An Eskimo with non-hairy, glabrous body; D. A Sioux Indian, with Mongoloid head hair and cheekbones, but non-Mongoloid nose and eyes. E. Indonesia-Malay.
A Batak tribesman from the island of Sumatra. Very likely he represents an ancient admixture
of Mongoloid and Negroid (C, D, E. Chicago Natural History Museum.)

purplish-blue areas of skin (**Mongoloid spots**) at the small of the back, but these generally disappear by adolescence. Comparable spots may also occur in Negroids. Among the best known of the Mongoloid races are the **"classic" Mongoloids** of Eastern Asia and the **Eskimo.** Important Mongoloid strains are also found within the mixtures that make up **American Indians** and the **Indonesian-Malays.**

E. SOME BALD FACTS ABOUT RACE

No matter how crude some of the traditional techniques of physical anthropology are now regarded to be, earlier workers in the field did make some valuable contributions to a scientific understanding of racial differences. From the outset they showed a marked determination to avoid preconceived notions and to deal with human variations with the same objective detachment that zoologists exhibit when classifying other animals. Some of their pronouncements on race are still valid and worth repeating.

All anthropologists are united in the belief that stock and race distinctions are biological, resulting from geographic isolation and the interplay of evolutionary and reproductive forces. Accordingly, differences of race or stock cannot possibly be expressed in terms of nongenetically heritable, nonbiological, or nonsomatic traits. Anthropology does not recognize such so-called "races" as Aryan, Latin, or Semitic, which are best regarded as linguistic groups; Mohammedan, Hindu, or Jewish, which most commonly refer to followers of particular religions; and Italian or British, which have primarily geographical or political significance. Students of man must never allow themselves to forget the fundamental distinction between inborn, biologically determined, lifelong, racial characteristics that one receives involuntarily at conception, and cultural attributes that are acquired by postnatal education. After all, a member of any stock or race may be taught to speak any language whatsoever; may learn to worship any god; may live in any part of the world, without altering his inherited biology; and may acquire citizenship in many a different country.

The anatomical features of individuals are always genetically predetermined at conception, but racial boundaries are not rigidly fixed, and some physical traits are constantly in the process of being modified or changed. In fact, races are sometimes thought to be

embryonic species, or units that are going through a process of
change which may ultimately convert them to new species.[15] More
than one study has shown that any given race of human beings
possesses so much **plasticity** that its members are likely to become
at least phenotypically different from each other if some of them
grow up in dissimilar environments. Practically, this amounts to saying, among other things, that the offspring of migrating members
of a race will vary considerably from the children of stay-at-home
members of the same race.[16] By itself, however, plasticity does not
seem sufficient to cause an individual to differ racially from his
parents. We do not know of a single case whereby, through plasticity alone, a full-blooded child has turned into a racial type that
differs from that of his father and mother.

No race or stock, taken in the aggregate, can be judged to be
more highly evolved than any other. Biologically speaking, a race
could be called superior if it proved to have more strength, vitality,
longevity, disease resistance, or fertility. After many years of research, anthropologists have reached the conclusion that in these
terms there are neither superior nor inferior stocks and races. In
all important anatomical details, all of living mankind is alike. At
the same time, there are indications of some lesser biological differences. Mongoloids appear to have a lower metabolic rate than
Caucasoids of corresponding sex and age, Negroids are the most
susceptible to sickle-cell anemia, and in the United States cancer
strikes an exceptionally high percentage of Caucasoids. So far the
data on this topic are too meager to permit the formulation of general laws, but comparative pathology is one of the most interesting
fields of research dealing with physical variations among differing
groups of men.

Neither race nor stock mixture produces harmful biological consequences and, contrary to opinions that prevail in some quarters,
they may even bring about beneficial results through the agency of
heterosis, or **hybrid vigor.** On this topic anthropologists speak with
assurance because members of the profession have studied the off-

---

[15] An elaboration of this concept, based on recent theories of human genetics, is
to be found in S. Garn, "Race and Evolution," *American Anthropologist,* Vol. 59,
1957, pp. 218-224, especially p. 219.

[16] This demonstration was first made over forty years ago by the very traditional
anthropologist, Professor Franz Boas, in *Changes in Bodily Form of Descendants of
Immigrants,* Washington, 1911. It was then verified by later workers and was given
a new statement by H. L. Shapiro, *Migration and Environment,* New York, 1939.

spring of a great many interstock matings in all parts of the world.[17] Nowhere have they found signs of physical deterioration resulting from intermixture. Even the descendants of such varied parents as Dutch (Caucasoid) men and Hottentot (Negroid) women turned out to be vigorous, fertile, and long-lived.[18] Popular prejudices often create difficult social and cultural situations for hybrid individuals or groups, but in strictly biological terms, race mixture produces no harmful results.

Less is known about the consequences of inbreeding, but the few investigations that have been made by unprejudiced observers have led to the tentative conclusion that it is not invariably dangerous. As far as can now be determined, inbreeding does no more than intensify the usual procedures of heredity. Therefore, if it occurs in a group with a good genetic background, it should do no harm, but if it takes place among people with many deficient genes, it may lead to biological disaster.

These findings have been directly opposed in our day to the exaggerated claims of unscientific speakers and writers on racial topics. The term **racist** has come into current usage to denote those who argue about race without reference to observed and known facts. It is to the credit of physical anthropology that it has provided effective material to counteract the extravagant statements uttered by unabashed racists.

To date, no convincing proof has been brought forward to show that the races of mankind differ in the *potentialities* of their mental equipment. Assuredly, vast differences of intellectual *performance* can be demonstrated, but when it comes to measuring potential the going gets harder and harder. The reason that anthropologists are more concerned with comparative ratings of mental potential rather than performance is because no one knows to what extent the latter is based on cultural conditioning instead of on biological inheritance. Varying scores on intelligence tests between American Negroids and Caucasoids, for example, have been shown to relate so directly to cultural factors such as the amount of education and social or economic status, that it is hard to tell whether the tests measure biological differences of mental capacity or differences of

---

[17] See, for example, L. C. Dunn, *Eugenics in Race and State,* Baltimore, 1923, pp. 109-124.

[18] Consult the famous study of E. Fischer, *Die Rehobother Bastards,* Jena, 1912. "Bastards" is inaccurate as the subjects were born of legally married parents. Its very use may connote a degree of cultural prejudice.

training and background. Until techniques are devised for evaluating intellectual ability without reference to cultural influences, it can only be maintained that no distinctions of basic mentality are known to exist among the races of man.

Inasmuch as human beings live bioculturally rather than biologically, it follows that wherever biological race mixture takes place, a degree of cultural mingling is also likely to occur. By no means is this to be regarded as detrimental. We in the United States are proud of the high level of culture that we have attained, but we tend to overlook the fact that our way of life is the product of a great deal of borrowing and mixture. Only too often do we forget, for instance, that Semitic-speaking peoples from Asia and Africa were the first to develop such basic features of American culture as the Christian religion, the Phoenician alphabet, and Arabic numerals. Nor do our textbooks of history give sufficient emphasis to the long list of items that our white settlers borrowed from the Mongoloid American Indians whom they contemptuously labeled "savages." When we were worried about our supplies of rubber and quinine at the time of Pearl Harbor, did we realize that these vital substances originally had been made known to us by the aboriginal inhabitants of Central and South America? And when, during the course of the Second World War, lines of eager people formed in the hope of purchasing cigarettes or chocolate bars, were they aware that they were paying indirect tribute to those hybridized Mongoloids known as Indians who had introduced tobacco and cocoa to the American pattern of culture?

Incomplete as this list of cultural items is, it should serve to remind us of the hybrid nature of our way of life,[19] and to make us aware of the great enrichment that results from the mingling of cultural traditions.

SELECTED REFERENCES

Boas, F., "Changes in Bodily Form of Descendants of Immigrants," *61st Congress, 2nd Sess., Senate document no. 208.* Washington, D. C., 1911.

Broom, R., "The Genera and Species of the South African Fossil Ape-Man," *American Journal of Physical Anthropology.* Vol. 8, 1950, pp. 1-13.

---

[19] Ralph Linton's "One Hundred Per Cent American," *American Mercury,* Vol. 40, New York, 1937, pp. 427-429, provides an amusing but factual treatment of this topic.

Broom, R., and Schepers, G. W. H., "The South African Fossil Ape-Men, the Australopithecinae," *Transvaal Museum, Memoir no. 2.* Pretoria, South Africa, 1946.

Count, E. W., *This is Race.* New York, 1950.

Hooton, E. A., *Up from the Ape,* rev. ed. New York, 1946.

Howell, F. C., "The Place of Neanderthal Man in Human Evolution," *American Journal of Physical Anthropology.* Vol. 9, 1951, pp. 379-416.

Keith, Sir A., *New Discoveries Relating to the Antiquity of Man.* London and New York, 1931.

Krogman, W. M., "The Concept of Race," *The Science of Man in the World Crisis,* R. Linton, ed. New York, 1944.

Morton, J. D., "Evolution of Man's Erect Posture," *Journal of Morphology and Physiology.* Vol. 43, No. 1, 1926.

Shapiro, H. L., and Hulse, F., *Migration and Environment.* New York, 1940.

Stewart, T. D., (ed.), *Hrdlička's Practical Anthropometry,* rev. ed. Philadelphia, 1947.

Straus, W. L. Jr., "The Riddle of Man's Ancestry," *Quarterly Review of Biology.* Vol. 24, 1949, pp. 200-223.

Von Koenigswald, G. H. R., *Meeting Prehistoric Man.* New York, 1956.

Washburn, S. L., "Thinking about Race," *Smithsonian Report.* Washington, D. C., 1946, pp. 363-378.

———, "The New Physical Anthropology," *Transactions of the New York Academy of Sciences,* Series II, Vol. 13, No. 7, 1951, pp. 298-304.

Weidenreich, F., *Apes, Giants, and Man.* Chicago, 1946.

4

BIOLOGICAL FOUNDATIONS
OF CULTURE

A. PREAMBLE

All of *Homo sapiens* reveals in its anatomy sure signs of close relationship with other eutherian mammals and Primates. Students of cultural anthropology must constantly bear in mind that the differences which distinguish the various groupings of mankind are far less in number and significance than are the genetically inherited traits, presumably retained from a common ancestry, that bind all present-day human beings into a single species. Moreover, the evolutionary record, which shows how man acquired his body by taking over various of the biologic traits first developed by preceding forms of animal life, is of the utmost importance to those whose main interest is culture, for culture rests on biological foundations and the biology of man not only sets up definite objectives that all ways of life must meet, but it also establishes specific limitations beyond which no culture pattern may go.

Accordingly, it is impossible to gain a full understanding of man's culture without knowing something of his biology. For instance, all of us know that societies everywhere will have food habits of one kind or another because of the basic biological fact that men and women have bodies that cannot supply them with the necessary nutrients for sustaining life. To carry the same idea a step further,

86

social scientists may not be able to foretell if a given society will have prostitution, but if it does have such an institution, they can predict with assurance that common prostitutes will invariably be women because only feminine bodies are biologically capable of engaging in frequently repeated acts of intercourse without desire.[1] These are only two illustrations of the ways in which unalterable biological traits may influence the cultural behavior of human beings. Wherever biocultural behavior is in evidence, biology may be said to call the tune, but it is culture that sets the pattern of the dance. Moreover, so much alike in gross anatomy is all of *Homo sapiens* that those who preach the universal brotherhood of man may be thinking in terms of biology; whereas those who maintain that "never the twain shall meet" may have cultural factors in mind.

Careful observers have long noted that the body of *Homo sapiens* has retained many generalized Primate characteristics. They point out that man's five-digited hands and feet are built on a ground plan that has undergone comparatively little modification since it was first developed in amphibians. Most human organs and members are neither exceedingly large nor exceptionally small, nor is their usefulness confined to a greatly restricted environmental range or a sharply delimited kind of function. Animals that are greatly specialized can survive only in the particular environmental settings that are best suited to their anatomical specialties. Hence, it is a biological principle that the more specialized a creature is, the less chance it has to survive and play an important part in the evolutionary process. It is most unlikely that the first hominids who engaged in extrabiological behavior had this principle in mind, but the ultimate result has been that the progressive evolution and increasingly widespread use of cultural devices has allowed man to get along with a highly generalized type of Primate body.

While studies of organic evolution have revealed that *Homo sapiens* shares many of his somatic features with other animals, it is equally true that man has a few bodily characteristics that are entirely his own. In view of the fact that culture is so intimately

---

[1] Readers must learn not to be confused by mere words. Male prostitutes have been sometimes reported in anthropological literature, but such men were not common prostitutes. Use of the same word for men and women who get paid for the use of their bodies obscures the fact that males can never be ordinary prostitutes because they simply cannot have sexual relations repeatedly, day in and day out. Biology thus sets limits that no amount of cultural conditioning can overcome.

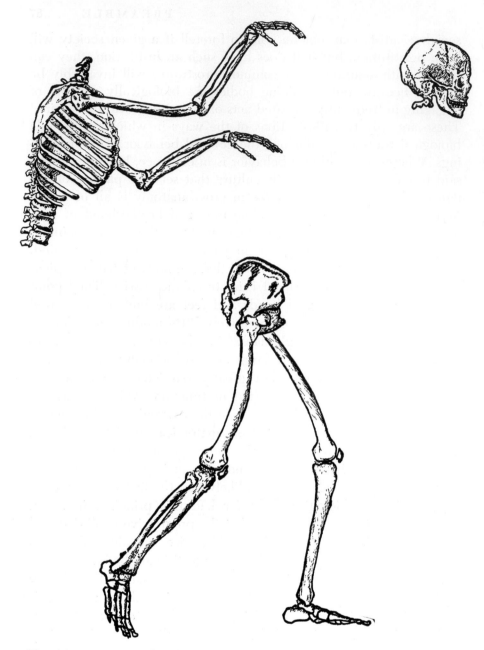

Fig. 4.1. Asymmetrical evolution. Each of the three areas appears to have had an independent evolution. Thorax and arms were the first to attain modern form, followed by pelvis, legs, and feet. The head and brain were the last to evolve fully. (S. L. Washburn, "The New Physical Anthropology," *Transactions* of the New York Academy of Sciences [May 1951].)

geared to biology, it stands to reason that the distinctive aspects of the human body must have an important bearing on his culture. We turn next to those bodily features that set man apart from the rest of the animal kingdom, or that furnish the biological foundations for his cultural behavior.

B. WALKING—NO HANDS!

The vast majority of man's anatomical distinctions seems to be concentrated in three of his body areas. They are the lower limbs, the forelimbs, and the head. Professor Sherwood L. Washburn, a distinguished physical anthropologist at the University of Chicago, is of the opinion that these three sectors did not evolve at one and the same time, but that the front limbs appeared first in their modern form, the lower limbs came next, and the head (with its enlarged brain) was the last to attain its present structure (see Fig. 4.1).

Homo sapiens is the only Primate that habitually walks on the ground in a bipedal or **orthograde** (upright) posture. On the one hand, this may be connected with the development and appearance

Fig. 4.2. Man's use of tools. A mechanic at work. His use of nonbiologic tools depends on the possession of such Primate characteristics as a prehensile grip, flexible wrists, opposable thumbs, and rotating forearms. (Courtesy of Eck Stanger, *The Ann Arbor News.*)

A   B

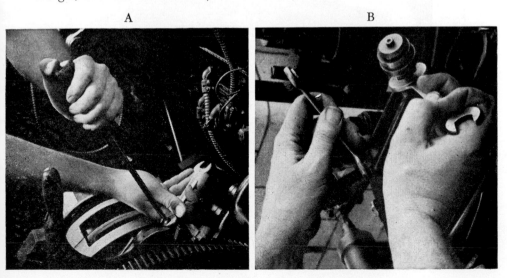

of his lower-limb structures, which seem to have become stabilized to the point where they can unassisted hold the body upright and move it about; and on the other hand, these structures came to do their job so well that other portions of the body were left free and could be devoted to other functions. This feature, which applies chiefly to the upper limbs and is conventionally described as the **emancipation of the forelimbs,** is of great importance in the forma-

Fig. 4.3. A baseball batter in action. Proper use of a baseball bat depends on features of Primate anatomy.

tion of culture. Primates who go about in a four-legged or quad-rupedal stance, and even those which may be considered partially bipedal, have muscle systems that bind the front or upper limbs, wholly or in part, to the support or movement of the body. Consequently, their forelimbs are not completely emancipated and cannot be freely used for nonpostural or nonlocomotor activities. On this score *Homo sapiens* differs markedly from all other Primates.

In other cases, man utilizes in his own way some of the body features that he shares with other Primates. Take, as examples, the customary manner in which *Homo sapiens* holds and uses a canoe paddle, can opener, hammer, saw, or screwdriver. In each of these instances and countless others involving the use of tools, the same bodily features (Fig. 4.2A), shared by humans and most other Primates, are brought into play. All of them, including the nerves that control their movements, provide the biological potential for such divergent activities as digging witchetty grubs or playing the piano, brushing one's hair, throwing a forward pass, knotting a necktie, beating drums, rolling out bread dough, steering an automobile, or using a variety of wrenches (Fig. 4.2B) and other implements. Without strong, firmly knit but flexible, and emancipated forelimbs, in conjunction with a collarbone or clavicle, powerful motions to the sides and rear of the body are also impossible. So, were it not for his distinctive and Primate anatomy, no baseball player could swing a bat hard enough to hit a home run (Fig. 4.3), no swimmer could do the backstroke well, and no tennis star could properly handle a racquet.

C. WATCH WHAT YOU'RE DOING

Increased reliance on the sense of sight is a noteworthy feature of biological evolution as we trace its story from fish to man. A world-famous neurophysiologist, Dr. R. W. Gerard, has estimated that approximately two thirds of all the nerve fibers that enter the human central nervous system come from the eyes. Any one of us, faced with the choice of losing either the sense of smell or the sense of sight, would unhesitatingly sacrifice the sense of smell.

Going a step further, we know that **stereoscopic** vision is just as important to human beings as is the accurate and rapid perception of simple light waves. Without the proper anatomical arrangement that makes possible overlapping or stereoscopic vision there would be no sense of depth, and without a sense of depth we could not tell a thin twig from a thick branch; it would be foolhardy ever to try to pass another automobile on the road; and motion-picture producers could save themselves the boundless costs of trying to perfect 3-D and similar devices for achieving the third dimension of depth.

Close coordination of hand and eye is likewise a prerequisite not only for successful life in treetops, but also for any human activity that involves the use of artifacts. Even so simple a matter as writing one's name becomes difficult if one tries to do it with his eyes shut.

Baseball coaches and golf instructors constantly remind players who are using bats or clubs to keep their eyes on the ball. Similarly, no one of us, if we had any say in the case, would accept the offer of a free operation at the hands of the most skilled of surgeons if we knew that he planned to operate while blindfolded.

Another important tie between the sense of sight and other body parts is involved in reaction speed, that is, the length of time that it takes for a message from the eyes to reach the brain, and for the brain to interpret the message and to send suitable instructions to the appropriate muscles that are to carry out a necessary task. Many people are prone to disregard reaction time and to think that body behavior and sight occur almost simultaneously. Not so with pilots of jet-propelled aircraft. As the speeds of their planes have increased, they have come to realize more and more how slow and imperfect are their own bodily mechanisms. No longer are they content to read instrument panels, to translate what they see, and to figure out what to do. What they want is a luminous screen that will show them at a glance the actual terrain towards and over which they are flying. And to further their sense of security, they would like this visual aid combined with a computer that would make all necessary calculations for them in only a few thousandths of a second.[2]

D. USE YOUR HEAD

It takes but a fraction of a moment to realize that every nonbiologic tool or artifact has to be made by a human being. Such things are so important for the ways of life to be found among all members of *Homo sapiens* that cultural anthropologists devote much effort to the understanding of how, when, where, and why they came into use; their methods of manufacture; and the ways in which they are utilized.

All clues once more lead back to Primate anatomy. Bipedal posture on the ground and the attendant emancipation of the forelimbs, together with the special construction of the front limbs, an amazingly large cranial capacity, and acute, stereoscopic vision, suffice to delineate the potential for tool usage, but it remained for a special kind of brain power to put that potential to work. A number of species of animals, far below the level of man in the evolutionary

---

[2] More details may be found in *Time*, October 22, 1956, p. 65.

sequence, are known to use bits of wood, stone, grass, earth, or other materials for a variety of purposes. In all such cases, there is clear evidence that extrasomatic devices are being employed as supplements to biologically inherited mechanisms; but as long as these things are used in their natural condition, it does not seem correct to class them as manufactured tools, even when they are combined into such complicated structures as nests.

To further the argument that extrasomatic items could have been in use before the appearance of hominids on earth, we have only to point to certain apes which, under experimental conditions, not only use tools but even show a limited capacity for making them. Credit for at least a small amount of manufacturing skill cannot be withheld from chimpanzees, which can bend flexible straws to make a stiff unyielding brush, fit two short sticks together to make a long one (Fig. 4.4), and can sometimes go so far as to chew on a thick stick until it is slim enough to penetrate a slender socket.

According to what we now know about the behavior of various beasts, it is evident that some tool-using and, possibly, tool-making ability is an ancient feature of life in the animal kingdom, and we may be sure that sticks and stones were used on occasion by man's ancestors. Not very long after the appearance of hominids, at the very latest by the time level of *Sinanthropus pekinensis* in the mid-Pleistocene, somewhere about 500,000 years ago, clear and irrefutable signs indicate that men were no longer living exclusively in the biophysicochemical world, but had entered into the realm of culture. The most conclusive proof rests on the occurrence of systematically manufactured stone tools that were found directly associated with skeletal remains. Regularly manufactured tools, it need hardly be emphasized, are not a part of any animal's biogenetic inheritance. They have to be fashioned with the help of a body, but they carry on an independent, extrabodily existence. We may speak of inheriting a kit of tools, but we realize full well that the manner of transmission is quite apart from sexual reproduction. By following all the implications of tool-making, it is possible to learn a great deal about how man came to use his inherited biological equipment for nonbiological purposes and in nonbiologically determined ways. It is the extraordinary elaboration and transmission of nonsomatic forms of conduct that most clearly marks the behavior of *Homo sapiens* apart from that of nonhuman beasts.

To make a tool requires the mental capacity to plan ahead freely without biological predetermination, to look unrestrictedly into the future, to deal with imaginary situations in the sense that all future events are imaginary before they have come to pass. Anthropologists have learned not to confuse the two different levels at which planning ahead may be found. One kind is biogenetically controlled, as

Fig. 4.4. Chimpanzee making a tool. Some credit for a degree of manufacturing skill cannot be withheld from a chimpanzee that can fit two sticks together to make an elongated implement with which to secure food. (From B. W. Köhler, *The Mentality of Apes,* 2d ed. New York, 1925. Courtesy of Harcourt, Brace and Co.)

when squirrels store nuts before the coming of winter, or when birds migrate from north to south and back again. The other kind is cultural and is neither biologically inherited nor a fixed response to environmental clues. The essential difference between these two levels of planning ahead is the matter of freedom of action. Biological planning ahead leaves almost no room for individual choice but is imposed, with only a little flexibility, on all the members of a given species. But cultural planning ahead permits each individual to act within a wide range of possibilities, and sets few limitations on how one may decide to meet a future contingency. Squirrels of a particular species must store nuts at certain times, in certain ways. Men, by contrast, may store any or no kinds of nuts, may decide to hoard instead potatoes or cans of soup, or may prefer to put money into the bank, or to go on relief when winter comes.

If it be granted that infra-human animals, particularly chimpanzees among the living apes, sometimes use and even manufacture tools, then it must be admitted that they too have at least a restricted ability to look ahead. This capacity has been proved in a series of revealing and sometimes amusing experiments. A vending machine, appropriately called a **Chimp-O-Mat,** was constructed in such fashion that by inserting a token comparable to a poker chip a raisin could be "bought." Experimenters showed the animals to be tested how to do a bit of work, operating a weight-lifting lever or pulling a sliding tray, by means of which a food token was earned. This was inserted into the Chimp-O-Mat and a raisin "purchased," and eaten.[3] Chimpanzees promptly caught the idea and were soon busily working for tokens and buying raisins (Fig. 4.5). Sometimes

Fig. 4.5. Use of the Chimp-O-Mat. A chimpanzee buying a raisin with a special token for which it has worked. This shows that it could plan ahead, in addition to recognizing a man-established, symbolic value. (Courtesy H. W. Nissen, J. B. Wolfe, "Effectiveness of Token-rewards for chimpanzees," *Comp. Psych. Monographs.* [Vol. 12, 1936].)

the Chimp-O-Mat was deliberately rendered out-of-order, but the apes continued to work for tokens, with somewhat diminished eagerness, in anticipation of going on a buying spree when the machine resumed operation. Chimpanzees also learned to discriminate valid discs from counterfeits. Tests yielding roughly comparable results have been carried out with a wide assortment of animals, not necessarily Primates.

By comparison with other creatures, man uses his ability to plan

---

[3] The short account given here is based on a combination of two reports, which may be found in J. B. Wolfe, "Effectiveness of Token-rewards for Chimpanzees," *Comparative Psychological Monographs,* Vol. 12, No. 5, 1936; and J. T. Cowles, "Food-tokens as Incentives for Learning by Chimpanzees," *idem,* Vol. 14, No. 5, 1937.

ahead so much more frequently and freely that it forms one of the most essential traits that separates him from the rest of the animal kingdom. Yet, there is a convention among ourselves that we cannot guess about the future, and all of us are familiar with remarks like, "No one knows what the future will bring," or "It's ridiculous to try to predict the future." Of course there are many vast and important areas in which prediction is futile, as in trying to guess who will be the President of the United States in 1990. Just the same, in spite of the wealth of proverbs and popular sayings to the contrary, human beings constantly indulge in predictions.

Every day, and at practically every moment of the day, huge numbers of men and women are constantly predicting, and to a great extent accurately predicting, many important future events. Countless school children select their colleges and professions years in advance; lovers decide to marry "when John gets out of the Army"; youngsters repeatedly make dates for "after school"; wives ask husbands each morning to bring something or other "on the way home from the office"; people make travel or hotel reservations months ahead; and invitations to great affairs go out long before they are scheduled to take place. Obviously, death or sickness or some other unforeseen contingency may upset one's predictions, but human beings persistently and to a large extent successfully base their lives on the premise that their plans for the future will be carried out.

It is time now to see how man's aptitude for planning and looking ahead applies to the making of tools. If one decides to manufacture even the simplest of implements, say a homemade toothpick of wood, he must plan for the future in several ways. He must know where he can get the necessary raw material and where he can secure the needed tools. More important still, he must have clearly in mind, before he begins manufacturing, the size and shape of the finished object that he wants to make. Unless he has in mind an advance blueprint of the completed product, he is unlikely to turn out even so elementary an implement as a simple, wooden toothpick.

Once he had developed the capacity to think ahead in ways that were not biologically predetermined or controlled, man was able to escape biophysicochemical limitations and to begin fashioning culture. Yet, he could not entirely divorce himself from biology, for if he refused to obey its imperatives, as by failing to breathe while manufacturing tools, he would surely die. Moreover, even if a man had the clearest of mental pictures of something he wanted to make, he would still require strong and flexible fingers, hands, wrists, and arms, accurate muscular controls, and keen hand-eye coordination in order to be a successful manufacturer. Thus can it be shown that cultural behavior must always utilize body parts, and that toolmaking is a biocultural activity.

E. WORDS AND SYMBOLS

Man's capacity to deal with future or imaginary situations calls for a kind of mentality that is, as far as is known, unique among animals. Because of this special ability the test of reality among human beings is no longer restricted to physical, chemical, or biological standards. This is what Emily Dickinson meant when she wrote her famous lines:

> "I never saw a moor
> I never saw the sea
> Yet know I how the heather looks
> And what a wave must be."

Man can and does deal with nonexistent or imaginary things with just about as much assurance as he does with tangible objects. Mermaids are not supposed to be real, but human beings can count them, paint or carve them, and write stories or poems about them. It is easy to give any normal human being verbal instructions that will enable him to go to some place where he has never before been and to take up an object which he has never before seen. I can readily tell a person who has never been to my house how to enter my study and remove the only black mask that hangs on the wall, but I cannot with speech alone similarly instruct any other animal.

One of man's most extraordinary mental accomplishments is his capacity for dealing with **abstractions.** By no test of bio-physico-chemical reality can one establish the existence of such abstract ideas as "pride," "civic duty," "loyalty," or "thoughtfulness"; yet, human beings have no trouble in grasping these intangibles, and even in measuring or comparing them, as when we say that one person has more or less pride than another. With the emergence of the mental ability to deal with abstractions, the way is opened for the development of higher mathematics, philosophy, poetry, religion, ethics, and similar fields.

Abstract ideas achieve a kind of reality, as a rule, only when they have been expressed in words. Accordingly, the human capacity for dealing with abstractions cannot be separated from the use of language. In essence, a spoken word is a sound or combination of sounds to which a group of persons (a society) has assigned a particular meaning. Take the sound "C" as commonly uttered in the English-speaking world. By itself it has absolutely no meaning, as any skeptic can discover if he will travel about the world saying, "C," "C," "C." Nor has this sound any specific meaning even to speakers of English. When used in one context the sound "C," spelled "see," means "look"; but if spelled and used another way the same sound, "sea," means "a body of salt water." "C" can just as well stand for the third letter of the alphabet, a note of our musical scale, an athletic award won at Colgate or Cornell, or a familiar form of address for a girl named Celia. How can the same sound "C" mean so many different things in English, to say nothing of meaning "yes" in Spanish or Italian, and "if" in French? Paradoxical as it may seem, the reason why "C" can mean all these things, plus whatever else human beings may choose to have it mean, is that in and of itself it has absolutely no meaning. Since it is entirely without meaning it does not restrict any society from assigning to it as many different meanings as it wishes. Even when this has been done with as much variety as in the English use of "C," no one of the ascribed meanings becomes permanently attached to the sound. We can still, if we like, change the meanings at will. In making up a code we can make "C" stand for an oboe or a windmill.

To deny that other animals are able to use *true speech* is not to deny that they can utter meaningful sounds. Birds, chickens, dogs, cats, most Primates, and many other creatures produce sounds that convey definite meanings, but on analysis it turns out that their sound-making ability is biologically inherited in its manner of production as well as in its content. Among all species below man the sounds are almost exclusively limited to the expression of generalized, subjective states like fear, hunger, joy, or sexual desire. There is no capacity for dealing with abstractions, and not even the most ardent of animal fanciers really expects a parrot to discuss philosophy. Moreover, not a single nonhuman creature can make sounds that apply to precise details. Even if one knows from the whine of a pet dog that it has been hurt, one realizes that the beast cannot utter detailed information about who injured it, when, or under what circumstances. To make meaningful sounds is a common aspect of animal behavior, but to use true speech is an exclusive, human ability.

The mental power to assign one or more meanings to something which has no meaning of its own is the basis of **symbolic behavior.** A standard dictionary definition of a **symbol** reads in part, "That which suggests something else . . . especially a visible sign of something invisible, as an idea, a quality. . . ." [4] A symbol does not necessarily have to be a sound. In fact, it is universally agreed that the invention of a mark for **zero** is one of the highest mental achievements ever made by man because it expresses the very essence of symbolism by providing something that stands for absolutely nothing. So extraordinary is this idea that anthropologists believe it has been separately hit upon only three times in the known history of the world's cultures. Only the Babylonians, Mayans, and Hindus are thought to have introduced symbols for zero into their mathematical systems as **independent inventions.** Wherever else zero figures occur they are considered to be borrowings from one of the three just-mentioned sources.

Anything at all can be endowed with symbolic meanings or values, and the meanings cannot be perceived except by members of the society who have been taught to know them. In purely physico-chemical terms two pieces of wood in the shape of a cross are nothing but two pieces of wood and will be so regarded by true pagans. But to believing Christians the symbolic meaning of a wooden cross is very real and of far greater significance than the chemical or physical properties of wood.

Ability to symbolize depends on a kind of mentality for which the term **algebraic** has been suggested.[5] This idea can easily be grasped if we think of the commonest statement used in algebra, "Let x equal." Whenever we use this expression the symbol x has no meaning of its own, but in problem after problem it can be assigned any meaning within the limits of human imagination. The symbol x can just as well equal 8 railroad cars, or ½ an orange, or 37 women, or

---

[4] *Webster's Collegiate Dictionary*, abridged, 5th ed., Springfield, 1948, p. 1010.

[5] W. Köhler, *The Mentality of Apes*, rev. ed., New York, 1925, p. 11, speaks of experiments with apes that require "a complicated geometry of movement." L. A. White has carried the concept a step further and describes human mentality as "algebraic."

14 pairs of green shoes, or 3 unicorns. Here again we find that no matter how many meanings are assigned to x, the symbol itself remains without fixed meaning and so stands ever ready to have any of its assigned meanings changed at the will of those who manipulate it.

Because the entire range of culture leans so heavily on the use of language and other forms of symbolization, scientists are eager to know if nonhuman animals have similar capacities, perhaps in a less perfect form. Experimenters have worked with a host of creatures to see whether or not they were able to symbolize. Claims of all sorts, some clearly extravagant and others hard to deny, have been made for beasts that seem to deal successfully with symbols. Seeing-eye dogs that stop at a red traffic light, apes that remember which of several identical doors was briefly lighted up as an indication that it led to food, mice that repeatedly run a difficult maze, numerous animals that "speak," and rats that learn to distinguish the symbol "A," leading to a reward, from the symbol "B," that leads to punishment, are only a few that have been cited. Yet, all the uncertainties that have been raised by these cases can be swept away if we take into consideration two factors.

In the first place, in every experiment of this kind so far devised, the symbolic value, such as a red light meaning stop, "A" signifying food, and "B" standing for punishment, has been thought up by a human being. There is no record of any other animal that has *invented* a symbolic meaning and arbitrarily assigned it to a particular sound, mark, color, or object. It is one thing to *recognize* a man-established symbolic meaning, which many animals can learn to do, but it is quite another matter to invent a symbolic value, which man alone can do. In the second place, all human beings, even small children, can learn to switch symbolic meanings about. If "B" stands for punishment today it can just as well stand for reward tomorrow. To fool an enemy, perhaps, we might decide to stop traffic on green and proceed on red. There would probably be some confusion especially at first, but it would not be too difficult for people to learn the new system. With nonhuman animals the situation is very different. Once they have learned to associate "B" with punishment, it is no easy matter to retrain them to link "B" with reward.

Beginners in cultural anthropology sometimes find it hard to understand the truly vital roles of symbolization and speech in the formation and continuation of culture. Luckily, their doubts can be resolved because every now and then persons more devoted to science than comfort have taken into their homes baby apes, treated them with the same care lavished on human infants, and tested them in every conceivable way. They have found their little charges capable of learning much that human children are expected to know and do before they begin to speak. Sometimes little Primates prove to be on a par with their *sapiens* fellows, occasionally they exceed them, and once in a while they fail to equal them. Now and then an over-indulgent "parent" is carried away by enthusiasm and claims to have taught an ape to speak, but careful investigation always reveals that the utterances are limited to a word or so, that they are not always clear to an unbiased observer, and that they are frequently used out of context as well as in their proper place.

A painstakingly thorough experiment of this general sort was reported over twenty years ago by Professor and Mrs. W. N. Kellogg, psychologists at Indiana University.[6] They took into their home and for nine months reared with their small son, Donald, a baby female chimpanzee named Gua (Fig. 4.6). With great care they gave identical treatment to the ape and their own infant, and both youngsters were subjected to various tests. Among other things, Gua learned to wear clothes, sit in a high chair, eat with a spoon, and respond to a number of spoken commands. Throughout the experiment's duration, ape and child ran neck and neck on most tests, but at the end of nine months Donald began to speak and to forge ahead rapidly, while Gua was unable to make further progress. Thereupon the Kelloggs returned her to a cage.

Although many of the psychological data published in 1933 are out of date, a few positive conclusions may be drawn that cannot be challenged today. The Kelloggs never claimed that Gua had learned to speak, and therein lies the key to the building or absence of culture. Lacking the ability to speak, Gua was utterly incapable of communicating to other apes a single item of her experiences in Indiana. She had no means of handing on any of her special knowledge either to her generation of chimpanzees or to any offspring that she might have borne. Whatever she had learned had, inevitably, to die with her. Had she been enabled to reconstruct the physical setting of the Kellogg home, she might conceivably have acted out some of her activities there and evoked imitation. Had this been the case, which is, of course, entirely fantastic, she might thus have transmitted part of her knowledge to other Primates, but this is a difficult and limited way of giving information.

Fig. 4.6. The ape and the child. Donald Kellogg is shown walking with Gua, who is dressed in human style. Although the young chimpanzee learned a great deal at the Kellogg home, she was unable, lacking true, symbolic speech, to share her knowledge with anyone else. (From W. N. and L. A. Kellogg, *The Ape and the Child*. New York, 1933. Courtesy McGraw-Hill Book Co.)

To bring the main issue into sharp focus, one has only to imagine Gua's situation in reverse. If a human being had lived for nine months among apes, the chances are that he would bore his listeners to tears with petty details. Through the use of speech he could reconstruct every aspect of his unusual experience, and with the aid of translations anything that he had learned could, theoretically, be made a part of human knowledge throughout the world. His words could be carried even to people who never saw or heard him in person, and who had never seen an ape. Sharing experiences with others, contributing to the sum total of human knowledge, and transmitting ideas and information to succeeding generations are things that normal human beings can easily do; but so long as they lack the ability to invent symbolic values and to assign some of them to sounds (speech), no other animals are capable of doing likewise. Whatever a nonhuman creature learns is almost certain to perish with it unless it can be biogenetically transmitted; whatever man learns can be spread about and handed on indefinitely and nonbiologically. The chances are nil that culture could have originated without speech, and it is equally certain that without speech there could have been none of that adding on or stockpiling of knowledge which is at the very base of culture growth.

Man and man only has the mental capacity to think up symbolic values, practically without limit; to assign them to anything whatsoever; and to switch about and change symbolic meanings if he so desires.[7] For these reasons anthropologists are convinced that none but humans have unqualified algebraic mentalities and true speech. At this point the scientific world finds itself baffled. Even if it is admitted that the use of symbols by *Homo sapiens* is a unique achievement, it is exceedingly hard to single out the particular aspects of man's anatomy which have given the species that special ability.

F. BIOLOGY AND ALGEBRAIC MENTALITY

Only one feature of human biology gives promise at this moment of holding the key to man's exceptional mentality, and that is his highly developed brain. Relative to the size and weight of the average body, *Homo sapiens* has by far the largest brain of any Primate. Correspondingly, the species has the greatest cerebral cortex of any related group. Within its manifold curves and wrinkles the human

---

[7] Once again must the reader be reminded that words may have a variety of different meanings assigned to them. Thus, a recent investigator has claimed that infrahuman Primates could symbolize because they could remember, after a lapse of time, which of several identical doors had been lighted up as a signal that it led to food. As the "capacity to symbolize" is used in this book, it is not equivalent to an act of memory. Moreover, it was not a lower animal but a human experimenter who first determined that a lighted door should be a sign of food. To this writer it seems clear that the truly symbolic behavior was carried out by a representative of *Homo sapiens* and not by some lesser Primate.

cerebrum lodges over nine billion cells, and it is perhaps possible that the combination of gross size and multitudinous cells, coupled with a rich blood supply and, perhaps, other physical traits, may some day yield a clue to man's most distinctive mental characteristic. At the moment, no one dares to speak with assurance about the relationship of gross brain size to symbolic behavior, but certain tentative suggestions may be advanced.

If it is true, as there is every reason to believe, that man alone has an algebraic mentality, then it may not be improper to point out that the average human has a cranial capacity of 1350 cc, which is two and one-half to three times that of a large gorilla. Running from the living apes through the man-apes and extinct hominids, there appears to be a continuum that spans the gap between the ape and human brain sizes. Somewhere along the line algebraic mentality is thought to have made its appearance, but no one knows exactly where. Because it is obviously impossible to observe the mental workings of extinct animals, scientists are forced to make comparisons between living humans and living apes, and that may explain why differences of brain size stand forth as seemingly all-important.

While increases of quantity do not invariably result in changes of quality, there are instances where more or less of something leads to a critical point or threshold beyond which a qualitative difference may be noted. An informal experiment, recently performed, may help to clarify the concept of critical points. A young man was asked to tear as many sheets as he could from a ream of lightweight paper. He had little difficulty until the pile of sheets reached 130. If we take the number 20 as a unit, it made little difference in the ranges 20 to 40 or 60 to 80; but the same unit from 130 to 150 made a critical threshold beyond which the subject's ability to tear a pile of papers could not go.

Another significant case of this kind is that of water temperature. When ordinary water at sea level is chilled below 32 degrees Fahrenheit, it becomes a solid, ice, and remains a solid no matter how much colder it gets. Between 32 and 212 degrees Fahrenheit there is a wide range without critical points, within which water retains the properties of a fluid. But 212 marks another threshold, above which hot water becomes converted from a liquid to a gas, steam. Solids, fluids, and gases certainly have different properties and different ways of acting and re-acting. Yet, in the case just cited, they are all composed of water, with varying quantities of heat added or subtracted.

By analogy with other substances, there is a possibility that cranial capacities may also have critical points. Tentatively stated, it may be that a healthy Primate brain which is normally less than 800 cc stands for a mentality that is incapable of true symbolization; between 800 and 900 cc may represent a threshold zone about which nothing definite is known; and any normal Primate brain well above 900 cc is probably fully capable of using symbolic speech and other features of algebraic mentality (Fig. 4.7). Once this point has been

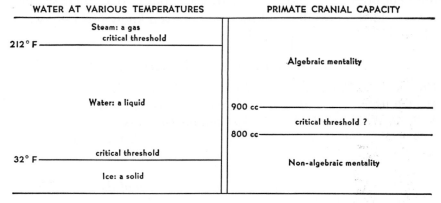

Fig. 4.7. A suggested analogy between water temperature and cranial capacity. Under certain conditions quantity may affect quality. The cranial capacity of healthy Primates may turn out to have a critical threshold between 800 and 900 cc. Below 800 cc, symbolic behavior may be impossible, but it is quite certainly possible when the cranial capacity exceeds 900 cc. If this should prove to be true, it would explain the origin of algebraic mentality.

reached, additional cubic centimeters of cranial capacity do not seem to affect the quality of mental behavior. No tests have ever demonstrated that a normal Primate brain size of around 1000 cc is any less efficient in dealing with symbols than one of 1600 cc or more.

The figures of 800 cc, below which algebraic mentality is dubious or impossible, and 900 cc, above which it is more than likely to be present, have not been capriciously chosen. In the case of the Australopithecines, whose ability to speak is very much subject to question, cranial capacities are variable, but probably average below 800. As to human infants, not enough studies have yet been made, but cranial capacities seem to average around 600 cc in the first twelve months, and to jump to about 950 cc at two years,[8] that is, at about the same time that speech may be assumed to have begun.

Advanced students of the human brain are inclined to think that something other than size differential has provided the basis for man's unique mentality. They feel that some day tangible factors that have so far eluded detection will be discovered and will provide more satisfactory solutions to the puzzles in which they are interested than sheer quantitative differences. In fact, some of them hold the opinion that speakers of different languages probably use different brain cells and neural pathways, but to date their searches have yielded no results, and they do not even know precisely where in the brain intelligence is lodged.

SELECTED REFERENCES

Crawford, O. G. S., *Man and His Past.* London, 1921.

Hooton, E. A., *Apes, Men, and Morons.* New York, 1937.

Kellogg, W. N. and L. A., *The Ape and the Child.* New York, 1933.

Köhler, W., *The Mentality of Apes,* rev. ed. New York, 1925.

Kroeber, A. L., "Subhuman Cultural Beginnings," *Quarterly Review of Biology.* Vol. 3, 1928, pp. 325-342.

Mettler, F. A., *Culture and the Structural Evolution of the Neural System.* New York, 1956.

Singer, C., *et al.,* eds., *A History of Technology,* Vol. 1, Chs. 1 and 4. New York and London, 1954.

White, L. A., "The Mentality of Primates," *Scientific Monthly.* Vol. 34, 1932, pp. 69-72.

Yerkes, R. M., *Chimpanzees.* New Haven, Conn., and London, 1943.

Yerkes, R. M. and A. W., *The Great Apes.* New Haven, Conn., 1929.

---

[8] F. A. Mettler, *Culture and the Structural Evolution of the Neural System,* New York, 1956, p. 3, table 2.

CHAPTER 5

EARLY FORMS OF CULTURE:

THE OLD STONE AGE

A. CULTURAL ORIGINS

Under test conditions it has repeatedly been demonstrated that apes, especially chimpanzees,[1] are not entirely limited in their actions to biologically determined channels. When hominids first came into being they seem to have been so similar to the big apes that it is probably correct to assume that anatomically they could do whatever their remote cousins could do, except for a few things specifically connected with arboreal life. It is apparently safe to assert, then, that the earliest men and women were at least on the threshold of culture.

To learn all that we can about the faint beginnings of humanoid culture we must turn to the findings of archeologists whose special province, let us recall, is the study of extinct or prehistoric cultures. In all likelihood the first objects used by pre-*sapiens* hominids to supplement their somatic equipment were sticks, bones, and stones as nature made and supplied them. Such things of stone, supposedly utilized but not manufactured by human beings, are sometimes known as **eoliths,** or "dawn stones" (see Fig. 5.1). Unfortunately,

---

[1] Young chimpanzees are the commonest ape subjects for testing because they are less surly, more cooperative, and generally more responsive to human attention than most other Primates.

we have no assured way of recognizing these objects, even if they should happen to come to light. Not until stones are systematically worked according to a regular plan or pattern, can we be reasonably sure of detecting them as tools.

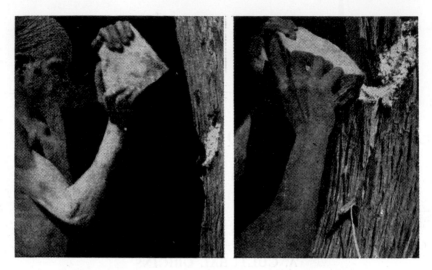

Fig. 5.1. Survival of an eolithic usage. An Australian aborigine, using a sharp but unworked stone for cutting into a tree. (Courtesy C. P. Mountford.)

As to those things that were made of organic substances like wood or bone, they would undoubtedly have disintegrated in the vast span of time since manlike creatures appeared on earth. That is why archeologists concerned with the first definitive signs of human culture rest so much of their case on discoveries of stone artifacts, and that is also why the first stage of human culture is known as the **Paleolithic** or **Old Stone Age.**

Conventionally, American anthropologists who deal with the Paleolithic use the terminology and the order of events that apply best to Western Europe, and more specifically to France. This is somewhat unfortunate because we are quite certain that neither hominids nor human ways of life began there; but the sequence of happenings is clearest in France, and since more is known about early forms of culture there than in any other region of the globe, we shall begin the story of culture in the usual manner.

As it is most often described, the Paleolithic sequence falls within the time limits of the Pleistocene or Ice Age, which started about a million years ago and came to an end around 20,000 B.C. In Western

Europe the Pleistocene was marked by alternations of wintry weather, when ice sheets covered vast stretches of the countryside, and periods of warmth, when the fields of ice melted or retracted. These fluctuations provide a rough basis for dating, because the four periods of major advances of glacial conditions are reasonably well charted. Between them came mild stages, called interglacial periods. In contrast to the various advances of the ice fields, which left permanent marks on the landscape and can, therefore, be studied with a fair degree of accuracy, the individual interglacial epochs are much harder to identify because their traces were far less enduring.

B. LOWER PALEOLITHIC INDUSTRIES

Hominids apparently entered Western Europe during one of the early interglacial periods when the weather was mild or hot. This is not surprising, for man seems to have originated in a warm climate, very likely in some place where forests bordered on grasslands. He was biologically ill-suited to cope with cold weather, and culture was far too rudimentary at the outset to afford much help in dealing with an unfavorable environment. The valleys of the Somme in France and the Thames in England have yielded many stone artifacts of the beginning or **Lower Paleolithic** era. It is customary to call the earliest series of man-made implements **Abbevillian,** formerly known as **Chellian,** and a somewhat later variety of stone tools, **Acheulian.**

Speaking very broadly, the term Lower Paleolithic may be applied both to the manufactured objects and the way of life practiced by early man before the onset of the fourth (**Würm**) glacial advance of the Pleistocene. Almost nothing is known of the kinds of hominids then alive, but there are suggestions to indicate that they were Archanthropinae, that is to say, pre- or non-Neandertaloids. There is also doubt as to the exact time involved, but in very approximate figures the climax of the Lower Paleolithic may be dated between 500,000 B.C. or a few centuries earlier, and around 120,000 B.C. Even in the matter of material accomplishments there is not much that can be said with conviction. All perishable substances from this remote era have long ago disappeared, and only a few stone artifacts have survived.

Throughout Western Europe the most typical Abbevillian implement was a **fist-ax**, also designated as a hand-ax or *coup de poing*. Most commonly it was a big, clumsy object, roughly pear-shaped, about 9 inches long and 4 or 5 inches across at its widest part. The rounded upper portion was probably designed to be held in the clenched palm, and the lower end culminated in a rounded or pointed tip (Fig. 5.2A). From the way it fits into the modern hand it

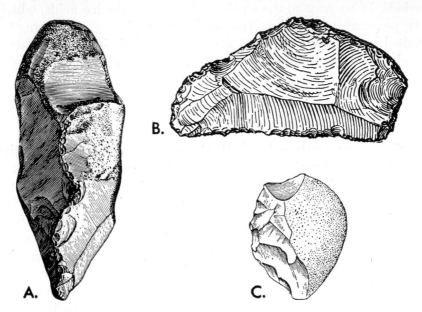

Fig. 5.2. Typical stone tools of the Lower Paleolithic. A. A crudely made fist-ax, percussion chipped on both faces. B. Flint knife or side-scraper. C. Chopping tool. (Courtesy of Peabody Museum, Harvard University, and British Museum of Natural History.)

is pretty clear that it was not at all like a conventional ax. The earliest fist-axes were made from an original core or nodule of a stone like flint, that fractures evenly into segments when it is struck, without crumbling to bits. A **percussion** technique was employed for the manufacturing process, which means that small chips or flakes were struck away from the original core. While it was being made, the implement was subjected to blows on each surface, so that Abbevillian fist-axes are usually described as bifacial. Workmanship was none too good, and the two long sides were often rough and unsymmetrical. Whatever flakes or chips were detached from the original core as it was being made into a tool were generally wasted.

Acheulian fist-axes are smaller than Abbevillian, oval or almond in shape, trimmed to a thin edge along the entire circumference, and have the center of gravity more clearly defined and located near the middle of the tool. Both types were made by similar techniques which called for the striking off of small flakes on both sides of an original core. Practically all the detached flakes were again wasted, but it is possible that some of the larger ones were themselves used as tools in the Acheulian phase. Often the flake tools that may well be the incidental results of core workmanship have one sharp edge and are called **knives** or **side-scrapers;** while broad, heavy scrapers are sometimes termed **cleavers.**

Archeologists who specialize in Lower Paleolithic studies distinguish flake utensils that are by-products of core techniques from tools deliberately planned to be made of skillfully detached flakes. Best known technique of the earliest flake industries is the **Levalloisian.** This required very careful preliminary shaping of a stone nodule in such fashion that when the initial work was finished, flakes ready for immediate use as tools could be detached with single blows. Pre-fashioned Levalloisian stones are called from their customary appearance **tortoise cores.** The more carefully they were prepared in advance, the more suitable for prompt service were the struck-off flakes. Thus does the Levalloisian method forcibly bring home the truth of the statement that tool manufacture calls for an advance blueprint in the mind of the workman.

Because of the manner in which they were detached, **Levallois** tools were always smooth on the inner surface, which remained unworked. As flakes, Levallois-made artifacts used up less raw material than did core implements, and because they required less trimming they saved working time. In its own humble way, therefore, the Levallois style may be said to have represented in its day an industrial revolution.

Not many years ago most archeologists believed that the divisions and sequences established for the Lower Paleolithic of Western Europe were typical of the entire Old World. This is no longer held to be true. Discoveries in Africa and Asia have made it clear that in many details the Western European scheme is valid locally but not universally. As a general rule, core tools are much alike wherever they may be found, but flake tools are apt to show great variations.

Quite distinct from the Lower Paleolithic industries of Western

Europe are a number of tool-making traditions from Eastern and Southeastern Asia. There are some early **chopping tools,** often made from pebbles, which may prove to be related to African types, but in Northwestern India, Burma, Java, and China, there is neither an Abbevillian-Acheulian core industry nor a recognizably Levalloisian style of flake manufacture. Instead, the commonest early tools have been described by Harvard's Professor Hallam L. Movius, Jr., as chopping tools, featuring **choppers,** and **hand adzes** (see Fig. 5.2C).[2]

Professor Movius has made a first-hand study of the stone tools found together with the bones of *Sinanthropus pekinensis* at Chou Kou Tien. He has named that industry **Choukoutienian** and has assigned it to the chopper, chopping tool, hand adze complex of East Asia, and not to any of the Lower Paleolithic cultures of Western Europe.

C. HUMAN LIFE IN LOWER PALEOLITHIC TIMES

Any effort to present a fully rounded picture of Lower Paleolithic life is pre-doomed to failure because of the meager evidence available. That men of those days lived in Western Europe while the climate was warm is very strongly suggested to us by the occurrence of Abbevillian-Acheulian implements in soils containing remains of elephant, rhinoceros, lion, and hippopotamus. Such an association reinforces an interpretation to the same effect based on discoveries of Lower Paleolithic tools in the beds of ancient streams. Throughout most of the world, Lower Paleolithic people probably camped outdoors. They seem to have made only temporary camps, and if they put up habitations at all they were apparently too flimsy and impermanent to have survived or to have left identifiable traces on the ground. At Chou Kou Tien, China, on the contrary, hominids are thought to have lived in caves. Here there is ample evidence that *Sinanthropus pekinensis* made and controlled fire, manufactured tools of stone, hunted deer and cracked their long bones for marrow, possibly hunted human beings and cracked their skulls for brains, and gathered and ate wild hackberries.

---

[2] For further details consult H. L. Movius, Jr., "Early Man and Pleistocene Stratigraphy in Southern and Eastern Asia," *Papers of the Peabody Museum, of American Archaeology and Ethnology,* Harvard University, Vol. XIX, No. 3, 1944.

A good synopsis and bibliography by the same author may be found in A. L. Kroeber, editor, *Anthropology Today,* Chicago, 1953, pp. 163-192.

For most of the Old World, even these few details are lacking. Men and women probably wandered in small bands along the banks of streams, fishing, hunting, and gathering edible plants, seeds, fruits, nuts, roots, and berries. They were at best collectors or gatherers of foods provided by nature; they were not food producers. Nothing is known of any system of symbolic values that might have prevailed, but there is indirect proof of algebraic mentality because of the size of cranial vaults and the ability these folk demonstrated for planning ahead while making tools. Similarly, their capacity for speech cannot be directly proved, but secondary evidence makes it likely that they could talk because by no other means could traditions and styles of manufacturing have been readily spread and maintained for countless generations over wide stretches of territory.

One can only guess at what use may have been made of perishable materials for building, clothing, or other purposes. There is much less need for speculation when it comes to the evidence provided by Lower Paleolithic artifacts of stone. Taking the entire range into account, there are found sturdy fist-axes of value for helping kill game or enemies, sharp knives for cutting up slain beasts or severing branches, scrapers capable of working wood or hides, and pointed implements suitable for stabbing or digging operations. Some archeologists regard well-made fist-axes as all-purpose tools, but the great number of knives, scrapers, points, cleavers, and choppers suggests that there was at least a modest preference for specialized implements based on the concept of a particular kind of tool for a specific purpose.

Even in terms of stone working, it is apparent that culture started slowly and remained relatively unchanged in the course of hundreds of thousands of years. True, archeologists know of many variations in the early lithic industries, but all of the manufacturing methods are but modifications of a single technique—the shaping of tools by knocking or pressing smaller fragments from a larger piece of stone. Dependence on a single method, most commonly a percussion technique, strictly limited man's use of the natural resources around him to fine-grained varieties of stone with cryptocrystalline structures, capable of segmenting evenly when struck or pressed hard. Some workmen were without question more skillful than others, but in a pinch any normal individual could turn out a reasonable facsimile of a satisfactory tool. The quantity of rather poorly made implements is so great that it is fantastic to think of Lower Paleolithic societies as having specialized workmen who devoted themselves fulltime to the making of stone products. Every man his own craftsman is much more likely to have been the rule.

Although it is the present contention that core-made bifacial implements and flake tools have always existed side by side, the fact remains that the preparation of core instruments diminishes with time and disappears before the Paleolithic has run its full course. It is interesting to guess at the meaning of this trend. If we apply modern economic ideas to the situation the termination of core workmanship may be explained on two counts. Making core tools is more costly because it requires bigger blocks of raw material to start with and because nearly all of the struck-off chips are wasted. Furthermore, core tools take longer to produce because they must be worked on both surfaces and can be finished only one at a time. Flake tools waste very little raw material, are worked only on one side, and are rapidly produced by single blows after a satisfactory preparation has been made. There can be little question but that flake techniques won out over core methods of production because they were more economical in terms of raw materials, muscular energy, and time. These technological trends, barely discernible in the Lower Paleolithic, become increasingly plain as we approach our own era.

As far as anyone knows, all of the Lower Paleolithic implements were meant to be used by hand. They had only slight mechanical efficiency of their own, and differences of effective use depended less on the skill with which a utensil was made than on the biological power and strength of the user. A weak little man holding an excellent fist-ax could not hope to stand up to a big brute of a fellow armed with a third-rate fist-ax. How different from today, when we demand efficiency and power in our tools rather than in our bodies. Even the most destructive of modern weapons can be fired by a person with weak muscles. Along similar lines, a Lower Paleolithic tool could not be hurled for any great distance, the amount of space covered being dependent once more on the anatomical power of the thrower. Judged by what we know of it, Lower Paleolithic culture was only in a very limited degree capable of serving man as an aid to or substitute for biology. In this regard, hominids were for several hundred millennia not much better off than other Primates of their size and strength. No imaginary observer who might somehow have been enabled to watch how slowly man was building his culture throughout Lower Paleolithic times would have been willing to bet that it would ever amount to much. Why *Homo sapiens* steadfastly persisted in maintaining culture during the thousands of years that it seems to have done him but little good, is a mystery that has not yet been solved.

D. NEANDERTAL MAN AND MIDDLE PALEOLITHIC CULTURE

The picture of hominid life which is so hazy and dim for the Lower Paleolithic comes into a much clearer and sharper focus in the **Middle Paleolithic** or **Mousterian** phase. Although the origins of Mousterian culture are still undetermined, it is believed to have flourished at its highest peak in Western Europe from approximately 120,000 B.C. to about 70,000 years ago. It is better known because it is closer to our own time and because its remains are found in caves where materials are likely to accumulate and be kept together. Its products are so often directly associated with Neandertal skeletons that it is hard to escape the conclusion that in Western Europe, at least, Mousterian culture was the way of life of Neandertal man. There the transition from Lower to Middle Paleolithic must be considered in relation to a change of climatic conditions. Toward the end of the Lower Paleolithic the weather shifted from warm to cool to cold. The continued lowering of temperature is connected with the advance of the Würm glaciation. Some of the earlier people may have adjusted their cultures to fit the oncoming Ice Age, but most of them probably died out or moved southward, possibly taking with them the core-biface tradition. Beyond speculations of this sort, nothing is known of the fate of Lower Paleolithic man. Several reputable archeologists feel that there are so many links between the Middle and Lower Paleolithic periods that they should not be regarded as different phases. However, enough new factors were introduced in the Middle Paleolithic to justify its treatment as a distinct stage of Old Stone Age life.

Mousterian culture continued to be based on a hunting-fishing-gathering economy, and its practitioners never learned to become food producers. Unrestricted wandering out of doors was impossible because of the cold, and Neandertal man is known to have had resort to caves. Judged by the location of his cultural remains, he preferred to live near the threshold of a cave where there was more light and fresh air than in the dank interior. So abundant are the remains of hearths and charred substances that fire must have been commonly used for light, heat, and the preparation of food. Life in heated caves and the consumption of cooked foods, afford testimony of Neandertal man's ability to sustain himself during the frigid Würm period by making cultural instead of biological adjustments (see Fig. 5.3).

From time to time it has been surmised that Neandertal man secured much game by trapping. Such a conjecture may well be correct, but not one of his presumed traps has survived. Granted

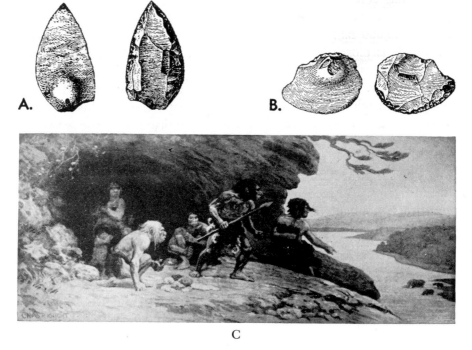

A.   B.

C

Fig. 5.3. Specimens of Mousterian culture. A. Back and front faces of a Mousterian point. There is a pronounced bulb of percussion, and the chipping on one face only suggests a connection with the Levallois technique. B. Reverse and front views of a Mousterian scraper. C. An imaginary scene of Mousterian life. Many of the details were supplied by the artist, but Neandertal man is known to have lived at the mouths of caves, and the manner in which a Mousterian point is hafted to a spear shaft is indicated by archeological evidence. (Courtesy of Peabody Museum, Harvard University.)

that the use of traps is unprovable, it still remains a fact that Middle Paleolithic man was able, with the help of some kinds of cultural equipment, to hunt down such enormous Ice Age beasts as the mammoth and woolly rhinoceros. He sometimes used their large bones for chopping blocks or anvils, but most of his implements continued to be fashioned from fine-grained stones (Fig. 5.3A, B). What use was made of skins, furs, or hides is not certain, but it seems reasonable to assume that some pelts were worn for clothing. Scraps of shells and tiny bones indicate that fish and shellfish were eaten, but there is little to tell how they were obtained; nor is anything known about the extent to which vegetable products were gathered and utilized.

Neandertal man's stone work was based on established Paleolithic percussion methods. Resemblances or relationships have been noted to core-made, Acheulian bifacial fist-axes, as well as to Levalloisian flake implements. For the rest, his stone tools consisted chiefly of side scrapers and small triangular points. Also found on occasion are rounded objects of flint, whose purpose is undetermined. They may have been used for hurling one at a time, and it is sometimes guessed that they may have been attached in small sets to leather thongs.

A nice problem arises when one tries to consider the possible use of the commonly found small triangular **Mousterian points**. If they were meant to be held in the hand, even of a very strong man, they could have had but dubious efficiency. Indeed, none of the Middle Paleolithic tools, held in hand, seems to have been capable of delivering a deadly blow to a mammoth. To have been effective, a Mousterian point must have been attached to a long handle to form a kind of spear. Neandertal man was thus confronted with a difficult problem of **hafting,** for a spear is worthless if it has a stone tip that is not securely attached to the shaft. In this instance the difficulty was increased by the fact that Mousterian points are straight across at the base and are therefore hard to affix to anything like a pole. The problem was very likely solved by notching the upper end of the shaft and wedging the stone point into the cleft. There is also a possibility that extra firmness was achieved by binding the notched portion, after the stone tip had been wedged in, tightly around the outside with strips of leather.

If it be assumed that Neandertal man successfully solved a difficult problem of hafting, and that he learned to use spears skillfully, it follows that he had devised a new kind of weapon which incorporates the principle of leverage. Thus, for the first time, were hominids able to add extrabodily mechanical power to biological strength. One can imagine a relatively weak man with a good, long spear, holding at a distance or jabbing to death a stronger man armed with a fist-ax that could be effective only at close range. Spears that could either be held in the hand or hurled would give many advantages to Neandertal hunters of big game. In such cases cultural efficiency was being used in place of biological force, or, to put it in colloquial terms, brain was being substituted for brawn. This is another important trend that is hardly noticeable in the Middle Paleolithic but which becomes more and more noteworthy as we approach modern times.

Once the usefulness of leverage, as applied to handles, became recognized, it was never dropped from human culture. Modern tools make such a widespread use of handles that we rarely bother to analyze their utility. And yet we know full well that it is comparatively easy to dig a hole with a long-handled shovel, whereas the same task would be exceedingly difficult if we had to use only the blade of a shovel, with no handle at all.

There is one more feature that marks Mousterian culture apart from the Lower Paleolithic. Some Neandertal skeletons have been found deposited in graves that were deliberately dug into the floors of caves. The most amazing of such discoveries was made at La Chapelle-aux-Saints, where a corpse had been laid out in a carefully excavated trench, and left surrounded by typical Mousterian implements. To appreciate the meaning of this find it is necessary to know that analogous customs still prevail in a great many primitive societies. Everywhere the habit of putting objects into graves is explained in the same way—they are for the use of the dead in the other world. By analogy, therefore, we are forced to conclude that Neandertal man must have had a belief in an afterlife. From what can legitimately be deduced from his burial practices, we get our first hint of Middle Paleolithic man's religious concepts, and no further proof of Neandertal man's algebraic mentality is needed.

E. NEOANTHROPINAE AND UPPER PALEOLITHIC CULTURE

No scholar can tell how long Neandertal man and Mousterian culture persisted after they had reached a peak around 70,000 B.C., but their survival in Western Europe was probably of relatively short duration. They seem to have been crowded out by a succession of important changes that were taking place in nearly every sphere. These were of such magnitude as to warrant distinguishing the new era, **Upper Paleolithic,** from the Mousterian that had preceeded it. Among the innovations, heavy emphasis must fall on radically different styles of workmanship and the replacement of Neandertal (Paleoanthropic) men by Neoanthropic varieties that culminated in the Cro-Magnons. A wide gap culturally and biologically is thus indicated between Middle and Upper Paleolithic, and if it is correct to associate the former way of life with Neandertal man, it is equally appropriate to link the latter with the Neoanthropinae.

Wintry blasts greeted the Neoanthropinae when they first showed up in Western Europe. The Würm glaciation had not yet ended, although it might have been wavering. By common agreement Upper Paleolithic culture is thought to have begun no later than the closing phases of the Würm and to have remained in effect until the end of the Pleistocene some 20,000 years ago. Thereafter the **Holocene (Recent)** geological period started and modern climatic conditions were established. No single kind of weather prevailed all through the late stages of the Pleistocene, but extended cold spells alternated with long stretches of warmth. It takes only a little reflection to realize that under such conditions Upper Paleolithic life must have varied from time to time and place to place. Three major stages of culture are conventionally recognized and they are named, in order, **Aurignacian, Solutrian,** and **Magdalenian.**

Upper Paleolithic tools of stone continued to be made of fine-grained varieties by percussion or pressure methods. Hunting-fishing-gathering pursuits still formed the basis of economic life, and there are no signs of food growing, animal domestication, pottery manufacture, or permanent settlement in large communities. Whatever cultural innovations were introduced failed to go beyond the general pattern of the Old Stone Age. A faster tempo of change was very likely inaugurated but the magnitude of Upper Paleolithic achievements must be considered small when compared to what was destined to take place after the end of Pleistocene times.

With the opening of Western Europe's Upper Paleolithic era the "contest" between core and flake tools was unconditionally resolved in favor of the latter, but the kind of flake utilized differed from anything made before. Essentially, it is parallel-sided, at least twice as long as it is wide, thin, and very sharp along the cutting edges. In this form it is known as a **blade** (Fig. 5.4), and comprises the

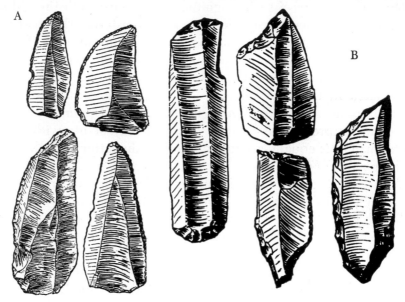

Fig. 5.4. Upper Paleolithic blade tools. A. Aurignacian types. B. Magdalenian specimens. All Aurignacian and Magdalenian stone work shows a vertical channel and is smooth on the inner surface. There is a close resemblance between these two styles. (Courtesy of Peabody Museum, Harvard University.)

basis for the commonest run of Aurignacian and Magdalenian lithic implements. Most of the blades appear to have been detached from a core by a blow on an accurately placed pick, whose point rested on the stone. Many blades were used exactly as struck off, although some had their working edges secondarily retouched.[3]

Aurignacian

Not only do the various stages of Aurignacian work in stone reveal some of the new features introduced by Upper Paleolithic crafts-

---

[3] For clever illustrations showing most of these forms and suggesting modern parallels, see R. J. Braidwood, *Prehistoric Men,* Chicago, 1948, pp. 62-65.

men but there is ample evidence that man had added to his earlier employment of raw materials a widespread use of bones (Fig. 5.5).

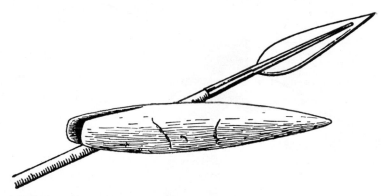

Fig. 5.5. Bone point of the Aurignacian period. It is split at the base to accommodate a handle. The manner in which it was fashioned into a spear is suggested in the accompanying drawing. (R. J. Braidwood, *Prehistoric Men.* Chicago, 1948. Courtesy of Chicago Museum of Natural History.)

Besides stone and bone, workmen of this era learned to handle ivory and reindeer horn, sometimes using lithic tools for drilling holes in or making javelin points from less resistant materials. Needles of bone made their first indisputable appearance in the Aurignacian and furnish a bit of indirect proof for the manufacture of some sort of clothing. Among the most important innovations is the spear- or javelin-thrower, usually fashioned of antler horn. Its appearance is deceptively simple, much like a stick with a raised hook at one end. When it is to be used, a spear or javelin is laid flat against the throwing device, with the butt end pressing against the raised hook (Fig. 5.6). This has the effect of increasing the stretch of the user's arm by the length of the spear-thrower, and gives him more mechanical power than his own body possesses. To be used successfully, a spear-thrower demands the mental ability to look ahead. No one can be expected to use this device properly at the first trial. This means that a user must be willing to practice without immediate benefit for the sake of a future reward.

In addition to the aspects already discussed, the Aurignacian marks a departure from the Mousterian by its flair for ornamentation and other expressions of the fine arts. These range all the way from lines that look like mere doodles, through engravings and sculptures, to exceedingly realistic paintings of animals. The cata-

Fig. 5.6. Use of a spear-thrower. A native of New Guinea illustrates how a fish-spear is hurled with the help of a spear-thrower. The use of this cultural implement has the same effect as would the lengthening of the man's arm. (From H. I. Hogbin, *Peoples of the Southwest Pacific*, New York, 1945-6. Courtesy Asia Press, Inc.)

log is long and cannot possibly be covered here, but one item demands special mention. Figure 5.7A shows a "necklace" made up of a combination of spinal bones of fish, perforated canine teeth of stags, and the drilled shells of gastropods. They are arranged into regular units, each one consisting of two sets of four vertebrae, three shells, and a tooth. The same grouping is duplicated over and over, thus showing that even at this early stage of art the concept existed of using fixed units made up of divergent parts, regularly or rhythmically repeated. It is hard to believe that in fashioning such a necklace, crude and unesthetic by present standards, some unknown Aurignacian artist had hit upon the basic principle of repetition coupled with variety that makes up the essence of so much modern art from poetry to music to architecture.

Archeologists have also been intrigued by outlines or impressions of mutilated human hands (Fig. 5.7B) made on cave walls in Aurignacian times. Their meaning can only be guessed, but hands with one or more finger joints missing immediately bring

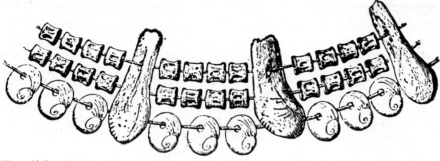

Fig. 5.7. Aurignacian symbolism. A. Upper Paleolithic necklace (after Verneau and MacCurdy). Each unit has two sets of four fish vertebrae each, three gastropod shells, and one canine tooth of a stag. The units are rhythmically repeated at fixed intervals, showing an appreciation of the esthetic principle, "repetition coupled with diversity." B. Hand imprints (after MacCurdy, following Cartailhac and Breuil). Such mutilated hands are common in various primitive societies, where fingers are offered as sacrifices. The preponderance of left hands furthers the notion that fingers were deliberately cut off with the right hand.

It should be remembered, however, that leprosy sometimes causes similar mutilations. (Courtesy Peabody Museum, Harvard University.)

to mind a well-known primitive custom. Several American Indian tribes regularly expected their men to lop off finger joints while striving to communicate with their deities. It is tempting to consider the possibility that similar practices prevailed during the Upper Paleolithic. Nevertheless, one should not overlook the possibility that diseases like leprosy can produce closely comparable disfigurations.

Widely known, too, are several stone carvings and statuettes of large-breasted women (Fig. 5.8). They are called, somewhat inappropriately, "Venuses." Many a scholar has tried to guess at their meaning, and the most frequently heard explanation refers them vaguely to a "fertility cult." Such an interpretation cannot be completely dismissed, but all that can be said with absolute certainty is that Aurignacian man, like his predecessors and successors, was interested in sex and reproduction.

Fig. 5.8. An Upper Paleolithic "Venus." A female figure, holding a bison horn, is carved of limestone in low relief. This sculpture, from Laussel, Dordogne, France, conforms to an Aurignacian tendency to neglect details of feet and face. (Courtesy of Peabody Museum, Harvard University.)

Far and away the most exciting examples of Aurignacian art are the paintings recently discovered on the walls of Lascaux cave, near Les Eyzies, Dordogne, France. A variety of large mammals is there depicted, often in motion, like plodding oxen or trotting horses. (See Fig. 5.9). Every observer has been taken with these splendid and vigorous paintings, some of which are monotone and some of which are in two colors.[4] There is much to admire in these

---

[4] For a fine study of the Lascaux paintings, consult F. Windels, *The Lascaux Cave Paintings*, New York, 1950, and H. Breuil, *Four Hundred Centuries of Cave Art*, New York, 1950.

pictures, even by the most rigorous of modern standards, but their original significance is not known.

However inadequate may be our speculations about its meanings, Aurignacian art certainly shows that in those days there was a great deal of concern with and aptitude for things nonmaterial and extra-biologic. A further indication along these lines is found in Upper

Fig. 5.9. An Aurignacian cave painting. A. This running horse is depicted in the Lascaux cave. (From F. Windels, *Lascaux Cave Paintings*. New York, 1950. Courtesy of Viking Press.)

Paleolithic burial practices. These are more elaborate than the ones noted in the account of Mousterian times. A number of deliberate burials have been found, each with some feature to suggest an interest in the fate of the deceased after death. This was expressed by daubing red clay, possibly to represent blood, on skeletal remains, or by leaving implements and ornaments in the grave. The high development of fine arts and the burial customs combine to show that *Homo sapiens* was making considerable use of algebraic mentality during the Aurignacian phases of cultural evolution.

Solutrian

Either as a result of the spread of new ideas from places outside of Europe or by virtue of an actual influx of different kinds of people, there next developed in Western Europe a distinct culture complex termed **Solutrian.** Wherever it may have originated and however it may have been carried to Western Europe, the manifestations of Solutrian culture usually follow the late Aurignacian. At this time the extremely frigid weather of the Würm glaciation had somewhat subsided, and the Solutrians lived under cold but open steppe conditions. Pitifully little is known of the total range of their lives, but they were doubtless hunters who slew and ate quantities of wild horse *(Equus przewalskii),* as well as reindeer and other animals of that day.

Accompanying the remains of Solutrian folk are numbers of Upper Paleolithic blade tools, but their really distinctive implements, fancifully called *laurel-* or *willow-leafed,* stand entirely apart. They were made by percussion from flakes or blades, retouched on one or both surfaces by pressure. So skillful were the craftsmen that by dint of precisely controlled chipping they produced symmetrical, ripple-like ridges across the entire face of an implement, and reduced it to remarkable thinness and delicacy (Fig. 5.10). All Solutrian tools of stone are pointed, but their size varies from as small as an inch to as large as a foot or more. They may also be divided into those that are pointed at both extremes, and those that culminate at one end in a tang, presumably for hafting to a javelin

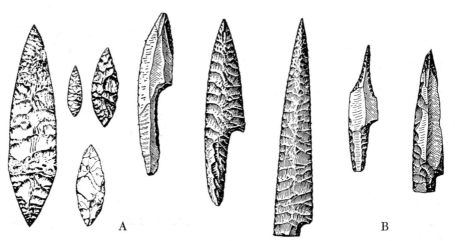

Fig. 5.10. Solutrian tools from the Upper Paleolithic. A. Flint points of the style known as laurel leaf. B. Willow leaf points. The notched shoulders are thought to have facilitated hafting. Solutrian lithic implements show the highest peak of Old Stone Age workmanship. The ripple effect is achieved by precisely controlled pressure-flaking. (Courtesy of Peabody Museum, Harvard University.)

shaft. Because they were manufactured with such skill, precision, delicacy, and symmetry, the Solutrian stone implements reached the greatest heights of Upper Paleolithic workmanship. They were supplemented by a few tools and ornaments of bone, horn, and ivory.

The duration in time and the geographic range of Solutrian culture are both restricted. Neoanthropinae are known to have been its carriers, but their appearance and disappearance in Western Europe are equally mysterious. Solutrian remains in Western Europe soon give way to the Magdalenian.

Magdalenian

Magdalenian culture, last of Western Europe's Upper Paleolithic series, falls in the terminal phase of the Pleistocene. The recession of winter conditions under which Solutrian man had been lucky enough to live was followed by a late glacial advance. Homes were again made in caves or within rock shelters, and animals that thrive in the cold were once more abundant. On scientific evidence it can be demonstrated that summers alternated with winters and that the Magdalenians were in the habit of leaving their winter residences to hunt reindeer at their summer grazing grounds. It can also be shown that arctic grouse and hares were occasionally caught, and there is ample proof of fishing for pike, trout, and salmon.[5]

No longer found as Magdalenian culture progresses are the exquisitely made Solutrian stone tools, and back on the scene come blade artifacts that are reminiscent of Aurignacian styles (Fig. 5.4B). But whatever loss of stone-working skill may be charged to Magdalenian craftsmen is more than compensated by an advance in handling bone, ivory, and horn. Needles, buttons, awls, and fishhooks of bone are common, and the use of horn javelins and spearthrowers, some of which are elaborately ornamented, becomes widespread (Fig. 5.11).

Occurring sporadically in deposits of earlier cultures but gaining prominence in the Magdalenian are tiny stone implements, suitably called **microliths,** that require mere bits of raw material. Many microliths are so small that they fail to cover an average man's fingernail, but each is carefully made and gives clear proof of

---

[5] For further details, see J. G. D. Clark, *Prehistoric Europe,* New York, 1952, pp. 26-27, *et passim.*

human workmanship. Ordinarily, microliths are sharp-pointed and suggest that they might have been inserted to form barbs for larger objects. There is also proof that they were sometimes hafted in rows to provide a saw-tooth effect, or worked into wooden shafts to make stone-tipped darts. All such implements continue to take

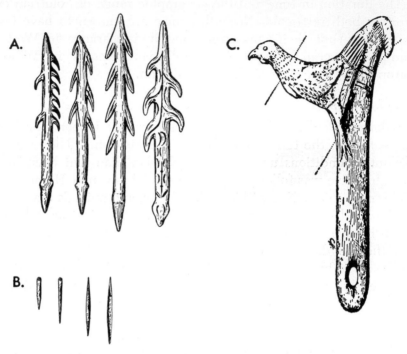

Fig. 5.11. Upper Paleolithic bone and horn tools (after MacCurdy, following Breuil). A. Several harpoons with double barbs, made of reindeer horn. B. Needles, with circular eyes, and awls of bone. C. An ornamental horn spear-thrower, from the Magdalenian stage of the Upper Paleolithic. The portions outside the dotted lines were reconstructed by Abbé Breuil. (Courtesy of Peabody Museum, Harvard University.)

advantage of hafts, based on the principle of leverage that was first utilized during Mousterian times. This provides an early example of the additive nature of human culture that grows by accretions of knowledge.

Archeologists formerly denied the use of bows and arrows among Upper Paleolithic people, but it is now pretty well conceded that such weapons were employed during Magdalenian times.[6] If one

---

[6] *Ibid*, pp. 30-31.

Fig. 5.12. Youthful archers. Pygmy Negro boys learning to shoot bows and arrows. Primate anatomy, close coordination of hand and eye, and much preliminary practice are required to make possible the skillful use of these weapons. (Courtesy of American Museum of Natural History.)

accepts this opinion, another exceedingly important forward step in cultural evolution must be acknowledged. Adequate use of a bow and arrow, like the skillful control of a spear-thrower, implies a fresh application of algebraic mentality, for no one can become a skillful archer without considerable practice. This means that Magdalenian man must have been willing to work long and hard without immediate compensation in order to gain worthwhile rewards at some time in the future. Moreover, a comparatively weak individual who had taken the trouble to become a crack shot could triumph over a much stronger person who had never practiced, or who was armed only with older types of weapons. Nor should it be overlooked that a good bowman could discharge deadly arrows while protected by rocks or trees. The mechanical proficiency of a bow is, beyond dispute, much greater than that of a spear-thrower. So it is that *Homo sapiens* was coming to depend on the effectiveness of his tools, and was learning to rely more on culture than biology to help him meet many of life's crises. Nor should it be overlooked that use of the bow is possible only to a Primate of human form. An archer must be able to stand firmly on his hind legs; and he must have at least a powerful shoulder girdle with a good clavicle, strong but flexible wrists and fingers, prehensile hands, rotating forearms, and keen coordination of hand and eye (Fig. 5.12).

Magdalenian interest in the nonbiologic is attested by the care taken with burials. Graves were more regularly and frequently dug than ever before, there was much use of red ochre, and bodies were often ornamented with shell necklaces or accompanied by numerous tools. Only the most unreasonable of skeptics would try to deny that the Magdalenians had some concept of religion, at least to the extent of belief in an afterlife.

Until the discovery of the Lascaux paintings it used to be thought certain that Magdalenian artists were far and away the best of the Upper Paleolithic. Even now the claim is by no means unfounded. There are countless ornaments, carvings, engravings, sculptures, clay figures, and paintings from this era, a good percentage of which are of breathtaking excellence. Many techniques, styles, subjects, and color schemes were employed, but the highest critical acclaim of our day is generally reserved for polychrome paintings cleverly shaded to give an illusion of depth or solidity. Two of the very finest examples are reindeer figures at Font-de-Gaume near Les Eyzies,

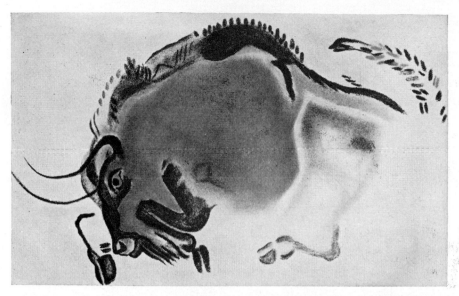

Fig. 5.13. Charging bison, Magdalenian cave painting from Altamira. This is one of the best-executed and most famous cave paintings found at Altamira. There is a marked contrast between the splendidly portrayed outer form of the animal and the crudely made heart represented by the diamond-shaped design. (Courtesy of Peabody Museum, Harvard University.)

and the bison (Fig. 5.13) depicted on the roof of the world-famous Altamira cave, near Santander in Spain.

Archeologists are seldom content to discuss Magdalenian art in purely esthetic terms. The very fact that some of the very best specimens are found in dim recesses of inaccessible caverns makes it unlikely that such art products were produced only for their own sake or to be admired by the general public. Once more one is tempted to have recourse to analogy with known primitive customs. Many peoples believe that ritual acts of slaying representations of animals will lead, on the principle of **mimetic,** or **imitation, magic,** to great success on an actual hunt. Religious interpretations of this kind are supported, in part, by occasional portrayals of wounded animals, or of realistically drawn beasts with crudely figured hearts on the outside, perhaps for use as targets. Also found among Magdalenian works of art is a tendency to paint one creature right over another. Such a custom, too, plays a part in some primitive religions. Once a spot has acquired a sacred character it is not likely to be readily changed, and wherever such a belief prevails it is not sur-

Fig. 5.14. Horse and hind, from Altamira. The figure of the horse is drawn on the same spot as, and right over, the figure of a hind. This may be due to a religious convention. Both figures are thought to be of Magdalenian age. (Courtesy of Peabody Museum, Harvard University.)

prising to find paintings superimposed on one another. There is always a possibility that archeological interpretations based on analogy with existing primitive procedures may be wrong, but there is scarcely a writer who touches on the subject of Magdalenian art without suggesting that it may have religious overtones (see Fig. 5.14).

With the end of the Pleistocene and the termination of Magdalenian culture in Western Europe, modern times begin geologically and, to some extent, culturally as well.

SELECTED REFERENCES

Breuil, H., *Four Hundred Centuries of Cave Art*. New York, 1950.
Burkitt, M. C., *The Old Stone Age*. Cambridge, England, 1933.
Daniel, G. E., *The Three Ages*. Cambridge, England, 1943.

DeLaet, S. J., (R. Daniel, trans.), *Archaeology and its Problems.* New York, 1957.

Kuhn, H., *On the Track of Prehistoric Man.* New York, 1955.

MacCurdy, G. G., *Human Origins.* New York, 1924.

Movius, H. L., Jr., "Old World Prehistory: Paleolithic," in *Anthropology Today,* A. L. Kroeber, ed. Chicago, 1953.

Nelson, N. C., "Prehistoric Archeology" in Boas, F. *et. al., General Anthropology.* New York, 1938.

Oakley, K. P., *Man the Tool-maker,* rev. ed. London, 1950.

Obermeier, H., *Fossil Man in Spain.* New Haven, 1924.

Senet, A., *Man in Search of his Ancestors.* New York, 1954.

Shapiro, H. L., ed., *Man, Culture, and Society,* Chaps. 2, 3. New York, 1956.

Windels, F., *The Lascaux Cave Paintings.* New York, 1950.

Zeuner, F. E., *Dating the Past,* rev. ed. London, 1946.

UPPER PALEOLITHIC CULTURE

CHAPTER 6

THE MIDDLE AND NEW
STONE AGES

A. MESOLITHIC CULTURE

Between the end of the Upper Paleolithic and the start of the Neolithic (roughly from 20,000 to 6,000 B.C.), there is a spread of about fourteen millennia during which man's cultural progress is but slightly understood. Until the turn of the present century this phase, currently known as **Mesolithic ("Middle Stone Age")** was rather contemptuously dismissed as a kind of Dark Age. Part of the low regard was due to ignorance of what man had then accomplished, and part of it was based on the patent fact that some of the highest attainments of the Upper Paleolithic were lost. No stone work in the Mesolithic reaches the perfection of the Solutrian, and there is no continuation of the splendid artistic creations of the Aurignacian and Magdalenian periods.

In all fairness to the human beings of Mesolithic times in Western Europe it must be recognized that they were living in an era of drastic environmental changes. The huge glaciers of the Pleistocene were shrinking, leaving enormous fields of melting ice that ultimately raised water levels throughout the region. When much of the water finally drained into the sea, the land was relieved of its heavy burden and began, in its turn, to rise. These fluctuations of

land and water levels, and the establishment of new equilibria between them, were greatly influenced by the mounting temperatures
that continued in force even after they had initiated the melting of
glaciers.[1] Under these conditions vegetation thrived and dense forests arose. Animals biologically adjusted to Ice Age weather could
not survive the increasingly warm climate and became extinct or
migrated far to the north, and new species took their place. At first
these fauna showed adaptations to tundra and steppe life, but forest types gained in prominence as the Mesolithic grew older. Only
Homo sapiens met the challenges of fundamental environmental
changes by adjusting his culture instead of his biology.

Obviously, over a long span of time during which took place so
many alterations of climate, fauna, and flora, no one form of culture
could have been universally appropriate. For the Mesolithic, even
more than for the Paleolithic, it is necessary to deal with local or
regional patterns instead of with one generalized way of life. Unlike the Paleolithic folk of Western Europe, who experienced similar glacial conditions in most of the places where they lived, the
Mesolithic people of the north found themselves in a markedly different climatic belt from those who dwelt in the central to southern
reaches of the continent. Those who hunted game in forests must
inevitably have differed from coastal folk who fished and collected
shellfish, and what was suitable for northern Denmark might
well have been unfit for south-central France. Such conditions provide the kind of setting in which diffusion operates whenever communications are established between two or more previously isolated regions of diverse culture. Combinations of ideas, objects,
and people move back and forth, thus enriching the prevalent ways
of life in numerous areas.

Attempts have been made to derive some of the Mesolithic cultures from specific Upper Paleolithic manifestations, but most of
them are far-fetched. Satisfactorily proved connections may some
day be demonstrated, because it is unlikely that all Upper Paleolithic cultures and their carriers were completely exterminated as
soon as the Pleistocene closed.

---

[1] Melting glaciers usually deposit in lakes twin soil layers or **varves** annually.
During warm weather a band of sand or silt forms and is overlaid the next winter
by clay. The number of varves in a glacial lake bed thus gives a clue to its age.
This method of dating has been well developed in Scandinavia.

B. THE MAGLEMOSE AND ERTEBØLLE PHASES

Much more is known of Mesolithic life in northwestern than south-western Europe, and the probability is strong that some Upper Paleolithic people from Spain or France moved northward in post-Pleistocene times. Most intimately adjusted to the changing times were a group of ax-using peoples in Denmark and the vicinity, whose main implements were hefty enough to cope with the growing forests. The best studied part of their culture is the **Maglemose** phase, which has left ample remains. People who followed Maglemose ways of life hunted elk, red deer, and wild pig; caught many pike and other fish from inland waters; did a considerable amount of fowling; and collected various edible plants. Also, they made stone tools that vary from microliths in many shapes to heavy-handled **core-built axes** (Fig. 6.1), roughly rectangular, and not to be confused with generally pear-shaped Lower Paleolithic fist-axes, as well as **adzes, picks,** and **chisels,** or **tranchets.** They also made harpoons and barbless fishhooks of antler and bone, in addi-

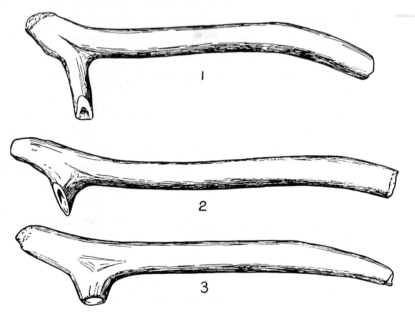

Fig. 6.1. Three Mesolithic tools. All three implements were made with handles of reindeer antler to which stones were fitted. Number 1 is in the shape of an ax; 2 was used as an adze, and 3 is simply a haft. (J. G. D. Clark, *The Mesolithic Settlement of Northern Europe.* Cambridge, England, 1936. Courtesy Cambridge University Press.)

tion to assorted items of wood. Among the most interesting Maglemose remains are a number of large paddle-rudders that point to a
knowledge of water transport, most likely in the form of dugout
canoes.

No doubt the Maglemose folk had the resources to deal with
forest life, and some think it was in connection with hunting in the
woods that they achieved their greatest cultural triumph, domestication of the dog. There is a question as to whether they originated
the idea or borrowed it from outsiders. In either case, this marks the
first instance in our outline of cultural evolution of man's use of a
lower animal for purposes other than food or as a source of raw
material. Accordingly, this seems to be the logical place to discuss
the concept of animal domestication, which was later to become
one of the most valuable principles on which modern culture is
based.

It is important not to confuse domestication with simple taming.
A completely domesticated animal must not only be so tame that it
will not attack people or run away, but it should also be dependent
on man for some of its food, as opposed to foraging on its own, and
it should be capable of breeding under conditions of captivity. If
a beast has been thoroughly domesticated its anatomical structure
may change, in which event paleontologists can usually tell the remains of a domesticated creature from those of its wild relatives.
It has been thoroughly established that dogs were the first beasts
to have been brought under domestication and that their ancestors
were wolves. There is no way of telling by what steps the dog was
domesticated, nor are the uses to which it was put at all clear.[2]
Even so, its presence stands out as an important event in the progress of Mesolithic cultures.

According to several experts, a salt-water sea was formed in
northern Europe in the course of time. Some of the Maglemose
hunters apparently moved there rather late in Mesolithic times
and settled permanently on its shores. Their culture at this stage is
called **Ertebølle** and is often, but not in every instance, represented
by huge mounds of debris known as **kitchen middens.** Kitchen middens consist of discarded shells, bones, earth, lost or rejected tools,
and other odds and ends densely packed together. Sometimes they

---

[2] The theory has been advanced, by analogy with known areas where livestock
are kept for social or religious purposes, that animal domestication may not have
started as a practical measure. This is an interesting but unproved hypothesis.

contain skeletal remains. Those who lived at the seashore long enough to build vast heaps of debris were probably permanent residents, for the kitchen mounds show enough fire hearths to suggest that the inhabitants stuck it out even during inclement seasons. Material remains of Ertebølle culture run closely parallel to those of the Maglemose, except for the addition of pottery vessels. The invention of pottery is an exceedingly important attainment, but Ertebølle is so recent a phase of Mesolithic culture that nearly everyone agrees that the concept was not original but came from some other area where Neolithic culture was already well advanced. All archeologists subscribe to the notion that at the time in question the cultural attainments of Northern Europe's inhabitants lagged far behind the accomplishments of many people who lived further south in the Old World.

Borrowed or not, Ertebølle pottery was far from handsome, and its methods of manufacture do not show great skill. All of the specimens that have ever been found seem to represent utility vessels. They were lumpy of texture, and were made of black clay **tempered** with coarse grit. When they were fired they took on a gray-brown color. Quite often, the pots were so badly made that they cracked open. Oval saucers and wide-mouthed jars with conical, pointed bases are the commonest remnants, and the prevailing style of decoration consisted of a series of fingernail impressions along the rim (Fig. 6.2).

C. INTRODUCTION TO THE NEOLITHIC

By 6000 B.C. *Homo sapiens* had gone through a long and diversified cultural apprenticeship. Throughout the hundreds of millennia of the Old and Middle Stone Ages the species had shown itself capable of adjusting to extreme environmental differences. It had devised a great profusion of tools made in a variety of ways from wood, fine-grained stones, ivory, horn, bone, and other materials. It had made homes in caves, under rock-shelters, in the open, in forested land, and at the seacoast. Fire was everywhere under human control, and ingenious methods of obtaining food from nature had been developed. Religious practices had been introduced, and examples of the fine arts occasionally reached marvelous heights. Before the conclusion of the Mesolithic the potential power of the human body had been greatly increased through the agency of such

Fig. 6.2. Mesolithic pottery. All the sherds pictured are specimens of Ertebølle pottery. It is always poorly made. Impressed designs may occur on the rims, and the bases are typically conical. (Courtesy of the Danish National Museum.)

extracorporeal things as sturdily hafted tools, bows and arrows, boats or canoes, and, perhaps, the domesticated dog. Also, during the Middle Stone Age the making of pottery introduced a new industry to Western Europe and led to an expanding utilization of natural resources. Nevertheless, despite the record of their achievements Old and Middle Stone Age cultures advanced at a painfully slow pace and cannot help but appear remote and drab to those who live in the second half of the twentieth century A.D. This picture, as we shall soon see, changed with dramatic suddenness when some groups of men entered the **New Stone Age** and became *producers* of plant and animal foods.

Ancient forms of culture doubtless survived in various parts of the world long after they had become outmoded elsewhere. This raises an interesting question about the situation as it developed some eight millennia ago. Viewed in universal terms, a previously unknown situation must have arisen in the Neolithic. For the first time in human history, there must have been groups of hunters and collectors of foodstuffs who looked with envy on prosperous, agricultural neighbors, particularly in late fall or winter when game was scarce and wild botanical products were unavailable. These are the very seasons of the year when farmers and keepers of livestock are likely, except under the most wretched of circumstances, to have food surpluses. A distinction must have arisen at such times between "have" and "have not" societies, and it seems reasonable to believe that large-scale raids or wars, as distinguished from sporadic assaults or occasional murders, must have had their beginning in Neolithic times. By way of partial proof, it may be noted that New Stone Age settlements fortified by ditches and ramparts are commonplace.

Consideration of the Neolithic also serves to bring out other points of theory. In tracing the march of culture we are dealing not with universal stages through which each local community must have passed, but rather with a synthesis that puts into an orderly sequence the highest levels of culture that were reached here and there by various units of people. No one race, tribe, nation, society, or corner of the globe showed the way at all times. It is vitally important to remember that around 6000 B.C. many spots in the Old World that are now regarded as "backward" were exerting vigorous cultural leadership and, conversely, that such a "forward" area as Western Europe was then far behind the times.

At this point it may be wise to repeat why the descriptions of Paleolithic and Mesolithic cultures were centered on events that took place in Western Europe. It was not meant to imply that during the Pleistocene Western Europe had either the earliest or the best-developed form of culture in the entire world. The one and only reason why data from Western Europe were emphasized is because the sequence of man's earliest efforts to live by culture has there been most intensively studied. When it comes to a consideration of man's progress in Neolithic times, however, it becomes necessary to shift the scene. Not Western Europe but the **Eastern Mediterranean Zone** best reveals the manner in which *Homo sapiens* made his way into the New Stone Age. This zone extends from Egypt's Nile River in northeastern Africa to the valleys of the Euphrates and Tigris Rivers in Western Asia. The Eastern Mediterranean Zone incorporates what is often called "the Fertile Crescent." It provides the environmental potential for the New Stone Age; and it is here, most archeologists believe, that Neolithic culture was born. That it did not spring into existence full-blown is readily acknowledged, but the immediate steps leading to its formation have never been discovered.

D. NEOLITHIC STONEWORK

Because "Neolithic" has become a time-sanctioned term for the new ways of life that started around 6000 B.C., it is appropriate to begin with a description of stone usages, although they were by no means the most important accomplishments of the era. Even during the antecedent Mesolithic of northwestern Europe, attempts had been made to handle stone in ways that were unknown to Paleolithic man. Most valuable of the new methods was a process of rubbing a bit of stone repeatedly over a rough abrasive substance such as sandstone, rough vegetal fibers, or plain sand. This technique, commonly known as **grinding** or **polishing**, produces a tool that has a smooth, highly burnished appearance. One can usually identify a Neolithic stone implement by its characteristically smooth surface.

In the Neolithic, grinding or polishing systematically displaced the older percussion and pressure methods of dealing with stone. Introduction of the new process is of deep significance because it greatly increased man's use of natural resources through his new ability to utilize hitherto valueless raw materials. No longer was it necessary to seek out flint, quartz, or other fine-grained stones of cryptocrystalline structure. Almost any kind of stone, regardless of grain or internal composition, can be ground into a tool. Even granites, which disintegrate when subjected to percussion or pressure flaking, can be rubbed into a desired shape. Polishing has the further advantage of producing sturdier working edges than the older methods, which turned out implements that often split or cracked after they had been used to strike a few hard blows. When a Paleolithic tool was damaged it could seldom be repaired and was likely to be discarded and replaced, but the working edge of a polished stone instrument can be resharpened or repaired by re-rubbing, pretty much on the same principle that is used to repair a metal tool on a grindstone. In the long run, therefore, Neolithic implements turned out to be more durable and economical than their parallels from the earlier ages. They enabled man to cut and shape timbers more efficiently than was previously the case, and they may well deserve credit for providing the means of establishing carpentry as a more important craft than ever before.

With increased reliance on techniques of grinding, the old distinction between flake and core tools grew meaningless. So little raw material was wasted by the Neolithic process that it made small difference if a craftsman started with a core or a flake. For the most part the same kinds of utensils continued to be made, but after a while Neolithic workmen came to show a preference for what is called a **celt** (Fig. 6.3). Only a glance at a typical celt is needed to convince one that when suitably hafted it is the prototype of our familiar hatchet or ax blade. Abandonment of tools designed to be held in the bare hand and worked through the agency of muscular strength is a very significant feature of the Neolithic and helps us to realize how persistently *Homo sapiens* continued to elaborate his culture while he allowed his body to remain unchanged and rather generalized.

Despite the almost undifferentiated use of stones made possible by Neolithic workmanship, there was a differing value put on various kinds of lithic substances. Stones that are today classified as semiprecious, as well as amber and sea shells, seem to have been regarded as valuable and were widely traded. Metals, including gold, silver, copper, and lead, were also known, but they were generally used while cold and were never melted or liquefied. It is probable that mining for particular varieties of stone went on in earlier times, but not until the New Stone Age is there evidence of large-scale mining activity, with such technological contrivances as sunken shafts and connecting galleries.

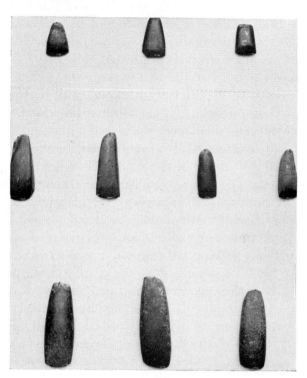

Fig. 6.3. Neolithic celts from the Swiss lake-dwellings. These celts represent the most common stone tools of the Neolithic. All were rubbed or polished until smooth. None was used without a handle. (Courtesy of Chicago Natural History Museum.)

E. POTTERY MAKES ITS APPEARANCE

Neolithic man learned to increase his material resources still further by coming to understand how to convert wet clay, which had hitherto been nothing but a nuisance in the form of sticky mud, into fine dishes and outlets for artistic expression. Invention of pottery making must be ranked as one of man's greatest cultural triumphs.

No better appreciation of the value of mental foresight can be gained than by trying to imagine the first person who saw in his mind's eye the possibility of turning clay into the kinds of ceramic vessels that have culminated in the Lenox, Wedgwood, and Spode products of our day. To become a successful potter is no easy matter, and many anonymous craftsmen must have made contributions that helped carry this art to perfection. Professor V. Gordon Childe, one of the greatest living archeologists, even regards pot-making as the beginning of science and perhaps man's first conscious utilization of a chemical change.[3]

Some of the basic complexities of this skill come to light even in a brief account of only a few of the steps involved. To begin with, a deposit of suitable clay, containing an adequate amount of silicate of aluminum, must be located. The clay must then be mixed with just enough water to form a paste that is plastic but not too sticky. It must then be carefully kneaded until it is perfectly uniform inside and out. To the clay paste must be added a small percentage of a **tempering substance,** such as chopped-up bits of straw, grains of sand, fragments of crushed shell, or minutely crumbled pieces of stone. At a later stage, while a vessel is being fired, steam or other gaseous by-products will escape through tiny outlets provided by the **temper,** and so prevent the clay body of a pot from cracking. A craftsman must make a neat calculation of the exact amount of tempering material he is using in order to get the desired effect without making the finished vessel as coarse as is the general run of Mesolithic pottery.

After the clay, water, and temper have been well worked together comes the difficult task of shaping a vessel. Early Neolithic potters were inclined to mold by hand such small objects as cups, somewhat in the fashion of sculpture. Larger things were often made by coiling, a process whereby a worker rolls out "ropes" of clay, then fits one above another until the shape desired has been achieved. The coil junctures may then be allowed to remain as ornamental effects, or else they may be obliterated by judicious squeezing and rubbing. Next, the outer walls of the vessel are carefully scraped or polished. A preliminary drying out-of-doors follows, after which the pot is at last ready to be fired. At a temperature of over 1100 degrees, Fahrenheit, the original clay loses its plasticity and bakes into a hard, waterproof, solid material, capable of retaining its shape, until smashed, in any environment whatsoever. Once having become waterproof, true pottery no longer reverts to raw clay when it is wetted.

Even this fragmentary synopsis, which says nothing about methods of decoration, or about firing, or handles and covers, should serve to convey some of the difficulties that must be overcome if

---

[3] V. G. Childe, *Man Makes Himself,* London, 1936, p. 101.

good pottery is to be made. A long time must have elapsed before pottery manufacturing reached a high degree of perfection, but the usefulness of pottery for storage and the cooking and serving of various foods, as well as its artistic possibilities as a background for design and ornament, was recognized very early. Broken fragments, known as **potsherds,** are always conspicuous in Neolithic remains. This provides a totally different kind of value that has come to be attached to **ceramics.** Although objects of pottery are notoriously fragile and easily broken, the resulting **sherds** are practically indestructible. Bits of broken pots are worthless to their owners and are usually left behind when a settlement is abandoned, to remain in place for untold centuries. Modern archeologists are eternally grateful to the unknown discoverer of the potter's craft. Highly specialized techniques of ceramic analysis have made possible scientifically accurate determination of clays, coloring substances, tempering materials, and firing temperatures and methods. The availability of detailed information along these lines often makes it possible for archeologists to tell where a given kind of pottery originated. They are thereby provided with clues to the study of migration, trade, and cultural diffusion.

F. THE NEOLITHIC BASES OF MODERN LIFE

The New Stone Age differs most widely from its predecessors because it involved the production, rather than mere gathering, of food. Farming made the big difference between Mesolithic and Neolithic patterns of culture, and farming could never have been started were it not for man's ability to plan ahead and to have confidence in his predictions. At the very least a farmer must, long before he can expect any benefit from his efforts, be willing to expend time and labor in clearing a bit of land, breaking ground, planting seeds, and removing weeds. Only those who are farsighted enough to work hard in the hope of gaining future compensation can ever become successful farmers, but when the rewards do come in they are apt, except in unusually bad years, to be very generous. Agricultural communities generally find it possible to raise more than they collectively need, and thus they develop a surplus which can be stored and used for purposes other than the satisfaction of hunger.

Closely affiliated with the idea of farming is the notion of animal domestication. Contemporary anthropologists do not accept the priority of **pastoralism** as a separate stage of culture, but are of the opinion that the cultivation of plants and the rearing of livestock took place at about the same time. Throughout the Eastern Mediterranean Zone **mixed farming,** as it is called, is found in very early Neolithic settlements. Cattle, sheep, goats, and pigs, in addition to dogs, were the first beasts to have been brought under domestication, and wild forms of all these species are known to have lived somewhere within the extensive region of supposed Neolithic origins. With the help of surplus agricultural products, farmers were able to feed livestock, in exchange for which they acquired a reliable source of meat, milk, hides and other raw materials, and creatures that could be trained to do much of their work for them. Through the judicious selection of animals for slaughter, coupled with careful supervision of breeding, Neolithic man found himself with another potential surplus in addition to what could be saved from his crops.

There is no reason to think that New Stone Age people gave up hunting, fishing, and gathering just as soon as they had acquired the arts of farming and keeping livestock. On the contrary, there is abundant archeological evidence that the new activities were simply added to the older ones. Hence Neolithic societies, unlike those with Paleolithic or Mesolithic cultures, grew less and less dependent for their welfare on the vagaries of nature. Food shortages and indefinite periods of want must have diminished when man became a successful food producer.

Domestication of plants and animals stimulated and called into being other practices, not necessarily directly concerned with the production of food. Devices for housing, feeding, tethering, and leading or guiding beasts, as well as the manufacture of agricultural tools, would be of this order. A less direct by-product that arose in the Neolithic is the textile industry, which necessitates the spinning of thread and the weaving of cloth. Each of the two major aspects of domestication played a part in this development. Domesticated plants included flax and cotton, which were grown because their fibers could be drawn out and spun into long threads from which linen or cotton cloths were made; and domesticated sheep provided wool, which was similarly converted into cloth. In neither case was the matter left to chance, for flax and cotton were specifically cultivated as non-food crops, and wool-bearing animals were systematically bred to produce a heavy fleece.

The essentials of weaving as established in Neolithic days have continued to serve mankind throughout the ages. Threads that are tied in place on a loom and made to hang vertically downward at regular intervals are known as the **warp.** Cloth is then woven by the act of introducing a moveable element (**woof,** or **weft**) which is passed horizontally over or under one or more warp strands at a time. Designs are produced by the coloring of threads or else by the order in which the warp strings are raised or depressed as the weft moves across them. Even the most complicated of automatic power-driven looms of our time still operate on the original plan that was figured out by some unknown Neolithic genius.

Much basketry is produced along the same principles as cloth weaving. When **twined** or woven objects are to be made, stiff vegetal fibers are fixed in position, without need for a loom, to serve as the warp, and similar elements are passed over and under them in the manner of a weft (Fig. 6.4). There is, though, another widespread basketry technique that is more like sewing than weaving.

Fig. 6.4. An Indian basket maker. This Pomo Indian woman, from California, is making a basket by a weaving technique. Note the warp elements that are fixed in place. (Courtesy of the Bureau of American Ethnology.)

This is the **coiling method,** in which a worker prepares rings of fibers and then stitches them into position, one above another. Specimens of both processes are known from Neolithic remains.

A

B

C

Fig. 6.5. Early means of transportation. A. A dog-drawn travois. Bundles were tied on the frame close to the animal. Although this picture shows a Blackfoot Indian travois, comparable devices may well have been used elsewhere prior to full development of wheeled vehicles. (American Museum of Natural History.) B, C. Ancient wheels, as depicted in the Near East. B is from a scarlet pottery vase found at Susa in Iran; C is from a limestone relief discovered at Khafaje in Mesopotamia. Both are dated in the Copper-Bronze Age. (Courtesy the Prehistoric Society, England, and Oxford University Press.)

Long before the New Stone Age reached a close, the principle of the wheel, which converts straight-line to rotary power, was discovered. Very likely its quality of reducing friction was soon recognized as suited for improving means of transportation, but its use was doubtless preceded by that of drags, sledges, or rollers (Fig. 6.5A). In order to appreciate the full and ultimate value of the concept of the wheel, one has only to think of its importance to modern industry. Not only are wheels placed on all sorts of vehicles from perambulators to airplanes, but they are also of prime importance to the operations of contrivances as varied as watches, record-players, and electric generators. The Neolithic inventor of the wheel could not have foreseen the consequences, but the idea of using rotary power has become one of the most valuable industrial notions of our day.

Man's adoption of weaving and the concept of the wheel serve to illustrate a distinction that some cultural anthropologists make between an **invention** and a **discovery.** Clothmaking, which represents an invention, does not exist in nature and could only have been worked out by a person of algebraic mentality who could foresee what would happen if fixed warp threads were crossed by moveable weft elements. Rotary power, on the other hand, does exist in nature, as whirling logs or rolling stones amply attest. Therefore, its incorporation into human culture called only for the discovery of an already existent principle.

As the Neolithic got into full stride, the social aspects of life inevitably came to differ noticeably from the interrelationships of the people who had remained at the earlier stages. Great advances in technology never fail to be accompanied by equally important shifts of social organization and religion. Farmers, particularly in the early days of their reliance on agriculture, are not always unwilling to migrate, but surely no human being in his right senses will sow a crop and then voluntarily move away while someone else reaps the harvest. Faulty environmental conditions, including wornout soils, may induce farmers to move, but assuredly their wanderings are negligible compared with those of the preceding Stone Age folk.

Besides their greater permanence, agricultural communities can support denser populations. Not until Neolithic times do archeologists find signs of settlements large enough to be called towns or villages, and with correspondingly big refuse mounds to suggest long occupancy. The very magnitude and stability of Neolithic communities must have raised some serious problems. Large numbers of people do not live for very long in close proximity without well developed social organization. Systematic rules for controlling the conduct of individuals toward each other invariably arise. Full-fledged ethical systems and repetitive ways of correct behavior are thus established, and that is how technology and social organization become interconnected.

As to religion, there is little of a tangible nature to guide conjecture, but certain implications are fairly evident. People invariably seek aid and comfort from their deities, and it stands to reason that societies which depend on farming and raising animals will not want the same sort of help that hunters and gatherers seek. There is nothing startling in the statement that hunters are likely to worship gods of the hunt, whereas farmers are more likely to worship agricultural deities. But such a statement also serves to reveal an intimate connection between a society's economic pursuits and its religion. This is the sort of linkage that may often be readily detected in a primitive group, but which is generally much less clear in a complex society.

There is also a profound difference in the degree of *reliance* on supernatural or religious aid between the two groups. When pre-Neolithic man was faced with a food shortage he could do little about it except pray for assistance. Neolithic man was not quite so helpless as his predecessors. There were, of course, many things over which he had no control, but when threatened by a food shortage he might not only seek supernatural aid but he might in addition increase his own diligence. If, for example, it was a matter of drought that bothered him he might pray for rain, but he might also seek to improve the situation by building irrigation canals or deliberately hauling water from a distant source. No one pretends to know how often Neolithic man followed one course or the other, and no one knows which he found more satisfactory, but the fact remains that potentially the people of the New Stone Age were more the masters of their fate than were those who lived by Paleolithic or Mesolithic forms of culture.

Neolithic communities are thought by Professor Childe to have been pretty self-sufficient, and as communities they probably were; but the same cannot be said of individuals. It is no great strain on the imagination to think of a Mesolithic or Paleolithic man who could carry out all the occupations demanded of a male by his culture: one who could make his own tools, hunt, fish, contrive shelters, build fires, and the like. It is quite another matter to try to picture a Neolithic person who could by himself make all his own polished stone tools, build his house and outbuildings, breed and care for animals, manufacture pottery, weave cloth, and fashion baskets, all in addition to raising crops. Undoubtedly the more complex forms of Neolithic life were carried on with the help of a more varied assignment of differing tasks to each of the sexes and between young and old, as well as of cooperation among them and their fellow-villagers, but it is almost as certain that incipient classes of specialists were emerging in the persons of those who could make better baskets, pots, or cloth than their neighbors. Full-time specialization could not arise until some folk regularly accumulated large enough surpluses of food to barter or trade them, in one form or another, for manufactured items. And as specialization increased, there would have to be regulations to control the orderly exchange of goods. Archeologists have no way of measuring the extent to which new social forms accompanied the advanced technology of the New Stone Age, but it is certain that by 6000 B.C. the good old days of simple biological behavior had been left far behind in New Stone Age settlements; and yet, the full complexities of modern life were just starting.

There is much that is solid and enduring in Neolithic man's accomplishments. The crops that he first brought under cultivation in the Old World, notably wheat, rye, barley, and oats, are still of prime importance throughout the world; the animals that he succeeded in domesticating, such as cattle, pigs, sheep, and goats, remain among the most valuable ever brought under human control; and the techniques of pottery-making, basketry, and weaving that he devised continue to form the basis of much modern industry. Only his stone tools have become entirely outmoded. It is probably correct to say that Neolithic life in the Eastern Mediterranean Zone so nearly resembled our own in agricultural areas that even the most up-to-date of our farmers would require only a short space of time in order to adjust himself to the life of a New Stone Age community.

Another way of coming to realize the persistence and the vitality of Stone Age ways of life emerges from a study of history. The highest levels of culture attained by any of the North American

Indian tribes before 1492 were only Neolithic; and Australian and Tasmanian bands had not even advanced so far when they were first encountered by Europeans.

Several important but unsolved problems of great theoretical significance plague archeologists who specialize in studying the remains of the New Stone Age. How many of the new traits must a site reveal to be classified as Neolithic? Is the occurrence of polished stone tools or pottery enough? If one of these features is not sufficient to warrant Neolithic classification, then how many are required, and in what combination? Were the New Stone Age traits invented only once and diffused elsewhere, or were they independently originated in several places and at various times? In either case, precisely when and where was each item first made a part of human culture, and exactly how did the new customs spread about? At what date did the Neolithic come to an end, or does it still persist in some areas?

These questions are posed not to bewilder the reader, but rather to suggest some of the leads that remain to be explored by future investigators.

SELECTED REFERENCES

Amsden, C., "The Loom and its Prototypes," *American Anthropologist*, Vol. 34, 1932.

Bibby, G., *The Testimony of the Spade*. New York, 1956.

Braidwood, R. J., "The Near East and the Foundations for Civilization," Condon Lectures. Eugene, Oregon, 1952.

Childe, V. G., *Man Makes Himself*, Chap. 5. London, 1936.

———, *What Happened in History*. London, 1943.

Clark, J. S. D., *The Mesolithic Settlement of Northern Europe*. Cambridge, England, 1936.

———, *Prehistoric Europe*. New York, 1952.

Coon, C. S., *The Story of Man*, Chap. 4. New York, 1955.

Holmes, W. H., "Origin and Development of Form and Ornament in Ceramic Art," *Fourth Annual Report, Bureau of American Ethnology*, Washington, 1886.

Mason, O. T., "Aboriginal American Basketry," *Annual Report for 1902, Smithsonian Institution*. Washington, 1904.

O'Neale, L. M., "Archaeological Explorations in Peru: Textiles of Early Nazca Period," *Field Museum of Natural History, Anthropological Memoirs*, Vol. 2, No. 3. Chicago, 1937.

Shapiro, H. L., ed., *Man, Culture, and Society*, Chap. 4. New York, 1956.

Weltfish, G., *The Origins of Art*. Indianapolis and New York, 1953.

CHAPTER 7

LATER DEVELOPMENTS

OF CULTURE

A. PRELUDE TO METALLURGY

For all its near approach to modern patterns of living, the Neolithic failed to make the grade. If one central factor were to be singled out to account for the failure, it would have to be the ignorance of **metallurgy.** This is not the equivalent of ignorance of metal. A good number of Stone Age peoples used gold, silver, lead, and copper from time to time, but they dealt with them usually while they were cold or warm, and always as solids, pretty much as though they were unusual varieties of stone. Not until man had discovered that metals undergo marked changes when melted did he develop true metallurgy. Only then were previously unsuspected secrets unlocked for further exploration and exploitation. So extraordinary was this accomplishment thought to be that early metallurgists were seldom taken for granted. Smiths were anything but common in those days, and they were so frequently believed to have supernatural powers that they came to be looked upon as gods or devils.

The first metal to come under man's control in molten form was **copper,** and all signs point to the Eastern Mediterranean Zone as the place where this event occurred. Scholars disagree as to whether copper was used in anything like a pure form long enough to warrant recognition of a **Copper Age.** Most archeologists believe that copper so rarely occurs without admixture of other metals or minerals that metallurgists from the start were accustomed to using adulterated copper. Whether by accident or design, it was not long before it was found that a combination of copper and tin made **bronze,** a more satisfactory substance because it is harder and melts at a lower temperature. Thereafter, bronze rapidly replaced pure copper as an important resource for manufacturing. By way of compromise we shall call the first Age of Metal **Copper-Bronze.** It lasted from about 4000 B.C. to about 1500 B.C., when some metallurgists, again in the wide Eastern Mediterranean Zone, found out that **iron,** soon compounded to **steel,** had many advantages over bronze. Thereupon was inaugurated an **Iron Age** that endured from around 1500 B.C. to the start of the Christian era. It is no longer necessary to study cultural evolution after that time by means only of imperishable artifacts, since written documents were by then abundantly available to provide source materials for other approaches. Archeologists can and do contribute much to an understanding of later developments, but in the study of human life during historic times their functions are greatly modified.

Before taking up the details of life in the **Metal Ages,** it is important to re-emphasize that human culture is additive (Fig. 8.3), and grows by the accretion of knowledge. Those societies that were among the earliest to learn the arts of metallurgy did not discard the many contributions of the Stone Ages. The new horizons of culture grew out of the preceding stages but did not necessarily break with them. Cold materials of long familiarity such as wood, stone, bone, ivory, and horn, continued to be important; hunting, fowling, and fishing remained significant; pottery-making, basketry, and the weaving of cloth became increasingly widespread; and, of course, farming and stock breeding still formed the essence of the economy. Progress was made partly by the improvement of older devices like the wheel, partly by the expansion of activities like crop raising, and partly by the introduction of brand-new practices.

As we trace the march of culture in the Metal Ages we are again making a synthesis of high-water marks. No single society encompassed within itself all the innovations and improvements of the new era. Only a few groups in restricted portions of the Old World took the forward strides, and the bulk of mankind remained at Neolithic, Mesolithic, or Paleolithic levels. This is much like saying that only a few contemporary nations are learning to deal with atomic energy, or like making the simple observation that in any of our cities it may be possible to see moving about at the same time pedestrians, bicycles, automobiles, and airplanes.

As was true in earlier stages the attainment of different forms of material culture and the establishment of a new technology did not make up the sum total of Metal Age accomplishments. Far-reaching changes accompanied the introduction of metallurgy in the less obvious fields of social and religious organization. In combination, all the fresh ideas and customs paved the way for our present scheme of life, which is firmly grounded on Metal Age antecedents.

Among the major Neolithic discoveries was the concept of the wheel. Yet, this concept received little practical application until the start of the Copper-Bronze Age. Among other uses the wheel was then applied to the manufacture of pottery. A lump of prepared clay would be thrown on the center of a revolving wheel, and as it spun the potter manipulated it until it took the shape he had in mind. Not only did the new method greatly speed up the technique of pot formation, but the action of the wheel resulted in a vessel of far greater symmetry than could be achieved freehand. By the same means a greater perfection of design was made possible. To produce a perfectly even, circular line that runs clear around a piece of pottery is exceedingly difficult if the vessel must be turned by hand a little at a time. But one need only hold a stylus, comb, or brush steadily in place while a potter's wheel makes a complete revolution in order to achieve a perfect circle.

There is also an important sociological correlate of wheel-made pottery that has no bearing on sheer mechanics or technology. Throughout the world hand-made pottery is usually the task of women, but wherever the wheel is used the manufacture of pottery becomes, almost without exception, a masculine occupation (Fig. 7.1). The reason for this state of affairs is not known, but it is certainly not due to any biological difference between the sexes.

An even more significant application of wheels was developed in conjunction with vehicles. Ponderous carts, with two or four wheels made of heavy wooden sections that turned with the axle, are known to have been in use soon after the end of Neolithic times, but only gradually, after the Metal Ages were well under way, were light but strong wheels made with spokes and rims of metal. Even

Fig. 7.1. Pottery-making in India. A, B. A woman making pottery by hand. C. A male potter using a wheel. In most primitive societies, the sexual dichotomy of pottery-making is the same as it is in India. (A, B, C. Courtesy of Museum of Anthropology, University of Michigan.)

so, full use of wheeled vehicles could not come about until strong animals had been trained to pull them.

That domesticated beasts had been employed to share some of man's labors as early as the New Stone Age is a safe assumption. Nevertheless, no draught animals could have been put to work before the invention of suitable means of harnessing. Few remains of such contrivances appear prior to the Metal Ages. Oxen were certainly among the first creatures set to the pulling of carts or wagons, but they must have proved too slow for many purposes. Asian asses were found better suited, and were commonly utilized in Copper-Bronze times. Horses do not seem to have been domesticated until the late Neolithic at best, and they remained unimportant until the early Metal Age. Horseback riding as a regular custom came late and may have followed driving by as much as a millennium.

Use of strong animals for pulling was not restricted to vehicles, but was also employed when plowing became widespread in the Eastern Mediterranean Zone. Again, it had first been necessary for suitable accessories to be devised. As the custom of plowing made headway, another interesting sociological transfer took place. When small fields were worked with a hoe, the task fell to women in practically all primitive societies, but when large farms had to be plowed, it became a masculine duty. In this case the greater muscular strength of men may have been a factor.

These are only a few of the ways in which the people of the Copper-Bronze Age expanded notions that had originated in the Neolithic. The examples also show how closely one invention may be interlocked with others and how frequently technological shifts affect social organization. Improvements and additions were made in every sphere of human existence. Indeed, so many items were added to the crops under cultivation that just about all the plants grown in the Old World before the discovery of America were being raised by Copper-Bronze Age farmers. There was also a new use made of grains, fruits, and cereals, in the form of alcoholic beverages. It is perfectly possible that barley beer was known in the New Stone Age, but not before the Copper-Bronze period does proof exist that the drinking of beer and of date and grape wines had become a fixed custom.

B. THE START OF METALLURGY

Above and beyond their elaboration of Neolithic concepts, the Copper-Bronze Age folk opened new cultural outlets by learning to exploit a previously undeveloped natural resource. Let us begin with some of the advantages gained from man's mastery of molten copper, the first metallic substance to come under his full control. When copper is heated to the melting point, it can be poured into a container, and upon cooling it becomes a solid in the shape of the container. The most exciting aspect of this simple fact is that the process is reversible, so that the same chunk of copper can repeatedly be made to go from solid to liquid to solid. Practically speaking, this means that man soon found out that he could rapidly and economically change the shape of a copper object without wasting any of the precious raw material. Once the basic principle had been grasped it became no trick at all to convert something in the shape of X to Y, or Z to A. This could not be done with any of the previously employed materials that had been used while they were cold or solid.

Knowledge of this basic physicochemical reaction soon gave rise to the technique of **casting,** or **molding,** whereby a receptacle is first prepared in the desired shape and size from stone, pottery, or some other heat-resistant substance. After that, a sufficient quantity of molten copper is poured into the **mold** and allowed to cool and harden. If proper advance precautions have been taken to prevent sticking, it is then an easy matter to turn the solid product out of the mold and to give it such minor finishing touches as may be needed. Usually, no more is required than a bit of hammering or rubbing.

Casting made possible the first steps leading to **mass production,** for a well-made mold can be used repeatedly, and a number of molds can be filled and their contents allowed to harden almost simultaneously (see Fig. 7.2). There is, furthermore, a fundamental distinction between the skill and intelligence needed to design and prepare molds and the crude labor which is all that is necessary for filling and emptying them. Thus do we get a glimpse of an embryonic system that was destined to culminate in the modern distinction between white-collar workers who devise machines and manual laborers who work on assembly lines. Here, then, is a further example of the way in which technological innovations may influence changes of social structure.

Another method of handling molten metal was probably developed at some time after the start of simple casting. This is the ingenious **lost-wax,** or **cire-perdue,** process. A wax model must first be made, correct in all the particulars wanted for the final product. Then the wax model is carefully covered with clay in which an

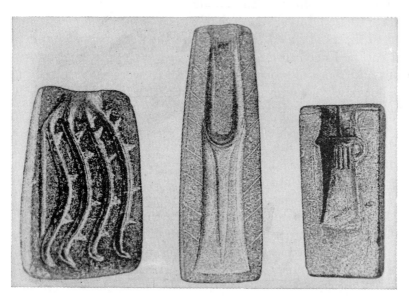

Fig. 7.2. Molds used for casting Bronze Age tools. Four saw-blades at a time could be cast in the form at the left, thus making possible mass production. (Courtesy of Peabody Museum, Harvard University.)

entrance hole and an outlet are provided. Next, the whole thing is subjected to firing, whereupon the clay hardens and the wax melts and runs out. The outlet is then closed, and liquid metal is poured into the space vacated by the wax. As soon as cooling has occurred, the baked clay is broken open and the metallic object comes forth as an exact duplicate of the original wax model. Although the cire-perdue technique is much more complicated than casting, it is better for making rounded objects or things that would otherwise have to be made in two parts and fitted together.

Awareness of the reversible nature of liquid and solid copper also made possible a great saving of raw material. Objects made from cold substances can be fashioned only by striking, cutting, pressing, or rubbing smaller bits from a larger unit, and whatever comes off is usually wasted. Not so with metals like copper or bronze. Any bits or scraps left over from manufacturing a particular object can be melted together and used afresh. There need be no wastage of chips, flakes, or shavings, no matter how small each particular fragment may be.

Another great advantage of copper is that it is **malleable** and can be pounded into sheets. True enough, certain kinds of bark can be similarly treated, but sheets of bark are woefully fragile when compared to sheets of metal. Again, copper heated short of its melting point can be forced through the hole of a die and drawn into wire. Strings and ropes of wool or vegetal fibers were undoubtedly used in earlier days, but wire is infinitely superior in strength and durability.

Also, copper can be coiled into springs that may be held taut or released at will. Only very rarely can spring coils be made with any of the common cold materials. Too, metal can be made without danger of breaking, into very slender forms with sharp points, as in pins and needles. It was necessary to combine the qualities of coiling and sharp pointing before the first safety pin, known archeologically as a **fibula,** could come into being. Once the trick was learned, man went in for an amazing degree of elaboration. **Fibulae** came to be made in great numbers, and in many sizes and shapes (Fig. 7.3). Quantities of brooches and clasps were manufactured on similar principles.

Among the early uses to which metal was put was the production of weapons and agricultural implements, notably swords, daggers, scythes and sickles, that call for sharp yet sturdy and durable cutting edges. The superiority of metallic blades for such purposes

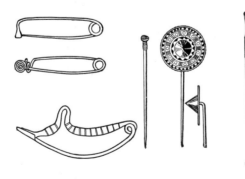 

Fig. 7.3. Pins and safety pins, or fibulae. These forms appeared for the first time in the Bronze Age, but some of them continued in use to the Iron Age and beyond. (Courtesy of Peabody Museum, Harvard University.)

was promply grasped, and copper celts, particularly, were produced in abundance. Methods of hafting remained to be worked out. An interesting series of metal celts can be arranged to illustrate various solutions to this problem (Fig. 7.4). Early Copper-Bronze Age celts

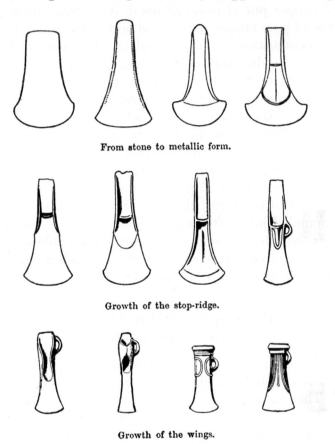

From stone to metallic form.

Growth of the stop-ridge.

Growth of the wings.

Fig. 7.4. From flat celt to palstave. Various kinds of metal celts are illustrated. They are arranged in logical order to show all the stages from flat shapes to ringed palstaves. (Courtesy of British Museum.)

were flat, and very similar to those of polished stone. These were presumably wedged into the cleft of a handle and may have been secondarily tied into place. Others had raised sides that formed a constricted channel into which a shaft could be tightly forced. Still others combined this feature with a horizontal bar or **stop-ridge** designed to keep a handle from slipping too far down. Most elaborate of all were **palstaves,** in which the sides rose and met each other to form a hollow socket. Some palstaves even had a ring added at the side to make doubly sure of a tight haft by wedging and tying.

Despite the wide range of new possibilities that the qualities of liquefied copper put at man's disposal, its softness made the continued use of pure copper impractical and it was soon displaced by bronze, a combination of copper and tin. This was made possible by yet another advantage of metallurgy, because by melting together two or more metals a blend, or **alloy,** can be made that has different qualities from any of the contributing materials. Bronze, the first alloy to come into wide use, added hardness and toughness to copper without detracting from its attractive properties. Very early specimens of bronze reveal great uncertainty as to the best proportions of tin to copper; but later a formula of about 10 to 15 percent of tin and 85 to 90 percent of copper became almost universal. One must not forget that bits of stone, ivory, or cold metal can be pounded into softer materials like wood or leather, but in such cases there is no fusion of properties; each cold substance retains its distinctive nature, and no new qualities emerge. Only molten materials can be truly blended into alloys.

C. SOME SOCIOCULTURAL CONSEQUENCES
OF METALLURGY

When we were dealing with the Neolithic, it was pointed out that specialization probably began as the range of arts and crafts increased. There is no longer any uncertainty about the growth of specialists during the succeeding Copper-Bronze Age. It was not long before free metallic copper on or near the earth's surface was exhausted. It then became necessary to mine copper ore. To do this called for **prospectors** trained to recognize and discover hidden cuprous deposits, **miners** to extract the ore, and **smelters** and **refiners** to separate the pure metal from its associated impurities. Even after these operations, it was no easy matter to acquire the skill and equipment needed for metallurgy. No individual could possibly carry out all the activities by himself, and anyone who wanted to make or acquire things of copper had no choice but to depend on others. Personal self-sufficiency, which was highest in the Old Stone Ages, dwindled in the Neolithic and came to an end during the Copper-Bronze era.

Much the same is true of community self-sufficiency, particularly after bronze replaced pure copper. Copper and tin deposits very seldom occur in the same locality. Hence, practically every society that advanced well into the Metal Age found itself compelled to import either copper, tin, or both. Thus was initiated an export-import business, and thus did community self-sufficiency reach a close. So much importance was attached to the metal trade that it always tended to become either a government monopoly or a private enterprise regulated by the state.

To secure the supplies required for bronze work, many things were necessary, chief of which was a surplus of something valuable that could be exchanged for tin or copper. By the year 3000 B.C. methods of mixed farming had improved to such an extent that well-favored settlements had the wherewithal to engage in long-distance trade. There then arose a new impetus to knowledge. Importers had to know where the supplies they wanted were located, and they had to learn ways of reaching the exact spot and getting home again. If trips were to be overland, an elementary knowledge of geography was essential. One had to know what rivers, lakes, forests, mountains, or deserts would be encountered and which were the best routes to take. If travel was to be by water, the art of navigation had to be understood. In each case, too, there was the need of providing a suitable means of transportation, animal-drawn vehicles or boats propelled by oars or sails. It is no coincidence that the rise of such intellectual pursuits as map-making and astronomy came into being at the very time when the ingredients for bronze were being sought.

But intellectuals are also specialists, and they cannot develop their skills to the utmost if they must work regularly to produce food and other essentials. Before they could function efficiently, other members of the community had to have extra supplies of food and the like, some of which they were willing to exchange for the fruits of intellectual labor. Other specialists who had to be similarly maintained by surpluses of vital supplies were boat builders, wagon makers, and travelers who made long-distance journeys.

Additional important consequences resulted from the establishment of export-import trade. No one would risk sending a load of valuable goods for the purchase of expensive raw materials unless his investment were protected. In minimum terms this meant that voyagers conveying costly cargoes had to have armed guards to prevent hijacking and piracy. So begins the tie-up between business and military and naval forces which is still of such great concern today.

Before many decades had elapsed it was found to be inefficient to send heavy loads back and forth to complete a single transaction. Instead of elementary barter, systems resembling **coinage** were devised, by means of which a great deal of value could be encompassed in a small item. Bars of silver were first used for this purpose. Their worth depended on weight and there was much concern over sharp practices of adulteration and short-weighing. Later, when **coins** replaced clumsy bars of precious metal, traders accepted them only if they were confident of the stability of the governments that issued them. From the beginning coinage was recognized to be a state rather than a private function, and that is one of the ways in which economics and politics became closely linked.

As commerce continued to expand, there was a strongly felt need for systems of standardized weights and measures. Every dealer had to know how large a return he could expect for a given amount of goods. The principle of so-much of this for so-much of that, which underlies all trade, cannot operate without standardized units of values, weights, and measures. And standardization along these lines cannot develop without mathematics. This was not the only practical application of mathematics in the early Metal Ages. Measures of distance were essential to geography, and the sciences of astronomy and navigation also have mathematical foundations.

With the rise of big business came a further need for precise notation. Records of all kinds had to be accurately kept to prevent chaos, and neither maps nor charts could be prepared without a means of writing. Ownership and identifying marks were indicated by impressions made with **seals.** Some seals were flat while others were cylindrical; both sorts were pictorial and carved out of hard material. Seals, like signet rings, had only restricted meanings pertaining to the person of the user and could not express all the details of a transaction. For the rest, it was necessary to have true writing, based on a **phonetic alphabet.** A phonetic alphabet implies that certain written symbols stand for particular sounds, thus making it possible to put into writing whatever meaningful sounds a given language utilizes. In Mesopotamia the earliest records were made by cutting wedge-shaped characters into soft clay tablets with a sharp-pointed stylus (Fig. 7.5), a style of writing known as **cunei-**

form. When the clay tablets were baked the cuneiform inscriptions became permanently fixed. Thousands of complete or fragmentary tablets have been dug up by archeologists from ancient settlements in Western Asia, and there are specialists among us who can read many of the antique scripts. Their translations reveal that an overwhelming proportion of the earliest written documents dealt with business and that smaller percentages were concerned with politics and religion.

Fig. 7.5. Model of a Mesopotamian clay tablet. A sharp-pointed stylus is thought to have been used for incising the cuneiform writing at the top. The scene below was made by pressing a seal into the soft clay of the tablet before it was baked. (E. Chiera, *They Wrote on Clay*. Chicago, 1938. Courtesy of University of Chicago Press.)

One of the fascinating aspects of archeology is to observe how a number of apparently unrelated traits may cluster together to help form a new device. An extraordinary instance of the process is to be found in the formation of a **calendar.** Whether based on movements of the sun, moon, stars, or the planet Venus, all calendars depend on some knowledge of astronomy coupled with mathematics. To keep accurate track of the passage of time, based on measurable activities of heavenly bodies, it is necessary to be able to write. So, in a sense, the calendar may be regarded as a combination of astronomy, mathematics, and writing. Its earliest uses, too, were composite, ranging from religious interest in the heavens to agriculture and the commercial importance of knowing the length of time involved in completing a business transaction.

Learning to write and read was a long and laborious process which ordinary folk were not expected to master. To serve them there arose another specialized group, **scribes,** who exchanged their skill for the necessities of life. Scribes worked for illiterate individuals, as well as for the state and its rulers, temples and their administrators, and businessmen. For the latter they drew up agreements which were signed with the seals of contracting parties in the presence of witnesses. Contracts were binding, and there were courts of law to see that their terms were carried out. The equivalents of our phrases "Put it in writing" and "I'll sue you" were everyday features of Mesopotamian Copper-Bronze Age life, and many of the courtroom procedures of that place and time are still current in our society.

A few additional comments may help to bring about a fuller appreciation of the significance of writing. Its introduction speeds up the building of culture, because it helps to prevent loss of ideas and so contributes to the formation of a larger and larger stockpile of human knowledge. Whatever is put down in writing acquires permanence and stands an excellent chance of being more accurately preserved than can be done by word of mouth. Whatever is written can easily outlast the lifetime of the author; with the help of translation and copying it can be spread throughout the world; and when signed with an official seal it has greater authenticity than a verbal message. If a postman in the United States were to tell a young man orally that he had been drafted, the chances are that the message would not be taken seriously. Not so if the postman delivered an official document containing exactly the same words in writing.

For the student of culture growth, too, the development of writing is of the utmost importance. With the help of written statements one can learn the full range of ideas, values, symbol systems, and abstract concepts that once prevailed in an extinct society. Archeologists working in historic periods are no longer confronted with the need of trying painfully to deduce these intangibles from material remains, and the record of the past emerges in greater detail and clarity than ever.

Even a brief synopsis serves to bring out the complexities of Copper-Bronze Age life. Mention has been made, no matter how scantily, of miners, prospectors, smelters, metallurgists, traders, travelers, drivers, sailors, geographers, astronomers, mathematicians, soldiers, scribes, lawyers, rulers, and priests, to say nothing of agriculturists, stock breeders, potters, weavers, and small merchants. No one of the specialists could have been a full-time farmer, and no full-time farmer could have doubled as a true specialist. Social distinctions based on wealth and occupation, as well as on sex and age, are everywhere in evidence, and differences between rural and urban folk come into prominence. Everyone who lived in a Copper-Bronze community was directly and deeply affected by the new technology and its consequences, but metal was so scarce and expensive that only a fraction of the populace regularly used things of copper and bronze; others had an occasional metallic object or so; and the average person's material culture continued to be no more than Neolithic.

A sage who was conversant with the entire world as it was known in the Fourth and Third millennia B.C. (4000-2000 B.C.), would have known for a fact that the latest advances of culture were to be found in the neighborhoods of Mesopotamia, Egypt, and the Indus River valley of northwestern India. By comparison with these centers the rest of Africa and Asia was certainly backward; Europe, any sane man of that time would have said, was too far behind ever to amount to much; and as for the Americas—what were they? Anyone nowadays who is concerned about the lack of progress in the underdeveloped regions of the world should find solace in the errors of past judgments. Far from having been a leader at all times, the Western world got its start toward dominance in the Copper-Bronze Age by diffusion from the Eastern Mediterranean Zone.

For one reason or another, very little is known of the varieties of mankind that were responsible for the formation of the earliest Copper-Bronze cultures. About all that can be said without quibbling is that they were members of *Homo sapiens*, that the Caucasoid stock played a major part, and that the Mediterranean race was strongly represented. The Negroid stock may have played a contributory role, but the presence of Mongoloids is not attested at the time.

D. IRON COMES ON THE SCENE

Somewhere around 1500 B.C. people living in the vicinity of present-day Armenia discovered how to manufacture things of iron. They did all they could to keep their knowledge hidden from others but they used the new metal for weapons, and as their armies made conquests the secret was automatically disclosed. Among the first to exploit the advantages of iron were the Hittites, followed soon after by the Assyrians. Both the Hittites and the Assyrians found the great and wealthy Copper-Bronze centers of the Eastern Mediterranean Zone extremely tempting targets for attack, and were soon coming down on them, in Byron's words, "like the wolf on the fold." The successes of the Iron Age invaders were due not only to their fighting ability and superior arms, but also to the internal collapse of the older societies. Assuredly, the Copper-Bronze Age communities carried within their own social systems the seeds of destruction. Throughout their existence objects of bronze remained out of reach of the general populace, and wealth tended to become concentrated in the hands of a few. Such was the case, too, with all the associated advances of knowledge and industry. Commoners worked hard, paid heavy taxes, and supported the state in every way, but got pitifully little in return. By and by rulers came to rely for support not on masses of loyal citizens but on slaves and mercenaries. It was no wonder that they could not offer strong resistance to invasion and attack.

Within a few centuries after 1500 B.C. every one of the great Copper-Bronze centers in Mesopotamia, Egypt, and India had collapsed. A kind of Dark Ages followed, but the accomplishments of the early Metal Ages remained to form a platform on top of which the Iron Age was built. At first the period of transition gives the impression of moving backward, but in the long run it appears that cultural progress was still being made as new and more modern forms of group living emerged.

In strictly technological terms it was not always easy for iron to displace bronze. Above all, it was necessary for new metallurgical skills to be acquired. Because of its internal composition, iron does not readily lend itself to casting, either in simple molds or by the lost-wax method; and cast iron is too brittle to be practical. Not until methods of **forging** (repeated pounding while hot) and **tempering** (sudden alternations of heat and cold) were figured out, could sturdy implements be made of wrought iron. Even so, forging and tempering remained freehand techniques, requiring a strong operator who could turn out only one object at a time. Other drawbacks were the quantities of fuel needed and the tendency of pure iron to rust. On the other side of the ledger, the new substance was far more abundant than copper, and even more so than tin. It could also be used by itself, thus making it much cheaper than bronze. Moreover, iron is tougher than bronze, and mixed with a small amount of inexpensive carbon or other elements it becomes still harder as well as rust-resistant. Suffice it to say that almost at once the advantages were found to outweigh the disadvantages, with the consequence that for the first time iron made possible the everyday use of metal implements. Iron was indeed the poor man's metal. With the use of metallic tools, forests and timber could more easily be cut, plowing and cultivating practices could be improved, every soldier in an army could be well-equipped, and cheap household instruments and ornaments became available to almost everyone.

The late start of the Iron Age also provided time for at least two of the Copper-Bronze Age traits to mature to a point where they could achieve widespread distribution. Writing, thanks to simplification of the phonetic alphabet, became somewhat less of a highly specialized craft. Universal literacy was far from being attained but many ordinary folk learned to read a bit and to write their names, and some small merchants began to find that they could keep their own accounts. Coinage, too, was brought to lower social levels than ever before. Coins of small denomination were minted, making it easier for people of little wealth to buy and sell, undertake to save for the distant future, to pay taxes more conveniently than in kind, and so to participate to some extent in the money economy of the total community. Without any formal planning, the Copper-Bronze Age had turned into an era of aristocrats, and the Iron Age was to witness the rise of the common man. Householders began to take it for granted that they would have metal knives, safety-pins, shears, scissors, razors, tweezers, hammers, saws, and even buckets (see Fig. 7.6). Farmers regularly had plow tips of iron, as well as metallic scythes and sickles; animal harnesses included many metal parts; and the wealthy came to protect their possessions with locks and keys. After death, burial in the ground was the rule throughout most of the period, but cremation appears before its close. Important men were on occasion interred with their chariots, and one famous

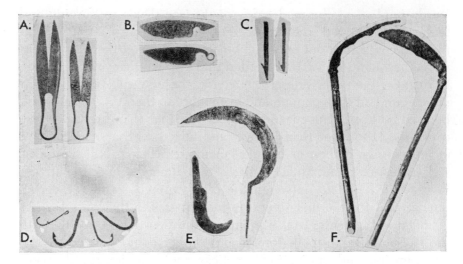

Fig. 7.6. Nonmilitary Iron Age tools (after MacCurdy, following Vouga). A. Scissors or shears. B. Razors. C. Harpoon heads. D. Fish-hooks. E. Sickles. F. Scythes. (Courtesy of Peabody Museum, Harvard University.)

grave of this sort also contained wine, several varieties of meat, iron spits, and a great carving knife (Fig. 7.7).

During the 500 years prior to the Christian era, the world's most important historical events were taking place not in Central or Western Europe but in Greece and the Eastern Mediterranean Zone. Darius the Great, of Persia, had by 500 B.C. subjugated all of Western Asia, and was looking for more worlds to conquer. Greece was the only European nation of the day that seemed worth bothering about, and in 491 B.C. Darius sent a huge fleet of six hundred ships against Athens. After unchallenged initial successes, the Persians reached Marathon where they were soundly beaten in 490 B.C. by a confederation led by Athenian Greeks.

It is beyond the scope of this volume to trace the rise of classical Greek culture that followed soon after Marathon. However, for the benefit of those who may look upon the archeologically established Iron Age as something distant and unconnected with modern times it may be well merely to list, with their dates, a small handful of the well-known historic figures who lived in Iron Age times. Herodotus, father of modern history, died in 425 B.C.; Hippocrates, father of modern medicine, was born in 460 B.C. and died around 370 B.C.; the great playwright, Sophocles, lived from 496 (?) to 406 B.C.;

Fig. 7.7. An Iron Age chariot burial. This presumed warrior from the Iron Age was buried under a two-wheeled chariot, with food and implements. The small rectangle in the foreground contained the remains of horse trappings. (Courtesy of British Museum.)

Socrates' life ran from 469 to 399 B.C.; the everlastingly famous Aristotle was born in 384 B.C. and died in 322 B.C.; the short but important lifetime of Alexander the Great ran from 356 to 323 B.C.; Cicero lived and died between 106 and 43 B.C.; and Julius Caesar was born in 100 B.C. and died in 44 B.C. So did the Iron Age witness the shift of world leadership from the Eastern Mediterranean Zone to the continent of Europe, and thus did it bring mankind to the threshold of our own era.

E. MAN AND CULTURE IN THE NEW WORLD

Despite the abundance of material already presented, very little has been said about the evolution of man and culture in the extensive territories of the Americas. From the point of view of learning the main steps leading to the formation of *Homo sapiens* and of becoming acquainted with the broad outlines of his cultural origins and progress, it may be enough to limit one's self to the Old World, but to arrive at a better understanding of the varieties and complexities of human behavior it is necessary to know something of the New World as well. Not that there is any direct contradiction between the main events that took place in the two areas, but there is a profound difference in details. It is only by examining the differences that a cultural anthropologist can gain an insight into the range of biological and cultural activities that may be found in widely separated and dissimilar environments. An impartial, comprehensive and universal science of man cannot be formulated if one hemisphere of the globe is left out of consideration.

Because of circumstances that are still inexplicable, there was no hominid evolution in the Americas, even though the general pattern of biological development followed much the same course up to the emergence of lemurs, tarsiers, and platyrrhine monkeys. Nowhere in the Americas, except for known importations, has anyone ever found a verifiable specimen, fossil or living, of any catarrhine monkey or ape. There is also a total absence of extinct hominids, which lends further support to the contention that man did not originate in America. And yet, there were several millions of Indians present when Columbus arrived. There seems to be no way of getting around the conclusion that man entered the New World from the Old at some time after he had evolved into *Homo sapiens*. A date of around 15,000-20,000 B.C., representing the latest phases of the

Pleistocene, is widely accepted as the approximate time when the North American continent received its first human inhabitants.[1] By then, it will be remembered, culture had progressed so far in the Eastern hemisphere that it is unlikely that cultural evolution in America should have started from scratch.

If man did not evolve in the New World he must have entered it from the Old. This unequivocal statement of fact, innocent as it seems, has given rise to a series of long-lasting, sometimes acrimonious, and completely unresolved debates among American archeologists. The problem of who the first Americans may have been is complicated by the fact that archeologists have as yet found no skeletal material that is unquestionably associated with the oldest recognizable artifacts. In other words, there have been discovered ancient stone specimens of undeniably human workmanship, but there is no way of telling who made them. Since the middle decades of the last century, reports have occasionally been made of skeletal remains supposedly pertaining to Pleistocene man, but in nearly every instance the claims were subsequently modified or rejected. Until the time of his death Dr. Aleš Hrdlička led a stubborn, and usually successful, campaign to refuse the label of Pleistocene antiquity to any American hominid specimen, particularly if it bore a resemblance to living Indians. Today, there is a complete willingness to accept as valid any human relics, regardless of their "modern" appearance, if they can be accurately dated by geological or other scientific methods.[2] Just the same no candidate for the honor of being the first American has been unanimously nominated, to say nothing of having been elected.

On the basis of present-day knowledge scholars accept the probability that the peopling of the New World began with the arrival of *sapiens* strains. They did not come in a single movement but in an indefinite number of waves of migration that lasted over many centuries. Most groups of American Indians are classed as Mongo-

---

[1] A strong protest against the acceptance of the traditional dates was published by Dr. George F. Carter in *Pleistocene Man at San Diego*, Baltimore, 1957. On the basis of archeological remains, Dr. Carter argues for a date of 100,000 years. The entire question of man's arrival in the New World is now being restudied, and it appears likely that in the future a date earlier than 15,000 to 20,000 B.C. will come to be accepted.

[2] For a discussion of this controversial problem, see, with the citations he makes, T. D. Stewart, "The Development of the Concept of Morphological Dating in Connection with Early Man in America," *Southwestern Journal of Anthropology*, Vol. 5, No. 1, 1949, pp. 1-16.

loid by virtue of skin color, hair form and distribution on the face
and body, and cheekbone configuration, but they are not at all identical and many subvarieties can be distinguished among the living
tribes.[3]

On the score of place of entry there is comforting agreement.
Only a rare dissenter, almost never a trained anthropologist, objects to the contention that man came to America from northeast
Asia, by crossing the Bering Straits into Alaska. A few disturbing
details remain to be clarified before high probability can be converted to established fact, but in most respects the Bering Straits
point of entry is satisfactory.

As to the question of what kind of culture the first occupants of
America brought with them, there is again no clear-cut answer.
Whatever they had that was intangible or perishable cannot be recovered, and whatever they have left behind of a durable nature
can tell only a partial story at best. Even so, archeologists would
be delighted if they could identify with certainty the material remains of the original migrants. Failing actual specimens, however,
recourse has been made to speculative reconstruction. Professor A.
L. Kroeber, dean of American anthropologists, has attempted to reconstruct the elements of original New World culture on the basis
of items that have been universally reported among the known
tribes. Kroeber feels, in theory, that traits which are common to
every one of the Indian groups may well have been retained from
the culture that was brought here at the beginning. His list of material items includes stone implements made by pressure or rubbing,
bone or horn objects fashioned by polishing, knowledge of hafting,
control of fire, making of baskets or nets, use of the spear-thrower
or bow, and possession of tamed (domesticated?) dogs.[4] Such a
list of traits fits the Old World pattern of cultural evolution at a
point that resembles the Mesolithic.

When all the evidence about the early Americas is put together,
it appears that the line of cultural development in the New World
ran parallel to the Old in broad outline, but differed in one essential
detail after another. In both vast areas there was a similar origin
in a hunting and food-collecting stage, featured by the manufacture

---

[3] Data concerning the variations that exist in the physical types of the American
Indians may be found in W. S. Laughlin, ed., "Papers on the Physical Anthropology
of the American Indians," *The Viking Fund*, New York, 1951.

[4] A. L. Kroeber, *Anthropology*, New York, 1948, p. 778.

and use of Paleolithic or Mesolithic tools. This was followed by the entrance of some groups into Neolithic levels and culminated in cultures that had acquired metallurgy. Compared with the Old World story the evolution of man and culture in aboriginal America is greatly compressed in time and scope. There is no telling what might have happened had the course of history been different.

Whether or not the first Americans remained in touch with their homelands in the Old World is a moot question. Archeologists in this country are reluctant to say that all contact was immediately broken, yet, as they study the evidence it looks very much as if the great bulk of later American culture went through an independent evolution in isolation. For example, a good number of groups moved into a Neolithic stage, but instead of relying on Old World plants and beasts we find them domesticating maize, beans, squash, tobacco, potatoes, and such New World creatures as the alpaca, llama, and turkey. Much the same may be said of pottery. Neolithic peoples in the New World manufactured an incredible variety of ceramic objects, but only a restricted number of their forms and decorations can be matched in the Eastern hemisphere. Similarly, some American Indians may have known the principle of the wheel, but at no time before Columbus was the concept put to practical use, and the rare instances of its occurrence are limited to little things that might have been toys.

One of the most startling revelations of American archeology is the greater height of cultural advance that was made once or twice by an essentially Neolithic people. Among the Maya Indians of Guatemala and Yucatan, who were in practically every regard Neolithic, are to be found an amazing collection of traits which, throughout the Old World, do not appear until the maturer phases of the Copper-Bronze Age. The Maya were grouped into city-states; founded great urban centers with many architecturally splendid structures; organized a complex social system featuring great rulers, commoners, and corps of specialists; and maintained a highly trained body of priests who had a knowledge of writing, mathematics, and astronomy and were capable of keeping track of an exceedingly intricate but accurate calendar (see Fig. 7.8).

Prior to 1492 there was a Copper-Bronze Age in America, but its effective range did not extend very far beyond the territorial limits

A

B

C

Fig. 7.8. Some aspects of Maya culture. A. A ruined temple at Uxmal, in Yucatan. B. the lower half of a carved stele in Chichen Itza, Yucatan. It shows the feet of a warrior, trampling on Ahpuch, the god of death. C. A few examples of Maya hieroglyphics.

of the so-called Inca Indians of Peru and Bolivia.[5] Only the Inca had some craftsmen who regularly used an alloy of copper and tin, but even they did not make quantities of everyday implements of bronze. One must not jump to the conclusion that America's Copper-Bronze Age was a duplicate of the Old World's. In some regards it was, but neither in writing, mathematics, nor the use of a calendar, did the Copper-Bronze Inca equal the attainments of the basically Neolithic Maya (Fig. 7.9).

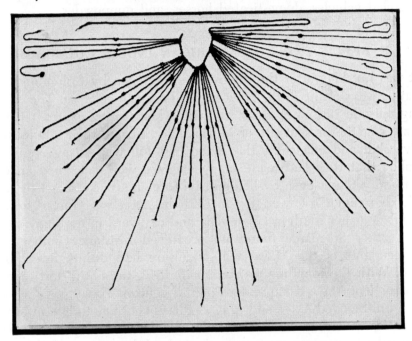

Fig. 7.9. A Peruvian quipu. Knotted strings served the Incas as accounting devices and comprised their method of keeping track of statistics. The Inca had no knowledge of true writing. (Courtesy Chicago Museum of Natural History.)

Thus does the archeological record of America teach us that there is nothing inevitable about the traits of culture that may accompany either the Neolithic or the Copper-Bronze Age. Still, it would be a serious error to go to the extreme of saying that technology,

---

[5] There is a good possibility that various American Indians in what is now called Latin America understood metallurgy, but that they worked with raw materials other than copper and tin.

Strictly speaking, the term Inca applies only to the aboriginal rulers of the Peruvian zone. However, it has become commonplace to use the term for all the native inhabitants of the area.

especially metallurgy in this case, has nothing to do with the total march of culture.

By way of another contrast with the Old World, the aboriginal metallurgists of America never learned to utilize iron. Whether they would have developed an Iron Age had it not been for European conquest and colonization will never be known. In any event, it is certain that the American Indians were the more readily defeated because they lacked such cultural devices as metal weapons, wheeled vehicles, domesticated horses, and gunpowder.

F. REFLECTIONS ON AMERICAN INDIAN CULTURES

It was not long after the discovery of America by Columbus that native ways of life in the New World began to collapse. The opening episode started as early as 1519, when Cortez confronted the Aztecs at the present site of Mexico City. For all their administrative skill and efficiency, the Aztec had followed so aggressive a policy that they had made many enemies who welcomed an opportunity to get even by helping the foreign attackers. A long and bloody struggle followed, but in 1521 the Aztec were forced to succumb. Further south in Guatemala and eastward in northern Yucatan, other Spaniards found no organized resistance among the descendants of the Maya, whose culture had disintegrated long ago. With the founding of Merida in 1542, the entire territory of the ancient Maya came under Spanish control. Today, several million full-blooded Aztec and Maya Indians continue to live in Meso-America, but they cannot read the ancient hieroglyphs, calculate the calendars, nor manufacture the splendid products of the past.

What may have been a mere accident paved the way for the conquest of the Inca domain. Huayna Capac, the last great ruler, died suddenly in 1527 without having named a successor. Two half-brothers, his sons by different mothers, promptly engaged in a civil war to determine who should rule. When Pizarro arrived, he cleverly took advantage of their bitter struggle and managed to defeat them, one after the other, by 1532.

Shortly after, in 1540, Coronado undertook the first Spanish penetration of the southwestern United States. He met resistance occasionally, but was soon able to win at least the nominal submission of the natives. There were no great stores of treasure to reward a conqueror, so little effort was made to subjugate the Indians thoroughly, and they continued to carry on much of their old culture even though they acknowledged the legal control of Spain. At the same time that Coronado was traveling through the Southwest, De Soto was leading an expedition into the Southeast. Here he found aboriginal patterns of culture still flourishing, but his coming began to upset the established ways of native life, and when the European colonization of the eastern seaboard started, the old Indian customs rapidly disintegrated. Much the same was true of the northeastern United States. The colonists who founded Jamestown in 1607, or who reached Plymouth in 1620, were confronted by tribes whose cultures were going concerns. But when colonial expansion started to move westward, aboriginal life quickly changed or vanished.

Within a hundred years after the discovery by Columbus there was not a region of high American Indian culture that had not been greatly influenced or submerged by Europeans. This century was not, except in rare cases, marked by good will or helpfulness on either side. From the standpoint of the Indians, the termination of nearly all of their old customs must have been a continuous tragedy. Yet, from a detached anthropological view, there is a lesson in cultural growth to be learned from the situation. At the cost, it must be admitted, of a deplorable amount of bloodshed and grief, each party's culture was enriched by the contact in several respects. Europeans learned to grow potatoes, corn, and tobacco, and Indians learned to raise wheat and oats. Europeans acquired knowledge of rubber and cocaine, and native Americans became acquainted with iron, steel, and wagons. Domesticated ducks and turkeys were introduced to the Old World, and the New found out about horses, sheep, and cattle.

Post-Columbian contacts of Europe and aboriginal America throw light on the way in which particular cultures grow. To some extent they develop from **local inventions,** but they also expand by accretions gained through diffusion, despite the basic hostility of the peoples concerned. Indeed, if one takes a world view, existing cultures are found to have a much higher percentage of diffused elements than of independent inventions.

From the interchange that took place after 1492 we may note that all groups of *Homo sapiens* are potentially capable of assimilating each other's customs. No biological or mental barriers stand in the way. Culturally imposed obstacles, it must be concluded, do far more to prevent the sharing of a given way of life than do any supposed deficiencies of mind or body.

SELECTED REFERENCES

Bennett, W. C., "A Reappraisal of Peruvian Archaeology," *Memoir, Society for American Archaeology*, No. 4. Menasha, Wisconsin, 1948.

British Museum, *A Guide to the Antiquities of the Bronze Age*. Oxford, 1904.

———, *A Guide to the Antiquities of the Early Iron Age*. Oxford, 1905.

Chiera, E., *They Wrote on Clay*. Chicago, 1938.

Childe, V. G., *Man Makes Himself*, Chapters 6 and 7. London, 1936.

———, *New Light on the Most Ancient East*. New York, 1934.

Delaporte, L. J., *Mesopotamia*. London and New York, 1925.

Hawkes, C. F. C., *The Prehistoric Foundations of Europe to the Mycenean Age*. London, 1940.

Martin, P. S., *et al.*, *Indians Before Columbus*. Chicago, 1947.

Morley, S. G., *The Ancient Maya*. Stanford, 1946.

Sayles, E. B., and Antevs, E., "The Cochise Culture," *Medallion Papers*, No. 29, 1941.

Singer, C., *et al.*, eds., *A History of Technology*, Vol. 1, Parts VI, VII, and VIII. New York and London, 1954.

Steward, J. H., ed., *Handbook of South American Indians*, six volumes. Washington, 1946-1950.

Vaillant, G. C., *Aztecs of Mexico*. New York, 1941.

Wormington, H. M., "Ancient Man in North America," *Museum of Natural History Publications*. Denver, 1949.

CHAPTER 8

BIOCULTURAL DYNAMICS

A. PROLOGUE

By the dawn of written history, *Homo sapiens* had brought culture to such a stage that its usefulness was plainly evident. Once patterns of culture were originated, however, they proved to follow laws of their own, occasionally without reference to the wishes of the individuals who lived by them. At the same time, man could not completely shake off the age-old imperatives of the biophysicochemical world. The chemical substances within his body continued to act in their accustomed ways, the laws of physics still operated as they always had, and the dictates of biology had to be observed. It is because these forces are so firm and insistent that no pattern of culture can ever be purely random, and that the values imbedded in any way of life can never be entirely arbitrary or capricious.

Students who are just becoming acquainted with the science of man frequently ask, "Why, apart from mere curiosity, should we have to learn so many details of man's cultural past?" This is a legitimate question, worthy of a careful answer.

Cultural anthropologists do not find it difficult to justify their interest in the data of archeology, even when the subject leads back to times so remote that few facts are available and all interpretations are open to question. Unless one takes the indefensible position that modern culture sprang ready-made into existence without antecedents, he must be willing to study what came before in order to understand what is going on now. Without such understanding we would have no inkling of the laws of culture growth, could make no predictions, and could establish no controls.

On one other important point at least, archeologists have already made a lasting contribution. No one knows, nor is anyone likely ever to discover, the stock or racial affinity of the very first fist-ax maker, potter, weaver, farmer, or metallurgist; nor is it probable that we shall ever learn the identity of the first person to have made use of a spear, bow and arrow, wagon, boat, alphabet, calendar, or coin. Archeologists have shown that no one race can truthfully take credit for having begun all these achievements, and that once they had become part of human culture they were utilized by all manner of people. From the start the building of culture has been a joint enterprise of mankind, and leadership in the movement has shifted without loss of progress from one region to another and from one hominid subdivision to another.

Archeology has also proved that everywhere on earth human beings have transcended the bio-physico-chemical realm and entered the sphere of culture. It has, in addition, brought to light the infinite variety of forms that particular cultures may take and has demonstrated how often a group of people in one locality may develop a way of life that is markedly different from that of their neighbors. It is easy enough to become bewildered by these facts and to come to the erroneous conclusion that the totality of culture is a chaotic hodgepodge which has followed no consistent pattern of development. But, a discerning student of man must learn to recognize the unity that underlies the mass of differing details. Today it can be shown that from the beginning a number of consistent trends have been operating along regular and therefore predictable lines. Once the existence of these trends has been recognized, their past courses can be charted, and if they show steady movement in a given direction it may be forecast that they will, until diverted, continue to go in the same direction in the near future. Archeology makes one of its major contributions when it provides the data from which trends may be charted. It is convenient to talk of trends as moving consistently in one direction, but trends generally move in zig-zag fashion even when they ultimately continue level or go up or down.

B. SOME LAWS OF CULTURE GROWTH

All sciences pass through a preliminary fact-gathering stage, after which efforts are made to discover which phenomena regularly occur together. These observations lead to the establishment of scientific laws of cause and effect which seek to describe the observed combinations and to explain how, when, and why they were formed. Then, laws that are found to have been long operative in the past are used in forecasting the future. Thus, anyone who has again and again watched blue litmus paper turn red when dipped in acid can predict that on future occasions blue litmus will redden on contact with an acid. The longer and oftener one can observe the operation of a presumed law in the past, the more certainly can he foretell its future course. Under such conditions prediction is no more than a projection into the future of a trend line observed in the past. So it is that anthropologists who want to know how culture is likely to act in the future must find out from archeologists how it has acted in the past.

However, there is at least one characteristic of laws in social science that makes them different from laws in other fields. Laws of any sort can be most accurately expressed only when all the factors under which they operate can be so rigidly controlled that they are practically invariable. The less control there is, and the higher the degree of variability, the less likely is it that trends will always function in regular and predictable ways. At present, for one reason or another, we have so little control of the circumstances under which biocultural trends function that the best we can do is to establish temporary laws. For instance, around 1800 A.D. a working week of 84 hours was by no means unknown in the United States. Gradually the hours of work were reduced to 63, 56, 52, 44, and 40. Now there is talk of a 35-hour working week, and on the basis of former happenings this looks like a manifestation of a law of diminishing hours of work. Yet, if such a trend continues indefinitely, it will some day reach the point of absurdity. We may applaud the reduction of working time to some extent, but what if the work week is cut to one hour, or twenty minutes, or ten seconds? At what point do we try to halt or even reverse a trend whose course can be so well plotted in the past? And how, if it should be desired, would we make an established trend move in the opposite direction? To some extent, as several observers have already pointed out, the "do-it-yourself" movement can be interpreted as a way of using up the excess of leisure which hangs heavy on the hands of many workers (see Fig. 8.1), but it must be admitted that such movements are no

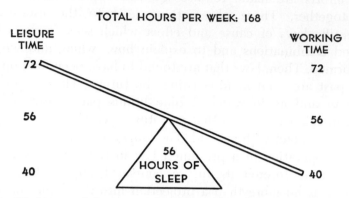

Fig. 8.1. Working and leisure time. Assuming that eight hours are devoted daily to sleep, the number of leisure hours per week rises in direct proportion to the shrinkage of working time. Leisure does not necessarily mean complete idleness. Therefore, as the working week gets smaller, the problem of what to do with leisure time gets larger.

better than makeshifts when it comes to dealing firmly with the question of reversing a strongly-directed trend. Few social scientists have as yet begun to study universal trends of cultural behavior, and too little information is available about some former cultures, but enough is already known to justify the cautious formulation of a few tentative laws. These formulations, even though they may not persist for all time, are among the most significant of the inferences to be drawn from archeology. Equally important is the fact that the recognizable and predictable trends which are expressed as laws can be shown to operate, not independently, but as integrated parts of one whole pattern of cultural evolution. Integration usually sounds like a good thing to us, but it can be a source of serious trouble when a pattern of culture must integrate, or keep in equilibrium, a number of conflicting forces.

An obvious clash arises whenever a hungry person is confronted with a forbidden food. He must, in all such cases, make a choice between observing biological or cultural values. He cannot, at the same time, observe both.

Or, take the case of a young American who has always been a devoted son while he was single. As soon as he marries he can no longer remain an equally devoted son without making a poor husband. If he gives all his attention to his mother, he must neglect his wife; and if he is completely attentive to his wife, he must become at least partially neglectful of his mother.

These instances serve to illustrate only two of the kinds of contradictions which all systems of culture must try somehow to reconcile. In addition, every successful way of life must maintain a dynamic balance between forces of stability, conservatism, or inertia, and forces tending to change or disintegration. No pattern of culture is flawlessly consistent, and the best it can do is to have the sum total of its cohesive elements outweigh its disintegrative factors. With these matters in mind we may now turn to a consideration of those laws that seem to be operative in the ways of life of all known societies.

1. The Law of Increasing Reliance on Culture

For all the grave doubts that may beset the student of human origins, it has been established that on their very first appearance the earliest hominids could, perforce, have utilized only such biologically inherited mechanisms as their hands and feet. Presumably, they quickly came to make some use of sticks and stones that could be manipulated by the organs of their bodies, but as the archeological record of the Lower Paleolithic bears witness, they were very slow in the beginning to develop an extrasomatic kit of tools. Thereafter they came to depend more and more on nongenetic equipment, and as they did **the law of increasing reliance on culture** began to operate.[1]

A minority element among us may self-consciously forego a bit of its group's culture now and then as by abstaining from all cooked foods, going about stark naked, refusing medical assistance, or bathing only in running streams, but mankind as a whole continues to rely increasingly on cultural mechanisms. Admittedly, there must be an ultimate limit to this trend. Increasing reliance on culture cannot advance so far as to eliminate human biology (Fig. 8.2). This is true, but it is not easy to foresee when or where the ultimate limit will be reached. Already mankind has begun to make cultural implements which greatly exceed the potentials of the human

---

[1] In order to keep the argument as unified and simple as possible, it will be assumed that every person has complete access to all the items available in his stage of culture. The reader must recognize that this is not the case in reality.

body. One aviation expert has thus described the situation: "Our flying machines are rapidly approaching capabilities that are penalized rather than aided by the presence of a human pilot." [2]

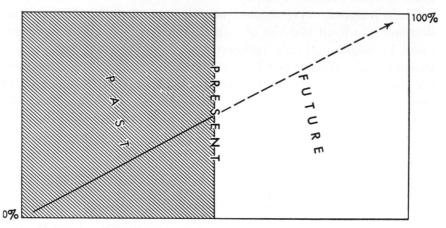

Fig. 8.2. The law of increasing reliance on culture. When hominids first appeared, they probably used biological mechanisms very much and culture very little. As time went on, they increased their reliance on culture and decreased their dependence on biology. However, *Homo sapiens* can never rely entirely on culture or completely eliminate his biology.

The law of increasing reliance on culture does not stand apart from other trends of cultural development. Among other things it makes possible man's shift from dependence on brawn (biological strength) to trust in brain (cultural efficiency). It also helps to level out the nonphysical differences between the sexes. Throughout the world it will be found that as cultures advance sex differences tend to diminish, except in matters directly related to biology. Any middle-aged citizen of the United States can recall cultural activities that were once regarded as entirely masculine and are now carried on by individuals of either sex.

2. The Law of Expanding Use of Natural Resources

It would not have been possible for man to have increased his reliance on culture had he not learned to make wider use as time went on of the raw materials provided by nature. This could have been accomplished only by a growth of knowledge, for no new ingredi-

---

[2] This statement was made by J. H. Kindelberger, and was quoted in the *Ann Arbor News* for June 13, 1952.

ents have been added to the composition of the earth since its formation. Whatever original substances or organisms have at times been formed in laboratories have always been recombinations or refinements of older ingredients. Basically, man has had the same physicochemical resources available to him from the time when hominids first appeared. Until 20,000 B.C. *Homo sapiens* was able to utilize only a small fraction of his physical environment, not much more than the air around him, wild plants and animals, water, and a few substances that could be used while cold. Then, in the Neolithic, grass and farm lands that had had no particular value in the Old Stone Age became highly important for grazing and agricultural purposes; certain kinds of clay changed from a detriment to valuable commodities for manufacturing pottery; and previously neglected fibers took on a new significance as the making of textiles developed. Later, metallic ores became greatly prized; and in our own day the rapid march of culture has given previously undreamed-of value to once negligible items like uranium. A couple of generations ago our grandfathers would have cursed anyone who might have dumped a ton of uranium in their backyards. Today, if one can imagine so much generosity, such a donor would be regarded as a rare benefactor.

While the law of expanding use of natural resources continually brings new materials to the fore, it also serves to render older things obsolete. The general point of this statement can be illustrated by an example from the United States. Around 1910 an investment in a municipally-owned trolley system would have been regarded as safe and the purchase of automobile stock as reckless. Today only a lunatic could be persuaded to invest in trolley cars, and automobiles are considered safe, even though it is reasonably sure that they will some day be outmoded. Not all of the natural resources that were of prime significance to *Homo sapiens* in former times lose their value at the same rate of speed, and the use of some things continues to be retained for many centuries; but whenever an object loses its importance, its manufacture tends to become a lost art.

To chart the past operation of the law of expanding use of natural resources (Fig. 8.3) is none too difficult, nor is it hard to foretell that some materials presently of little worth will some day turn out to have exceedingly high value. At the same time, it must be recognized, man's increasing ability to utilize the potentials of his

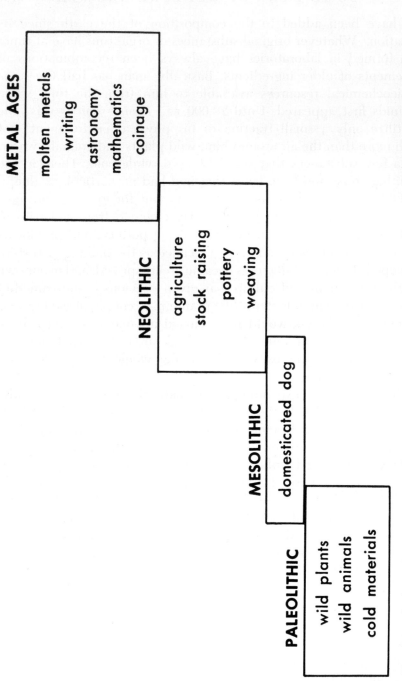

Fig. 8.3. The law of expanding use of natural resources. Although the figure illustrates man's expanding use of natural resources, it also brings out the additive nature of human culture.

environment has had much to do with increasing the speed of culture growth. Early Stone Age man, it has been demonstrated, was slow to build and expand culture, but from 6000 B.C. the tempo has become increasingly fast. Our own era is distinguished for its amazing speed of culture growth, especially in the field of technology. Whether or not man will forever go on expanding his use of natural resources is a question that only the future can answer.

Since cultures grow only a little by means of local invention and very much through the agency of diffusion, quick progress is aided by the speed and frequency of contact between a given society and many others. With the modern perfection of means of communication, an item invented in one place can almost instantaneously be spread throughout the world. All societies with progressive cultures, whether on friendly or hostile terms, strive to keep in touch with each other; and the surest way to cultural decline is through a policy of isolation.

3. The Declining Percentage of Individual Knowledge and Its Corollaries

As the human ability to take advantage of a steadily mounting number of natural resources continues, the sum total or stockpile of knowledge available in a progressive society becomes too great for any one person to encompass. So there comes into play **the law of declining percentage of individual knowledge** (Fig. 8.4B). In order to understand how this law works we must imagine a stage when every human male knew all there was for men to know and when every female knew all that pertained to the members of her sex. Such unspecialized levels probably existed at the very dawn of cultural evolution, and at that time each individual may be said to have had 100 percent of all the knowledge available to his sex. For contrast, we have but to consider the present state of affairs in our own society. What man or woman of today knows how to raise and prepare all the food that he eats, fashion all the utensils and dishes needed for cooking and serving, make all the garments to be worn, build his own house, cure his ailments, and build and service his own radio, television set, refrigerator, and automobile? Far from knowing how to do all these things for ourselves, we rely on numerous others to do most of them for us. And to the extent that this is the case we exemplify the law of declining percentage of individual knowledge. It must be admitted that in our society and culture one person, no matter how brilliant he may be, can have only a tiny fraction of the total knowledge to be found among all of us.

Whenever such a stage is reached in any society the only way that its culture can be maintained is by a process of compartmentalization, which means that its stockpile of knowledge is divided up, with particular subgroups or specialists assuming responsibility for particular fractions of the total. Wherever the law of declining percentage of individual knowledge goes into effect, therefore, it is invariably accompanied by a **law of increasing specialization** (Fig. 8.4A). Once more, it is archeology that supplies the necessary

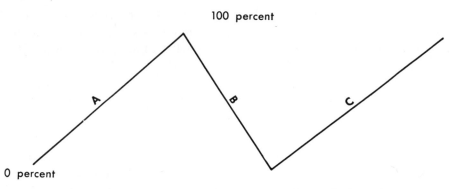

Fig. 8.4. Three interconnected laws of culture growth. A. The law of increasing specialization. B. The law of declining percentage of individual knowledge. C. The law of necessary cooperation. These three laws usually work together.

proof. Neolithic communities always have more classes of specialists than those of the Old Stone Age; Metal Age societies have even more; and modern social units have the greatest numbers ever known in the history of mankind.

The law of declining percentage of individual knowledge, together with its corollary, the law of increasing specialization, gives firm support to the ancient jest that "a specialist is one who learns more and more about less and less." These laws also apply to tools, for the more highly specialized a tool is, the more restricted is its range of usefulness. No builder would want to erect a house with nothing but surgical instruments, nor would any normal patient voluntarily trust himself to a surgeon who operated with a butcher knife and a carpenter's saw.

The law of declining percentage of individual knowledge and the accompanying law of increasing specialization bring into action still another trend that may be described as the **law of necessary cooperation** (Fig. 8.4C). To prevent a very complex culture from collapsing, each individual participant must be assured of the cooperation of specialists who can fill in the gaps of his own knowledge. Where each person knows only a tiny percentage of his total culture, he cannot possibly insist on complete independence. So essential is mutual interdependence that it may not be left to chance. Hence social regulations that are designed to further the law of necessary cooperation are found in every advanced culture. We could no more maintain our way of life with a Paleolithic form of social organization than we could keep up our industrial production with Old Stone Age implements, techniques, and raw materials. Any society that fails to pay full attention to the law of necessary cooperation is bound to find its culture getting out of balance and veering toward disintegration.

4. The Laws of Conservation of Time and of Human Muscular Energy

Neither the expanding utilization of natural resources nor increase of specialization is a random matter. Consciously or not, each was developed in the interests of greater efficiency. No matter in how many ways efficiency may be defined and evaluated, it can always be measured with reference to material culture by standards of time consumption and the expenditure of human muscular energy.[3] Throughout the march of culture, an implement that could perform a given task in less time than its predecessor would, in the course of events, always displace the earlier tool. This is equivalent to saying that insofar as two instruments could do the same task, mankind has invariably selected the one that accorded with the **law of time conservation** (Fig. 8.5A).

More dramatic still is the **law of H.M.E. conservation** (Fig. 8.5B). This is one of the most clearly demonstrable and most surely predictable of all the laws of culture growth. Whether one is dealing with a progression of cutting implements and weapons, from stone knives and fist-axes to spears, bows and arrows, revolvers, machine guns, and atom bombs; or with the evolution of means of transportation from foot, to horse, to automobile, to airplane, the same

---

[3] As another instance of a labor-saving device, the letters H.M.E. will be used for the phrase, Human Muscular Energy.

principle applies. The primary determinant is the recognition, explicit or implicit, of the fact that more can be accomplished if mechanical efficiency is increased and the expenditure of H.M.E. decreased. We demand and praise effectiveness in our cultural implements, not in our biological structures. When our eyes begin to fail we try to get adequate corrective glasses, rather than resort to operations on our genetically inherited optical systems. Only in sports and recreational pursuits is a great output of H.M.E. given high prestige.

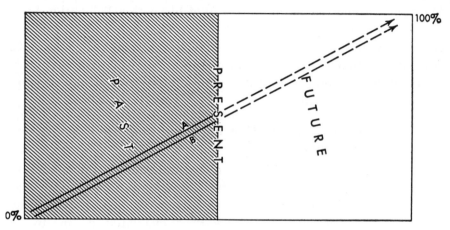

Fig. 8.5. The twin laws of conservation. A. The law of time conservation. B. The law of human muscular energy conservation. As culture grows, man consistently tries to save increasing amounts of time and human muscular energy.

Even when analysis is restricted to a single technological device, like an automobile, the law of H.M.E. conservation may be seen to operate constantly and consistently. The first automobiles manufactured had to be cranked by hand, at a considerable cost in H.M.E. Today, they begin with the push of a finger on a starter. Shifting gears manually, which was once universal, is now an almost obsolete practice. Tires that had to be laboriously blown up on hand pumps are rapidly and effortlessly filled with air by the use of readily available pressure pumps. Even car windows that had to be raised or lowered by turning a handle can presently be operated by touching a button.

In combination, the laws of time and H.M.E. conservation have worked, in the past, with unfailing certainty. One may be positive that in the foreseeable future no invention will succeed if its use calls for an additional outlay of time and human effort. With equal assurance one can forecast that a time and energy-saving contrivance has an excellent chance of ultimate acceptance. No shrewd businessman can be persuaded to finance the production of anything that goes against this combined trend. As a matter of fact, a new item may not look or taste as nice as something it is trying to replace, but if it saves time and energy it stands a good chance of succeeding. Any manufacturer of prepared foods or "mixes" can vouch for the truth of this statement. So much importance does mankind attach to the laws of time and H.M.E. conservation that objects conforming to these principles are likely to be widely purchased even if their manufacturing costs are high. Still, one can imagine a day when these trends may come to an end or be reversed.

C. FORCES OF CULTURE AND BIOCULTURAL INSTITUTIONS

There is much yet to be learned about the laws of culture growth, but it is encouraging to know that a start toward understanding them can already be made. It is entirely unlikely that the first hominids to have used extrasomatic implements had any inkling that what they were doing had some connection with forces of culture, any more than they are likely to have known about the forces of biology, physics, or chemistry. In fact, so few highly sophisticated people of our own day have any awareness of the existence of abstract forces of culture that we must assume that early man had no knowledge of them. Yet, much that he did was shaped by these forces. When fixed responses became established as customary ways of behaving, they formed the basis for what social scientists generally have in mind when they speak of social, cultural, or biocultural **institutions.**

Once they have come into being, the institutions of any society tend to have an independent existence and to follow their own rules. They are, therefore, legitimate objects for study, even if a student has little interest in the forces that may have brought them into being. Institutions customarily include not only fixed ways of acting, but also the people who are expected to behave toward one another in prescribed, repetitive ways. Quite commonly, too, as in the case of religious institutions, set ways of acting are associated with particular kinds of external objects, such as garments, insignia, implements, or structures.

Rarely are institutions neutral in terms of being regarded by the members of the societies in which they are found as neither good nor bad. Far more commonly institutions are connected with systems of values. Not all societies develop the same institutions, nor do they all ascribe identical values to similar institutions. Likewise, as societies grow large, complex, and heterogeneous, some of their members come to live by one set of institutions and values, whereas others may live by quite different ones. Variable though social or cultural institutions and systems of values may be when one compares group with group, they all stem from identical chemical, physical, biological, and cultural forces. These are relatively so invariable that their study promises to yield more valuable information than an examination of biocultural institutions. On the other hand, we can expose and examine underlying forces only by studying the particular institutions through which they make themselves manifest.

D. CULTURAL CONFIGURATIONS

Cultural anthropology teaches us that the major features of any society's institutionalized way of life neither stand by themselves nor fall into a shapeless arrangement. It may not be possible to give a full pattern of culture a single graphic expression, such as a geometric form, that is satisfactory to every social scientist, but a sense of order may be achieved if only the minimum essentials are portrayed. Even if such a procedure is accepted, there may still be a measure of disagreement. Some may wish to picture a culture pattern as a pentagon, with one side each devoted to man's dealings with his environment, interpersonal relations, religion, language, and value system. Others may consider values to be subsumed under religion and may accordingly prefer to show a way of life as a square or rectangle. Still others, including the writer, in their search for absolute minimums, would reduce the figure further and give it graphic representation as a triangle. Far more important than the actual number of lines used is the fact that they should always be shown linked together, for the various facets of biocultural behavior never remain separate but always form a connected pattern.

In a **biocultural triangle** (Fig. 8.6) one must imagine a spring placed at each juncture where two lines meet. This will make it easier to appreciate why heavy pressure on, or a marked change in the direction of, any one side is bound to induce changes in the total configuration. Stated graphically, a biocultural triangle may look thus △ at one stage, and like this ◿ under different circumstances.

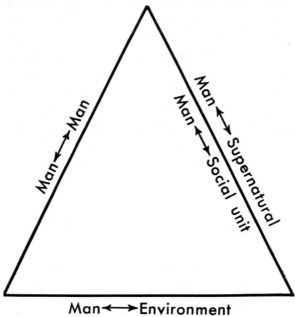

Man ⟷ Environment

Fig. 8.6. A biocultural triangle. The three sides are always integrated, but do not receive equal emphasis in all societies. Some aspects of biocultural behavior are not included in the triangular configuration.

Although every feature of a society's way of life is not necessarily encompassed within a biocultural triangle, a high percentage of vital traits are always included. Cultural anthropologists who have learned to think in terms of such a configuration have found that it gives them an objective way of arranging their material when making field studies anywhere. Also, the use of this device puts into concrete form the abstract concept of a pattern of culture and makes possible point for point comparisons between the behavior of one group and that of another.

If it be true that the three principal segments interlock, then it makes little difference, in a specific culture, at which spot an investigator starts his studies. A careful follow-up of any lead should take him all around the three sides of the figure. For instance, a cultural anthropologist is unlikely to arouse initial resentment if he shows a friendly interest in the daily work of a potter. Without fail, inquiries along these lines will take him well into the Man←→Environment aspects of the tribe's culture, after which it is but a simple step to seek information on the potter's background. This will include questions about the sex, age, and relationship of the potter's teacher, the age when training began, and other attributes of Man←→Man conduct. Quite often, too, it will be found that some pots are made specifically for use in sacred contexts, and that design elements on others have religious significance.[4] By following such leads, an alert field worker can gain valuable information about a tribe's Man←→Supernatural beliefs. This demonstrates how all parts of a biocultural triangle may fit together and shows how an alert investigator may learn much about social and religious customs even if he starts out with simple questions about the technique of pottery making.

E. PROBLEMS OF CULTURE CHANGE

Whatever particular pattern a society develops never remains perpetually the same. Only as a kind of delusion, comparable to stopping a motion picture film on one frame so that it looks like a still, does a way of life appear to be static. There are, of course, periods when changes are more noticeable or more rapid than at other times, but even if a group lives in total isolation from the rest of mankind, the pressure of internal forces of culture inevitably brings about change. Many **internal changes** seem to arise simply as people add to their collective stockpile of knowledge. With the passage of time the members of any society are likely to learn more and more about the external environment in which they live. This results in a different and, usually, a wider and more efficient use of natural resources. In turn, this leads unfailingly to some modification of technology. These technological shifts then impel some people to develop new skills, and very often to make novel tools. If the new devices are to become a permanent part of a society's culture pattern, their use must be taught to others. The resultant changes, therefore, may begin with man's relations to his physical setting

---

[4] R. L. Bunzel, *The Pueblo Potter*, New York, 1929, p. 92. Nos. 1 and 2 describe prayer-meal bowls, and a design element on no. 4 is interpreted as a prayer for rain.

but are likely also to enter the zone of interpersonal relations. Nor is anything basic apt to stop there. Frequently, important changes in these spheres are reflected in a group's dealings with its supernatural agents, as well as in its system of values.

Much more striking than the alterations that arise internally are those **external modifications** that result from the contact of one group of humans with another. Prerequisite to this kind of change is a breakdown of isolation. Most often this is brought about by the building of a new road, but any new form of transportation or communication may have the same effect. As long as a society lives in complete isolation, it cannot possibly receive any stimulus to **external changes** of culture; nor can it have the opportunity to compare its own customs with those of different people. However, just as soon as one society comes into contact with another, a potential for comparison arises. Without fail, through the operation of some process whose workings social scientists do not always understand, a trait from one society comes to be more highly esteemed than its counterpart in another. When this happens, a choice is made, and preference is given to that feature which has come to be rated higher.

At present there is hardly any society which has not felt the impact of a culture different from its own. It is to the process of the intermingling of cultures that the name **acculturation** has been given.[5] While the main idea of this term is closely related to that of diffusion, and while the term can be used for whole or partial mixtures of any different ways of life, it is most commonly applied to the study of the influence of a Euro-American culture on that of a nonliterate, relatively isolated group.

The most obvious approach to research in acculturation is for an observer to list the kinds and numbers of recognizably foreign objects, such as cast-iron stoves or sewing machines, to be found in a primitive society. A survey of this sort, considered by itself, has only superficial value, but it can afford a basis for studying the history of culture contacts and the nature of diffusion. Reports of acculturation gain in value as they contribute to an understanding of

[5] Those who wish to explore this topic further should consult: M. J. Herskovits, *Acculturation*, New York, 1938; H. G. Barnett, *Innovation*, New York, 1953; H. G. Barnett, L. Broom, B. J. Siegel, E. Z. Vogt, and J. B. Watson, "Acculturation: An Exploratory Formulation," *American Anthropologist*, Vol. 56, 1954, pp. 973-1002; and E. M. Bruner, "Differential Culture Change: Report on the Interuniversity Summer Research Seminar, 1956," *Social Science Research Council Items*, Vol. II, No. I, March 1957, pp. 1-3.

cultural processes. Some ethnologists have begun to examine such dynamic aspects as the differential emphases that the people of a lending society may give to various parts of their culture. Quite often representatives of one society may want a different group to adopt their religious beliefs, but in other cases those who establish the initial contacts may strive to introduce instead such economic features as the use of power-driven vehicles or a system of working for cash rather than for goods. Other cultural anthropologists have begun to investigate the motives which may influence adoption of some new items and rejection of others. Students of culture are also inquiring into the ways that new features are modified or left intact and how they are fitted into a native culture pattern. Valuable results can likewise be obtained from a study of the degree of compulsion that might have forced peoples to accept a foreign trait against their will; from an analysis of the effects of the borrowed item on individuals of different sex, age, occupation, or social standing; and from efforts to understand the nature of the contacts between members of the giving and receiving group. It is now well realized that the process of acculturation may affect those who give as well as those who take.

A few rules of general cultural behavior have already emerged from **acculturational** investigations, broadly considered. Unless there is a great deal of violence involved, a receiving society is likely to accept only such items as fill a conscious need, particularly if the new things can be interpreted as modifications only of existing traits. Most readily borrowed are objects of material culture whose use will result in a great saving of time and human muscular energy and whose effectiveness can be most readily demonstrated, grasped, and accurately measured. Nonliterate people are rarely articulate about their motives for borrowing, but even a simple list of Euro-American things accepted by a number of primitive groups confirms such a conclusion. Metal tools and weapons seldom fail to supplant similar implements of stone or wood, especially if their use does not require long training and the acquisition of new motor habits. Also, manufactured garments can always be counted on to replace home-made clothes. Women are more likely than men to cling to native forms of dress, and religious personages are even more conservative. For the most part, though, "store-bought" clothing soon becomes the rule for those who have sufficient money. The acceptance of new material traits cannot be considered apart from the degree of success with which individual natives enter into the money economy of the Euro-Americans with whom they have contact.

Nonmaterial traits are more likely to meet with widespread initial resistance. Nevertheless, even the acceptance of a purely technological trait is likely to alter a society's social and religious structure. Realization of this fact, though usually implicit rather than explicit, lies behind the refusal of many "backward" nations to accept offers of material assistance from the United States. In the nonmaterial realm, Euro-American forms of religion are apt to be rejected at first, although they may later be accepted through missionary and other pressures. Anthropologists have found Christianity to be surprisingly flexible. Sometimes it is deliberately molded to primitive shape by evangelists who hope by this means to gain ready converts, and sometimes it is given strange twists through the ignorance of native practitioners.[6]

One of the areas of greatest resistance to acculturation is in the field of speech. Many a people who seem to be thoroughly acculturated in other respects continue to speak their native tongue in addition to a Euro-American language. At the present time the Araucanian Indians are practically indistinguishable from their nearby Chilean neighbors in physical appearance, dress, occupations, and the use of material objects, but every person who considers himself an Indian speaks Araucanian at home. In another part of the world the Japanese provide an outstanding example of the same phenomenon. Throughout the course of centuries they borrowed all sorts of cultural items from China. They even began their system of writing by employing Chinese characters as a basis. Still, at no time did spoken Chinese offer the slightest challenge to the continued use of Japanese speech.

Food preferences also change slowly. People everywhere are reluctant to give up foods to which they have grown accustomed. Nevertheless, whether or not the individuals concerned like it, diets do change along with other aspects of culture. Inevitably, even the most conservative persons, or their offspring, find themselves unable to get the things that they once esteemed, and all that remains as they adjust their tastes to new menus is a vague longing for the foods that mother used to make.

---

[6] A great many examples of this point can be found in E. Nida, *Customs and Cultures*, New York, 1955.

As might be expected, a strong group seeks to impose its system of cultural values on a weaker one. If the difference of strength is very marked, the latter cannot resist; and if the stronger society appears to be better adjusted and more prosperous, the weaker one may actually show eagerness to accept the other's ideas. But a value system does not exist apart from an entire configuration of culture, and it is often impossible for the imitating society to take over the complete way of life of the dominant people. There must then follow a sad period of transition, during which the weaker society continues to lose faith in its own traditional values, but lacks the means to adopt the more desirable ones. At such times a marked feeling of **dysphoria** prevails, and the members of the society faced with the need of a changeover appear to be disturbed, insecure, and unhappy.

Since biocultural forces usually exist in a dynamic equilibrium, some account must be taken of the differing rates of speed at which various segments of culture are likely to change. Also, pressures for modification are balanced against forces of inertia, but in the course of acculturation, existing equilibria always become upset. It is when this happens that an era of uncertainty is most likely to set in and to endure until a new equilibrium has been established. The symbolic values that had previously been affixed to all aspects of life no longer apply, and new sets of values have not yet emerged with any degree of clarity or fixity. Nor is it easy for an individual to readjust himself and to accept new values after he has already learned to live by a different set of standards. This is perhaps the basis of the universal human tendency to look back nostalgically to the "good old days," when everything had its place in what seemed to be a permanent scale of values. By the same token this may be why oldsters everywhere tend to be conservative, to look askance at innovations and innovators, and to feel that the contemporary world is "going to the dogs."

F. THE DANGER OF BIOCULTURAL UNCONFORMITY

Because the values of biology and those of culture can, and occasionally do, run counter to each other, there arises a source of potential conflict in human affairs that is entirely missing in the activities of other animals. As long as a society's ways of life correspond reasonably well to the biogenetically determined requirements of its individual members, there need be little difficulty, but if a group's symbolic or cultural values diverge widely from basic biological considerations, a sort of **biocultural unconformity** develops, which is a possible source of great danger. (Fig. 8.7). Several aspects of Euro-American life illustrate the grave importance of this principle.

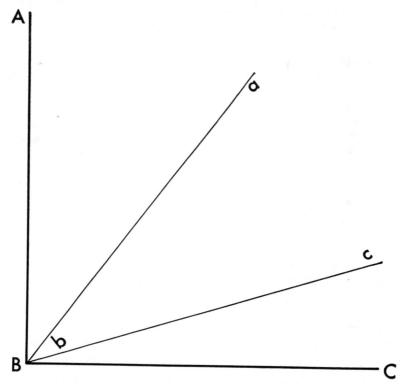

Fig. 8.7. Biocultural unconformity. The heavy lines are for the biological forces that underlie human behavior and the light lines represent cultural responses. Trouble spots arise whenever ab diverges from AB, or when bc is too far removed from BC. The further the gap between them, the greater is the likelihood of trouble.

Many agencies in the United States, including all branches of medical practice, are dedicated to the saving and prolongation of human life. Our system of cultural values gives high esteem to these objectives. Every time a life is saved or mortality rates are lowered we are inclined to cheer. Tables, such as the one in Fig. 8.8, showing a steady rise of life expectancy in the United States, make us very proud. What we often overlook is the patent fact that these accomplishments are limited to matters of biology and are not always accompanied by cultural advances in the treatment of the aged. Illogically, we are making a successful biological effort to produce, for the first time in our history, a growing body of oldsters, but culturally we do not know what to do with them.

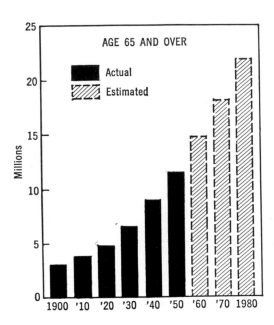

Fig. 8.8. Increase of older people in the United States. Actual figures are indicated by solid columns; projections into the future are shown in the stippled columns. (Courtesy of U. S. Department of Labor: Bureau of Labor Statistics.)

Much the same applies to many patients in mental hospitals. Thanks to some splendid and dramatic advances in therapy, the staffs of many institutions annually cure physically thousands of disturbed persons who were once regarded as incurable. Unfortunately, there still persists in our society a **cultural stereotype** that makes something shameful of mental disease. Consequently, many patients who have become well continue to remain in hospitals because they are culturally unwanted by their relatives and friends.

Biocultural unconformity may also manifest itself in a society's symbolic values toward parenthood. Every biologically normal adult desires sexual intercourse at one time or another, and every social unit wants to have children born to its members. Yet, there is no society known on earth that is willing to leave these matters entirely to the powerful promptings of biology. Instead, each group approves of sexual relations only between certain people under specified conditions and sanctions the birth of children only to selected persons. It is a quirk of biocultural behavior that cultural approval may be given to these activities quite apart from the biological fitness or readiness of the individuals most concerned.

Hardly any society chooses to make a theoretically vital distinction between those who are biologically best suited to have children and those who are culturally best equipped to rear and train them. With pitifully few exceptions, an unproved assumption is made that those who produce children are competent to raise them. Hence, in practice, no distinction is drawn between biological parenthood and what may be called cultural parenthood. The tendency to treat the two factors as one and the attendant danger of failing to recognize the existence of a potential for biocultural unconformity is illustrated by the fact that many American schools with "advanced" ideas devote much time to teaching youngsters the facts of biological conception through sexual intercourse, which really requires a minimum of knowledge and skill, but virtually neglect the far more difficult problem of how to rear a child properly. Only the USSR and Israel, among modern nations, are reported to have tried separating biological from cultural parenthood, but at the moment no reliable information on the success of their efforts is available.

Two aspects of juvenile delinquency in the United States may be better understood, at least in part, in the light of the difficulties that may arise from biocultural unconformity. At present we do not know all the biochemical ingredients and interactions that are contained in each body, but enough is known to suggest that no two persons are exactly alike,[7] and that the ingredients that compose one's body may have some bearing on one's temperament and, accordingly, on his behavior.[8] There is a good chance, therefore, that people are biologically greatly varied even at birth, yet our school system fails to take account of this probability. All children in the United States must, by law, attend school until about the age of fifteen or more. No consideration whatsoever is given to the possi-

---

[7] The promise of getting badly needed information along these lines is held forth in the researches of recent workers who call themselves chemical anthropologists.

[8] Dr. W. H. Sheldon has argued that people of endomorphic (fatty) build tend to be viscerotonic (interested in body comfort and digestion), whereas those who are mesomorphic (muscular) are apt to be somatotonic (interested in physical exercise and active forms of behavior) and those who are ectomorphic (tall and thin) are likely to be cerebrotonic (interested in mental processes and the use of the brain).

Sheldon and Eleanor Glueck, Physique and Delinquency, New York, 1956, pp. 226, 227, have found that mesomorphic youngsters are the most likely to run afoul of the law.

bility that some children may be biologically well suited to this cultural requirement, whereas others might be better fitted, biologically, for roaming outdoors than for attendance at school. If this be so, there is no use in lamenting the restlessness of some children in classrooms or their indulgence in truancy. Since they cannot change their inherited biologies, it would seem wiser for societies to modify their cultural requirements and to make them more flexible in order to eliminate some of the sources of biocultural unconformity.

More dramatic still are those aspects of biocultural unconformity that constantly arise in the United States from our attitudes toward sexual relations. Boys and girls throughout the world reach biologic sexual maturity somewhere around the age of fifteen, and for the next five years males, especially, are at the height of their potency and desire. During those very years our ways of life provide not a single culturally approved outlet. Youthful marriages are deprecated, particularly for men, and are often unfeasible for economic or other reasons; irregular love affairs, or the "sowing of wild oats," are so frowned upon officially that they are often punishable as illegal; consort with prostitutes is forbidden and widely condemned; and homosexuality, sodomy, and masturbation are considered thoroughly despicable. On the score of sex, then, our culture is entirely unrealistic and illogical, permitting a wide gap to open up between the facts of biology, particularly as they apply to young men aged fifteen to twenty, and the symbolic values that these self-same young men are taught to hold high. Small wonder that the statistics of criminality show that the age-group in question gives far more than its proportionate share of trouble. It would be naive to assume that young adult males commit only crimes of sex, for psychologists have shown that sexuality can be sublimated or directed into numerous channels. It is too bad that we have no way of determining the number of antisocial acts that may originate from biocultural unconformity.

Biocultural unconformity poses a threat to stability not only when one deals with the operations of whole societies, but also when one considers the reactions of particular individuals to the patterns of culture within which they grow up. If it were a fact that all cultural systems stress the same symbolic values and if it were true that all neonates are born with precisely the same biological mechanisms, it would be relatively easy to bring biology and culture into line in such a way that the dangers of biocultural unconformity would be lessened or eliminated. Unfortunately, no two ways of life emphasize exactly the same qualities, and no two children are likely to be born with exactly the same genetic inheritance. Biocultural configurations vary widely in the traits that societies most esteem and reward, and babies differ in their ability or willingness to accept restrictions and to tolerate frustrations. Over the years it always happens that some infants are better suited for life in one type of system than another.

In all cases where there is a presumed discrepancy between inborn temperament and cultural values, an individual finds himself facing a critical situation. If he is to conform to his society's standards, he must run the risk of internal or personality maladjustment; but if he elects to follow such dictates of his biological leanings as run counter to his group's approved code of behavior, he is in danger of external conflicts with his fellowmen. So does the threat of biocultural unconformity confront each of its potential victims with an insoluble dilemma. As it happens, few people and few patterns of culture run to extremes. Most individuals have mixed temperaments, and most ways of life stress a variety of themes for success. Among us, for instance, a great scholar, actor, or professional athlete, can live equally well. Beyond question, one of the greatest advantages of living in a big, culturally heterogeneous community is that its code provides a variety of satisfactions for all manner of persons.

SELECTED REFERENCES

Beals, R., "Acculturation" in *Anthropology Today*, A. L. Kroeber, ed., pp. 621-641. Chicago, 1953.

Benedict, R. F., *Patterns of Culture*. Boston, 1934.

Broom, L., *et al.*, "Acculturation: An Exploratory Formulation," *American Anthropologist*, Vol. 56, 1954.

Clark, J. G. D., "Archeological Theories and Interpretation: Old World" in *Anthropology Today*, A. L. Kroeber, ed., pp. 343-360. Chicago, 1953.

Herskovits, M. J., *et al.*, *Acculturation: The Study of Culture Contact*. New York, 1938.

Kluckhohn, C., "Patterning as Exemplified in Navaho Culture," in *Language, Culture and Personality*, L. Spier, *et al.*, eds., pp. 109-130. Menasha, Wisconsin, 1941.

Kroeber, A. L., and Kluckhohn, C., "Culture," *Papers of the Peabody*

Museum of American Archaeology and Ethnology, Vol. 47, No. 1. Cambridge, 1952.

Murdock, G. P., "The Common Denominator of Cultures," in *The Science of Man in The World Crisis,* R. Linton, ed., pp. 123-142. New York, 1945.

Opler, M. E., "Themes as Dynamic Forces in Culture," *American Journal of Sociology,* Vol. 51, No. 3, 1945, pp. 198-206.

Steward, J. H., "Cultural Causality and Law: A Trial Formulation," *American Anthropologist,* Vol. 51, No. 1, 1949, pp. 1-27.

White, L. A., "Energy and the Evolution of Culture," *American Anthropologist,* Vol. 45, 1943, pp. 335-356.

Zipf, G. K., *Human Behavior and the Principle of Least Effort.* Cambridge, Mass., 1949.

CHAPTER 9

THE STUDY OF PRIMITIVE
SOCIETY AND CULTURE

A. SOME CHARACTERISTICS OF PRIMITIVE SOCIETY,
AND A DEFENSE OF TRIBAL STUDIES

Physical anthropologists concentrate their efforts on the study of man's biological characteristics, and archeologists deal with the origin and growth of universal and local manifestations of past cultures, but the interplay of living people with one another as well as with their physical settings and the sum total of their cultural phenomena is the primary concern of cultural anthropologists. Each society has a distinctive manner of living that incorporates a number of regularly repeated acts of behavior, as well as a set of extra-biological, symbolic values, by means of which the conduct of its members is regulated.

There is no mathematically precise way of defining a society, but in general it may be said to consist of a group of individuals of both sexes who reside in one locality, recognize the same administrative authority, live according to the same standards of values, and interact or cooperate for the attainment of common goals. On each score a considerable amount of variation is possible. Using the people of the United States as an example, one might question whether they constitute a single society. One might justifiably ask whether residents of northern Maine really follow the same way of life as the inhabitants of southern California around Hollywood, or whether the folk in Delaware truly interact with those in Idaho for the attainment of common goals. Only in times of great events like national elections or wars are we conscious of any important degree of cooperation among all the citizens of the United States.

As it happens, many of the doubts that trouble students of large and complex communities are less grave in the case of those who deal with primitive societies, and cultural anthropologists have traditionally worked with the latter. "Primitive" is also a difficult term to define, but anthropologists agree that it should not be taken to mean inadequate, immature, deficient, savage, or backward. Perhaps the best way to sense the anthropological concept of primitive is to equate it with nonliterate,[1] that is, with societies whose cultures do not include the regular use of a written language.

Primitive societies differ from others in several essential regards. The differences need not be caused by an absence of writing, but on the whole it has been found that each nonliterate society is small and racially much alike and that it occupies only a limited range of territory, with boundaries that are well-known and seldom transgressed. Within the territorial limits, outsiders are rarely met, with the result that constant interaction with total strangers, so prominent a feature of our own lives, is rarely necessary. Living together with a restricted number of racially similar people whom one knows fairly well makes cooperation for the achievement of common goals comparatively easy. Furthermore, a primitive community is likely to have a relatively uniform language and religion, and a fairly homogeneous way of life. Rarely will it show great linguistic differences, significantly divergent political loyalties, allegiance to conflicting religious systems, or profound variations of symbolic values. Small societies, with relatively homogeneous forms of culture, usually function in such comparatively simple ways as to provide an investigator with a chance to discover their underlying structures and the main-springs of their people's actions. There is something comforting and satisfying in this situation. It affords a sharp contrast to the difficulties that must be overcome by those who study large, literate, culturally heterogeneous societies. These customarily have such complex systems of technology, economics, religion, politics, and social organization in general that it is very hard to find the princi-

---

[1] It is essential not to confuse nonliterate with illiterate.

ples according to which they operate. It might even be argued that a budding social scientist ought to learn something of the simpler forms of human life in society before going on to an analysis of more complex and complicated social structures.

Cultural anthropologists, then, aim to discover and record the basic mode of behavior or pattern of culture that makes up a group's design for living together. It does not take much experience to realize that even within a small, nonliterate, relatively homogeneous society, more than one culture pattern must prevail. As an irreducible minimum, one is unlikely to find an identical way of life prescribed for grown males and females, and it is hardly to be expected that a single design guides the conduct of infants and adults. There is also little cause for surprise if one finds varying patterns being followed by those of markedly divergent social backgrounds, greatly advanced age, and widely different occupations or places of residence, even within a single zone.

Since, then, every society has a number of differing designs for living, what is a cultural anthropologist to describe? Shall he report a great number of culture patterns, each of which applies only to one particular segment of a society; or shall he try to present a single, over-all pattern that may not be representative of all concerned? Anthropologists usually get around the dilemma by reporting in detail the commonest pattern of culture that applies to normal adults of either sex and by indicating whatever significant variations customarily apply to others.

Studies of contemporary primitive societies have proved to be of inestimable value for filling gaps in the archeological record. For example, when we were dealing with the Old World's New Stone Age it was possible to describe many details of material culture, but very little could be said of the intangible aspects of human behavior. Since primitive societies whose ways of life are essentially Neolithic still exist, one can determine from watching them how men and women probably behaved in the ancient New Stone Age.

Assuredly, it would be wrong to assume that every known group of human beings has passed through each of the earlier stages of culture depicted by archeologists. Yet, it seems certain that as a whole *Homo sapiens* did move progressively from reliance on stone to reliance on metals, from the collection of food to its production, and from nonliterate to literate levels. From this point of view there is much to be learned of man's cultural past by an examination of primitive societies. After all, the ultimate target of social science ought to be the behavior of the whole of mankind, and it would be a fatal error to leave out of the reckoning those aggregates of people who happen to be primitive.

Before going further, a serious student of cultural anthropology must memorize two fundamental axioms of the science of man. Every society seeks to perpetuate itself biologically through the birth of offspring to its members, and every society strives to continue its pattern of culture indefinitely by teaching infants to know and accept its ways of life. Reproduction is a social as well as an individual concern, and the establishment of long-lasting cultural traditions is not entirely a private matter. No society willingly looks forward either to biological or cultural extinction.

B. FIELD METHODS

Unlike many other scientists, a cultural anthropologist cannot bring his subjects into a laboratory. Instead, he must go to visit them wherever they may happen to reside. This may be inconvenient, but it has the advantage of giving him a chance to study a people's manner of living in its customary setting. Whenever possible, one should select for investigation a primitive society whose culture gives promise of throwing light on some particular problem of social science. Before departing for the field, an investigator should familiarize himself with whatever has already been written about the group and region he is going to study.

When cultural anthropology was in its infancy, the matter of making contact with a primitive folk was often a serious problem. Virtually all of the workers were Caucasoids of the Jewish or Christian faiths from Europe or America who were strange, and sometimes terrifying, to the people they wanted to observe. Conditions are much easier at present. There is hardly a tribe [2] left that has not become known to some government official, military officer, missionary, traveler, teacher, trader, or former anthropologist. Moreover, practically all primitive groups now number among their members some individuals who have received training in a European tongue. Intermediaries and interpreters are therefore customarily available and, in some cases, published materials contain

---

[2] As used in this book "tribe" is synonymous with primitive society.

linguistic information by means of which it is even possible to learn in advance a good deal about a language whose speakers have no means of writing.

Equipped with a background based on his reading and training, and aided by local residents who deal with the natives he intends to study, a cultural anthropologist nowadays rarely has difficulty in establishing contact with a primitive group. Whenever conditions permit, he makes arrangements to live right within the community whose customs he has come to investigate. Once he has settled in a suitable place and attended to the satisfaction of his daily needs, a field worker is ready to begin the dual tasks of making himself acceptable to the point where his presence is taken for granted by his neighbors and of noting everything that goes on about him. An anthropologist quickly senses whether his subjects distrust writing in their presence or the taking of photographs, and he guides himself accordingly. No detail should be deliberately omitted from his notebooks simply because it seems trivial, for the commonplace often has greater value than the spectacular in yielding understanding.

Collection of cultural data by an anthropologist in some ways resembles the collection of coins by a beggar. If a hundred people each give a beggar a nickel, no one of them feels that he has given more than a trifle, and each contributor would probably be surprised to know that in the end the beggar has received five dollars. So it frequently is with the cultural anthropologist. No native need give him more than a scrap of information at a time, yet if the anthropologist diligently writes down all that he is told on a given topic, he may at the end of a field trip find that on many subjects he has accumulated a sizable fund of valuable data, of whose existence none of his informants may be aware.

Apart from recording all that he chances to see and hear, an ethnologist finds it wise to question selected informants on particular topics. When interviewing, he must avoid asking leading questions and must allow subjects to wander from the point of inquiry as much as they like. Digressions frequently prove more rewarding than straightforward answers. At first a field worker must rely on interpreters, but he should take pains to learn the native language as well and as promptly as possible, so that he gradually becomes less and less dependent on what translators choose to tell him. Some cultural anthropologists supplement the data they get in interviews with answers to prepared questionnaires or standard psychological tests. Besides yielding a wide assortment of facts, these may be administered personally or by one's associates. They thus make extended coverage possible, but not all students of culture employ them.

Most of the anthropologists who deal with living people and cultures make use of the **participant-observer** technique.[3] This means that a man will seek to share in the activities of the male natives whereas a woman will try to take part in the daily life of members of her sex. A participant-observer is enabled in this way to acquire much first-hand information and to learn to see things from the tribal point of view. Critics sometimes object to this approach because they fear that it makes a field worker so much a part of the very thing he is studying as to deprive him of the detachment and objectivity essential to the scientific method. All that need be said in reply is that the danger appears greatest to those who have never tried to become participant-observers of a culture different from their own. A cultural anthropologist is in more danger of being kept an outsider who cannot get the local viewpoint than he is of being allowed to become too thoroughly immersed in the life around him. Overcoming the biases of one's own culture is a greater challenge than the risk of going native.

At the end of a lengthy stay in the field, an ethnologist should have gathered a mass of detail which he must later prepare for publication as a monograph. He must, of course, systematize his material in some sort of logical arrangement, by putting under a given heading all the data that seem pertinent. He must also provide whatever analyses and interpretations he can. Never should he omit contradictory items, nor pad out such gaps as may occur. Above all, he must be alert to check the validity of his findings as thoroughly as he can. It is from the comparative study of many particular ways of life that cultural anthropologists concerned with theory construct their hypotheses and attempt to merge the details of many locally functioning cultures into a grand scheme of human, cultural behavior.

Some scholars are still to be found who believe that experimenta-

---

[3] For more details regarding field methods, see the articles by J. Henry and M. E. Spiro, and by B. D. Paul in A. L. Kroeber, editor, *Anthropology Today*, Chicago, 1953, pp. 417-451. Consult also F. R. Kluckhohn, "The Participant-Observer Technique in Small Communities," *American Journal of Sociology*, Vol. 46, 1930, pp. 331-343.

tion is essential to the development of any science. According to their reasoning, studies of society can never be scientific. Cultural anthropologists have done much to overcome this kind of criticism. Admittedly, they cannot make experimental studies of tribal groups, but they know of so many different primitive societies that by careful comparison they can approximate the sort of experimentation that depends on the change of one variable factor at a time. The enormous diversity of nonliterate societies and cultures permits the comparative analysis of many units which may differ from each other in only one or two regards.

C. HOW DO YOU KNOW YOU'RE RIGHT?

Any inferences drawn from field data are bound to be wrong if the original material is faulty. Consequently, it is up to every cultural anthropologist to make sure that the information he publishes is as correct as possible. There are several ways of achieving reasonable accuracy. No one of them is self-sufficient, but all together they serve to keep a worker from making gross errors.

The most common practice is to question **multiple informants** on the same topic. There is no way of telling in advance whether a native is representative of his society or abnormal in some way, or whether he is truthful, willing to talk, and competent to speak on the subject under study. Accordingly, it is wise for a field investigator to question several informants. The informants should be as varied as possible, and they should be unaware of what others may already have said. If the statements of multiple informants show much agreement, the investigator may feel fairly certain that he is getting at the truth. If there is marked disagreement, he must note the fact and try to figure out what it signifies. Material obtained from a single informant is always suspect.

There is also a need for checking the **internal consistency** of one's data. If, to cite a hypothetical case, an anthropologist discovers that his informants insist that their society never indulges in violence, yet finds in his notes frequent instances of assault and murder, he is faced with a marked lack of internal consistency and must seek its explanation. On one occasion, when the writer was compiling a census of the Hopi Indian pueblo of Old Oraibi in Arizona, his informants claimed at first that divorce was practically unknown among their people. Later, when their attention was tactfully drawn to much contradictory evidence they cheerfully admitted that they had been in error, and provided data that indicated as high a divorce rate as 34 percent.[4] The second set of data proved the more accurate when compared with the statements of other informants.

Another method of avoiding mistakes is to make sure that one's description of a way of life covers **the yearly round.** Many peoples practice different customs at various seasons. Ideally, a worker should stay in the field at least for a whole year, but if this is impractical he should make certain to obtain from informants full accounts of the group's behavior all through the yearly round.

The author has long been an advocate of still another device for insuring accuracy, which he calls **the divided field-trip.** Essentially this means that a cultural anthropologist is wise to make more than a single visit to a society under study. Even if his total time in the field is limited to a few months, he would do well to leave the area for a while and to return to it after a lapse of time. The outstanding value of the divided field-trip is that it enables an anthropologist on his later visit to overcome some of the deficiencies of the first. On his initial arrival he might, without knowing it, have been introduced by someone whom the natives heartily disliked; he might unwittingly have dealt with unreliable informants; he might sometimes have been told deliberate untruths; his very presence might have been resented; and he might, through ignorance of local customs, have offended some members of the community. All of these faults are capable of being remedied on a return trip. Now the cultural anthropologist may join the society without any intermediary; he knows which informants are apt to be cooperative and trustworthy and which are better to be diplomatically avoided; few people are able to remember and repeat long after whatever deliberate misstatements they may earlier have made to an investigator; if he has previously acted properly, he will find the community pleased to have him return; and he is most unlikely to give offense through ignorance of the society's symbolic values. On the whole, the advantages of the divided field-trip are so varied and numerous that they far outweigh the disadvantages of losing a few working days in the field. Besides what has already been mentioned, the divided field-trip gives one an undisturbed chance to study his notes

---

[4] In this case the informants may have been trying to please the ethnologist by making their culture seem to conform to the expressed standards of his own. One cannot be sure that there was any deliberate attempt to deceive.

carefully, to discover such inconsistencies as may require further checking, to find out which topics have not been sufficiently investigated, and, in general, to lay plans based on the knowledge already obtained for a more adequate research program when work is resumed.

D. THE NATURE AND VALUE OF FIELD WORK

More than anything else, a cultural anthropologist on a field-trip must never forget the fact that he is an unexpected guest in a society made up of sensitive human beings whose system of values is entirely different from his own. His job is to learn all he can about the other culture, not to modify or reform it. It is for him to adjust to native ways, not the other way around. Even though the period of living in a strange cultural world is temporary, all anthropologists agree that it provides an exciting and deeply rewarding experience.

Many years of research have made it clear that some topics are best avoided at the outset. It is improbable that the members of any society will be willing to discuss freely with a stranger their deep-seated religious beliefs or the intimate details of their sex life. A beginner is well advised not to plunge into such matters prematurely. Information of this kind may be sought indirectly, or after one feels that he has won the confidence of "his people." It is usually best to start field work with commonplace technological activities, with the collection of word lists, or with any other subject that is known to be regarded as neutral.

A cultural anthropologist may aim at more than one goal. He may be chiefly interested in the local design for living of a single society, or he may be more concerned with the whole range of human culture. Again, he may in either instance wish to study culture at one time period, or else he may prefer to trace the development of culture from its beginning to the present. Most investigators feel that, whatever their approach happens to be, the broad outlines of man's cultural growth can be understood only if comparative studies are made of many particular cultures in all parts of the world. Each investigation thus makes a contribution toward the understanding of culture as a whole.

What every cultural anthropologist hopes to publish after returning from the field is a full and objective account of the prevailing pattern of culture in the society that he was visiting. Of necessity, this pattern will be a composite, made up of the ways of life of many individuals. It will also have to be a kind of average, and like all averages it will have to be carefully checked to make sure that it is truly representative of the whole society. It is practical to look upon a culture pattern as a generalized abstraction. It may have no more independent existence than the concept of righteousness. One can point to many examples of righteous behavior, but it is impossible to show righteousness by itself. So, too, with a pattern of culture. Many acts of cultural behavior can be shown to follow a pattern, but the pattern itself exists only as an abstract concept. Nevertheless, if field workers failed to organize their material into patterns, all efforts to construct theories of culture would be lost in a maze of details.

Sooner or later the thought is apt to arise: Why cannot the operator of an excellent moving picture camera and a perfect sound recorder produce a better report of a primitive culture than can a cultural anthropologist? A moment's reflection should provide part of the answer. Many people are averse to being photographed, and even if everyone were willing, it would be impractical to keep the needed equipment in continuous operation for months, possibly for a year or more. Besides, many activities take place indoors, at night, during periods of bad weather, or in spots where extraneous noises may drown out what is really important. Nor would a finished sound track convey much meaning to audiences that did not know the native life and language. Furthermore, one must not forget that mechanical devices can record only sights and sounds, whereas a human field worker uses all his senses.

No instrument has yet been invented that can make discriminating selections of cultural materials, and a trained anthropologist can certainly pick out significant items better than the most proficient of cameramen. Wherever possible, an investigator does not fail to supplement his notes with photographs, but indiscriminate picture-taking can be more harmful than helpful. Similarly, many workers take sound-recorders into the field, but once more the material to be recorded has to be carefully chosen.

Without a cultural anthropologist to marshal them into systematic order, facts remain in a hopeless jumble. Coherence emerges only when similar data are fitted together according to a consistent scheme. The more a field worker knows in advance what he intends to study and the kinds of questions he is going to ask, the more certainly will his material lend itself to adequate classification and intelligent analysis. Above all, it is the function of a cultural anthropologist to make his data meaningful to others. No matter by what techniques 'he acquired his information, it is up to him to provide explanations of his field material. Only a human being can make meaningful interpretations of culture. The success of a published monograph can best be measured by the light it throws on the behavior of people in a given society and by the extent to which its material makes possible the building of new theories pertaining to the universal workings of biocultural behavior.

Social scientists other than cultural anthropologists sometimes wonder why the latter appear to be preoccupied with primitive peoples and their forms of culture. Actually, many field workers trained in anthropology have begun to study modern, highly literate communities, and they have brought to their task some of the techniques and ideas drawn from their knowledge of primitive life. A surprising number of behavioral forms whose importance was first recognized in primitive tribes have been found to exist in literate, contemporary societies; and numerous students of human life in nonprimitive settings have expressed their indebtedness for fresh insights to the contributions made by cultural anthropologists.

E. CULTURAL EMPHASES

Besides varying in the details of which they are composed, biocultural configurations, taken as units, reveal different kinds of emphases. One society may reward with prestige and honors all manifestations of strongly aggressive conduct, but another may frown upon and punish aggressors. The late Ruth Fulton Benedict in her famous book, *Patterns of Culture*, selected to illustrate this point certain societies whose ways of life reflected strongly marked differences in basic attitudes. She described as **Apollonian** those forms of culture that showed high regard for sobriety and restraint, and she called **Dionysian** those which honored intemperate and reckless behavior.[5]

---

[5] R. F. Benedict, *Patterns of Culture*, Boston, 1934. Prof. Benedict also inaugurated a trend, still followed by some contemporary anthropologists, towards differentiating "guilt" from "shame" cultures. In the former, an individual feels uneasy if he becomes aware that any of his actions deviates from the approved moral code of his group; in the latter, a person regards transgressions lightly unless he happens to be caught.

Certainly it is true that some cultures have a dominant tone that seems to color the activities of all their participants. Orthodox Jewish males who lived in Eastern Europe during the late nineteenth century were Apollonian to the extent that they could achieve the most treasured honors of their communities only if they were great scholars who devoted themselves to the study of the sacred writings and their commentaries.[6] At the same period of history, far off in the Great Plains region of the United States, the Crow Indians favored Dionysian modes of action and reserved their highest admiration and rewards for men who were fighters.[7]

Since the publication of *Patterns of Culture*, other cultural anthropologists have pointed out that only a small handful of carefully selected societies are plainly dominated by a single cultural motive. Far more often, it is argued, group ways of life reveal the influence of multiple motivations. Professor Morris E. Opler has suggested that instead of having one guiding principle most cultures are organized around a number of interrelated themes.[8] Whichever may be the more accurate view, it is now fully recognized that varying culture patterns do show different emphases in setting up standards of approved behavior for the members of particular societies to follow, and every field worker is sensitive to whatever emphases seem to prevail in the culture he is studying.

Societies also vary in the degree to which their cultures seek to minimize the strictly biological parts of biocultural behavior. Measured in biological terms, there is little difference between the functioning of a mid-Victorian female's body and that of a contemporary Hopi Indian woman. But culturally there is a profound gap. The cut of an old-fashioned Hopi dress often discloses the left breast, and Hopi women openly suckle infants before either sex. Victorian women, we are told, were even reluctant to admit that they had breasts. Traditional Hopi pueblos had no toilets or outhouses of any kind, and passersby could not help but observe females in the process of elimination. Can anyone imagine a proper Victorian woman urinating or defecating in public? If one had sufficient data,

---

[6] M. Zborowski and E. Herzog, *Life Is with People*, New York, 1953, pp. 74 ff. *et passim*.

[7] R. H. Lowie, *The Crow Indians*, New York, 1935, p. 215.

[8] M. E. Opler, "Themes as Dynamic Forces in Culture," *American Journal of Sociology*, 1945, Vol. 51, pp. 198-206. A year later Professor Opler carried his ideas still further in "An Application of the Theory of Themes in Culture," *Journal of the Washington Academy of Sciences*, 1946, Vol. 36, pp. 137-166.

one could probably construct a trend line in which Hopi culture would appear much closer than Victorian to a biological level of behavior. There is some indication that culture in general has been moving from a 100 percent biological start in the direction of (but without being able to reach) a zero point of biology. In the absence of complete information, however, it is not possible to establish a law of cultural development based on this postulated trend.

F. THE REALITY OF CULTURE PATTERNS

Those who doubt the reality of abstract concepts may wonder if culture patterns actually exist. It can be shown that they do, even if the people most directly affected by them are not aware of their existence. Let us take an example from American food habits. Suppose a wealthy but eccentric individual decided that he wanted a breakfast of beet soup, raw oysters, and sassafras tea; in what restaurant could he get them? At the opposite extreme, Americans who order fruit juice, eggs or cereal, toast, and coffee may feel that they are expressing their personal desires, but restaurant keepers know that a pattern is being followed. Probably the most successful restaurateurs are those who most completely anticipate the patterned food habits of their patrons. What chance of success would a restaurant owner in the United States have if he catered to the unexpected whims of people who might breakfast on beet soup, raw oysters, and sassafras tea, but failed to stock fruit juices, eggs, cereals, toast, and coffee?

Storekeepers of every description realize that no matter how much Americans pride themselves on independence they actually do follow repetitive institutionalized practices in their buying habits. Few are the purchasers, though, who realize that they are not expressing strictly individual preferences when they buy things without obvious coercion. Yet so strong is cultural compulsion that whenever culture patterns change, people usually have no recourse but to adjust their tastes to them. Many a woman who feels herself to have been best suited by a fashion that prevailed two or three years ago finds it impossible to obtain what she wants in shop after shop that carries only the latest styles. To such a person the reality of a culture pattern is no idle matter.

For those who must deal with what is called "the public," the existence of patterned behavior is a great comfort. Not only merchants but police officials would find themselves at a loss if all the residents of a city suddenly abandoned their customary patterns of conduct in order to follow purely individual dictates.

Life in society would be just about impossible were it not for the existence of regularly patterned and therefore predictable ways of behaving. They are usually taken for granted by individuals, and they do not always function without a degree of variation; but think how difficult life would be if a person never knew what forms of behavior to expect from a spouse, parent, child, or neighbor. To appreciate this point, one has only to compare the assurance that an individual feels when he says, "I know how to handle him. I can anticipate every move he'll make"; with the distracted state of mind of the person who is forced to say, "I can't do a thing with him. I never know what he'll do next."

Two of the most interesting but difficult problems of social science are to determine how patterns of culture become changed and to discover the extent to which the behavior of people is based on individual will or motivated by the patterns of conduct that prevail in their society. Sometimes the forms of culture change, apparently in response to forces of their own, and run in systematic cycles that do not seem to be inaugurated by any identifiable person. Professor Kroeber and Jane Richardson have shown that styles in women's clothing change in cyclic fashion,[9] presumably in response only to internal forces of culture, and without noticeable reference to the wants of their wearers or the whims of dress designers. Unfortunately, the implications of this topic have not yet been fully explored. Despite the manifold problems of interpretation that await analysis, modern field workers invariably base their programs on the assumption that patterns of culture do exist.

G. OVERT AND COVERT

Some of the difficulties involved in ethnological studies grow out of the aforementioned existence in one society of a number of different biocultural configurations. It has already been indicated that what might be correct for men may be wrong for women, and that what is fitting for adults may be unsuitable for youngsters. Apart from these and other variable standards based on a number of tangible

---

[9] A. L. Kroeber and J. Richardson, "Three Centuries of Women's Dress Fashions, a Quantitative Analysis," *Anthropological Records*, Vol. 5, No. 2, 1940.

factors, there exist in all societies what Professor Clyde Kluckhohn of Harvard has discussed as **overt** and **covert** patterns of behavior.[10] By modifying his usage slightly, we may designate as overt standards those somewhat idealized notions that one consciously thinks of as typical of his culture and which are promptly recited in response to questions. Covert patterns may represent somewhat more realistic guides to conduct, but one is less sure to be immediately aware of them and less likely to express them readily in words. Something of the difference between them is reflected in our sayings about preaching one thing and practicing another, but when we mention a contrast of this sort there is usually a hint of deceit. Such is not the case in the distinction between overt and covert with which we are dealing. A native informant does not have to be a liar or a hypocrite to say that a given way of behaving is typical of his culture but to act most of the time according to a different pattern.

SELECTED REFERENCES

Benedict, R. F., "Anthropology and the Abnormal," *Journal of General Psychology*, Vol. 10, 1934, pp. 59-80.

———, *Patterns of Culture*. Boston, 1934.

Bennett, J. W., "The Study of Cultures: A Survey of Technique and Methodology in Field Work," *American Sociological Review*, Vol. 13, 1948, pp. 672-689.

Firth, R., "Contemporary British Social Anthropology," *American Anthropologist*, Vol. 53, 1951, pp. 474-489.

Hallowell, A. I., "Use of Projective Techniques in the Study of Socio-Psychological Aspects of Acculturation," *Journal of Projective Techniques*, Vol. 15, 1951, pp. 27-44.

Henry, J., and Spiro, M. E., "Psychological Techniques: Projective Tests in Field Work," in *Anthropology Today*, A. L. Kroeber, ed., pp. 417-429. Chicago, 1953.

Kluckhohn, C., "The Place of Theory in Anthropological Studies," *Journal of the Philosophy of Science*, Vol. 6, 1939, pp. 328-344.

Kluckhohn, F. R., "The Participant-Observer Technique in Small Communities," *American Journal of Sociology*, Vol. 46, 1940, pp. 331-343.

LaBarre, W., "The Cultural Basis of Emotions and Gestures," *Journal of Personality*, Vol. 16, 1947, pp. 49-68.

Paul, B. D., "Interview Techniques and Field Relationships," in *Anthropology Today*, A. L. Kroeber, ed., pp. 430-451. Chicago, 1953.

---

[10] C. Kluckhohn, "Patterning as Exemplified in Navaho Culture," *Language, Culture and Personality* (L. Spier *et al.*, eds.), Menasha, 1941, pp. 109-130.

10

MAN'S RELATIONS WITH HIS

PHYSICAL ENVIRONMENT

A. LET'S EAT!

Like those of other animals the bodies of human beings are made up of protoplasm which is not equipped either to store indefinitely or to replace from within itself the ingredients necessary to sustain life. This means that without fail members of *Homo sapiens* must regularly get from some external source whatever their bodies need. Adequate amounts of air, as well as those solids and liquids customarily consumed as food, generally provide each person with all that he requires to live and function properly. We have here the source of a universal aspect of all cultures, for no way of life can endure if it fails to deal satisfactorily with the problem of providing its carriers with a sufficient supply of oxygen and food. Yet, no two societies have exactly the same eating and drinking preferences. Truly has it been said that one man's meat is another man's poison.

In a few cases the bodies of other persons can provide much or all that an individual needs. Suckling babies everywhere derive most of their nourishment from their mothers or wetnurses; and cannibals sometimes consume the bodies of other humans for food. But the period of nursing never makes up more than a small fraction of an average life span; and anthropologists have found true cannibalism to have been important only in restricted parts of Africa, in the tropical areas of the New World, and on some of the South Sea Islands. Far more commonly, human beings get what they need in the way of oxygen, food, and drink, not from one another but from their physical settings. So incontrovertible is this requirement and so unfailing is this practice, that man's interrelations with his environment must form the base of every biocultural configuration.

Oddly enough, although we are dealing with an essential biological necessity for all mankind, the evaluation of food as good or bad is often illogical or nonlogical according to the scheme set forth on page 15.[1] There is no society known, including our own, which has first made a thorough scientific analysis of all the nutritive elements in its environment and then given preference in the order that items were shown to be best suited to man's biological needs. Instead, cultural anthropologists find everywhere the existence of food preferences based on symbolic, man-made values that may oftentimes have nothing to do with nutrition as such. A poor family of Caucasoids in the United States might bewail its inability to afford meat, but would nevertheless reject a gift of plump, nutritious gophers, which Navaho Indians regard as a delicacy. Even cows' milk, which is widely held to be an excellent food, was until recent years despised by Chinese, Koreans, Japanese, and other residents of the Far East. As late as 1934 the writer knew a Hopi Indian, hospitalized with an advanced case of tuberculosis, who insisted on returning to his native village because he was sure the hospital attendants were trying to poison him by making him drink milk.

Symbolic values are so basic to the use of all human foodstuffs that as many shortages are due to the scarcity of culturally approved items as are due to a real lack of nutriments. While World War II was being fought, teams of scientists tried to persuade Allied peoples whose customary rations were in short supply to substitute other highly nourishing foods. In practically every case where the substitution failed to conform to culturally determined standards of taste and color, it was strongly resisted, in spite of scientific assurances of its biological value. An interesting example of the same principle turned about is the practice of a soft drink company which

---

[1] A good deal of information about the acquisition and preparation of foodstuffs by particular tribes may be found in R. L. Beals and H. Hoijer, *An Introduction to Anthropology*, New York, 1953, pp. 271-310; and in E. D. Chapple and C. S. Coon, *Principles of Anthropology*, New York, 1942, pp. 127-138, 142-197, *et passim*.

retains an attorney who can eat various insects without harm. Whenever a suit is brought by a plaintiff claiming to have been made ill by a bug in his drink, the lawyer eats a similar specimen to disprove the claim. Apparently, juries are so impressed by this feat that they fail to consider the possibility of culturally induced damages and therefore dismiss the case.[2]

There is no substance to which seemingly arbitrary cultural values cannot be assigned. Sometimes foods come to be regarded as better suited for men or women, without reference to the actual physical differences of the sexes. Although we do not adhere rigidly to such a distinction, we still recognize an unscientific tendency to associate a taste for salads with females and a craving for thick steaks with males. A cultural concept, unknown in our society but widespread among Indian peoples of Latin America, is the notion that foods may be hot or cold regardless of their temperature or physiological properties. One of these nonlogical classifications lists as cold such diverse items as mutton, fish, maize, rice, chocolate, bread, butter, milk, sugar, and barley beer; whereas hot foods include beef, turkey, sweet potatoes, coffee, mangoes, and chickpeas.[3] People may cling to beliefs of this sort long after the basis for the classification has been forgotten. Anthropologists cannot always explain the origin of the hot or cold concept, but they can show that it is cultural and not biophysicochemical. Professor George M. Foster has tentatively traced some of these notions to the teachings of Hippocrates and Galen. They are likely to be associated with a belief that various ailments may be hot or cold. Quite often, in such cases, cures are thought to be brought about by resort to opposites, so that cold remedies and foods are used against hot illnesses, and vice versa.[4]

Foods may also be socially ranked as high or low. Sometimes this may be determined by expense, which may rest on a nutritional base, as when cream costs more than milk. Just as often, high class foods may be more costly but of less nutritional value, as in the case of polished and unpolished rice. Other rankings may disregard economics and biological worth altogether. Many American house-

---

[2] On June 27, 1953, the *Ann Arbor News* carried an Associated Press dispatch describing the victory of a lawyer who ate a cockroach in court.

[3] J. Gillin, "Moche: A Peruvian Coastal Community," *Smithsonian Institution, Institute of Social Anthropology*, No. 3, Washington, 1945, p. 54.

[4] G. M. Foster, "Relationships between Theoretical and Applied Anthropology: A Public Health Program Analysis," *Human Organization*, Vol. 11, 1952, p. 8.

wives would be ashamed to serve guests a Sunday dinner of hamburgers and onions instead of roast beef and potatoes, even though the former might conceivably be more expensive and nutritious than the latter. As an experiment, the writer asked five Japanese to rank a list of assorted foods in the order in which a traditional Japanese would have preferred to serve them to an honored visitor. All of them, as might have been anticipated, placed rice first. That they were thinking in terms of cultural values is made clear by the fact that a nutritional study of the same foods ranks rice last.[5]

There are as many variations of eating etiquette as there are food preferences. Despite the simple fact that the final aim of all feeding customs is to put food into the mouth, societies favor an incredible series of preliminary maneuvers. Another interesting distinction between biologic and cultural factors can be made on this score. It is a stark fact that the etiquette of eating seldom goes beyond the point where food is actually swallowed. Thereafter, in all societies, the matter of digestion becomes a biological activity, virtually free of cultural controls. To some extent, as is indicated on p. 15, culture may interfere with the biochemistry of digestion, but such interference is rarely a matter of fixed etiquette.

Very seldom does one find a culture pattern that gives high value to the serving of food in the same vessels in which it was prepared. Instead, human beings almost without exception try to eat their food from containers other than cooking vessels. As a matter of fact, there are many among us who pride themselves on the expensive array of dishes, covers, and table settings that they interpose between the preparation and consumption of food. Yet it must be admitted that these highly prized things have only doubtful value when it comes to the basically biological needs of ingesting and digesting nutritious substances. In contrast to those Euro-Americans who feel that correct dining demands a wide assortment of utensils, many inhabitants of Eastern Asia can get by with a pair of simple chopsticks (Fig. 1.2). Well-mannered Hindus eat with freshly-washed hands from individual trays, but many American Indians dip into common bowls with unwashed hands. Some societies regard postprandial belching as good form; others as bad;

---

[5] The list of foods, presented in alphabetical order, consisted of barley, beef, chicken eggs, milk, and rice. The biological or nutritional evaluation of these foods is taken from R. J. Williams, *What to Do about Vitamins*, Norman, Oklahoma, 1945, pp. 50-54. I am indebted for this reference to my colleague, Professor James N. Spuhler.

Americans as variable. Among us babies are aided to burp; a belch in polite company is a matter for apology; but a loud reverberating belch may be a matter for prideful boasting in a group of masculine beer drinkers.

Extrabiologic attitudes toward food are well brought out in a consideration of prescribed forms of restraint. Many societies have differing schedules for taking meals, and individuals learn to adjust their wants to cultural norms. Virtually never, except for babies fed on demand, are the proper times for eating left to the cravings of individual appetites. No matter how ravenously hungry a well-bred American may be, it would never occur to him to rush into a kitchen and begin eating before a hostess was ready to serve. Similarly, in distant Tierra del Fuego, a half-starved Ona woman may be eager to pounce on a guanaco brought home from the chase by her husband, but etiquette prescribes a pause and a show of indifference before cooking operations may begin. Obviously, in all cases of this kind, symbolic, cultural values carry far more weight than the pangs of biological hunger. Much the same applies to matters of quantity. The amount that a person consumes is not always commensurate with his appetite or the needs of his body. Eating or abstaining out of politeness are very real habits.

An inspection of rules of etiquette in the case of food consumption, as well as in many other areas of human behavior, shows that they are expected to operate in the sphere of culture except as noted on page 15. The reason etiquette regulations are limited primarily to the realm of culture is that their values and procedures are symbolic and man-made. Accordingly, they are subject, at least in theory, to human control. Basic biological processes, by contrast, are unalterable and are not subject, even in theory, to man's complete control. Hence, rules of etiquette tend to be inoperative in matters of strict biology. From one social unit to another the *proportions* of biological and cultural features affecting man's interrelations with his environment may vary greatly, but it will always be found that there is some *combination* of the two elements in every manifestation of biocultural behavior. Never can cultural factors be expected to displace completely the workings of biology; and since the values assigned to extrasomatic items depend on the workings of algebraic mentalities, they can never achieve the fixity and predictability of the biologic.

That food habits are directly connected with other aspects of the

biocultural triangle may be readily shown. Eating together at cele-
brations like weddings always has strong sociologic implications,
and the feeling that no party can be successful unless food is served
is widespread. Perhaps a trifle less apparent, but equally common,
is the use of food as a symbol of social status. The positive aspect,
indulgence in luxury items that are not necessarily nutritious, is
well known to all, but fewer people are aware of a negative side,
conspicuous waste.[6] In our culture we look down on those who
serve portions rigidly measured to the number of diners. Covertly
we feel that more than exactly enough food ought to be offered.
A similar notion is carried to even greater extremes among the Tro-
briand Islanders who live near New Guinea. One of their principal
staples is the cultivated yam, and on occasion farmers display
heaps of yams, many of which form a surplus and will be allowed
to rot. Not only is this an expression of conspicuous waste, but it
is also a measure of social standing, for convention decrees that no
native may pile up as many yams as does the village chief.[7]

The manner in which all three segments of a biocultural triangle
are interconnected is further exemplified by the manifold religious
implications of food. Practically universal are the beliefs that some
substances may fittingly be offered to supernatural powers, usually
in the form of sacrifices, and that foods blessed by deities or religious officers have great extranutritional value for humans.

Almost all cultures, too, incorporate a religious notion that certain foods are prohibited or tabued to ordinary men and women.
Sometimes the prohibitions admit of no exceptions, and sometimes
they apply only at particular times or under special circumstances.
In our sophisticated society the existence of religious food tabus
frequently causes embarrassment. Because of the high cultural value
we ascribe to being rational and logical, many of our religious people are somewhat reluctant to admit that they subscribe to tabus
which have been aptly described as based on culturally standardized unreason. Accordingly, they make great efforts to rationalize
their beliefs. Some Christians maintain that Lenten prohibitions
reflect a time when it was dangerous to eat in spring foods that had
been stored from the preceding fall. Along similar lines there are

---

[6] As here used, the concept is modified from Veblen's original usage. See *The
Portable Veblen,* Max Lerner, editor, New York, 1948, p. 136.

[7] B. Malinowski, *Argonauts of the Western Pacific,* second impression, London,
1932, p. 61.

Orthodox Jews who argue that they do not eat pork because it may anciently have caused illness in hot countries. When viewed in the light of all the food tabus involved in the faiths mentioned, these explanations prove to be unsatisfactory. They do not explain why many Christians who eat meat regularly on Thursdays and Saturdays must abstain on Fridays, and they fail to throw light on the Jewish custom of allowing dairy products to be consumed immediately before meat but not directly after. Religious attitudes toward diet are extraordinary phenomena of culture and are not always brought into line with biology. Their persistence into the twentieth century serves to demonstrate how consistently man gives preference, short of inducing death, to cultural rather than biological values. At the same time the contradictions involved in so many of man's attitudes toward food show why it is necessary to think of each pattern of culture as maintaining a dynamic equilibrium between conflicting forces.

B. DWELLINGS AND OTHER STRUCTURES

Housing is another essential aspect of material culture that is part of man's interaction with his external surroundings. By learning to build and occupy houses, man lessened the need of making biological adjustments to the weather. To the extent that habitations keep out rain, frost, wind, and direct sunlight, they serve to stabilize the environmental conditions under which mankind must live. As is the case with all biocultural activities, different societies may erect different kinds of dwellings even if they happen to reside in an identical setting (Fig. 10.1). On a joint reservation in Arizona the Hopi Indians occupy rectangular dwellings of stone and adobe, traditionally clustered into communal pueblos, whereas the Navaho live in individual, dome-shaped structures made of heavy timbers and earth.[8] Cultural values always dictate which of a range of available materials a group will select for building, and there is no established rule that enables one to predict from the nature of a region the kinds of houses that its occupants will construct.

What is true of building materials is also true of architectural styles and household furnishings. Physical environments never com-

---

[8] For further information on variations of house types, see Beals and Hoijer, *op. cit.*, pp. 328-334; Chapple and Coon, *op. cit.*, pp. 104-110; and E. A. Hoebel, *Man in the Primitive World*, New York, 1949, pp. 115-130.

pel the use of a given shape or size, although they may impose limitations on the choice of substances employed. Anthropologists can show numerous illustrations of housing practices that, in terms of our logic, seem to make clever adjustments to their setting, but they can also point out examples of dwelling styles that appear to be out of keeping with their surroundings. Eskimo igloos are excel-

A   B

Fig. 10.1. Contrasting house types in one environment. In Arizona and New Mexico the stone and 'dobe terraced structures of the Pueblo Indians (A) contrast vividly with the timber and earth hogans of the neighboring Navaho (B).

lent adaptations, by our standards, to Arctic lands where snowfall is heavy, but the windbreaks of the Ona near Antarctica fail to keep out the bitter cold to which these people are subjected for many months of the year (Fig. 10.2). Occasionally, specific methods of building homes or of making furniture become so thoroughly identified with particular societies that minute details of construction may be used for tracing tribal movements or contacts.

In this connection cultural anthropologists usually call attention to use of the **false,** or **corbeled, arch** as opposed to the **true arch.** Corbeled arches, which may be used to enclose large, free spaces, are constructed by a system of overlaps, so that the sides stick out and serve as counterweights to the arch or vault. The need for sidewise projections makes a corbeled arch appear massive and clumsy, with a good deal of solid construction in relation to the area of free space. Corbeled arches presumably originated in the Copper-Bronze Age in Greece, and independently among the Maya Indians in the New World. From these centers the trait seems to have diffused widely.

A   B

Fig. 10.2. Contrasting house types in cold environments. The snow house (igloo) of the Arctic Eskimo (A) is very different from the Ona windbreak (B) in Antarctica. By our standards, the Eskimo house is infinitely more logical. (A. G. de Poncins, *Kabloona*. New York, 1941. Courtesy of Reynal & Hitchcock Co. B. Bureau of American Ethnology.)

True arches are built in such fashion that their parts are self-supporting, especially when a **keystone** has been slipped into place. They do not require massive counterweights at the sides, so that they can be slender and graceful. Mesopotamia is generally accepted as their place of origin in the Old World, and in the New World the principle of the true arch is found among some of the Eskimos, who managed to construct domed igloos without supporting scaffolds or counterweights.

Like houses themselves, certain aspects of home furnishings are institutionalized responses to physical forces. Even the most scantily furnished of dwellings are likely to contain cooking vessels, dishes, dining implements; chairs, stools, cushions, or mats; as well as beds or their equivalents. The first three items on this list reflect ways of meeting the pangs of hunger. The next set, on which people sit, kneel, squat, or recline when they want to rest (Fig. 10.3), are necessitated by the fact that the muscles involved when standing become strained and weary in time and achieve relaxation when a person lowers his body. As to beds, it is an observable fact that all normal human beings must sleep for a part of each day, although physiologists have not yet determined precisely why sleep is necessary. Simply because some aspects of household furnishings can be shown to satisfy biophysicochemical needs, it does not follow that all of them do. Esthetic, social, and religious considerations may likewise be important in this connection.

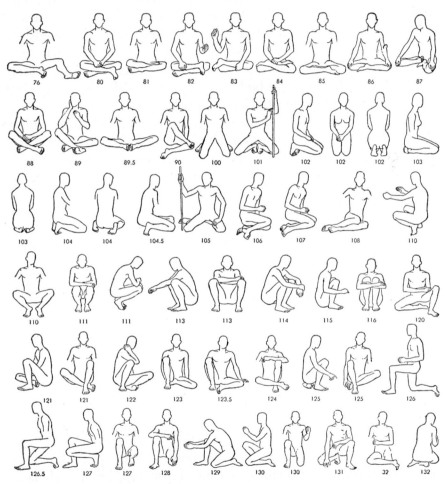

Fig. 10.3. The anthropology of posture. Resting customs indicate not only a variety of objects that are drawn originally from a group's physical setting but also a great diversity of culturally conditioned ways of holding the body. These are part of each society's motor habits. (From Gordon W. Hewes, "The Anthropology of Posture," *Scientific American*, Feb., 1957. Courtesy of the author and Scientific American.)

Structures that are meant for living quarters are found universally, but almost equally common are supplementary buildings devoted to other purposes. These, too, may vary in materials employed, methods of construction, elaboration or ornamentation, contents, size, and shape. Again, like residences, they may show varying degrees of compliance with the natural environment.

The clearest reflection of man's relations to his environment is to be found in the uses to which supplementary buildings are put. Commonest of all are those designed for storing surplus foods, tools and equipment, or materials to be used in manufacturing various things. Places for sheltering and feeding domesticated animals are widespread, and so, too, are working arrangements that may vary from mere covered platforms to elaborate factories. Less widely distributed, but very important on many Pacific islands, are distinct outbuildings for the preparation of meals.

As to the interactions of man to man with respect to secondary structures, the best examples are clubhouses of various kinds. Some are for the exclusive use of adult men, some are open only to members of a **secret society,** and others may be reserved for women. Special living quarters for unmarried warriors comprise an outstanding feature of Masai culture in East Africa, and large, communally maintained guesthouses are found regularly throughout Southeast Asia. It is often difficult to decide whether the functions of a building should be classified as social or religious. In a great many parts of the primitive world, females are expected to resort periodically to menstrual lodges, but this requirement is usually connected with a supernatural fear of blood. Sudatories or sweathouses are also very common, and their use generally has socioreligious implications.

More clearly religious in purpose are buildings in which major supernatural activities are regularly held. These may not be as elaborately constructed in primitive societies as are many churches, cathedrals, temples, synagogues, mosques, and shrines, but they serve much the same purpose. When they are not clearly differentiated from dwellings, observers unfamiliar with a particular culture may fail to recognize them as houses of worship, but members of a given society will ordinarily detect some bit of symbolism by which to identify them. Even when they are built with the same kinds of materials and along similar lines as homes, such places will be regarded as sacred because they are supposed to house

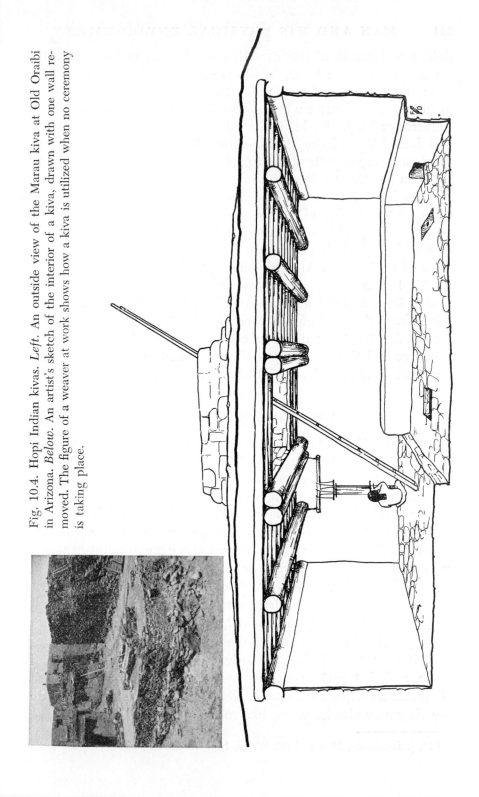

Fig. 10.4. Hopi Indian kivas. *Left.* An outside view of the Marau kiva at Old Oraibi in Arizona. *Below.* An artist's sketch of the interior of a kiva, drawn with one wall removed. The figure of a weaver at work shows how a kiva is utilized when no ceremony is taking place.

deities or because of the rites that are known to be held within them. On the other hand, buildings with primarily religious functions, like the **kivas** of the Pueblo Indians (Fig. 10.4), may be used as informal clubhouses when no rituals are in progress.

Professor M. J. Herskovits has also shown us how the structures and furnishings of the Bush-Negroes in Guiana, South America, touch on many aspects of their patterns of culture.[9] As he describes the situation, these natives live in rectangular, gabled houses, woven of palm-fronds. Each dwelling unit is part of a complex of structures, and a number of such complexes constitute a village. Doorposts of village elders are carved with symbolic designs, and men of wealth store their possessions in secondary buildings with open sides of latticework. All who please may look in, but only males related to the owner may enter, on pain of death from a potent charm. Even so brief a synopsis indicates ways in which materials taken from the environment are linked with social and religious factors. All structures and their correlated furnishings, especially in primitive societies, are likely to illustrate the ties that bind together the three sides of a biocultural triangle.

C. CLOTHES MAKE THE MAN

There was a time when the human habit of wearing clothing was unfailingly attributed to the promptings of comfort, modesty, the sex urge, or love of decoration. Then ethnologists began to report numerous instances of garments that were inadequate for comfort by our standards, that deliberately exposed body parts which Euro-Americans sought to conceal, or that appeared to Westerners hideous rather than ornamental. Examples also came to light of women who wore alluring garments or accessories, yet rejected the advances of all males. In many parts of the world a woman would be embarrassed to be seen without something, like a lip plug, that we might regard as largely ornamental, but would not feel ashamed at the exposure of what we call "private parts."

It is now agreed that the origins of clothing habits are obscure, and that various motives may prevail in different cultures. Garments sometimes are used to keep their wearers warm and dry, but they may also be worn, like summer furs, for purely symbolic

---

[9] M. J. Herskovits, *Man and His Works*, New York, 1948, pp. 217-220.

Fig. 10.5. Clothing customs among the Witoto. The Witoto Indians live in the tropical forest of the Amazon drainage. Men, women, and children all dress differently. On festive occasions, in particular, adult women use painted decorations in place of garments that conceal body parts. (Courtesy of Paul Fejos and Bureau of American Ethnology.)

reasons. Aboriginal Australians are occasionally said to betray deficient mentalities because they may wear too little for comfort even when thick pelts are available. With equal reason these natives might wonder about the mentality of Occidentals who wear far too much when it is almost unbearably hot.

Although human jaws, teeth, or hair may be worn (usually as ornaments) in many societies, the entire body of another person never serves as a complete garment. There is thus brought into play another aspect of man's relation to his physical setting. Plants and animals are always counted upon to supply needed materials. Nor should it be forgotten that all tools used in the making of clothing likewise originate in the natural environment.

Fig. 10.6. A Muslim bride. An Iranian bride is pictured in the costume typical of her status. She bears two lit candles that symbolize long life. (Courtesy Three Lions.)

Habits of dress never fail to have chronological and sociological connotations (Fig. 10.5). Sometimes these differences have demonstrable biological bases, but this is not always the case. The location of zippers toward the rear of skirts in our society rests on the fact that women's forearms are constructed anatomically differently from men's, so that they can more easily reach back; but biology fails to explain why skirts are worn by females in societies like ours, but by males in other areas, such as in parts of China or New Zealand. Makers of articles of clothing also tend to be of one sex or the other, and many of the body movements that distinguish males from females are associated with the making and wearing of different garbs. To an American, a man knitting dainty garments is always a comic figure.

Important distinctions of rank, wealth, occupation, and status are often expressed in wearing apparel (Fig. 10.6), ornaments, insignia, accessories, or hair styles. During the Copper-Bronze Age in Mesopotamia only priests were allowed to wear beards, and Buddhist religious officers always have shaven heads. Unmarried females among the Hopi traditionally had their hair done up in circular buns (**butterfly wings**) at the sides of the head; but married women wore their hair in two braids (Fig. 10.7).

Throughout Eastern Asia, fans and umbrellas of many kinds had marked sociocultural significance, and in Malaya a man felt improperly dressed without a dagger-like weapon conventionally known as a **kris.** Moreover, the kind of a kris, particularly its handle, gave an immediate clue to the wearer's status. Commoners had to be content with plain handles, but men of the upper classes went in for elaborate handles, featuring inlays of pearls, gold, or other precious materials. Possibly related to the Malay custom of wearing a kris was the Japanese tradition that permitted aristocratic warriors, **samurai,** to carry two swords. This privilege was so highly regarded that never did a samurai forget to carry his swords, and never did he carelessly put them aside. Commoners in old Japan were never allowed to wear swords.

Headgear often played an important role in setting apart one unit of society from another. In ancient China and Japan there were formal ceremonies, sometimes conducted by the Emperor in person, which granted honored people the right to wear a particular kind of hat or cap that showed where they stood in the social hierarchy. Americans are inclined to disregard the cultural impli-

A

Fig. 10.7. Hair styles of Hopi women. A. Girl with her hair in "butterfly wings," the coiffure worn by unmarried females. (Courtesy Bureau of American Ethnology.) B. Woman grinding corn. The two braids at the side of her head indicate that she is married. Her face is dark, presumably because it was smeared with purplish corn meal. The cut of her dress exposes her left shoulder and breast. (Courtesy American Museum of Natural History.)

B

cations of head coverings, but even so they associate mortarboards with academic titles, and graduates of nursing schools go through an impressive capping ceremony.

Study of clothing customs always leads an investigator into the field of supernaturalism. Religious officers customarily wear distinctive and often archaic garments when they are performing their rites, and lay worshipers often put on special clothes, such as the prayer-shawls of Orthodox Jewish men, while attending services. Quite commonly, religious symbols are worn as mute prayers by laymen, and Lumholtz once described the Tarahumara Indians of northern Mexico as being literally clothed in prayer.[10] Cultural conventions regularly prescribe gestures or body motions connected with wearing apparel during worship, as when Hindus or Moslems take off their shoes in sacred places, while Christian males bare their heads and Jewish men cover them. Such usages must be classed as nonlogical, for all attempts to rationalize them prove unconvincing except to members of the faith that practices them.

D. TECHNOLOGY

Industrial arts form a major portion of every society's **material culture.** Anthropologists generally study them under the heading of technology. Ingredients are so seldom drawn from the human body that the topic always becomes an integral part of any effort to understand man's relations to his environment. The commonest arts and crafts, in addition to those concerned with food, shelter, household furnishings, and clothing, are devoted to the manufacture of domestic utensils (including pottery and basketry containers), agricultural implements, weapons and cutting tools, and means of transportation.[11] Careful consideration of the materials used, working processes, correlated implements, and methods and styles of decoration provides a large body of factual data which cultural anthropologists find of the utmost importance for making comparative studies.[12]

Never does the technological aspect of a group's material culture stand by itself. Commonest of all sociologic connections is a di-

---

[10] C. Lumholtz, *Unknown Mexico*, New York, 1903, p. 827.

[11] Specific details on each of these topics may be found in the previously cited works by Chapple and Coon, Beals and Hoijer, and Hoebel.

[12] The most recent anthropological book that covers many aspects of this vast topic is G. Weltfish, *The Origins of Art*, Indianapolis, 1953.

vision of work between men and women, ordinarily described as **sexual dichotomy.** In practice this means that each society sets aside the teaching and performance of some occupations for males and reserves others for females. When these culturally assigned activities have been in operation for a long time, they come to be so intimately associated with a particular sex as to give the impression that they are biologically determined. Thus, in our society, we are inclined to think that women are better suited than men for sewing with needle and thread, baking cookies, dusting furniture, diapering babies, or nursing the sick. To whatever extent this may be true, it is much more likely the result of cultural conditioning than of biology. This may be seen from the number of men who are professional bakers, tailors, nurses, and valets; from the great changes of female occupations, without attendant changes of body structure or function, that have taken place in the last fifty years; and from the fact that the same pursuit may be feminine in one society and masculine in another. Surely, it is not because of anatomical differences that the making of bark cloth is the work of males in African Uganda but is left to females in the Polynesian Islands of the eastern Pacific. Except in terms of culture, it would be impossible to explain why the Hopi Indian men of northeastern Arizona weave rugs, dresses, and blankets, whereas all weaving among the neighboring Navaho is done by women (Fig. 10.8).

Sexual dichotomy has an effect on a group's way of life similar to that of specialization. It enables different people to devote themselves to different aspects of community living, and it demands cooperation if each sex is to benefit from the labors of the other. This helps to explain why technological and material considerations, rather than "love," are so often primary factors for the arrangement of marriages. As a Hopi Indian once said to a "white" bachelor who had just announced his forthcoming wedding, "Good. Now you'll have someone to cook for you."

In the case of all cultural phenomena, biological matters set definite limitations to the assignment of tasks for the two sexes. After all, it would be nonsensical to deny that only female bodies are capable of conceiving, bearing, and suckling infants; or that women alone are subject to menstruation, which in many societies is regarded with abhorrence and leads to the temporary withdrawal of females from their customary tasks. Because of inescapable physical facts, therefore, the duties of women tend to center about home and family, and rarely are women expected to roam as widely as men or to carry out the principal tasks on which the very life of a community depends. Even here, though, surprises sometimes await a Euro-American investigator. In a small number of societies, tasks that to us appear quite important, difficult, or burdensome are assigned to females, despite their occasional biologically determined infirmities.

Religious factors may also control a person's occupation. Shamans who practice curing because they are thought to have received a supernatural call are, as a rule, of one sex or the other in different societies. Even more to the point is the case of the Plains Indians

Fig. 10.8. Sexual dichotomy in weaving. Men are weavers among the Hopi, but women do all the weaving among the neighboring Navaho. (A. Courtesy of Chicago Natural History Museum. B. Courtesy Museum of Anthropology, University of Michigan.)

who used to inhabit the United States just east of the Rocky Mountains. Their young men were supposed to seek visions during which the spirits dictated their future careers. Every now and then a youth who was thoroughly masculine would find himself ordered to do the work of a woman. Such men were known as **berdaches.** Cases of this sort show that it is improbable that sexual dichotomy is based on anatomical factors. Instead, they establish a strong presumption that patterns of work, except in matters directly concerned with the biology of sex and reproduction, are determined on the basis of symbolic, cultural values.

E. WHAT MAN GIVES TO HIS ENVIRONMENT

So far, in this chapter, attention has been focused on what human beings draw from their physical setting, but a look at Fig. 8.6 will show that man's dealings with his environment are represented by a double arrow, indicating that man also gives things to the area about him. Ordinarily, what he gives most systematically consists of body wastes. All hominids must draw into their lungs great quantities of air that contains oxygen, and must exhale carbon dioxide, which the vegetation around them utilizes. Equally universal is the need to eliminate waste products, either as urine or feces. In most societies these substances are allowed to interact directly with the soil; but in Asiatic countries east of India, body wastes, euphemistically termed **night soil,** are utilized as fertilizer and are even placed directly on plants that later serve as food. Only a few Euro-American groups which have highly advanced technologies remove from bodily excretions all substances that are harmful to human beings before they are given to the environment.

Many differing cultural values may be associated with the act of elimination. Our society, which consistently ascribes the lowest of values to purely biological behavior on the part of humans, holds up as an ideal the separation of the sexes and privacy. Other societies may separate the sexes but show less regard for privacy. Still others may seem unconcerned on either score.

One must not jump to the conclusion that people who appear indifferent to urination or defecation are necessarily immodest. Anthropologists have learned to give due weight to what is known as **cultural blindness.** By this is meant any custom which induces people not to register or remember what their eyes see. Many a man in the primitive world observes a female in the act of elimination, but his brain records no apparent impression of what he has seen. In such cases, the phenomenon of cultural blindness may be just as effective for preserving modesty as are locked toilets. Incidentally, cultural blindness need not be restricted to the excretory process. In our society men whose eyes are perfectly sound are apt completely to forget what manner of clothes were worn by people whom they had seen only a few moments ago. Psychologists now recognize that human perception is not merely a matter of sound optics, but that it also involves the cultural conditioning and temperament of a viewer. No one in our culture would be greatly surprised to discover that a farmer and a business executive looked at the same bit of land in different terms.

Wastes eliminated from the body are by no means the only things that men and women give to their physical settings. Garbage, ashes, broken or discarded implements of all kinds, and the bodies of the dead are some of the other objects that people regularly donate, directly or indirectly, to the environments in which they live. Nor should we overlook the important fact that farmers, especially, are likely to add to a particular locality more water, insecticides, and soil nutrients than nature provides. All in all, it is easy to demonstrate that man takes many things from his setting but that he also gives other things to his environment in exchange.

SELECTED REFERENCES

Chapple, E. D. and Coon, C. S., *Principles of Anthropology*. New York, 1942.

Du Bois, C., "Attitudes Toward Food and Hunger in Alor," *Language, Culture, and Personality*, L. Spier, *et al.* eds. Menasha, Wis., 1941, pps. 272-281.

Forde, C. D., *Habitat, Economy, and Society*. New York, 1934.

Foster, G. M., "Relationships between Theoretical and Applied Anthropology: A Public Health Program Analysis," *Human Organization*, Vol. 11, 1952, pp. 5-16.

Gillin, J., "Moche: A Peruvian Coastal Community," *Smithsonian Institution, Institute of Social Anthropology*, No. 3. Washington, 1945.

Kroeber, A. L., *Anthropology*, rev. ed. New York, 1948, Chapter 12.

Mead, M., *Male and Female*. New York, 1949.

Morgan, L. H., "Houses and House Life of the American Aborigines," *Contributions to American Ethnology*, Vol. 4. Washington, 1881.

Richards, A. I., *Hunger and Work in a Savage Tribe*. London, 1932.

Sayce, R. U. *Primitive Arts and Crafts: An Introduction to the study of Material Culture*. Cambridge, England, 1933.

Singer, C. *et al.*, *A History of Technology*, Vol. 1. New York and London, 1954.

Williams, R. J., *What to do about Vitamins*. Norman, Okla., 1945.

11

CULTURE AND ENVIRONMENT

A. CULTURAL DETERMINANTS OF ENVIRONMENTAL USE

One of the most striking aspects of human behavior is man's universal unwillingness to deal with his external environment in purely biophysicochemical terms. Other animals when motivated by the force of hunger, let us say, interact directly with their physical settings to procure whatever biology tells them to eat (Fig. 11.1A). For *Homo sapiens*, considerations of biologic worth are not enough. Man never responds to the force of hunger by consuming everything nutritious in his territory. Wherever we choose to look, we find people utilizing only selected items from the region they inhabit, in accordance with the symbolic values that prevail in their society's way of life. Man, therefore, interposes a set of cultural institutions between any such biological force as hunger and the external environment which might satisfy it.

This kind of behavior may give hominids many satisfactions, but it may also endanger their existence. That is to say, culture may increase man's utilization of his environment under some circumstances (Fig. 11.1B); but it may, under other conditions, greatly restrict his use (Fig. 11.1C). Human beings, so far as is known, never eat raw grains or cereals. Accordingly, those aspects of agriculture that involve the growing of plants such as wheat or maize depend for their value on man's prior addition of controlled firemaking to his culture. Thereafter, cooking makes possible his use

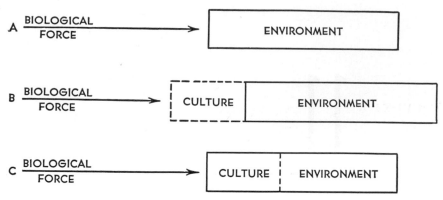

Fig. 11.1. Biology, culture, and environment. A. All infrahuman animals re-spond to certain biological forces, such as the pangs of hunger, by entering into direct relations with the environment. Man alone deals with his environment through a screen of culture. B. Sometimes cultural matters have the effect of enlarging his natural environment. In other cases, C, cultural factors, such as etiquette regulations or religious prohibitions, serve to reduce man's effective use of his environment.

of grains and cereals. Similarly, many tribes in the northern half of South America consume large quantities of a poisonous form of **manioc.** Only when the poison has been thoroughly squeezed out by a cultural device (Fig. 11.2) is this kind of manioc suitable for human consumption. These examples show how the adoption of culture may expand the worth of things that man gets from his surroundings. Nevertheless, to get a fully-rounded picture of the situation, one must give due recognition to the fact that symbolic, cultural values may also seriously curb man's use of his environment. That helps to explain why, if culturally approved meats are scarce and expensive in our society, it is pointless to urge a poor family to dine cheaply on rats that may be demonstrably clean and nour-ishing. We know very well that bread would be rejected among us if it were green and so crumbly that it could not be evenly sliced, even if it were scientifically established that such bread contained more food value than what we customarily consume.

Likewise, in regard to its clothing habits, no society is utterly indifferent to the materials used for making garments, quite apart from their biological effects on the wearer. Similar considerations apply to man's use of construction materials or resources needed for manufacturing.

To the extent that a pattern of culture restricts a group's utiliza-

Fig. 11.2. Manioc squeezer. With the help of cultural devices like these, many South American Indians are enabled to utilize a highly poisonous variety of manioc. This has the effect of making possible a greatly expanded use of the environment.

tion of its environment, it cuts down on what is available and thus creates a potential source of trouble. Many a traditional Chinese has starved to death in the presence of milch cows because his culture tabued the use of milk; and many a Hindu suffers from lack of meat within sight of a sacred cow.

From what has already been said on the subject of man's dealings with his environment it should be apparent that human beings never live in a world of bare physical objects. Everything about them may have a symbolic value. Invariably people learn to hold culturally standardized ideas about everything in their physical setting. Thus does it happen that every social unit makes the environment a part of its system of ideas. No outside observer can hope ever to understand thoroughly another group's ideology unless he becomes familiar with its cultural attitudes towards its external surroundings.

The existence of cultural ideas which direct a person's attitudes toward the world about him is only one of the essential ways in which *Homo sapiens* differs so widely from the rest of the animal kingdom. Just as significant is the lack of direct relationship between individual physique and treatment of the environment. A well-trained zoologist knows from an examination of a creature's anatomy whether it eats flesh or grasses, or lives in water or on land; but there is nothing in the structure of the human body that provides a clue to the details of man's interactions with his setting. No scientist of any kind can tell from examining a person's body if he is a vegetarian or a good swimmer. Furthermore, accurate knowledge of the activities of a single nonhuman creature affords an excellent clue to the behavior of the bulk of its entire species, but this is not true of human beings. Of course many animals show a degree of individuality, but in general they lack the wide choice of individual responses that culture has made possible for *Homo sapiens.*

B. SEX, AGE, SOCIOECONOMIC STATUS, AND LOCALE

Culturally approved ways of behaving are never exactly the same for all the individual members of a society. What is considered proper for the wealthy and powerful may well be regarded as improper for the poor and powerless. Nor are cultural values likely to remain unchanged throughout a person's life span. In homely language, it makes a world of difference if a child soils itself at nine months or nine years of age. Many an American parent does not hesitate to place a six-month-old daughter over his shoulder and to aid her to burp in the presence of onlookers; but who ever heard of assisting a sixteen-year-old girl to burp publicly? Except where simplification is essential, it is inaccurate to speak of a single pattern of culture that regulates the interactions with the environment of a total society. The major variables depend on a person's sex, age, socioeconomic status, and, in large societies, his place of residence. An example relating to dress should help to make the point clear.

If, with reference to American society, one were to say, "I know a thirty year-old mother who makes all the clothing that her five year-old daughter wears," the remark would cause little comment. How different the statement sounds, though, when we change some of the factors involved.

It is easy to imagine the amazed reaction of hearers to the remark that, "I know a thirty year-old father who makes all the clothing that his five year-old daughter wears." And the surprise of listeners would reach a peak if someone said, "I know a five year-old daughter who makes all the clothing that her thirty year-old mother wears."

This example indicates how likely it is that more than one way

of life prevails in any given society. It also shows that the human
utilization of environment is delimited not only by one overall set
of symbolic values, but by a number of value systems, each of which
may apply to the behavior of different persons. Rough parallels regarding behavioral differences for differing kinds of individuals are
not unknown in infrahuman societies, but they probably rest on
physical rather than biocultural distinctions.

An evolving society is likely to increase in numbers and expand
in territory. As the process continues, a tendency toward fragmentation arises, with the result that the male and female residents of
particular regions or neighborhoods form subgroups which may develop ways of life that can be designated as **subcultures.** If the
values of the subcultures are in agreement with those of the larger
culture within which they exist, no special difficulties need arise.
Unluckily, this is not always the case. Our culture frowns officially
on men who have many love affairs, but in some subgroups a man
who has "a way with women" may be esteemed and admired. Ideas
of this kind underlie our references to the right and wrong sides of
the railroad tracks.

It is when the symbolic values of a local subculture diverge
widely from those of the dominant way of life that trouble is most
likely to follow. Nudists and polygamists, for instance, may run
afoul of the law even when their behavior is perfectly acceptable in
their own communities. Many a person who lives up to the values
of his subculture finds himself arrested for failing to observe the
values of the greater society of which he is a part. The need of
reconciling over-all standards with those of subcultures is one of
the most troublesome problems in all large, modern societies.

Hardly anything gives more point to the existence of numerous
subcultures within the confines of a single society than consideration of **statuses** and **roles.** Most peoples are inclined to rank their
members on a scale of some sort, giving high status to certain individuals and low to others. As the late Professor Linton has pointed
out, status may be **ascribed,** or **automatic,** or else it may be
achieved. Typical of the former are those cases in which a person
is born as a noble or an aristocrat. Indicative of the latter are self-
made men and women.

With each status, whether it be ascribed or achieved, goes a
fixed way of behaving that Professor Linton has termed a role. Unless a person acts in the manner considered proper for his status,

his rank in a society may go unrecognized. Nor is the behavior unrelated to objects originally drawn from a society's external environment. People of high status are expected to dress and eat differently from those of low, to dwell in different kinds of houses or neighborhoods, and to carry or wear distinctive objects or insignia. As Professor Herskovits tells us, an aristocratic Dahomean from West Africa was distinguished from an inferior by the facts that he wore sandals, walked in the shade of an umbrella, smoked a long pipe, and proudly handled his great toga-like cloth and wand of office.[1] It is probably safe to say that even within the limits of a single society different patterns of culture, often involving different interactions with the physical setting, apply to those who have high or low status.

We can even go a step further. Each adult, regardless of his status, is usually expected to play a variety of roles in his society. A man may be a warrior at one time, a husband at another, and a farmer at a third. Seldom does a grownup find it hard to slip quickly from one role to another. In fact, we are likely to poke fun at a person who cannot readily change his behavior to suit changing circumstances. We find it amusing when a professional baseball player tries to maintain professional standards while playing "catch" with a young son, and we ridicule a college professor who "lectures" to his wife. We do not expect inflexibility of behavior in a normal human being.

As a general rule, the higher a person's status the less likely is he to exert much muscular energy, particularly in his dealings with the environment. Chinese gentlemen of old cultivated exceedingly long fingernails to show that they never had to work hard with their hands. We, too, differentiate between manual laborers and white-collar workers. In keeping with the human policy of holding in low esteem whatever savors of animal biology, we give small salaries and assign low status, in the vast majority of cases, to those whose occupations call for purely physical exertions.

If a group of people share similar statuses they form a **class.** Ordinarily a class implies a degree of **sociocultural mobility,** which means that a person can somehow achieve the status of a class different from the one into which he was born. A class thereby differs from a **caste,** which usually has fixed boundaries that cannot be crossed after birth. As we know it from India, whose caste system

---

[1] M. J. Herskovits, *Man and His Works,* New York, 1948, p. 210.

has been best described, a person who is born in a caste must stay within it for life, marry another member of the same caste, and practice only the occupation that his caste has traditionally followed. Proponents of this social arrangement argue that it is a good thing because craftsmen who follow the same pursuits for generations develop into fine specialists and because it reduces unrest and competition by ordering society so rigidly that "everyone knows his place." Opponents counter that competition is a good thing, that some occupations, like sweeping, do not require lengthy apprenticeship, and that many previously unknown or new pursuits cannot be reconciled with traditionally assigned tasks. Under modern conditions of rapid technological change the caste system is breaking down in many parts of India.

C. CULTURE AREAS

Long before the variability of any group's way of life was adequately recognized, many anthropologists, particularly in America, used to divide the world into a number of **culture areas.** Such classifications were originally made to enable museum visitors to envision, with the help of native specimens, how different peoples lived in various portions of the globe. Arrangements of this kind generally rested on the expressed or implied assumption that people living in a single environmental zone would develop distinctive ways of life,[2] or, conversely, that no culture pattern could succeed if it failed to utilize the materials provided by its immediate setting. Assuredly, one would have to search far and wide to find examples of people who refused to interact, more or less directly, with the natural habitats in which they lived. No wooden houses are likely to be built in a region where timber is unavailable. It is certainly true that many customs appear alike in one part of a continent but change markedly as one turns to a distant region; yet, modern anthropologists feel that the generalizations involved in the culture area concept are too broad to be useful except for very limited purposes. Members of many societies may use identical or

---

[2] The best available treatment of this aspect of the topic may be found in A. L. Kroeber, "Cultural and Natural Areas of Native North America," *University of California Publications in American Archaeology and Ethnology,* Vol. 38, 1939. It must not be thought that Kroeber is simply an economic or environmental determinist of the type that believes a given setting inevitably produces a given way of life. Clark Wissler, *The American Indian,* rev. ed., New York, 1938, is generally credited with having originated the concept of culture areas.

nearly identical environments in greatly varying ways, and, sometimes, remarkably similar things are found among people who dwell in vastly different settings. Another important criticism rests on the difficulty of establishing precise lines of demarcation that show where one environmental region ends and another begins.

Some anthropologists used to establish culture areas primarily but not always entirely on the basis of single items, such as the principal food-getting techniques or house types that prevailed in various spots (Fig. 11.3).[3] Once more, it would be hard to deny that the environment sets limits on what a society can utilize for food and related requirements. Certainly, it would be ridiculous to expect desert dwellers to try to live on fish. Nonetheless, the principle of culture areas is today used very cautiously because it underemphasizes the ingenious ways in which people may select different things from similar settings and because it fails to take into account the important part played by adherence to varying sets of symbolic values.

At the time when the concept of culture areas loomed large in the thinking of many American cultural anthropologists, efforts were occasionally made to derive the relative ages of various traits from their distribution within or between the culture areas in which they were found. Generally speaking, the assumption was made that each item of culture originated in one spot or center and then spread to the periphery. On this basis it was assumed that a trait was older in its place of origin and more recent elsewhere. This method of analysis, occasionally known as the *age-area* concept, has fallen into relative disuse because it is often difficult to determine where a given cultural item originated, because the centers and peripheries of assorted culture areas are far from clear, because it is now believed that archaic forms of a trait may sometimes be carried to the margins of an area, where they may persist long after they have been abandoned at the center, and because of the possibility that two virtually identical items might have been produced as independent inventions at two widely scattered spots. A further problem arises from the difficulty of determining whether a complicated cultural activity like farming should be treated as a single thing or as a **trait complex.** Also, under the heading of **stimulus diffusion,** Professor Kroeber has discussed the possibility that

---

[3] *The American Indian,* by Clark Wissler, rev. ed., New York, 1938, exemplifies this approach very well.

an idea may be diffused from one zone to another, but that it might be expressed in entirely different forms in the two regions concerned. It would be impossible in the light of Kroeber's illustrations to deny that stimulating ideas can spread as well as can material objects, but where the same concept gives rise to two or more different things it is extremely hard to trace what has actually spread from one place to another. A further difficulty arises from the fact that nonmaterial traits may have a vastly different distribution

INDIAN HOUSES
AND TEMPLES

Fig. 11.3. Areal distribution of structures in the aboriginal New World. Many diverse kinds of structure were built in pre-Columbian times in various regions or areas of the Americas.

from material items which are thought to have spread from the same source.

For all the criticisms that may currently be leveled against it, the culture-area approach was a useful construct when it was first developed. Not only did it make possible the orderly arrangement of much heterogeneous material that had previously remained unorganized, but it also served to draw attention to the basic fact that human societies cannot endure unless they enter into successful relationships with their external environments. More than one contemporary student of culture is of the opinion that exploitation of the environment, particularly in terms of the food quest, may be a major factor in the development of human societies. Some would even go so far as to say that friendly relationships, such as the sharing of food or other goods with non-kindred, has led to the formation of ever-larger political aggregates. We believe so firmly at present in the interrelationship of levels of technology and levels of social organization that we expect to find only small bands with rudimentary forms of material culture occupying a sparse region. Never do we find large empires under these conditions. Moreover, if the members of two societies live in similar environments and follow similar pursuits with similar tools, they are likely to worship similar deities. All of this implies that within the limits of any given culture area one is likely to find only a restricted number of biocultural configurations.

Archeologists, as well as some ethnologists, still utilize the culture-area concept, but in modified form. They customarily think in terms of **phases** arranged in chronological order to show evolutionary trends, if one phase is thought to have grown out of an earlier one. Among contemporary American archeologists there is much talk, also, of **co-traditions.** Co-traditions refer to the shared relationships to be found, through time, between entire phases or whole cultures, rather than between single elements. As is to be expected, one cultural continuum, with each phase growing out of the preceding one, is most likely to be found within the limits of one culture area. However, archeologists caution us that it is possible for people with a given cultural tradition to migrate from one culture area to another.[4]

As a general evolutionary rule to which, admittedly, a few excep-

---

[4] A fuller discussion of this point may be found in I. Rouse, "Culture Area and Co-Tradition," *Southwestern Journal of Anthropology*, Vol. 13, No. 2, 1957.

tions can be found, the lower a people's technology the smaller will be the number of men and women who habitually live together in societies; the more directly and biologically will individuals interact with their environment; the less specialization of occupations will there be; and the greater will be the proportion of time that the total membership devotes to the stark business of getting enough to eat.

The concept of **territoriality,** which may some day turn out to be closely related to the notion of culture areas, has of late been given serious consideration by a number of biologists. They have found that fish, reptiles, birds, and many kinds of mammals show **territorial** behavior. In most cases, this is connected with the driving off of intruders, even of the same species, if they are judged to be rivals of the occupants in securing food or sex partners. As to Primates, they too show many features of territoriality, according to Dr. C. R. Carpenter, who has studied howler monkey life in Panama. The concept of living a certain way in a particular region seems to be so basic to many animals that something resembling the culture-area notion has been postulated for the forerunners of *Homo sapiens.*[5]

D. MOTOR HABITS

One of the most intriguing approaches for studying the interplay of individual and group behavior, as well as cultural conditioning and relationships with the environment, lies in the field of **motor habits.** This phrase refers to any customarily repeated movements of parts of the body that are much alike for all members of a social unit, and often has reference to the ways in which the people of a particular society manipulate their physical settings or else to the accustomed manner of handling objects or materials that were drawn, originally, from a group's external surroundings (Fig. 11.4). Motor habits may pertain to the way in which adults employ tools, roll cigarettes, grasp the handle of a tea kettle, use a knife and fork, or sit on a sheepskin stretched on the ground. Some writers think that gestures and facial expressions may belong in the same category. To illustrate only a few of these items, American woodworkers push planes away from their bodies, but Far Eastern carpenters pull planes

---

[5] M. Bates, *The Prevalence of People,* New York, 1955.

A

B

Fig. 11.4. Motor habits and sexual dichotomy. A. In India the task of carrying bricks is assigned to women, who balance loads of bricks on their heads. B. In the United States bricks are carried by men. Formerly, bricks were put into hods that were placed on the shoulder. The different methods used for handling objects that originated in the physical environment illustrate divergences of motor habits and sexual dichotomy.

toward them; all Hopi Indians roll cigarettes by moving the thumbs upward, but Navahos turn their thumbs down; Americans pick up and pour from a tea kettle with the palm down, but Japanese grasp and use it with the palm up; and residents of India mean "yes" when they shake their heads halfway in the manner that Euro-Americans use to signify the negative. In some parts of Italy people are summoned by moving the fingers with the palm out, much as when we wave good-bye; but in other parts of the same country folks are called by using the hand with the palm in, just as we do.

Motor habits are usually different for each sex in a given society or subculture. This is connected with sexual dichotomy. As men and women are taught to deal differently with their environments, they learn to use their bodies in different ways. In some cases the motor habits that distinguish the sexes are outgrowths of biology, but often they are not. Biology may dictate that only women must learn all the actions that go with the nursing of babies, but there is nothing in the biology of sex that forces women to wash dishes. There are far too many educated people who fail to take account of the difference between biologically determined and culturally as-signed activities.

An adult who may be eager to change his accustomed way of life by adopting an entirely new culture often finds that acquisition of correct motor habits gives him more trouble than anything else. In times of war, spies who could otherwise pass for enemy nationals are likely to give themselves away by mistakes in motor habits. We usually look quite awkward when we try to eat with chopsticks, but most Far Easterners are clumsy when they try to eat with knives and forks. Only those who have made a detailed pursuit of this fascinating topic are aware of the extent to which seemingly individual body movements turn out to be standardized within the limits of particular patterns of culture.[6]

Dr. Gregory Bateson and Dr. Margaret Mead have made many studies and interpretations of the way in which various peoples move and use their bodies.[7] Dr. Mead even believes that it is pos-sible to identify different patterns of culture by analyzing single activities, such as the bathing of babies (Fig. 11.5). Along similar lines, Professor Gordon W. Hewes has made investigations all over

---

[6] Many further details may be found in W. LaBarre, "The Cultural Basis of Emo-tions and Gestures," *Journal of Personality*, Vol. 16, 1947, pp. 49-68.

[7] See, for example, G. Bateson and M. Mead, *Balinese Character*, New York, 1950.

Fig. 11.5. Bathing a baby in New Guinea. The manner in which parents handle a baby while it is being bathed is often standardized for an entire tribe. In this way motor habits may provide a clue to a group's identity. (Courtesy of Asia Press.)

the world of what he calls "the anthropology of posture." He regards the ways in which men and women hold and utilize their bodies to be biocultural activities, compounded of human anatomy and culture (Fig. 10.3). Many rugged individualists are amazed, when shown pictures of the motor habits that prevail in their societies, to discover how culture-bound they really are.

E. CULTURAL MODIFICATIONS OF ENVIRONMENT

Statements are sometimes made to the effect that a society's environment remains stable except under extraordinary conditions. This cannot be true if people are constantly interacting with their settings. Quite apart from drastic shifts that may be brought about by such nonhuman agencies as temperature and rainfall fluctuations, volcanic eruptions, floods, droughts, and erosion, there are a number of environmental changes that can be traced to cultural activities. In fact, it may be stated as a general rule that the more advanced is a group's technology, the greater are the alterations of physical setting that will be made. Thus, gatherers, hunters, and fishers make relatively few lasting changes in their environment; farmers and herders make more; and highly industrialized societies make the most.[8] Careless plant-gathering practices, indiscriminate use of grazing grounds, and large-scale mining operations are some of the ways that man may interact with his environment to bring about changes that may be detrimental to his future welfare.

There are also other cases wherein a society's whole way of life is affected by its interactions with its environment. The best known of such instances are those in which farming methods so exhaust the soil that people are forced to move periodically and so to become what cultural anthropologists call **shifting cultivators.** Likewise, settled communities which depend on wood for fuel, house construction, and other purposes, always face a critical situation when nearby sources of timber become depleted. The Iroquois-speaking Indians who lived east of the Appalachian Mountains provide a case in point. Although they used to inhabit permanent settlements, they were in the habit of moving their villages approximately every twenty years, in order to get closer to a forest. Indeed, when they first made contact with European colonists, they are said to have asked if these had come to a strange country because they had run out of wood in their homelands.

There is still another kind of interplay between culture and environment, by means of which certain unchanging features of a landscape may achieve a greatly altered significance through the agency of a group's level of culture. Let us suppose that a steep mountain peak, eight thousand feet high, stands midway between two communities. As long as the two settlements have no means of land travel except foot, the peak imposes a well-nigh insurmountable barrier to intercourse between them. If a road comes to be built over the mountain and animal-drawn conveyances or riding horses become available, the barrier grows less insurmountable. With the advent of power-driven vehicles, the difficulties of communication dwindle still more; and for those who can use up-to-date aircraft, an eight-thousand-foot peak is no obstacle at all.

What is true of mountains likewise applies to oceans, wide streams, broad deserts, and dense jungles. In each case, the environmental feature may remain exactly as it was, but its functional significance will vary with different stages of culture. The ultimate

---

[8] This subject has been comprehensively treated in W. L. Thomas, Jr., ed., *Man's Role in Changing the Face of the Earth*, Chicago, 1956.

effect is the same as if it were the landmark itself that had changed. That is what is really meant when people speak of the shrinking of the present globe or when Americans refer to the dwindling of the oceans that separate them from the Old World. From a long-range point of view it is a mistake for a cultural anthropologist to treat any environment with which human beings interact as if it were static rather than dynamic.

SELECTED REFERENCES

Bates, M., *The Prevalence of People.* New York, 1955.

Bateson, G., and Mead, M., *Balinese Character.* New York, 1950.

Hewes, G. W., "The Anthropology of Posture," *Scientific American,* Vol. 196, No. 2, 1957.

Hoebel, E. A., "The Nature of Culture," in *Man, Culture, and Society,* H. L. Shapiro, ed., Ch. 7. New York, 1956.

Kroeber, A. L., "Cultural and Natural Areas of Native North America," *University of California Publications in American Archaeology and Ethnology,* Vol. 38, 1939.

La Barre, W., "The Cultural Basis of Emotions and Gestures," *Journal of Personality,* Vol. 16, 1947, pp. 49-68.

Linton, R., *The Study of Man,* Ch. 8. New York, 1936.

Rouse, A. I., "Culture Area and Co-Tradition," *Southwestern Journal of Anthropology,* Vol. 13, No. 2, 1957.

Thomas, W. L., Jr., ed., *Man's Role in Changing the Face of the Earth.* Chicago, 1956.

Wissler, C., *The American Indian,* rev. ed. New York, 1938.

CHAPTER 12

INTERPERSONAL RELATIONS

A. A CHILD IS BORN

The second leg of our biocultural triangle (Fig. 8.6) is devoted to the relations that exist between a man and his fellows who live in the same society.[1] This is just as essential a part of any group's way of life as is the need for people to interact with their environments, and it, too, has undeniable biologic foundations. Once again, the genetically inherited forces that impel each person to deal with others are invariably channeled by each society into cultural institutions which are valued as good, whereas violations are branded as bad. Relationships between human beings, therefore, are truly biocultural; and when they are institutionalized they may serve as guides to conduct either for particular individuals, such as a chief, or for groups of people, such as all fathers or all mothers.

Barring the restricted possibilities of artificial insemination, adoption, or the recruitment of new members from the outside, a society can perpetuate itself indefinitely only through the continuous operation of sexual reproduction. Consequently, each social unit's pattern of culture must make adequate provision for the birth of children among its members. Every normal female, regardless of whether she is an opera singer, waitress, stenographer, or professional athlete,

---

[1] As used by anthropologists, man is synonymous with *Homo sapiens* and includes representatives of both sexes. This has given rise to the oldest joke in the profession—a definition of anthropology as "the science of man, embracing woman."

is a potential mother, and every normal male is a potential father. Just the same, no society is content to leave the bearing of offspring to chance or to the powerful urgings of sheer biology. A balance is always struck between the total range of a group's potential for begetting and bearing offspring and a set of cultural restrictions on parenthood. This is the way in which having babies becomes a biocultural phenomenon in all human societies. Popular writers sometimes make sensational references to widespread sexual promiscuity among native peoples, but cultural anthropologists have never found a group whose way of life permitted completely unregulated relations between the sexes.

What they do find is a widespread difference of moral values or standards. Some tribes allow a great deal of premarital license; others insist on prenuptial virginity, especially for girls. Some demand that cousins must marry; others forbid such unions. There is no uniformity of symbolic attitudes toward mating among mankind, but some features are universal. All societies distinguish socially permissible marital relations from other forms of sexual activity, all have culturally based preferences for the selection of proper mates, and all specifically forbid cohabitation between certain individuals. The most widespread of all prohibitions, **incest regulations,** are designed to prevent intercourse between parents and their children and between **siblings** (brothers and sisters). Historically, only Peru, Egypt, and Hawaii apparently permitted some brothers and sisters to mate and have offspring, but even in these places permission was not granted to the entire society. Instead, it was limited to members of ruling families. Cultural anthropologists are unable to explain in full detail how incest rules first arose, but they can show that they are cultural rather than biological in character. Again and again, people who happen to be unaware of their relationship may be attracted to one another and engage in copulation, only to be overwhelmed with shame and dread if they later discover that they are close kin. If the horror of incest were truly biological, forbidden unions could scarcely take place and there would be little need of cultural regulations to prevent them.

Marriages may be encouraged or prohibited on many grounds. Almost anything—kinship, race, religion, economic status, degree of education, place of residence, or occupation—can be used as a basis for discriminating for or against the choice of mates. When cultural anthropologists describe a custom that compels people to marry within a given unit, they call it **endogamy,** whereas a rule that forces individuals to find spouses outside a particular group is known as **exogamy.** These terms may apply to a total society or to any of its subdivisions. In Western societies most marriages are **endogamous** with respect to nationality and religious affiliation, but **exogamous** in regard to the family circle.

So many diverse forms of approved cohabitation are known that anthropologists have trouble in agreeing on a single definition of marriage. Most widely accepted, at the present moment, is a statement to the effect that marriage consists of the sanctioned union of one or more men with one or more women. Implied in such a definition, but not directly expressed, is the added fact that any children born of such a union will be recognized as "legitimate" and will be entitled to the care and training that will fit them to live in the society where they were born. Looked at in this way we find that throughout the world wedding regulations are designed not only to direct sexual activities into culturally approved channels, but also to encourage the propagation and rearing of children. The long-drawn-out helplessness of human infants is an inescapable fact and parents, particularly mothers, are everywhere charged with the responsibility of caring for babies at least until they can look out for themselves. If no parent is available a substitute, or **surrogate,** must be provided. In the words used by an Araucanian Indian from central Chile when we were discussing the problem of getting wetnurses for an orphan, "Nohow will they let the baby starve!"

Scientists have not yet determined the proper classification of the craving for offspring. As far as an individual is concerned, it may very likely be due to a combination of biological, psychological, and cultural elements, and in primitive societies sterile couples are particularly apt to be unhappy and to seek natural and supernatural help. But apart from anyone's private desires there is also the interest of society as a whole. Society never allows parents to do away with their children just as they please, and punishment is generally greater for one who illegally subtracts a person from a social group than for one who adds a member to it, no matter how disapproved may be the manner of propagation. Openly or tacitly, every social unit is pleased when children are born to its members although

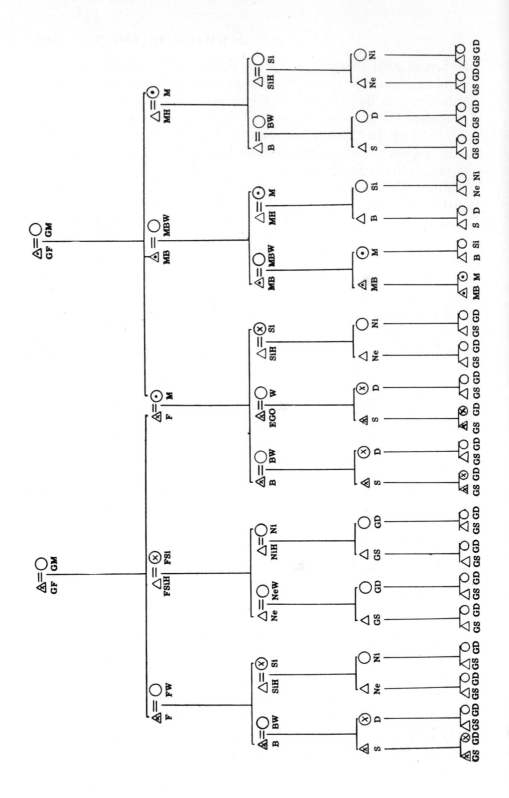

under special conditions, usually involving shortages of food, **infanticide,** the killing of babies, may be allowed.

B. SYSTEMS OF RECKONING KINDRED

As was pointed out in the preceding section, marriage regulations almost universally forbid certain kin to mate, and they quite often prescribe the union of other relatives. Wedding rules and methods of reckoning kindred are thus seen to be closely associated and to be basic to every society. An anthropological convention divides ways of naming relatives into **descriptive** and **classificatory** categories. Descriptive systems, like ours, are supposed to use a separate term for designating each particular relative, usually in the direct line of one's descent, such as his father or mother. Classificatory arrangements never restrict the use of a term to a single individual, but unfailingly employ one term to designate a class or group of persons, some of whom are lineal kin and others collateral. Thus, for example, the term for father might be applied both to one's father, and also to the father's brothers. Even if we grant that there is usually some overlap between the two methods,[2] it is still true that Occidental societies show a strong tendency to use descriptive terminology, while primitive groups reveal a marked preference for classificatory systems.

The manner in which a society identifies and labels relatives is an integral part of its **kinship system** and can readily be diagrammed as a sort of genealogical table (Fig. 12.1). Because each person is

---

[2] Professor Kroeber years ago drew attention to the fact that we group several different individuals under the designations of aunt or uncle, and that as many as 32 different persons may be called cousin. See A. L. Kroeber, "Classificatory systems of relationship," *Journal of the Royal Anthropological Institute,* Vol. 39, 1909, pp. 77-84.

Fig. 12.1. The Omaha kinship system. In this figure and the ones immediately following, the triangle stands for a male, the circle for a female, the equal sign for a marriage, and a vertical line for descent. The letters represent English words, so that "F" is for father, "Si" for sister, "MBW" for mother's brother's wife, "Ne" for nephew, "Ni" for niece, etc. An x designates members of *Ego's* own clan, and a dot indicates members of *Ego's* mother's clan. The Omaha system is associated with patrilineal clans or strong patrilineal emphasis. *Ego's* father and *Ego's* father's brother are merged, but *Ego's* mother's brother is differentiated by a separate term. *Ego's* mother's brother's male descendants are merged under a single term, thus overriding generation levels.

variously related to a number of people, as when I call "uncle" the selfsame man that my father calls "brother," cultural anthropologists find it essential to present each kinship system from the viewpoint of one particular individual. This personage is labeled **Ego** and customarily represents an average, adult male.

People in Euro-American societies generally trace kinship **bilaterally,** through the mother's and father's lines alike, but in a great many primitive cultures relationships are reckoned **unilaterally,** or **unilineally,** by way of one parent or the other. Where kinship is unilaterally counted only through males, the kinfolk make up a **patrilineal clan,** or **gens;** where kinship is unilaterally reckoned only through females, the relatives comprise a **matrilineal clan,** or **sib.** A clan may be defined as a named group of relatives who trace their descent in one sex line from a common ancestor or ancestress. All clanmates are taught to believe that they have a common ancestry, even when their supposedly shared lines of descent cannot be genealogically established. Clans are sometimes found to be subdivided into **lineages** (Fig. 12.2). A lineage may be described as a segment of a clan, between whose members informants believe actually demonstrable ties of descent do exist. Occasionally trouble arises in trying to separate a clan into its component lineages. This may happen when a field worker has decided that a certain clan contains two distinct lineages headed, let us say, by two presumably

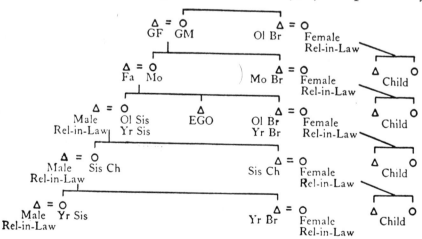

Fig. 12.2. A Hopi (Crow) lineage. The diagram shows his mother's matrilineal lineage, from the viewpoint of a male *Ego*. All members of *Ego*'s own clan and lineage are connected by short, vertical lines that indicate descent ties. (Courtesy of Fred Eggan.)

unrelated individuals, x and y. If, on the basis of later information, it develops that x and y are really siblings and have the same parents, a clan that was once said to have two lineages would turn out to be composed, in actuality, of a single lineage. Despite the danger of such confusions, anthropologists generally try to distinguish lineages from clans, because in some societies lineages are plainly recognized and in others a clan honor or object may be found to be transmitted not within the entire clan but within only a particular segment or lineage of it.

Since they are believed to be descended from the same personage, lineage or **clanmates** are usually regarded as brothers and sisters and are forbidden to intermarry. As a rule, their line is supposed to have been established at some time in the dim past when their original founder mated or had an intimate experience with a supernatural personage, plant, animal, object, or celestial body—ordinarily but not invariably identified as a **totem**—whose name the clan bears, and with which it feels itself intimately connected. This connection may be expressed by a symbolic design that may be used only by members of the appropriate clan, or else it may be emphasized by rituals intended to increase the numbers of the totem, or by tabus forbidding **clansfolk** to injure, kill, or eat representatives of their totem. By way of a concrete example, the members of a Rabbit clan may not marry one another, may look upon rabbits as siblings, perform ceremonies for the multiplication of rabbits, wear rabbit designs, abstain from rabbit hunts, mourn slain rabbits, and refuse to eat rabbit meat. In some cases clans may also have religious, political, or economic attributes, such as owning in common lands, houses, ceremonies, or rights to chieftainship.

As for clan methods of designating kindred, two principal variants are widely recognized. Patrilineal clans that have separate terms for mother's brother and father's brother, but which unite under a single label mother's brother, mother's brother's son, mother's brother's son's son, and so forth, are said to use the **Omaha** system (Fig. 12.1). Matrilineal clans that distinguish mother's sister from father's sister, but which group together the father's sister and her feminine descendants through females (Fig. 12.3), are said to use the **Crow** system.[3] In each of these instances, students must come

---

[3] Kinship terminology is called **bifurcate-merging** when some relatives are clearly set apart while others are grouped together. For much additional information on all the points treated in this chapter, see R. H. Lowie, *Social Organization*, New York, 1948.

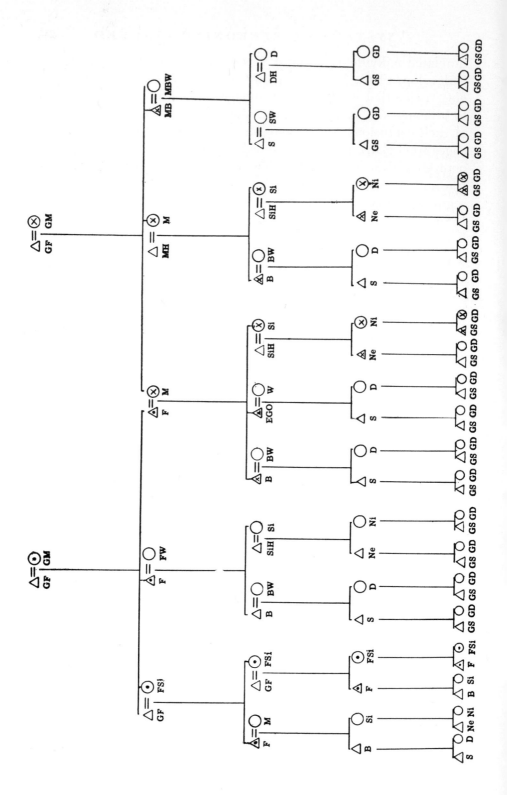

to realize, the lines that set some of the generation levels apart are occasionally disregarded in the terminology. There are thus at least two features common to classificatory forms of kinship nomenclature that are not found in ours. An adult *Ego* may find himself with a whole cluster of fathers, mothers, and grandparents; and some of these may be mere infants.

To a cultural anthropologist from a Western society on his first field trip, it comes as a shock to have an adult point out a small child as his father or grandfather, but this is a logical outgrowth of any kinship system that disregards generation lines. Similarly, it strikes us as incredible that a grown man should not know the identity of his real mother, but in certain of the classificatory arrangements under discussion no distinction in terminology need be made between the mother and her sisters. The result is that the women whom we call mother and aunts may become confused in a number of primitive societies. Whatever complexities may arise from such usages are compensated by the ease with which surrogates take over the functions of a missing parent. A child who has learned to call and regard as mothers many women is very likely to accept one of them as a true parent in the event of the death or loss of his natural mother.

Broadly speaking, the easiest way to grasp the workings of any clan system of kinship nomenclature, not only those that employ Omaha or Crow terminology, is to start with the premise that within a clan all persons of the same sex and approximate generation are identically designated. Where such practices exist *Ego* is likely to call his father and all of his father's brothers, "father"; his mother and all of her sisters, "mother"; his own agemates, "brothers and sisters"; and their offspring, "children." There are numerous variations of the basic clan method of labeling relatives, but their type names and distinctive characteristics may safely be left to specialists.

In many instances, a number of clans are found combined into larger groupings known as **phratries.** As a rule, a **phratry** may be de-

---

Fig. 12.3. The Crow kinship system. This is found associated with matrilineal clans or wherever a society has a strong matrilineal emphasis. *Ego*'s father's sister is distinguished from his mother's sister, but all *Ego*'s father's sister's female descendants are merged in the terminology, thereby disregarding generation lines.

fined as an unnamed exogamic unit consisting of two or more clans. Quite often, but not always, the members of a phratry share all the rights and obligations of their constituent clans. The earliest student of primitive kinship, Lewis H. Morgan, believed that phratries arose from the segmentation of clans either as a result of migrations or through the pressure of numbers. On the basis of his own field work, the writer inclines to Morgan's point of view. The late Professor Robert H. Lowie, on the other hand, who was a very astute student of the topic, favored the concept that phratries arose when originally unrelated clans merged for some purpose such as the carrying out of a ceremonial obligation. In either case, the definition of a phratry holds good as given.

If an entire tribe is divided into two parts, each of which is generally exogamous, each half is called a **moiety.** A moiety may thus consist of a number of phratries or else of a multiplicity of clans and their component lineages.

Kinship terms may be used in direct address, as when we say, "Father, I want to tell you something." They may also be used for reference, as when we say to a third party, "I told something to my father." Another usage, rare among us but often found in primitive societies, is called **teknonymy.** Teknonymy means that a person is identified by stating his relationship to someone else. So a wife might inquire for her husband by asking, "Where is my son's father?" Or a little boy might say, "I'm going to play with Jane's younger brother."

More than one system of kinship nomenclature may operate simultaneously. Men in the United States regularly apply the term "brother" to a male sibling, to a fellow member of a fraternity, and, sometimes, to a masculine co-religionist. In primitive societies, bilateral modes of labeling kin may operate side by side with unilateral practices. A highly important result is that family and clan ties may both be recognized. Where matrilineal clans are found, a man very rarely joins his wife's clan at marriage. Consequently, he is usually of a different clan from his wife and offspring, yet his children will call him "father" and acknowledge him as their male parent. When important clan functions are being held in a matrilineal society of this kind, a man may be excluded from his wife's and children's group, but in daily life he need not be treated as an outsider.

Whatever may be a society's method of designating kin, therefore, it will generally be found that full importance is given to a father, mother, and their unmarried offspring. These relatives comprise the unit widely known as the **primary, limited, conjugal,** or **nuclear family.** A social unit's habit of labeling kindred along only one sex line or the other does not mean that the nuclear family is being overlooked or slighted. The pull of bilateral family ties within a matrilineal clan structure was forcibly brought home to the author during a study of a village split that broke the Hopi pueblo of Old Oraibi into halves in 1906. With rare exceptions, conjugal or nuclear family groups sided together, and exclusively unilateral clan loyalties were almost entirely disregarded. Although the Hopi were grouped into exogamous matrilineal clans and regularly observed matrilocal, postmarital residence customs in those days, only four married couples out of several hundred were separated by the split. As among the Hopi, it will be found that throughout the world recognition is likely to be given to the nuclear or conjugal family, even if it is embedded within some larger segment of a social structure.

There are many writers who believe that the nuclear family is so nearly a universal feature of human societies that they regard it as having been derived from those of man's animal forerunners whose bodies come closest to his in build and function, particularly with respect to a year-round ability to perform the sex act. This ability would have induced a male, it is often argued, to have remained permanently with a female and might thus have been the basis for the formation of family groups. Assuredly, many interesting and fruitful suggestions for an understanding of the noncultural aspects of family life in *Homo sapiens* can be obtained from careful observation of nonhominid Primates, but one must use such data with caution. Scientists do not believe contemporary man to be directly descended from any of the living Primates, and human families are so full of cultural, symbolic overtones that it seems self-evident that only limited understanding can be achieved from studies made of cultureless creatures.

One of the major functions of the nuclear family in virtually all human societies is to acquaint youngsters with the details of the way of life to which they are expected to conform. Families thus have an important educational aspect by means of which patterns of culture are transmitted from one generation to another. Many other people ordinarily supplement the training that parents give to their children; but even if no one else lends a hand, the parents are expected to bring their offspring up properly. A child gets its cultural bearings, so to speak, within the confines of its nuclear family; and that is why this unit is sometimes called the **family of orientation.** This affords a marked contrast to the **family of procreation,** in which a mature *Ego* occupies a different position when he weds and has children.

Two other kinds of families are known to cultural anthropologists. One, found especially among the Hindus, is called a **joint family.** Its base consists essentially of a number of nuclear families, all related in one sex line or the other and all sharing a common residence; but servants and other nonrelatives may also live under the same roof. Sometimes, a similar grouping of kinfolk and retainers, generally called an **extended family,** may be found, with each of the related nuclear families occupying a separate home. When the consanguineous members of a joint or extended family trace their descent unilaterally, as they often do, they are hard to distinguish on this score from clans or lineages.

C. CONSANGUINITY AND AFFINITY

Regardless of what system of kinship nomenclature a society uses, it will be found that each person's relatives are somehow connected with him by "blood" or marriage. "Blood" ties, whether they be real or fictitious, are described as **consanguineous,** and relationships through marriage are called **affinal. Consanguinity** is supposed to denote descent from a common parent or parents, but in many cases it cannot be proved and has to be assumed. Primitive people are much less likely than Euro-Americans to insist on proof of "blood" connection, and they make little effort to separate real from fictional consanguineous kin. A husband is assumed to be the father of his wife's children, even if the wife is known to have been occasionally unfaithful. Nonetheless, primitive folk do not take the ties of "blood" lightly, nor are they indifferent to the links established through marriage. It is everywhere recognized that when two people wed they develop a new set of relationships not only between themselves but also among their respective kinfolk. This is no idle matter, and many wedding customs express a sense of reluctance on someone's part whenever a marriage takes place. The gravity of entering into a new set of affinal relationships is one of the reasons why the blessings of a deity, also known as **supernatural sanctions,** are sometimes sought at weddings. Another compelling reason for invoking religious aid is to ensure that the union will bear issue.

Primitive attitudes toward the birth of offspring are likely to be based on practical considerations as well as on emotion. Feelings of love for children are as widely prevalent as among us, but factors that we submerge or fail to recognize may be more openly expressed. There is no failure to realize that a consanguineous line can be maintained only by sexual reproduction, even though some earlier writers have expressed opposite views, and where offices or property must be transmitted to "blood" relatives, the extinction of a consanguineous unit may be deplored as a tragedy. This is all the more true since the economic costs of having babies are negligible in primitive societies. It does not cost much, if anything, for medical help; it is not a serious problem to feed another mouth or to clothe an extra body; and nonliterate people have no cause to dread the expenses of education. Formal schooling hardly exists, and informal instruction is freely given as occasion warrants. Moreover, children are very often the equivalent of old-age insurance. Many an aging pair finds it comforting to realize that they have numerous progeny who will look after them as a matter of course. Unwanted or rejected children are exceedingly rare in the primitive world.

The acceptance of affinal relatives is another matter, for one never knows how they will turn out, and they do not have to be involuntarily accepted from birth as do consanguineous folk. Yet, the operation of incest and exogamic regulations makes it necessary for each social division to take a chance on some outsiders when it comes to choosing spouses. A degree of unwillingness to undertake the hazards of matrimony may be expressed by individuals in the form of **ceremonial coyness,** or it may be reflected in a group's behavior. This may be inferred from the variety of ways in which two units that have once succeeded in providing each other with mates will continue to do so as long as possible. Such customs, known to all cultural anthropologists, as having two brothers marry sisters, or the **levirate,** whereby a widow marries a brother of her late husband, or the **sororate,** which permits a man to marry a sister of his deceased wife, or the requirement that a son must take over his dead father's spouse or spouses may all be interpreted as efforts to keep in force affinal bonds that have already been established. Even cross-cousin marriage (see page 274), may be partially interpreted in the same way, for its continuous operation results in having off-spring take mates either from the mother's or the father's social unit, instead of from another group made up of strangers.

The loss that one group sustains when a member marries and moves away is compensated as a rule by the other's payment of goods, money, or services. When it is a girl's consanguineous kindred that receive compensation, it goes by the name of **bride-price;** recompense received by the groom or his relatives is known as a **dowry.** One or two instances of true **wife capture,** in which men regularly carry off brides without prearrangement or payment, are authentically reported, but more often, as in the case of so-called mock rape among the Araucanians of Chile, all details for the "capture" of a bride are settled in advance, the bride and her people make only a token show of resistance, and adequate compensation is later provided. Very seldom does a wedding take place in primitive society without an attendant transfer of valuable items, and in some instances marriage payments prove to be costly and highly involved transactions.

D. KINSHIP AND MARRIAGE

Kinship systems not only stipulate how relatives are to be labeled, but they also prescribe forms of correct behavior between various sets of kin. Each recognized degree of relationship carries with it certain rights and privileges as well as a number of duties and obligations. Knowledge of these functional requirements is what gives life to the study of kinship systems, for in this way the cultural anthropologist comes to understand how all manner of people are expected to act toward each other in repetitive, prescribed ways. Among the most important regulations affecting the behavior of kinfolk are those pertaining to marriages. Practically universal in primitive societies is the aforementioned rule of exogamy that forbids clanmates to wed or to have sexual relations. Almost as common, except in Moslem societies, is an incest tabu directed against the mating of **parallel cousins** (offspring of two brothers or of two sisters). Such a prohibition is sometimes counterbalanced by a society's stated preference for **cross-cousin** marriage, which unites the children of a brother with those of his sister. In communities where this custom prevails, young cross-cousins of opposite sex may be brought up with the notion that they are potential mates, and they are sometimes allowed a large measure of intimacy that may even go as far as nonmarital intercourse. Lesser degrees of familiarity, sometimes between members of the same sex, may be formalized into **joking relationships.** Joking relationships ordinarily refer to culturally permitted and generally standardized forms of familiarity in speech or action that prevail between particular kinds of relatives. In a few societies brothers and sisters habitually tease and joke with one another, but more often grown brothers and sisters are taught to treat each other with formality and circumspection. Professor Lowie believes that joking relationships are most common among potential mates,[4] but Professors Fred Eggan and Sol Tax are inclined to regard the joking relationship as affording relief for some of the restraints and tensions caused by other features of a kinship system.[5]

A very interesting variation of cross-cousin marriage is found among the Arunta, or Aranda.[6] The Aranda are Australian aborigines who once inhabited the center of their continent and whose social organization affords a contrast to their simple material culture. The entire tribe is divided into exogamous halves, or moieties, each of which has two sections. If we call the moieties A and B, and their subdivisions 1 and 2, we find that the Aranda are grouped into four sections among which the following rules of marriage and descent prevail (Fig. 12.4). An A-1 man must marry a B-1 woman, and the offspring become A-2 (the other half of the father's moiety). An A-2 man must wed a B-2 woman, and their children are A-1. A B-1 man must take an A-1 wife, and their offspring will be B-2; and a B-2 man must marry an A-2 spouse, and their children will be B-1. Complicated though these arrangements may appear at first glance, they are really no more than a modification of cross-cousin marriage, as may be seen from a study of Fig. 12.4.

Because the Aranda use a classificatory method of reckoning kin, the rule of preferential cross-cousin marriage does not unduly restrict one's choice of mates. Each male has a whole group of fathers, any one of whose sisters' daughters he is eligible to marry, as well as a number of mothers with any of whose brothers' daughters he may wed. Among these people the kinship and marriage regulations provide the basis for a whole network of behavioral forms.

---

[4] R. H. Lowie, *Primitive Society*, New York, 1920, p. 102.

[5] F. Eggan, ed., *Social Organization of North American Indians*, Chicago, 1937, p. 76.

[6] G. P. Murdock, *Our Primitive Contemporaries*, New York, 1935, Chap. 2, contains a short sketch of Aranda culture.

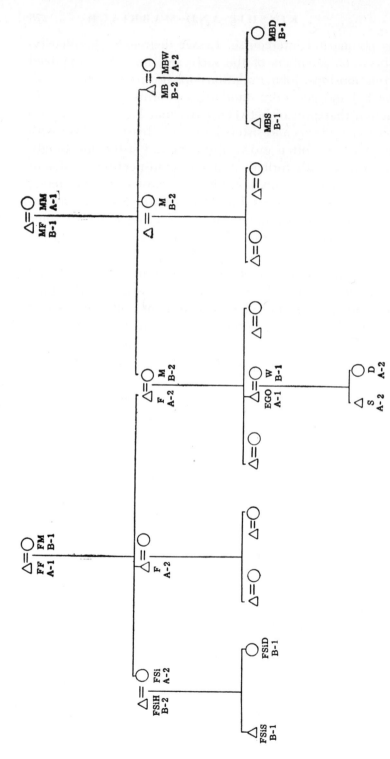

Fig. 12.4. Marriage pattern of the Arunta (Aranda). This Australian tribe demands that every A-1 male must wed a B-1 female. If a man marries either cross-cousin, his mother's brother's daughter or his father's sister's daughter, he will automatically make a proper marriage. Note, too, that a man falls into his son's son's category and a woman into the same division as her daughter's daughter. Cross-cousin marriage may thus go hand-in-hand with alternate generation harmony.

Beginning early in life, an A-1 male is taught to treat all older A-2 men as fathers, all older B-2 women as mothers, all B-1 females of his own generation as possible wives, all older A-2 women as potential mothers-in-law, and so forth. A young Aranda is not expected to treat exactly alike all the men and women whom he is taught to call father and mother. On the whole, though, his behavior toward these people is supposed to be modeled on his dealings with his own parents. Even a stranger from another district fits easily into the scheme as soon as his section becomes known, and violations of the code of behavior that regulates the conduct of each subgroup toward the others may be severely punished.

E. PLURAL MARRIAGES AND CONCUBINAGE

We are so accustomed to thinking of marriage in terms of our own concepts that it is easy for us to overlook the great variety of attitudes that may exist in other cultures. Americans, whose sense of morality stems from Judeo-Christian beliefs, find it very hard to avoid the feeling that a society which permits an individual to have multiple spouses at one time is somehow inferior and wanton. An ethnological report of a wife who nags her husband into taking another partner never fails to strike an American as being so incredible as to appear ludicrous. Yet plural marriages of one sort or another are widespread in primitive society.

When a man is allowed to have multiple wives, the custom is termed **polygyny,** but if a woman is permitted to have more than one husband concurrently, it is called **polyandry.** Together these customs are known as **polygamy.** Cultural anthropologists have found polygyny to be exceedingly common, but polyandry is reliably reported only among the Toda of southern India, in parts of Tibet, and in a small number of other places.

Marriage customs are not unitary but may better be likened to a rope that consists of independent strands braided together to form a single object (Fig. 12.5). Varying societies do not always select the selfsame strands for weaving the rope of marriage, and it is difficult for us to realize that each of the various segments may be assigned by a man to a separate wife. If a man weds several women simultaneously or in succession, each for a different purpose, polygyny automatically results.

To be more specific, Occidental men expect one wife to have at least four functions: to gratify her husband's sexual desires, to bear and rear his children, to conduct his household affairs, and to provide him with feminine companionship. We find it difficult to realize that these four elements of marriage are separable and that it is possible for each of them to be entrusted to a different woman.

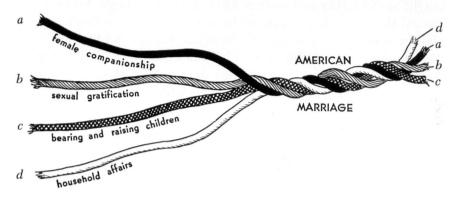

Fig. 12.5. The rope of American marriage. From an American husband's standpoint, the rope of marriage consists of at least four separate strands. Other societies may combine the same or other strands in different ways. Sexual gratification, and the bearing and rearing of children are the two factors that most commonly occur.

To us it is common knowledge that many a wife is delighted to have servants to help her with domestic duties, but we would hardly expect her to want her husband to marry her maids in order to make sure of retaining their services. In other parts of the world, on the contrary, plural marriage under such conditions is the accepted custom.

A man's spouses, even within a culture that freely permits polygyny, do not necessarily have equal status. Much more commonly, the first wife is regarded as the principal one. She outranks the others and generally has charge of running the household in which she resides. This was the case in ancient China, where a man's first wife had the greatest prestige and dominated all other females who might come to share her home through marriage to males who resided therein. Since, however, the only true test of a successful marriage by Confucian standards was the birth of a male heir, a Chinese woman who failed to bear a son fully expected her mate to take secondary wives or concubines.[7] In many parts of Africa, on the

---

[7] It would be unrealistic to think that Chinese men took concubines solely for

other hand, even a mother of many sons might scold her husband for neglecting to marry additional wives who would relieve her of difficult household chores.

Long before the publication of the Kinsey reports, men had come to realize that the sexual desires of their wives did not always correspond to their own. Some of the difference may be a matter of biology, for a young man's desires tend to be steady and continuous, whereas a woman's are more apt to be variable and cyclic. This depends, it is thought, on **hormone** production, which varies at different stages of the menstrual cycle. In any event, male and female sexual wants do not always coincide. From this point of view, it would be easy to explain why some well-to-do French women cheerfully help prepare their husbands to spend a night with a mistress. Unfortunately, this would not explain why females from other societies tend to be less cheerful under similar circumstances. Within the scope covered by the French example, sexual activity can be separated from other aspects of marriage, but the phenomenon is anything but customary and universal and it appears to be culturally rather than biologically conditioned. This interpretation is supported by the customs of the Nayar of southern India, among whom a woman lived for only a few days with her husband, after which she might openly dwell with a lover.

When it comes to the separation of providing feminine companionship from other wifely duties, old Japan furnishes an excellent example. Men who could afford it were expected to seek female companionship, not always including sexual indulgence, from the professional group called **geisha.** While some geisha undoubtedly granted sex favors to selected patrons, they were not as a class synonymous with prostitutes. Thanks to the geisha, Japanese wives were not called upon to perfect the arts of singing, instrument-playing, dancing, and making witty conversation that were the province of the professional entertainers. And when a geisha married, she no longer kept up her old skills but concentrated on meeting the other requirements of a good Japanese wife.

If one takes a worldview, it turns out that human multiple matings are highly complex and variable. Sexual impulses may underlie many of them, but they are neither the entire nor the only

the purpose of begetting sons. Still, a child born to a concubine might by a legal fiction be taken as her own by a barren wife. The difference between a secondary wife and a concubine usually depended on the woman's social standing.

reasons for entering plural wedlock. On the whole, such marriages among human beings turn out to be complicated biocultural arrangements, of which all the motivations have not yet been scientifically determined.

F. LIVING TOGETHER

As soon as a marriage has been made, the newlyweds must face the problem of where they should live. Only three possibilities are widespread under normal conditions. A bridal pair may settle in a place that is new to each of them (**neolocal residence**), they may go to live where the groom resides (**patrilocal, or virilocal, residence**), or they may settle in the vicinity of the bride's home (**matrilocal, or uxorilocal, residence**). Because of the strong sentiments of attachment that a person develops for the place where he was raised and for the people among whom he grew up, the choice of habitation that every wedded pair must make is a matter of grave concern. So, too, is the distance and availability of the new site with reference to the old. Professor Ralph Linton has urged cultural anthropologists to take pains to indicate the precise degree of isolation from a parental home that postmarital residence entails, but unfortunately his advice has seldom been followed. Among some tribes, the rules of postmarital residence are variable, and in others a period of dwelling with one set of in-laws is followed by a term of living with the second set. Frequently, the birth of a first child to a couple signals the time for a change of residence.

Perhaps of still greater significance is the question of whether a bride and groom establish an independent household or join an already existing residential unit occupied by the parents and other relatives of either the husband or wife. When merging takes place, the custom may aptly be described as forming a **unilocal household**. Valid distinctions may thus be drawn between patrilocal and matrilocal arrangements that are either unilocal or **multilocal.**

The most telling aspect of unilocal habitation results when newlyweds actually move into a house where live the kin of the bride or groom. Such a proceeding cannot fail to exert a profound influence on the married pair and on any offspring that may be born to them. If the principle of unilocal residence is consistently followed in a patrilocal setting, it inevitably leads to the formation after several generations of a social unit consisting of a man, his sons, grandsons, and so forth, together with their respective spouses and unmarried daughters. The males will form a permanent nucleus, occupying the same quarters from birth to death, bringing wives in from outside, and sending their daughters off at marriage. Where matrilocal customs prevail, the same results will ensue with the sexes reversed. The exact correspondence of such units (Fig. 12.6) with patrilineal or matrilineal clans (Figs. 12.1 and 12.3) was first noted many years ago, and there is a good likelihood that the unilateral classifi-

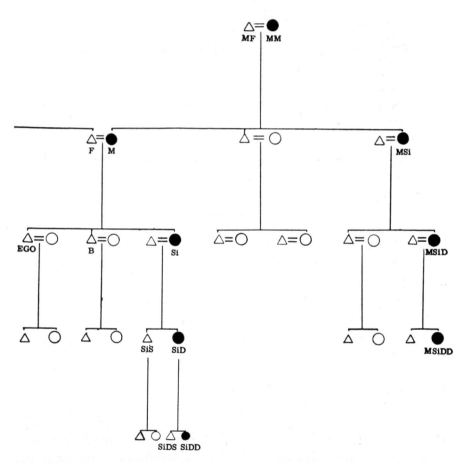

Fig. 12.6. A unilocal residence group in a matrilocal society. The natal members of a single household, who would normally reside under the same roof from birth to death by virtue of matrilocal residence, are shown in solid black. This alignment of coresidential kin is the same as that of a matrilineal lineage (Fig. 12.2) and closely resembles a segment of a matrilineal clan (Fig. 12.3).

cation of kindred was originally based on ties of common residence, rather than on bonds of consanguinity.[8]

Another feature of unilocal residence is the hardship it imposes on one party to a marriage. In a matrilocal society, as among the Hopi and Zuni, the women are so firmly placed in their households that they can, if they choose, make their husbands feel like privileged boarders who can be dismissed at the will of their wives. When a man is divorced in such societies he must rewed, return to the house of his mother, or go to live with a married sister. Conversely, in such patrilocal societies as that of the Araucanians or of the traditional Chinese, a girl was uprooted from her natal home at marriage and found herself forced to live out her adult life among strangers. In settings of this kind, young brides often found themselves unhappily subservient to their mothers-in-law or forced to show the greatest of respect to their fathers-in-law. Chinese literature is full of stories concerning the difficulties of recent brides in dealing with their mothers-in-law; and among the Araucanians older women who had married into the same patrilocal household frequently watched over a new wife to keep her from running away or committing suicide.

One of the commonest methods of preventing undue familiarity among affinal relatives who are forced by residence customs to live in close proximity is to prescribe a great show of respect or **avoidance.** This may take many forms, of which the most widely found is the custom, avidly seized upon by Euro-American comedians, of **mother-in-law tabu.** In reality, there is nothing amusing about a mother-in-law tabu in primitive society, because its violation arouses the displeasure of one's tribesmen and may even cause serious illness or death. This is the case among the Navaho, where a woman's married daughters live in nearby *hogans,* and yet their husbands are forbidden either to speak or to look upon the mother of their wives. Among the Navaho, childless brides or young children serve as intermediaries and warn people who might inadvertently violate the prohibition. Nevertheless, instances are known where a man's sickness is attributed to the fact that either he or his father once broke the mother-in-law tabu. Avoidance regulations, similar to the mother-in-law tabu, may be applied to other relatives.

---

[8] A detailed discussion of this topic may be found in M. Titiev, "The Influence of Common Residence on the Unilateral Classification of Kindred," *American Anthropologist,* Vol. 45, 1943, pp. 511-530.

G. SPACE AND KINSHIP

Kinship systems, including both the methods of labeling relatives and the prescribed forms of behavior that regulate their conduct, are so diversified and so basic to an understanding of social structures that they have been eagerly studied by cultural anthropologists for the better part of a century. To date, the most widely used approach has rested on the assumption that primitive groups designate kindred according to some method of real or assumed "blood" or genetic connections. Most of the traditional students of kinship have assumed that since every child must have a father and a mother, ties of descent always provide the basis for a kinship system. This is not invariably the case. It was recognized long ago that native peoples are not always interested in "blood" or descent, and that they are entirely unaware of genetic transmission.

In the light of these facts, it seems best to look upon kinship systems as parts of each group's culture, and, like other aspects of culture, designations of relationship may be regarded as symbolic rather than real. In this respect, kinship nomenclature is a human "invention." Ties of descent are not apparent to the naked eye, and it is not at all unusual to find in the primitive world ceremonies that are designed to establish the kinship relations (including parenthood) of a newly born child. That an infant and the other members of his society might not otherwise know the baby's father is an old, old notion among us, and we think nothing of it when we read that a man's paternity has to be culturally announced in one way or another. We are likely to think, however, that the biological bonds of mother and babe are so close that the kinship relations between them are automatically established. This is far from being the case, for there is absolutely no sure way that a mother can recognize her own infant. Among us, many a woman is delivered in a hospital and is hazy or unconscious at the exact moment of parturition. Under such conditions, relationship ties cannot and do not begin between a mother and her child until someone in the conventional garb of a hospital attendant hands a neonate to a just-delivered woman. Thus, it is not improper to say that motherhood as well as fatherhood is a sociocultural "invention."

Very often, in analyses of kinship, we fall into the habit of assuming that use of a given term, such as father, triggers a fixed sort of behavior or role. It is equally possible for the reverse to be true, namely, that a man may be called father because he behaves toward *Ego* in a certain way. Thus, kinship terms may be applied to people who regularly help or feed one, quite apart from matters of descent and regardless of whose genes one happens to carry. Once again does the matter of physical space enter in, for no man or woman can possibly act as a parent unless he is, at least on occasion, within reach of a child. Parenthood at a distance is absolutely impossible in any society.

A sharper distinction than is customarily made needs to be drawn between **natal kin,** who comprise one's relatives by "blood" and who are *involuntarily* acquired at birth, and the marital or affinal kin whose selection is made *voluntarily* in postnatal life, as a result of someone's choice. Natal kin can then be further subdivided into those who customarily share a common habitation with a newly born *Ego* and those who do not. If such a subdivision is made, it will be found that incest tabus apply to those of one's natal kin and their offspring who, under aboriginal conditions, might have been expected to have lived in *Ego's* household when he was born.

To avoid making an incestuous marriage, a masculine *Ego* must then take a spouse from a household different from the one in which he has resided from birth. If it be admitted that primitive people are reluctant to establish marital bonds with a great scattering of persons, the safest course for our hypothetical *Ego* to follow would be to marry someone from the same household whence came his mother or his father. In a matrilocal society a male *Ego* would thus wed his father's sister's daughter, and in a patrilocal setting he would marry his mother's brother's daughter. This system is known as **unilateral cross-cousin marriage,** and accords with Crow kinship nomenclature in the first instance, and with Omaha terminology in the second.[9]

Besides providing a different way of trying to understand the wide prevalence of cross-cousin marriage in primitive societies, and in addition to whatever value it may have for explaining certain ways of designating kindred, the method of analysis in terms of space and common residence may also contribute to a better understanding of the phenomenon that cultural anthropologists know as **alternate generation harmony.** By this it is meant that people in a

---

[9] An elaboration of the viewpoints expressed in this section may be found in M. Titiev, "The Importance of Space in Primitive Kinship," *American Anthropologist,* Vol. 58, 1956.

grandparental generation are warm and kindly to their grandchildren, whereas there may be a good deal of tension and strife between successive generations, that is, between parents and offspring. Sometimes, as Figure 12.4 demonstrates from Arunta data, grandparents and grandchildren, thanks to cross-cousin marriage, fall into exactly the same social divisions. This may facilitate the harmony of alternate generations. In the case of people like the African Ashanti this factor gains additional importance from the native belief that the spirit of a deceased grandparent can be reborn only in a child resulting from cross-cousin marriage.[10]

One further point should be kept in mind when dealing with the mating of cross-cousins. Incest tabus forbid a sister and a brother to become parents of the same children, but through the operation of cross-cousin marriage they become parents-in-law of one another's offspring.

For all that has already been discovered, there is much yet to be learned about primitive kinship. Recent students are both thinking along lines that were unknown to their predecessors and building their analyses on ideas put forward by their forerunners.[11] Some of them are focusing attention on **kinship sets,** which may be defined as categories of relatives bound together by one or more relationship ties. Others take the position that no terminological analysis is complete unless it partitions the whole universe of kin types into as many segments as there are terms of relationship, with each segment corresponding exactly to the range of a single term. New kinds of diagrams are displacing the conventional charts that look like genealogical tables, and fresh approaches are everywhere in evidence. These are healthy signs, and they show that cultural anthropologists still regard the study of primitive kinship to be of prime importance for an understanding of human behavior.

SELECTED REFERENCES

Edmonson, M. S., "Kinship Terms and Kinship Concepts," *American Anthropologist,* Vol. 59, No. 3, 1957, pp. 393-433.

Eggan, F., ed., *Social Anthropology of North American Indian Tribes,* rev. ed. Chicago, 1955.

Fortes, M., *The Web of Kinship Among the Tallensi.* London, 1949.

---

10 *Idem.*

11 See, for example, M. S. Edmonson, "Kinship Terms and Kinship Concepts," *American Anthropologist,* Vol. 59, No. 3, 1957.

Goodenough, W. H., "A Problem in Malayo-Polynesian Social Organization," *American Anthropologist*, Vol. 57, 1955, pp. 71-83.

Kroeber, A. L., "Classificatory Systems of Relationship," *Journal of the Royal Anthropological Institute*, Vol. 39, 1909, pp. 77-84.

Lévi-Strauss, C., "The Family," in *Man, Culture, and Society*, H. L. Shapiro, ed., Chapter 12. New York, 1956.

Lowie, R. H., *Primitive Society*. New York, 1920.

———, *Social Organization*. New York, 1948.

Morgan, L. H., "Systems of Consanguinity and Affinity of the Human Family," *Smithsonian Institution, Contributions to Knowledge*, Vol. 17, No. 218, Washington, 1870.

Murdock, G. P., *Social Structure*. New York, 1949.

Radcliffe-Brown, A. R., "The Social Organization of Australian Tribes," *Oceania*, Vol. 1, 1930.

Rivers, W. H. R., *The History of Melanesian Society*. Cambridge, England, 1914.

Titiev, M., "The Importance of Space in Primitive Kinship," *American Anthropologist*, Vol. 58, 1956.

———, "The Influence of Common Residence on the Unilateral Classification of Kindred," *American Anthropologist*, Vol. 45, 1943.

CHAPTER 13

SOME NONKINSHIP ASPECTS
OF SOCIAL ORGANIZATION

A. KINDRED AND STRANGERS

Primitive people always differentiate between relatives, no matter how they are identified and labeled, fellow villagers or neighbors, and total strangers. For the most part the latter are so seldom encountered that there may be no established ways of dealing with them. At the opposite end of the scale, etiquette rules may be exceedingly detailed and may call for very lengthy preliminaries before one deals with strangers. In some parts of the Orient it is expected that three days will elapse before a stranger states his business.

Those of us who are accustomed to dealing regularly with strangers, such as clerks in stores, and who even entrust our lives to strangers without giving the matter a second thought, as we do whenever we take a bus or a plane, ride in a train or taxicab, eat in a restaurant, or sail in a ship, often fail to appreciate what it means when a stranger appears among a closely-knit group of primitive people.

When the state of Israel was receiving migrant Jews from all parts of the world, the question of dealing with strangers became a practical matter. European Jews who applied for housing had no trouble in giving officials their names, the size of their families, and

similar information. Oriental Jews, on the other hand, found themselves embarrassed and uneasy when they had to give personal
information to strange receptionists. They could not bring themselves to reply quickly even to routine questions, and they often
caused long delays simply because they were unaccustomed to
dealing promptly with strangers.

It is not surprising that under conditions of isolation strangers
are regarded with a mixture of fear and hostility. Still, it does not
necessarily follow that these feelings are the only causes of wars.
Civil wars are not entirely unknown in the primitive world; and warfare is sometimes regarded more as a means of gaining honors
than as a way of expressing aggression against strangers. The Plains
Indians of North America are famous for the frequency with which
their young men went on the warpath, but study of their customs
shows that they fought more to gain the esteem of their fellows
than to inflict damages on their enemies.

Many of the Plains tribes had systematic grades of prestige to
be won in war. One of these systems is widely known as **counting
coup,** and higher honors were won, because of the degree of daring
involved, for touching a live foe than for slaying an enemy. Similarly, some of the same tribes gave high prestige, after 1492, to a
successful horse thief. Once again the boldness of the feat far out-
weighed the practical considerations. It was much more honorable
to steal one horse that was tethered within an enemy encampment
than it was to drive off a number of horses whose owners were nowhere in the vicinity.

Some cultural anthropologists, including the famed student of
kinship, Professor G. P. Murdock, believe that it can be demonstrated that warfare is sometimes closely connected with polygyny.
If warriors are successful, they may carry off enemy women and
force them to become secondary wives. But if a war goes badly,
many men are likely to be killed, whereupon the survivors may
marry several of their tribeswomen to keep them from going entirely husbandless. When warlike tribes are pacified, the sex ratio
returns to normal and tends to approximate one to one. Thereupon,
monogamy is likely to replace polygamy, a change which illustrates
the operation of an internal force of culture as opposed to such external pressure as might result from the teachings of Christian mis-
sionaries.

In terms of over-all social organization, distaste for strangers is often counterbalanced by a fear lest groups of kindred become so thoroughly self-sufficient that they will deal only with one another, to the disregard of other members of the community. If this should happen, the overemphasis on relatives would weaken the larger social structure of the entire settlement. An equilibrium must be struck in this matter, as in many others, whether or not people are consciously aware of the need.

Considerations of this sort may help us to understand why incest regulations and other forms of exogamy are so widespread in human societies. If they do nothing else they force the near of kin to seek mates from other groups, weakening kinship ties and enforcing a degree of cooperation with other social units. In a broad evolutionary sense, the more primitive a society is the more likely are its individuals to depend on kin for the satisfaction of all their wants; and the further "advanced" a society is, the less do its members limit their interactions to kindred.

B. ASSOCIATIONS

Apart from the involuntary links of consanguineous relationships that await each child at birth, and different from the affinal bonds formed at marriage, there exist in primitive societies a large number of ties arising from membership in voluntary **associations.** They may be entered at different times, at various ages, in divergent ways, and for a variety of reasons. Joining may be purely optional or may result from social pressures that are so strong as to leave an individual little or no choice. Admission to associations may depend on the biological factors of sex or age; on general considerations of culture like rank, prestige, or marital status; on specific elements like occupation or the possession of a given amount of wealth; or on a combination of all three, as in the case of masculine, unmarried, warriors. For all their diversity, associations show three virtually universal features. They are almost never made up entirely of a unit of consanguineous or affinal kin; each is exclusive because it never admits all the people of a given society; and each develops strong bonds of attachment among those nonkin who are admitted to membership. A good idea of the variety and complexity of primitive associations may be had from a brief account of several particular examples.

1. **The Cannibal Society of the Kwakiutl Indians.**[1] One of the most colorful areas of the aboriginal New World ran along the Pacific seaboard of Canada. This is the region described in anthropological literature as the Northwest Coast. Here, among others, lived the Kwakiutl Indians, whose customs were carefully studied by Franz Boas in the decade prior to the start of the present century.

During the summer season the social organization of the Kwakiutl was based on ties of descent that sorted the people into clans, but in the winter months there prevailed an entirely different grouping, which depended on membership in secret societies. Individuals from each clan had a number of these societies from which to choose, but one of the most popular and highly regarded was the **cannibal** society, *hamats'a* (see Fig. 13.1).

---

[1] F. Boas, "The Social Organization and Secret Societies of the Kwakiutl Indians," Washington, 1897.

Fig. 13.1. A cannibal dancer. Among the Kwakiutl Indians of the Northwest Pacific coast, the cannibal society, *hamats'a*, was very popular. Members dressed in elaborate costumes when they danced in public. (Courtesy of the Museum of Anthropology, University of Michigan.)

Young men who were about to enter the cannibal society were whisked away early in the course of the rites. For four days they were kept in total seclusion. At this time they were supposed to be visiting the home of their unit's guardian spirit, who taught them certain songs, dances, and other bits of sacred and tribal lore. While they were absent their sponsors, usually their own fathers, were expected to provide feasts for their society mates. At the end of four days the initiates were lured back to the everyday world and entered the dance hall in a state of frenzy, because they were supposedly possessed by their guardian spirit. As cannibals, the novices bit people and acted madly until they were calmed down by the older men of their fraternity. Thereupon they sang and danced, presumably in the fashion learned from their guardian spirit, and gradually they again became integrated with the daily world.

Boas believed that the cannibal society was originally connected with warfare. In more general terms, however, all the secret societies of the Kwakiutl seem to have fulfilled a number of similar purposes. Each group sought to emphasize its spiritual origins, and tried to strengthen itself by re-enacting its traditional way of behaving. At the same time, it also saw to it that its initiates learned some of their tribal mysteries but ended up by accepting the everyday values of the tribe. Finally, membership in a secret society invariably encouraged strong bonds of fellowship among nonkin and served clearly to differentiate the initiated from the uninitiated.

2. **Masai Warriors' Societies.**[2] Under aboriginal conditions the Masai occupied a portion of East Africa. Each male, soon after attaining puberty, was subjected to **circumcision.** All those who had gone through the operation in any four-year period were combined into a **warriors' group,** which acquired a distinctive name and the right to use special insignia (Fig. 13.2). For an indefinite time the members lived in a special structure, away from their families, together with paramours who were unmarried women of about their own age who had in the last four years been subjected to **clitoridectomy,** an operation that involves an incision of the clitoris. After a dozen years or so, individual members of the warriors' group would begin to leave the common habitation, marry, and

---

[2] A. C. Hollis, *The Masai*, Oxford, 1905, p. xvi, *et passim.*

Fig. 13.2. Members of a Masai warriors' group. These men lived together as long as they remained unmarried. During this time they formed a distinctive unit within their society. (Courtesy of British Information Services.)

settle down in the expectation of becoming tribal elders. When the last of a warriors' group had taken these steps, the unit was officially dissolved, but the former members retained their distinctive name and continued to share a few common interests for life.

3. **Crow Indian Military Societies.**[3] Quite different in nearly every way were the **Lumpwoods** and **Foxes,** two military societies that were very popular among the Crow Indians who used to live in the

[3] R. H. Lowie, *The Crow Indians,* New York, 1935.

Plains area of the United States. Each was led by elected officers who were distinguished warriors, and every spring the leaders invited about a dozen promising young men to join their organization. Membership was for life, and each society had exclusive rights to the use of a characteristic song and dance. Members lived at home and were permitted to marry, their wives sharing in a few of the public functions like feasts. From time to time each association would serve as a police force, and feats of military daring were regularly performed for the greater glory of one's club. Fierce rivalry prevailed between Lumpwoods and Foxes, and once a year each side paraded in public whatever mistresses it had made among the wives of the rival outfit. Convention forbade a cuckolded husband from punishing his spouse or betraying anger, but in most cases a faithless woman soon found herself abandoned both by her lover and her mate. Membership in the Crow military societies was so greatly coveted that, if a man died, his family brought pressure to have him replaced by a relative.

4. **Banks Islands Sukwe.**[4] On the Banks Islands of the Western Pacific every man sought to join the **Sukwe** society. Admission might be had at any age upon payment of a fee of shell money to those who already belonged. The Sukwe met in a clubhouse of its own in each village, and the structure functioned as a combined recreation hall, dining room, and dormitory for men only (Fig. 13.3). All Sukwe buildings were carefully partitioned into graded sections, and no man dared enter a higher portion than his own on pain of death. Members of each unit prepared and ate meals together, and it was every man's ambition to get into the highest branches of Sukwe. Since heavy payments had to be made for each advance, few natives got to the very top, and those who did were held in the greatest esteem. For a man to be out of the Sukwe altogether was a social disgrace, and those who remained in the lowest grades for life were regarded as failures. Stories of success on the Banks Islands, comparable to our tales of going from rags to riches, are told about men who overcame obstacles to reach the highest levels of Sukwe.

---

[4] W. H. R. Rivers, *The History of Melanesian Society*, Cambridge, 1914, Vol. I, p. 61 ff.

Fig. 13.3. A *gamal* on the Banks Islands. Within such structures members of the Sukwe society held their meetings. Each gamal was partitioned into graded units, one for the members of each degree. Trespass into a higher section was punishable by death. (Courtesy of Cambridge University Press.)

5. **The Hopi Indian Marau Society.**[5] As the examples already summarized indicate, a majority of associations in the primitive world are designed for men, but women's groups are not unknown. Among the Hopi Indians of northeastern Arizona every town or pueblo has its populace divided into a number of **secret societies,** each of which is responsible for conducting an important ceremony for the good of the tribe. Many of these associations have lapsed, but a few remain active. At the village of Old Oraibi there used to be three feminine associations, of which the most popular was the **Marau.** Admission was entirely voluntary and was almost never denied when requested. Despite the ease with which it might be joined, the Marau was a highly regarded aggregation of females. It had its own kiva at Old Oraibi, carried out its own initiations, performed secret rites for the promotion of rainfall, good crops, health, and fertility, and annually staged a public dance in distinctive costume (Fig. 13.4). In the eyes of the Hopi the Marau observances were a regular part of the ceremonial cycle, and the prayers of the women were as greatly prized as those of the men.

Additional associations are well known, and a full account of

---

[5] H. R. Voth, "The Oraibi Marau Ceremony," *Field Columbian Museum, Anthropological Series,* Vol. II, No. 1, Chicago, 1912.

Fig. 13.4. Marau dancers. The Marau was the most popular of the three associations for women among the Hopi. In their public performances, the members of these associations always ranged themselves in circular form. (Courtesy of the Chicago Natural History Museum.)

their operations would reveal a bewildering profusion of eligibility requirements for members, underlying motives, forms of initiation, and methods of operation. Because participation is practically never limited to a single group of kin, membership in associations cannot help but create bonds that cut across ties of relationship and serve to knit firmly together many unrelated members of a society. Some associations carry on strictly practical activities, but even then they usually bring a splash of color and excitement into the lives of their community. People everywhere seem to enjoy opportunities to get away from their customary surroundings and routine duties, to learn secrets not shared by their fellows, to perform strange actions and rituals, and to wear elaborate costumes that differ greatly from conventional garb (Fig. 13.5).

Fig. 13.5. A Duk-Duk assembly. On New Britain, in Melanesia, the Duk-Duk was an important secret society. Its members dressed in elaborate costumes, very different from their daily wear. (Courtesy of the Museum of Anthropology, University of Michigan.)

C. INSTITUTIONALIZED FRIENDSHIP

Among ourselves, friendships occasionally play the part that relationships do in primitive societies; and in modern Japan there is a popular proverb, capable of being variously translated, that says in effect: "A friend close at hand is better than a far-off relative."

For all our recognition of the value of friendship, though, our type of society has never thoroughly institutionalized it. In many regions of Africa, however, as well as on a number of South Pacific islands and in other parts of the primitive world, dealings with friends are systematically regulated and play an important part in holding together unrelated members of a society.

One of the best-known ways of establishing close bonds among individuals who need not necessarily be kindred is an institution closely resembling **godparenthood,** which is known to various native peoples of Latin America as a **compadre** relationship, and which may call for such fixed patterns of behavior among those concerned as to lead to the formation of what have been termed **"padrino groups."** [6] Where the institution of *compadre* is highly formalized, very little is left to chance. **Godparents** take their obligations seriously and come much nearer than is often the case among us to acting like substitute parents to their **godchildren.**

[6] E. H. Spicer, *Pascua, A Yaqui Village in Arizona,* Chicago, 1940, pp. 91-116.

Somewhat resembling the foregoing is the custom found among various American Indian tribes of the Southwest, who live in towns, or **pueblos,** of establishing ties of quasi-kinship between a child and its **ceremonial parents.** As a rule this refers to that individual and one of his relatives of the opposite sex who sponsor a youngster's admission into a **sodality** or secret society, which performs an important rite. (See the description of the Marau, above.) Parents do not lightly select a ceremonial father or mother for their offspring. They are so conscious of the fact that the person chosen may be called upon to act as a parental surrogate that they weigh his qualifications very carefully.

It is not at all uncommon for institutionalized friendship to bind together for life two unrelated members of the same sex. Such men or women pledge themselves to cooperate at all times. The use of these alliances as a substitute for kinship connections is well brought out in a consideration of the Plains Cree Indians of Canada.[7] Among them, two boys who pledged friendship would address each other's parents as father and mother; and if one died, the survivor always lived for a time in the home of his deceased friend, where he was regarded as a sort of adopted son. Likewise, should two friends marry, their wives would call each other sisters, as do the wives of true brothers.

Most widely publicized, although it occurs but sporadically in primitive society, is the custom known as **blood-brotherhood.** In one form, practiced in medieval Europe and in parts of Africa, the principals would draw blood from their arms, allow it to mix in a container, then drink the contents. Other tribes may not establish blood-brotherhood quite so literally, but in all cases something is done publicly to show that the two parties, and sometimes all their relatives as well, are henceforth to be regarded on the same basis as real "blood" kin. Customs of this sort emphasize the importance that many societies attribute to the need for establishing close bonds among those who are not automatically related by descent.

Somewhat less telling is the custom of recognizing **age-groups** or **age-sets.** Recognition may be completely informal or highly systematized. It is based on the idea that people of the same sex and approximate age are somehow alike and ought to develop the solidarity of a social group. Actually, many males and females are sub-

---

[7] D. G. Mandelbaum, "Friendship in North America," *Man,* Vol. 36, 1936, pp. 205-6.

jected to similar codes of behavior and share many experiences that serve to bind them together. Where age-groups are explicitly recognized, the members are usually expected to help and befriend one another whenever necessary. In some instances societies anticipate that age-mates will act together, and they may even go so far as to assign tasks to be carried out by an age-group rather than by particular individuals or some other social unit. (See the Masai Warriors' Societies, above.)

Each biocultural triangle may now be seen to be faced with the need of striking an equilibrium between opposing forces. Bonds of kinship are never allowed to become all-sufficient. This compels people, for the good of society as a whole, to develop links with nonrelatives. Various kinds of associations, institutionalized friendships, and age groupings provide mechanisms by means of which warm and close ties can be formed among members of a society who do not happen to be kin.

D. PRIMITIVE LAW [8]

If a social unit wishes to keep itself going, its pattern of culture must contain something approximating a legal system. That is why cultural anthropologists do not regard primitive societies as anarchical even when they lack formal agencies for making and enforcing laws. By definition, nonliterate peoples cannot have written judicial codes, and it is most unusual to find them with clear-cut legislative and executive bodies. Nevertheless, their standards of conduct are usually known to all and punishment for offenses committed is not rare. One of the objectives of an ethnological field trip might well be to work out from the observed customs of a tribe whatever legal principles it seems to follow.

Law enforcement implies a degree of social compulsion, tinged with a threat of authorized physical force, that makes an individual regulate his personal conduct to comply with the values, norms, or mores of his group. It is as though each society said to its members, "Conform, or be punished." Beyond the acceptance of this universal concept there is no world-wide agreement on what constitutes a violation of proper conduct or on the punishment to be

---

[8] Professor Hoebel, of the University of Minnesota, is the foremost anthropologist who specializes in primitive law. For his presentation of some of the points made in this section, see E. A. Hoebel, *Man in the Primitive World,* rev. ed., New York, 1958, chapter 27.

inflicted. The cultures of some societies permit and even encourage forms of behavior that other groups may severely condemn. A distinction may be drawn between groups that have something approaching a **state** and which exercise controls through the agency of bodies of **police** or other formal enforcement units, and those groups whose social controls are effective only through the operation of traditional usages as expressed in public opinion or reaction. It is never easy to draw a fine line between these two types of society, or between those nonconformists whose deviations are subject to some form of punishment and other nonconformists or innovators whose departures from established codes become accepted as models for new ways of behaving.

Once in a while laws are based on considerations of biology. Human females are capable of having sexual relations at all times, without desire. This is not true of men. For this reason all legal systems recognize that rape and criminal assault can be committed only against women. Except for a greatly restricted number of such cases, social regulations appear to be based more on symbolic, cultural values than on matters of biology, and some biocultural traits, as has already been indicated, may even give the appearance of running counter to biology. For instance, no one doubts that men everywhere are incapable of bearing offspring, yet some societies, notably in the tropical portions of South America, practice the **couvade,** a custom in which men do the lying-in after their wives have given birth. In extreme forms of the couvade, males may even pretend to undergo the pains of labor and may simulate parturition.

Then, again, in any society men are likely to be stronger of physique than most women, but where such cultural mores as mother-in-law tabus prevail, a bold and powerful man may be genuinely afraid even to glance at his wife's mother. Along similar lines, it is entirely likely that on the Banks Islands some wives henpecked or dominated their husbands at home, but never would women have dared to follow their spouses into a men's clubhouse.

On the whole, as these cases make clear, symbolic, cultural determinants play a greater part than biological factors in establishing what rules individuals of either sex are expected to observe.

Perhaps the most widespread of all legal regulations are those concerned with the sanctity of **property rights** and of **human life.** Property may be intangible, like ownership of a specific design or tune; it may have such real value as would a well-made spear; or its worth may be completely symbolic, as in the case of shell money. Moreover, property may be individually or collectively held, and it may be either zealously guarded or freely loaned. Such factors make little difference. In all these instances there is present a concept of ownership, and violations of proprietary rights are punishable.

Since no society likes to face extinction, it follows that there will always be laws to prevent the killing of people, especially if they are members of one's own group and capable of parenthood. A small percentage of tribes allow infanticide or permit the killing of the very aged or the hopelessly sick, but most societies regret the loss of a member under any circumstances. Distinctions may be drawn for all kinds of reasons between abortion, infanticide, suicide, murder, and various degrees of manslaughter, and some means of causing death may be condoned while others are not. In our society, the safest tool for a killer to use is an automobile. Should an intoxicated man shoot several people, he might be charged with murder and executed if found guilty; but if a drunken driver kills an equal number of people, he may be found guilty of involuntary manslaughter and sentenced to a relatively light prison term.[9] Other societies may make different discriminations. In many tribes a man who kills an adulterous wife caught in the act may not be charged with any offense at all, but if he is thought guilty of having bewitched a woman, he may be put to death.

There is no universal touchstone, either, for evaluating how severe the same form of punishment will be judged to be by peoples of different cultures. Cutting off the nose of a culprit might be regarded as unbelievably brutal in one society and as moderate in another. A slap across the face would humiliate and infuriate an adult male in the United States, but would have been taken in stride by a recruit in the Imperial Army of Japan. We might regard social ostracism as light punishment for a serious offense, but most primitive groups would tend to consider rejection by one's fellows as a fate worse than death.

Responsibility for carrying out retribution seems to follow a definite trend when one compares various social systems. Where cultures are relatively uncomplicated, the matter of inflicting pun-

---

[9] The *Detroit Free Press*, October 20, 1950, p. 12, carried a story of a youth who, while drunk, drove through a red light and crashed into a car, killing two people and one of his own passengers. He was convicted of "involuntary manslaughter."

ishment on offenders is likely to be left to the kinfolk of those who were injured, but in societies and cultures of greater development and complexity, the administration of justice is left more and more to impersonal agencies or nonrelatives. In simple societies a murderer may be called upon only to pay a fixed sum, **weregild,** to the surviving kin of his victim. In other cases a murder may start a **blood-feud,** in which bereaved relatives try to kill an equivalent member of the other side's kinfolk. On the whole, punishment for murder is likely to be more drastic in literate than in primitive societies.

Methods of evaluating evidence and determining guilt are also highly variable. They may range from a tendency to regard as guilty anyone against whom an accusation is brought to very elaborate procedures for weighing evidence, and even for the punishment of those who bear false witness. A favorite device is to subject a suspect, and, once in a while, his accuser as well, to an **ordeal.** Much as they may differ in details, all ordeals are based on the setting up of a trial or contest situation in which victory is always supposed to go to the innocent. Whether the test consists of being immersed in water, grasping a white-hot iron, drinking poison, swallowing a hard crust, or trial by combat, the underlying idea seems to be that an incorruptible power, usually regarded as supernatural, will always make its decision clear by allowing the guilty party to suffer injury or defeat (Fig. 13.6). That mortals might "frame" the ordeal situation to favor or condemn a particular party is an idea that could be entertained only by an unbeliever. The swearing of oaths, and a variety of divinatory practices, are other ways of asking supernatural powers to determine the guilt or innocence of accused persons.

Whatever other attributes they may have, all legal systems are meant to help hold a society together and to maintain its accustomed way of life by preventing conflicting interests from coming to an open clash. Here obedience to law and patriotism or loyalty to one's social unit fuse into a single concept. The law-abiding person, whether primitive or not, is expected to put his social responsibilities above his personal desires, and so, too, is the patriotic individual. In this connection, the highest legal authority in most primitive societies is vested in the head-man or chief, who is also the tribe's political leader. When so much power is lodged in a single personage he is likely to be equated with a deity, and the notion of divine rulers is exceedingly common. Under such conditions violations of the accepted mores of a tribe may be regarded at one and the same time as political crimes and religious sins. It should occasion little wonder that an investigation of this aspect of man's relations to man in a primitive society regularly brings a student to a consideration of man's dealings with the supernatural, for orderly, patriotic, and religious conduct are constantly blended.

Fig. 13.6. An ordeal by hot water. Among the Ifugao, in the Philippine Islands, guilt was often determined by subjecting a suspect to an ordeal by hot water. It was believed that an innocent person would be unharmed by such a test. (Courtesy of the Museum of Anthropology, University of Michigan.)

E. A REVIEW OF MAN'S RELATIONS TO MAN

Man's interactions with his fellows cover a host of topics, but they fall into a systematic arrangement if they are viewed in the light of the twin axioms that all societies seek to maintain themselves and their cultures indefinitely. Sexual reproduction is the only way, directly or indirectly, of continuously replenishing the supply of human beings that constitute a social unit, and on this point biological factors cannot be disregarded. All normal females are capable of bearing children, and every society encourages them to have offspring under regulated conditions. Cultural considerations also affect the recognition and naming of kinfolk. Every anthropologist realizes that consanguinity may be assigned as well as inherited. A Toda baby in southern India accepts as its father whatever man ritually presents its mother with a bow, regardless of whose genes it actually carries. Until modern times the Chinese considered all people who had the same surname to be bloodkin and forbade them to marry even if no trace of genealogical connection could be established. On the other hand, we must not forget that wherever unilateral systems of kinship nomenclature are in force, even "blood" relatives as close as one's own father or mother might, under some circumstances, be left out of the reckoning.

Primitive societies show a marked preference for the use of classificatory terminology, for unilateral methods of labeling kin along only one sex line, and for the occasional overriding of generation lines. Literate societies, in general, employ descriptive terms and trace relationship bilaterally, by way of both the father's and the mother's lines. Accordingly, unilateral groupings such as lineages and clans, sometimes clustered into phratries or moieties, are commonplace in primitive society but rare or nonexistent elsewhere. Two of the best-studied systems of unilateral descent terminology are the Omaha and Crow, but others are known to specialists.

Even when a tribe labels kindred unilaterally, however, it is likely to give some recognition to nuclear family groups consisting of parents and their unmarried offspring. Nuclear family units, since they include both fathers and mothers, are usually bilateral, but their existence may be recognized even in societies that use unilateral methods of nomenclature.

All social groups differentiate between consanguineous relatives, supposedly bound together by involuntary ties of descent, and affinal kin who become joined to an *Ego* through someone's marriage. In all societies, too, the matter of postmarital residence is of great importance. Primitive peoples often, but not always, expect newlyweds to live with or near the same sex line that is used for labeling relatives. Thus, although a few exceptions are known, patrilocal residence goes hand in hand with patrilineal descent, and matrilocality is most commonly found with matrilineality. As societies evolve toward more modern conditions, newly married couples tend more and more to establish independent, neolocal residences, away from the kin of either principal.

Marriage customs everywhere consist of the weaving together of numerous, individual strands. Differences arise because different societies combine varying strands in a variety of ways. If there is an evolution of marriage practices, it runs from polygamy to monogamy, and the cessation of warfare may provide one stimulus for this trend.

To be successful every society's way of life must strike a balance between encouraging bonds of cohesion to develop among some of its members and preventing tightly-knit groups from giving up their allegiance to the social whole. Bodies of close relatives, such as natal kin, are particularly prone to form self-contained and self-sufficient cliques that may threaten to become independent of the rest of their society. As a rule, incest and other exogamic regulations, membership in scattered associations, institutionalized friendships, and authorized dealings with strangers, are enough to overcome the dangers of large-scale segmentation. Then, too, individuals must occasionally be held in line for the good of the total society. This can ordinarily be accomplished through legal restrictions and appeals to patriotism. Where such measures prove insufficient, recourse may be had to supernatural beliefs that reinforce socio-cultural sanctions and so help to bring about the formation of strong bonds of attachment to one's total society.

SELECTED REFERENCES

Boas, F., "The Social Organization and Secret Societies of the Kwakiutl Indians," *Report of the U.S. National Museum for 1895*, Washington, 1897.

Hoebel, E. A., *Man in the Primitive World*, rev. ed., chapter 27. New York, 1958.

———, *Primitive Law*, Cambridge, 1950.

Hollis, A. C., *The Masai*, Oxford, 1905.

Lévi-Strauss, C., "The Social and Psychological Aspects of Chieftainship in a Primitive Tribe: The Nambikuara," *Transactions, New York Academy of Sciences*, series II, Vol. 7, 1944, pp. 16-32.

Lowie, R. H., *Primitive Society*, chapter 10. New York, 1920.

———, *Social Organization*. New York, 1948.

Mandelbaum, D. G., "Friendship in North America," *Man*, Vol. 36, 1936.

Rivers, W. H. R., *The History of Melanesian Society*, Vol. I, pp. 60-79. Cambridge, England, 1914.

Spicer, E. H., *Pascua, A Yaqui Village in Arizona*, pp. 91-116. Chicago, 1940.

Titiev, M., "Old Oraibi," *Papers of the Peabody Museum of American Archaeology and Ethnology*, Cambridge, Massachusetts, Vol. 22, No. 1, 1944.

Voth, H. R., "The Oraibi Marau Ceremony," *Field Columbian Museum, Anthropological Series*, Vol. 11, No. 1. Chicago, 1912.

14

GROWING UP IN A CULTURE

A. PROLOGUE

Not so long ago it became apparent that something vital was being omitted from traditional studies of culture in terms of biocultural configurations. Progress was being made in the identification of trends or laws of culture growth, sharper analyses of the dynamics of cultural processes were being formulated, and there was an increasing understanding of the interplay of various forces within every pattern of culture. It thus became a truism to say that each society had one or more approved forms of behavior and to point out that this implied a system of values which made every conceivable act right or wrong in the eyes of a given social unit. But it ultimately dawned on some cultural anthropologists that studies along these lines, while highly important, paid little attention to the individual men and women who, in all instances, were the sole carriers and transmitters of patterns of culture. Particularly was it felt that the impact of culture on the personalities of specific individuals was being neglected. If every human being must learn to adjust his behavior to the sanctioned values of his society, the very process of adjustment cannot fail to have a weighty effect on his total personality.

Today there is increasing reluctance to deal with biocultural configurations as if they existed in a vacuum. More and more attention is being devoted to efforts to understand what happens to the

personalities of people as they learn to conform to the culture patterns that prevail in their societies. To be truly valuable, these
studies require detailed investigation into the lives of many particular individuals. Resort to generalities, averages, or types is considered of small worth in this kind of approach. A host of modern cultural anthropologists, including Kluckhohn, Mead, Benedict,
Hallowell, and Linton, whose names are best known to the general
public, have made important contributions toward an understanding of the ways in which socially sanctioned mores affect the conduct and temperaments of specific persons. Professor Kluckhohn
has neatly characterized this aspect of the science of man as being
concerned with the "person-in-a-culture."

All researches into personality formation owe much to the hypotheses so convincingly advanced by Sigmund Freud. Even those
who most violently disagree with parts of his teachings or methods
are likely to take for granted some of his ideas. Over the years many
criticisms have been made of Freud's concepts, but a number of his
most fundamental tenets have never been proved wrong. This is
certainly not the place for a complete review and evaluation of
Freudian doctrine, but two of his cardinal points have stimulated
a great deal of research on the part of numerous cultural anthropologists. These are the concept of infantile sexuality, which seems
to be inborn and which perpetually seeks gratification, not necessarily intercourse and orgasm; and the notion that feelings of love,
hate, anger, and frustration that are experienced in early life may
be buried for years before expressing themselves overtly in ways
that may not necessarily reveal their true causes. These features of
Freudian doctrine have led investigators to devote much attention
to child-rearing customs and, since toilet training and weaning are
widely interpreted to induce frustration in babies, great stress is
laid on studying these practices in varied societies. A few extrem-
ists have read far more meaning into toilet training and swaddling
habits than the average cultural anthropologist considers to be
justified. Nonetheless, it is pretty well agreed that the experiences
of early childhood are apt to play important parts in the formation
of adult personalities.

For determining what grievances, resentments, hatreds, delights,
or loves an individual may carry below the level of his conscious
thoughts and attitudes, it is customary to use **projective tests.** These
fall into several groups. One type asks a subject to perform tasks,

like drawing a man or a horse, wherein the things that he emphasizes or omits may provide clues to his innermost traits of personality. Another kind confronts a person with a series of vaguely-defined pictures, based on inkblots or deliberately ambiguous sketches, which the subject is asked to explain or interpret in any way that he pleases. A third sort requires a subject to judge the behavior of people in standardized situations, such as that of a man who beats his wife, or to tell what values or associations a given list of words brings to his mind.[1]

Answers obtained from projective tests of these kinds have been found to reveal about a person many things that lie below the threshold of consciousness. A number of ethnologists now give projective tests as part of their research programs in the field. Sometimes they turn the results over for analysis and interpretation to third parties, and in a surprising number of cases, psychologists unfamiliar with the individuals and cultures concerned, have made diagnoses of personality that closely agree with the independently formed judgments of the field workers.

A few psychologists and psychologically-oriented anthropologists go so far as to try to explain the nature of culture itself as a reflection of individual personality traits. This reflects a time, for instance, when the emphasis on war that characterizes numerous societies was attributed to the workings of a "death instinct" in the populace. Most modern scholars are reluctant to make such assumptions, and the origins of cultural emphases are usually left unexplained. Contemporary anthropologists are content to agree that each newly born child is faced with a pre-existent society and culture to which it must learn to adjust its built-in, biologically inherited mechanisms. Put another way, it amounts to saying that every baby must learn to conform to its society's sanctioned patterns for group living. What is called **learning theory** is thus involved, and to this vital subject many research workers have turned their attention. A common interest in learning theory is only one of several fruitful mergers between cultural anthropologists and psychologists.

Another area of joint activity concerns the awareness that the

---

[1] Best known of the tests based on indefinite pictures is Murray's Thematic Apperception Test (T.A.T.). Standardized ink-blots are used in Rorschach tests. A discussion of this subject may be found in H. H. and G. L. Anderson, *An Introduction to Projective Techniques*, New York, 1951.

psychological potentials of a human being can be realized only if he is given the chance of interacting with other representatives of *Homo sapiens*. Ordinarily, these representatives will be found to stand in definite relationships to a child, and to accept the obligations of attending to his physical needs and of teaching him the systems of values that are essential ingredients of their way of life. The instructional responsibilities are conventionally entrusted in the first instance to parents or their surrogates; but other kin, friends of the family, neighbors, teachers, playmates, and religious or political officers always supplement parental instructions. Through the combined efforts of all concerned, the sum total of the cultural norms of his social unit is brought home to a neonate, and as he grows older he becomes increasingly aware of the forms of behavior which are expected of him. Anthropologists firmly hold to the belief that an individual's personality can be understood only if one knows as much as possible about the whole cultural system in which he lives.

B. THE PROCESS OF ENCULTURATION

Although there are a great many definitions of culture, it is generally agreed that cultural concepts cannot be transmitted through genetic inheritance, so that each child must start to learn the culture of its group after it has emerged from its mother's body. In any study of neonatal development, therefore, an anthropologist must begin with the assumption that a child is born with a set of complicated biological organisms but without a shred of culture. However, from the first moment of its birth a human baby begins to feel the impact of culture: in the way it is delivered, the mode in which its umbilical cord is cut and tied, the fashion in which it is washed and handled, and the manner in which it is swaddled or clothed. Somewhat later, a newly-born infant begins to behave bioculturally, and as it matures it will find itself playing down the purely biological aspects of its conduct and stressing cultural values. It is as though each child began postnatal life as a 100 percent biological mechanism and thereafter tried to reduce its biological conduct to a hypothetical vanishing point (Fig. 14.1). In reality, of course, biological activities can never be totally eliminated from human behavior.

For the process of adjusting individual responses ever increasingly to a society's patterns of culture, Professor Herskovits has chosen the fitting name **enculturation.** Enculturation may be regarded as the manner in which each society molds the biological organization of its neonates to a set of pre-existing cultural norms.

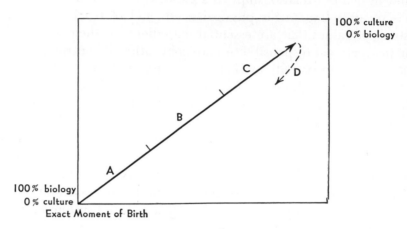

Fig. 14.1. The process of enculturation. In every society each neonate must go through the process of enculturation. This is divided into four stages. "A" stands for infancy, "B" for adolescence, "C" for adulthood, and "D" for old age. It should be noted that in each society "A" has the highest percentage of biological behavior and that "D" reverts somewhat to "A."

If it be granted that a baby's very first activities in postnatal life cannot be other than biological, it follows that many of its earliest experiences with the process of enculturation will be restrictive or frustrating. No matter how eager societies and their cultures may be to satisfy infantile demands, there is no group of human beings that drops everything instantaneously to feed a child at the first sign of hunger, or allows it absolutely unlimited freedom of muscular movement, or everlastingly permits it to excrete when and where it will. Sooner or later each child must learn to eat, move, and eliminate in accord with the culturally determined set of rights and wrongs that prevails in its society. As it learns to conform, every baby must experience restrictive checks on its biological behavior. No doubt neonates differ in the degree to which they can tolerate restriction, but no human infant can completely avoid developing some feelings of displeasure or hostility as it reacts to enculturation. There is an assumption that a child reared under easygoing conditions that hold in check very few of its activities, cater to its wants, and permit toilet training and weaning to occur without signs of grown-up impatience or distaste, will develop into a well-adjusted adult. Unfortunately, there has been little proof of the truth of this assumption. On the contrary, it is now known that Navaho men and women, brought up in an atmosphere that seems highly permissive to us, show as many maladjustments of personality as do mature individuals in other types of society. Plainly, the influence of childhood training on adult character is a subject that is not yet entirely understood.

Studies of enculturation may throw new light on such traditionally Freudian concepts as the important **Oedipus complex.** Hitherto, it has been assumed that a male child got so much loving attention from his mother that he grew up to hate his father as a sort of rival whom he hoped to displace in his mother's affections. Now it can be shown that a baby also resents the **enculturators** who impose cultural checks on his actions. In the vast majority of known societies, the biological or quasi-biological parents of an infant are its earliest and most important enculturators, but this need not always be the case. Theoretically, at least, a neonate may grow up to hate his enculturators, but may have no resentment at all toward his father.

Most of the requirements of enculturation are patterned similarly for all normal children of comparable age, sex, social background, and place of residence. Other demands are regularly repeated and apply to nearly everyone, with little distinction. They are the ones that can be predicted without much difficulty by any competent observer who is well acquainted with a particular society. Thus, we know that all girls among us will be taught not to reveal their breasts when wearing street dress, and we anticipate that boys will show an interest in athletics. Furthermore, patterned regularities of conduct may even be imposed on children who have been subjected to unexpected conditions, as when an American youth is injured so severely that he can neither play nor watch sporting events. Such random experiences may place a severe strain on the formation of individual personalities, yet the demands of cultural conformity are so relentless that something approximating normal adjustment is expected despite all handicaps.

All in all, the process of enculturation may be envisioned as a continuum, marked into a number of stages (Fig. 14.1). The first stage, labeled "A," shows a neonate beginning to move away from the strictly biological condition in which he was born. Throughout the beginning phases of this stage, an infant is the helpless and passive recipient of whatever forms of culture its handlers may choose to inflict upon it. At this time, too, a baby cannot be made significantly aware of its sex, socioeconomic status, or locale. Only gradually does it become conscious of the differences that these factors may cause or imply. Nor, at the outset of postnatal life, can the adult members of a society place too many restrictions on a neonate's biological behavior. Dr. Gesell and others have satisfactorily shown that physical maturation proceeds by degrees in infancy. Accordingly, it would be impossible to toilet-train a youngster before his brain was capable of giving the appropriate orders to those organisms that control the bladder and sphincter muscles.

Children born into any society must go through a stage "A." What differs from one group to another is the detailed forms of the culture that will be imposed on a neonate, the manner in which they will be applied to him, the severity with which transgressions will be punished, and the time when a child is assumed to have entered stage "B." Wherever, figuratively speaking, a social unit may decide to put the first dot on the continuous line that depicts the **enculturational process,** and no matter how unobtrusively or indefinitely it may be placed, the dot always represents a critical threshold, after crossing which a child is no longer expected to behave as it did in "A." This is what underlies the remarks, so often heard in our society, that run somewhat as follows: "Cut it out, you're not a baby any more!"

Broadly considered, stage "B" of Figure 14.1 covers the period of adolescence. This is always a difficult stage because a twofold series of changes is taking place simultaneously. Not only is the body undergoing numerous alterations, involving no one knows how many physical strains and stresses, but at the same time an adolescent must conform to a new set of cultural forms. Too often are adults likely to underestimate the cultural trials and tribulations of adjusting to stage "B." No grownup would view without alarm the necessity of changing his manner of speech, as well as his food and clothing habits, methods of movement, and so forth. Yet, in no society is an adolescent expected to talk, eat, dress, move, or excrete in the fashion of a baby. Of course, the changes required in "B" are not immediate. Time is generally allowed for them to take place, and youngsters are usually forewarned that they will someday have to modify their habits, but even so it is no trivial matter to adjust to so many changing ways of life at the same time that one's body is in a state of biological turmoil.

Stage "C" may be said to represent full maturity and is quite often marked by marriage. Once more a degree of variation exists in establishing this threshold, but again every society insists that adult behavior must be recognizably different from adolescent conduct. In some ways the transition to "C" is less difficult than the move into "B," but it is not without its problems.

On the assumption that marriage takes place in stage "C," as it usually does, a striking change takes place in every newlywed's way of life. Before marriage an individual ordinarily lived in his family of orientation (see p. 272). Here, if he had a brother and sister, he found himself forced to establish reciprocal ties of behavior with each of his parents and each of his siblings. Within his family of orientation, too, *Ego* was subordinate to his father and mother but more or less on a par with his brother and sister. At marriage, and particularly after he has begotten children, all this changes. Now a person finds himself occupying a different status in a family of procreation. Not only must he develop and maintain new bonds with his spouse, but he also finds himself dominant over his children.[2] Complications are likely to arise because a person is not expected to cancel all of the old ties in his family of orientation when he assumes new responsibilities in his family of procreation.

What has been said so far about "C" applies universally to all human societies. But in the United States additional strains may arise from our lack of fixed standards of values regarding the change-over from one family system to the other (Fig. 14.2). Suppose, in the case of a son, that his father were elderly and sick. As long as a male *Ego* continued to live in his family of orientation he would be expected, from the time that he was old enough, to help support his father. But if the father were still living when *Ego* married, what then? *Ego* is obligated to look after his wife and children, he is probably living away from his natal home, and he may not be earning enough to continue paying for his father's care. Most Americans would agree that a man's first duty is toward his wife and children, but they would also insist that it is not right to neglect a sick and aged parent. Not all societies permit conflicts of this kind to arise. In Japan, a man's obligations to his father are

---

[2] W. L. Warner, *American Life: Dream and Reality*, Chicago, 1953, pp. 81-83.

paramount and remain fixed. A filial son would neither feel upset nor arouse social criticism merely because he favored a parent over his wife and children. This is not to say that all Japanese cultural values are permanently fixed, but the values in this particular case are.

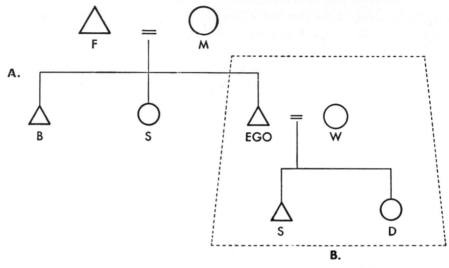

Fig. 14.2. Families of orientation and procreation. While *Ego* is unwed, he re-sides in his family of orientation (A), where he is equal to his siblings but sub-ordinate to his parents. When, at marriage, he shifts to his family of procreation (B), he becomes dominant over his children.

Last of the stages of the enculturational process is the one marked "D" on Figure 14.1. It is entered in old age, as any society chooses to define senescence. Ordinarily, a person who crosses this point is assumed to have a fairly complete knowledge of his group's culture. Thus, as he approaches a greatly advanced age he is no longer ex-pected to add still more cultural factors to his conduct. On the contrary, as Figure 14.1 indicates, a very old person is permitted in all societies to revert somewhat to the biological behavior of a neonate. Our popular sayings about second childhood reflect an awareness of this reversion. If an extremely aged person soils him-self or exposes his "private" parts, not much more is thought about it than if a small baby does the same things. Some of the behavior manifested in "D" may be rationalized or considered unavoidable because it is an outgrowth of physical change, but all cultures make allowances for such changes. As a rule, death intervenes to halt the complete reversion from "D" to "A."

C. INTERIORIZING CULTURAL VALUES

As a baby grows up in any society, it learns that much of what it was permitted to do as an infant it is not allowed to do at a somewhat later date. Such teachings take the form of negative statements directed to a youngster by older people. "Don't do this," "Don't be naughty," "Don't do that," "You mustn't," is what a child hears repeatedly. Consciously or not, a baby finds itself recurrently put into a hostility-fraught situation wherein it will gain rewards for yielding to the demands of grownups, but will arouse adult displeasure if it persists in following its own dictates; and adult displeasure, it soon learns from experience, leads to punishment in one form or another. Yet, an infant will not be emotionally content if it is constantly prevented from doing what it wishes. Psychologists have found that the commonest way out of the inescapable dilemma is for a child to bring itself to identify its views with those of the more powerful grownups, until it gradually acquires the feeling of *wanting* to do what they think it *ought* to do. When this stage has been reached, the instances of open hostility diminish and the youngster may be said to have **interiorized** the cultural values of its society. Much of the earlier antagonism may persist in the subconscious levels of personality, but on the surface, conformity without compulsion seems to prevail. Studies of personality formation, as well as analyses of the interplay between individuals and their cultures, must take into account the process of **value interiorization.** In reality, a child's formation of a **social conscience** may amount to no more than the internalizing of its group's standards of values.

A number of psychologists believe that the process of personality formation starts with the experience of birth. They hold that the first month or so of a baby's postnatal life is for the most part directed to an effort to re-establish the conditions under which it had lived in the womb. Members of some societies, for which the term **fetusphilic** has been proposed,[3] do give the appearance of attempting to make the transition from prenatal life easier for a baby by reproducing the physical conditions of its life while it was within

---

[3] See S. Bernfeld, *The Psychology of the Infant,* New York, 1929, p. 7.

its mother's body. They give a neonate warm baths and wrap it in soft garments. By way of contrast, people in other societies, which may be called **fetusphobic,** act in opposite fashion by dousing a child with cold water and wrapping it tightly or harshly. These variations of neonatal treatment are thought to reveal some of a society's standards and to affect an infant's degree of security or anxiety. How different must value interiorization be, if the process has been properly identified, under such contrasting conditions!

Interiorization is most successful when a person comes to carry out the teachings of his culture without conscious thought. If the welfare of a society depends on promptness, it would never be enough for each individual to have to remind himself continuously that he must be on time. Only when everyone concerned has so completely interiorized the value of promptness that he no longer has to think about it can promptness be taken for granted by the society as a whole. This type of thoroughgoing interiorization provides the only guarantee that a pattern of culture will function properly.

Because the processes of enculturation and value interiorization go on simultaneously or nearly so, they are sometimes regarded as one and the same. They are not, however, alike. During the earliest stages of enculturation, a baby has no option but to allow himself to become enwrapped, as it were, in its society's culture. On the other hand, interiorization is an active process, and an infant has a small degree of choice with respect to the selection of the items it will interiorize, as well as to the method, time, and order in which interiorizing will take place. A crude analogy may help to illustrate the essential difference between the two processes. A neonate may be likened to a child with a cent in a candystore. The money represents its limited facility for coping with a culture. When the storekeeper, who stands for parents or enculturators in a society, puts out a few bits of penny candy (cultural traits) it is *he* who makes the choice of what to offer, and his actions correspond roughly to the manner of enculturation. He may even go so far as to push one particular piece forward, which the little purchaser is very likely to choose. When the child makes the selection and actively takes the candy into itself by sucking, chewing, or gulping, it is as though it were interiorizing an item of culture.

To drop the analogy, we seem to have arrived at a pair of universal laws governing the interplay of an individual and his culture. Each society insists that its neonates adjust themselves to the pattern of culture which begins to enfold them as soon as they have been born, and value interiorization is one of the major mechanisms by which every baby makes the compulsory adjustment. Within the limits of even a single segment of a society and its particular subculture, the process of interiorization is complex and multidimensional. It appears to be compounded from at least three sets of variables which probably differ for each infant. The first variable is biological, for it cannot be assumed that each neonate begins life with exactly the same genes and inborn equipment. This may help to account for the differing degrees of acceptance, or **thresholds of frustration,** that have been observed in babies. Experiments with very young children have proved that they react differently to stimuli that are physically precisely alike. The second variable is sociological, for every additional child that is born to a family occupies a different place in respect to its siblings and confronts its parents at different stages of their age and experience. The third variable is cultural, inasmuch as patterns differ from one social unit to another and no design for group living remains static forever. Hence, what a child first learned to regard as wrong, it may later be taught to accept as proper. Half a century ago, for instance, it was illegal and daring in New York City for women to smoke in public, but today such behavior is commonplace.

This discussion may also serve to throw light on why a pattern of culture may, in theory, be treated as something that has an existence independent of the people who are its bearers. For one thing, patterns of culture are transmitted from one generation to another quite apart from the life and death of particular persons. They can also be more or less completely accepted and interiorized in different ways by various people. Moreover, the laws which govern their origins and changes are not entirely controlled by the wishes or desires of the persons whose conduct they help to regulate. How subtly a culture pattern can affect individual behavior is strikingly brought out by the studies of Dr. Gesell. The maturational sequences of an infant's physical development which were carefully worked out in his clinic at Yale University,[4] and which were as-

---

[4] A. Gesell, *Embryology of Behavior,* New York, 1945.

sumed at first to be universal for *Homo sapiens* and entirely biological, were later found to be partly cultural and to have their best application to children of middle-class parents in New Haven.

Early in the book the point was made that a human baby-to-be can exercise no choice over the genetic elements that it will receive from its parents at the moment of conception. This situation was contrasted with an infant's postnatal acquisition of culture with respect to which it could exercise a measure of selection. Theoretically, a growing child can decide to accept, modify, or reject any trait of culture whatsoever. Why, then, do people so seldom fail to accept and interiorize the values of their culture, even if many items are personally uncongenial or distasteful? The answer revolves around a few basic points. In the first place, enculturation begins at so early an age that a baby must be a passive recipient, without much capacity for active agreement or disagreement. In the second place, it is impossible during the early stages of life to reject a culture without repudiating parents, kinfolk, and other members of the society on whom one's welfare depends during the very time that he is learning the only way of life in his range of experience. In the third place, it is neither easy nor quick for an individual to learn a pattern of culture thoroughly. We know full well that if we were asked to name an informant who could properly explain our culture to an outsider we would suggest neither a young child nor an adolescent, but a mature person twenty-five years of age or older. This is equivalent to saying implicitly that we think it takes at least a quarter of a century to learn a single manner of living. Even though, grantedly, a second way of life might be learned more rapidly, it would still be extremely time-consuming and difficult for an adult who had been brought up in one fashion to learn flawlessly the requirements of speaking a new language, forming new motor habits, adopting new eating habits and preferences, and accepting a new set of outlooks on life, including new political allegiance and the practice of a new religion. The sheer hardship of learning another culture pattern thoroughly is enough to discourage all but a small number of people from voluntarily forsaking the way of life that they learned as children. Immigrants, it is true, often make drastic changes of culture, but it generally takes an exceptionally strong expulsive force to get them to leave their home societies.

D. THE INTERACTION OF INDIVIDUAL TEMPERAMENTS
AND PATTERNS OF CULTURE

In all investigations of enculturation and value interiorization there is one question that always stands forth prominently. What does each child bring into the world with which it must confront its society's culture? No matter what reply is made, one fact seems indisputable. Owing to the complexities of human reproduction, the likelihood is slim that any two offspring, excepting identical twins, will have inherited precisely the same genetic composition. To this extent it may be said that no two neonates face the world with exactly the same inborn equipment.[5] Even if they found themselves in absolutely identical societies and cultures, which is impossible in practice, they would still react in different ways. Yet, each would seek air, food, warmth, dryness, and stability; each would respond to some stimuli by crying and to others by falling asleep; and each would digest food and excrete waste matter in fairly predictable ways. In the most minimal and essential aspects of its bodily activities, therefore, each infant somehow reaches an equilibrium between its unique nature and the conformity of behavior that applies to its entire species. As it grows older, another kind of balance will have to be struck, this time between the child's inherited biological character and the culture pattern to which it must mold itself.[6] By the time it has reached maturity each youngster will have learned to conform reasonably well to the standards set by its culture, but it should not be assumed that all children end up exactly alike. It is much more likely that each child will have retained a measure of individuality, and that each will have paid a different price in terms of suppressions and repressions. Cultural conformity is a hard taskmaster, and it has been known to exact high fees in the shape of warped personalities.

Individual personality is the product of an inherited biological character modified by the demands of culture. From this standpoint it becomes clear that variations in people may result either from the effects of a similar pattern of culture imposed on different organisms, or else from the impact of essentially dissimilar ways of life

---

[5] Much new light is being shed on this topic by the investigations of Dr. Roger J. Williams, who has published some of his findings in *Biochemical Individuality*, New York and London, 1956.

[6] A great deal of information on the biochemistry of child growth may be found in I. G. Macy and H. J. Kelly, *Chemical Anthropology*, Chicago, 1957.

on reasonably similar biological entities. The possibilities inherent in these situations may be illustrated by combining some of Dr. William H. Sheldon's notions with some of the late Professor Benedict's. According to Sheldon,[7] people of mesomorphic type, who are muscular and sturdily built (Fig. 14.3), are somatotonic of temperament and like physical exercise, show a love of daring and boldness, seem indifferent to pain, and are assertive and aggressive, especially when under the influence of alcohol. These temperamental characteristics agree quite well with Benedict's portrayal of Dionysian patterns of culture, which honor aggression and reckless conduct in men.

Almost exactly opposite are the personality traits of those whom Sheldon calls ectomorphic. They are thin and fragile in anatomical structure (Fig. 14.3) and have cerebrotonic dispositions. Their actions are restrained, they are inhibited in dealing with others, hypersensitive to pain, and resist alcohol and other drugs. On the whole their temperaments are in accord with Benedict's account of Apollonian culture, which rewards self-restraint and sobriety.

If a male of mesomorphic build and a somatotonic temperament should happen to be brought up in a Dionysian culture, it seems likely that he may conform easily, without conflict and with little cause for psychological maladjustment. Similarly, there seems to be little reason why an ectomorph who is cerebrotonic cannot be expected to adjust smoothly to the requirements of an Apollonian way of life. But youngsters of all kinds are born into every sort of society, which suggests that somatotonics might find it hard to suit themselves to Apollonian patterns and that cerebrotonics would suffer where Dionysian standards prevailed.

The use of Sheldon's and Benedict's terminology does not mean that the author accepts their teachings without reservation.[8] He firmly believes that there is a grain of truth in their analyses, and

---

[7] Dr. Sheldon is one of the pioneers in a field that is sometimes called *constitutional anthropology*. He believes that a person's biological inheritance, as expressed by his body build, always conditions his reactions to culture. Dr. Sheldon's ideas are not accepted by all anthropologists, but they are widely used by students in other fields. Most of his concepts, and the terms he employs, may be found in the following works: W. H. Sheldon, *et al.*, *The Varieties of Human Physique*, New York, 1940; W. H. Sheldon, *et al.*, *The Varieties of Temperament*, New York, 1942; W. H. Sheldon, *et al.*, *Atlas of Men*, New York, 1954.

[8] Several details stand in the way of the author's full acceptance of either Sheldon's or Benedict's viewpoints. For example, the Hopi Indians are not at all ectomorphic in body build, yet their culture and behavior are typically Apollonian.

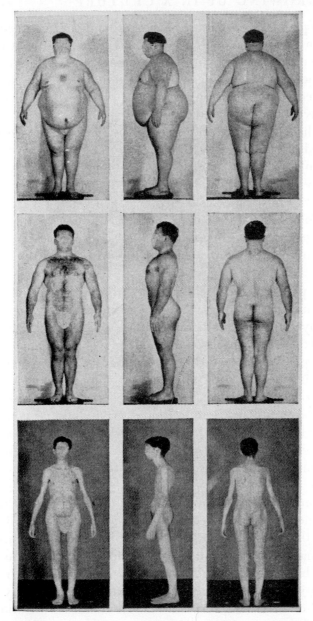

Fig. 14.3. Extreme varieties of somatotypes. At the top is an extreme endomorph, who is viscerotonic in temperament. The center shows an extreme mesomorph, with whom a somatotonic disposition is associated. The bottom pictures an extreme ectomorph, a type that is generally cerebrotonic. (W. H. Sheldon *et al.*, *The Varieties of Human Physique*. New York, 1940. Courtesy of Harper & Bros.)

that some peoples and cultures can be found that conform to their descriptions. At the same time he is convinced that what they have brought out applies best to extreme cases and has less application to the majority of individuals and patterns of culture, which tend to be mixed rather than purely of one type or the other. The extremes have been used only to bring the main issues into sharp focus.[9] What psychological price do individuals physically given to one kind of behavior pay when they force themselves to conform to a way of life that is uncongenial to their innate temperaments? How many maladjusted and neurotic individuals in any society result from the unspoken insistence that everyone, regardless of his inborn, biologically determined disposition, must regulate his conduct in agreement with predetermined cultural norms, which he may find unpleasant, but over which he can exercise little or no control?

At this point the danger of biocultural unconformity (p. 201) again looms large. Suppose an American father, whose son was neither physically nor temperamentally suited for athletics, insisted that the boy become a good football player. In such a dilemma, what is a poor child to do? If he disobeys his father, he runs the risk of losing his affection and support; but if he obeys, he is in danger of becoming internally upset. So it often is with the requirements of culture. From time to time every individual is placed in a situation where he offends his fellowmen if he follows his own personal leanings, but where he must take a chance on personality maladjustment if he makes himself conform to the dictates of his society.

A program ought to be undertaken to discover exactly what happens to a neonate's biological system as a child modifies it in keeping with the requirements of his culture. At the moment it is conventional to say that cultural restrictions induce feelings of frustration in babies, who cry because they are prevented from doing what they would like. Professor Norman R. Maier, a psychologist, suggests a contrasting interpretation. He defines frustration as "behavior without a goal," [10] and asks whether infantile crying may

---

[9] In *Physique and Delinquency*, New York, 1956, the authors, Sheldon and Eleanor Glueck, utilize many of Dr. Sheldon's concepts. Like him, the Gluecks believe that body structure holds a clue to biologically determined attitudes toward culture. They have found that an undue proportion of juvenile delinquents, particularly in America, are aggressive mesomorphs.

[10] N. R. F. Maier, *Frustration: The Study of Behavior Without a Goal*, New York, 1949.

not be a "problem-solving technique." Perhaps Professor Maier is right. It is just as likely that infants cry deliberately for the express purpose of being taken out of an unpleasant situation as that they weep only to express resentment and helplessness. Answers to vital questions of this sort will never be found so long as students of personality and culture continue to start with personality structures that are fully or reasonably well formed and then try to deduce the kind of childhood training that a subject may have had. Such a deductive method puts investigators of personality on the level of medical researchers before the causes of most diseases were well known. In those days doctors could not recognize an ailment until it was well advanced, which made cures exceedingly difficult and preventive medicine impossible. Only if they reverse their approach and begin to examine inductively the mechanisms by which newly born infants adjust their inherited biological natures to prescribed standards of culture will students of personality reach the scientific goal of knowing how personalities are formed at such an early stage that corrective measures can be applied, where necessary, before it is too late.[11]

E. PERSONALITY FORMATION AND CULTURE CHANGE

There is no reason to believe that only abnormal children encounter difficulties in moving from one enculturational stage to another. Normal youngsters, too, find it no trifling matter to grow up properly in any society and culture. Enculturation is a difficult process, and it is high time that we stopped regarding as abnormal every person who stumbles and requires help somewhere along the line.

Once the distinctions between biological and cultural conduct are understood, we may find ourselves supplied with better tools than are now available for making some fundamentally important distinctions that should lead to more accurate diagnoses and better curative procedures. To be specific, let us take the problem of homosexuality. As presently defined, a homosexual is an individual who seeks sexual gratification from another person of the same sex. At

---

[11] Claims have recently been put forward for psychological tests that enable investigators of youngsters to detect future alcoholics. Proponents believe that if these tests are given early enough, proper diets can keep susceptible children from becoming chronic alcoholics later on. These claims have not yet been substantiated, but such tests are indicative of a trend toward discovering and correcting defects of personality before they are fully formed.

the moment, it is not customary to distinguish between those who are biologically incapable of enjoying heterosexual relations and those who are culturally induced to become homosexuals. Even in jail populations, where the two sexes are carefully kept apart, a homosexual is a homosexual. Absolutely no distinction is made between those who actually prefer to make love to members of their own sex and those who may long to be heterosexual but are forced by prison conditions to become homosexual. This is no indictment of prison administrators; the writer knows full well that they are already confronted with an overwhelming number of problems. But if the people of any society wish to remedy some of the difficulties brought about by homosexuality, they will first have to differentiate between biological and cultural causation in order to know which corrective techniques should be used.

Enculturation is a hard enough process when a society's cultural values are clear and stable. It is made even harder, though, when socially sanctioned values are indistinct and subject to rapid change. Consequently, every individual should be prepared to shift his standards of values whenever necessary. But it is not easy to make such shifts, especially if the new values run counter to the old, and little time is provided for making the transition (see Fig. 14.4). A child who has thoroughly interiorized the belief that a particular way of life is right cannot quickly accept the opposite premise. Not enough attention has heretofore been given to the problems created by pressures to accept new, and sometimes contradictory, standards of values on short notice.

American marriage counselors are all familiar with the phenomenon of **marital frigidity** on the part of numerous wives. Many advisers have long realized that the problem is more often cultural than biological. Yet, they do not seem to have given enough weight to the difficulties of making quick shifts of culture values. We are naive if we think that every girl who has been taught to cherish her virginity and resist all the advances of men for twenty years or so can without uneasiness give herself to her husband one night later, simply because she has been officially married to him earlier that day. No wonder a number of wives find it hard to make such a rapid change-over and that feelings of shame or guilt regarding sexual relations so often arise even in the legally married.

Up to the present it has been customary for psychoanalysts and others who try to correct such difficulties as marital frigidity to seek the causes along the line "AB," as shown in Figure 14.4. "Perhaps," it is said or implied, "the patient once experienced an emotional block in her premarital upbringing and has transferred her hostility from the man who caused the block to her husband."

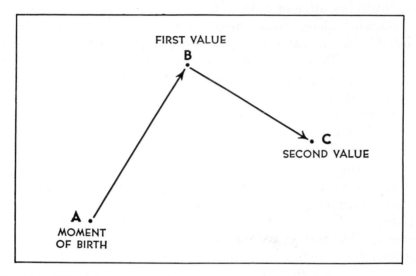

FIRST VALUE
B

C
SECOND VALUE

A
MOMENT
OF BIRTH

Fig. 14.4. Value changes. As a person grows up, he must inevitably change some of his values. Adjustments become harder in proportion to the length of time that a first value has been held, in regard to the thoroughness with which a first value has been interiorized, and in relation to the degree of contradiction or opposition between "B" and "C," and in accord with the preparation and length of time allowed for a change.

Theoretically, it is just as possible that the source of trouble lies along line "BC" instead of "AB" on Figure 14.4 and is due to socio-cultural insistence on an immediate reversal of what had previously been considered wrong. The causes of personality maladjustments need not be sought exclusively in one direction or the other.

F. MODAL PERSONALITIES AND NATIONAL CHARACTER

Despite the feeling that studies of persons-in-a-culture should be conducted on specific individuals, some writers have tried, in a manner of speaking, to combine the results of the investigations of numerous individuals into a kind of average, usually known as a **modal, or basic, personality type.** Apart from the convenience of grouping a large number of studies under a single head, efforts to establish modal personality types have some scientific justification.

Doubtless, it is to be expected that people who are brought up in the same patterns of culture and subjected to the same systems of values will show, at least on the surface, a number of common personality characteristics. These are what descriptions of modal personality types attempt to depict.

Following along similar lines, there has recently arisen in the United States an interest in what is often called **national character.** Such studies do not restrict themselves to small, culturally homogeneous, tribal groups, but undertake to deal with large, literate, and heterogeneous social units on the scale of the United States or the Soviet Union. They are based on the assumption that all citizens of a modern nation are exposed to so many uniform cultural institutions, such as public schools, newspapers, economic regulations, and patterns of federal government, that they develop similar characteristics of personality and behavior. Efforts are made to delineate national character in terms of regularities of conduct which can be predicted. It is also assumed that all members of a society who share an identifiable pattern of culture will show similarities of intrapsychic structure. If a certain action is condemned by a given society, it is said, then all the people in the group will show shame if they perform the disapproved action. Underlying this approach is the hope of developing a new psychocultural theory that will explain how human beings embody and learn to live by the cultural norms of their society.

Proponents of national character studies, led in the United States by Dr. Margaret Mead, are confident that this is a legitimate branch of cultural anthropology. They recognize that big societies tend to divide into subgroups, but they claim that it is possible to reconcile the customs of the smaller divisions with the established ways of life of the larger unit. One American is more like another American than he is like a Balinese, they insist, whether the American is a New England textile worker or a Texas rancher.

As for the use of cultural anthropologists in this type of research, it is felt that they have much that is valuable to contribute. They are supposed to be able to make disciplined studies of small, homogeneous, primitive societies which may serve as models for analyzing large nations; their research tools and techniques should prove applicable to social units of any kind; they are accustomed to integrating the various aspects of culture into one whole structure; they have been schooled to discount their personal biases and prejudices;

and they are so intimately acquainted with many diversified ways of life as to make possible valid intercultural comparisons.[12] At the same time it is realized that one observer might be competent to make a singlehanded study of a small community, but that he would be unable to handle all the complexities of a nation-state. For this reason teams of investigators are recommended, at least one of whom should be thoroughly acquainted with anthropological concepts and methods.

As in the case of all personality and culture studies, it is suggested that a thorough knowledge of culture patterns should be acquired before research on basic personality formation is begun. Child-training practices, especially, whose effects are thought to be essential to the development of each individual's adult personality, are supposed to be carefully studied, not only for their own sakes and the understanding of personality formation that they may yield, but also because they may be expected to provide clues to a society's system of values. Plots of popular films and novels, autobiographical accounts, and large-scale projective tests may likewise throw much light on national outlooks, values, and emphases. Ultimately, it will probably be found that while all cultures and subcultures appear to be unique when studied one at a time, they are likely to reveal many similarities when examined on a comparative basis. Once we have acquired an understanding of the universal elements that exist in all patterns of culture, we shall have in our hands the potential for a better control of the biocultural behavior of all mankind.

SELECTED REFERENCES

Benedict, R. F., *Patterns of Culture*, Boston, 1934.
———, "Psychological Types in the Cultures of the Southwest," *Proceedings, Twenty-third International Congress of Americanists*, 1928, pp. 572-581.
Gorer, G., "Themes in Japanese Culture," *Transactions, New York Academy of Sciences*, Series 2, Vol. 5, 1943, pp. 106-124.
Hallowell, A. I., "Culture, Personality, and Society," in *Anthropology Today*, A. L. Kroeber, ed., pp. 597-620. Chicago, 1953.
Herskovits, M. J., *Man and His Works*. New York, 1948. (Look up references to enculturation in the index.)

---

[12] Several anthropologists have for many years been assembling data from all over the world for the Human Relations Area File, at Yale University. These data are arranged by topics as well as regions, and make possible a large number of cross-cultural comparisons.

Hilgard, E. R., *Theories of Learning*, rev. ed. New York, 1956.

Honigmann, J. J., *Culture and Personality*. New York, 1954.

Hutt, M. L., *et al.*, "Social Values and Personality Development," *Journal of Social Issues*, Vol. 5, No. 4, 1949.

Jones, E., *The Life and Work of Sigmund Freud*. New York, 1953.

Kardiner, A., *The Individual and his Society*. New York, 1939.

———, *Psychological Frontiers of Society*. New York, 1945.

Kluckhohn, C., and Murray, H. A., eds., *Personality in Nature, Society and Culture*. New York, 1948.

Linton, R., *The Cultural Background of Personality*. New York, 1945.

Mead, M., "National Character," in *Anthropology Today*, A. L. Kroeber, ed., pp. 642-667. Chicago, 1953.

———, "The Implications of Culture Change for Personality Development," *American Journal of Orthopsychiatry*, Vol. 17, 1947, pp. 633-646.

Newcomb, T. M. and Hartley, E. L., eds., *Readings in Social Psychology*. New York, 1947.

Sapir, E., "The Contribution of Psychiatry to an Understanding of Behavior in Society," *American Journal of Sociology*, Vol. 42, 1937, pp. 862-870.

Sheldon, W. H., *et al.*, *The Varieties of Human Physique*. New York, 1940.

———, *The Varieties of Temperament*. New York, 1942.

CHAPTER 15

MAN AND THE SUPERNATURAL

A. PRIMITIVE RELIGION AS A SOCIOCULTURAL FORCE [1]

The very existence of symbolic, cultural values creates difficulties, unknown to subhumans, with which every humanly devised pattern of group living must successfully deal lest it be torn apart. These difficulties may be of various kinds, but some of the most important ones always concern shortages and their consequences.

If we examine the first two sides of a biocultural triangle, we find that with respect to man's interactions with his environment, cultural values, expressed chiefly as preferences, often diminish the impartial use of all that nature provides. Similarly, in the matter of interpersonal relations, cultural values, in the form of moral or ethical rules, serve to lessen at least the number of potential outlets for sexual expression. When the situation is thus viewed, *Homo sapiens* is seen to be faced with the threat of two kinds of shortages, those originating from environmental or biological deficiencies and those arising from cultural restrictions. Primitive people know pitifully little about overcoming the one or changing the other.

---

[1] Religion is a broad subject to which many volumes have been devoted and on which numerous books are sure to be published in the future. Since the space for treating the topic in this text is limited and since the author does not feel competent to discuss all aspects, it is only fair to the reader to explain the viewpoint that is to be followed. Every effort has been made to bring out the sociocultural implications of the subject and to analyze religion as a powerful cohesive force in society. Entirely omitted from consideration are such important features as individual motivations and the feelings of pleasure or comfort that worshipers may derive from religious practices.

No matter what their origin, shortages invariably cause unhappiness to some members of a society. Accordingly, in terms of biocultural dynamics, shortages may be said to give rise to disruptive forces that endanger the continued existence of every pattern of culture. To prevent dissolution, each biocultural configuration must, therefore, contain one or more cohesive elements (sides) strong enough to outweigh the forces of disintegration. Perhaps that is why some sort of religion is a universal feature of all societies whose cultures have been studied. In certain cases, patriotism, or the overriding loyalty of each individual to his social unit, is enough to supply the needed cohesion, but in most primitive communities the bonds of patriotism are reinforced so closely by supernatural sanctions that in many instances patriotism and religion cannot be told apart.

Even in the United States, where the separation of "church" and "state" has long been a cardinal operating principle, we still hear phrases like "the flag is sacred"; and children daily pledge allegiance to "one nation, under God." Yet, Americans are forbidden by their Constitution to have a national religion. They cannot, as a result, utilize the doubly cohesive bonds of patriotic and religous loyalty that are so common in primitive societies (see Fig. 15.1A). There are thus made possible in the United States two different kinds of loyalty. Americans may belong to tightly-bound international religions whose teachings take precedence, in some matters, over national allegiance (Fig. 15.1B), or else they may maintain national loyalties despite differing religious ties (Fig. 15.1C). Neither of these arrangements provides as much unified cohesion as do the dual bonds of patriotic and religious unity (Fig. 15.1A) that are characteristic of tribal groups. Interestingly enough, the modern totalitarian nations featuring nazism, fascism, or communism have tried to bind their citizens closely together by imitating the twice-bound sociocultural structures of primitive societies. This they have attempted to do by merging political loyalty with worship of the state and by seeking to deify the head of the state. The United States has tried to achieve much the same effect by doubling the ties of loyalty (Fig. 15.1D). That is why, in times of crisis, when the threats of internal separatism or social disintegration loom large, Americans double their efforts to arouse effective patriotism by calling for more and more tokens of loyalty, increased expressions of sentiments of attachment to the social unit in terms of enforced

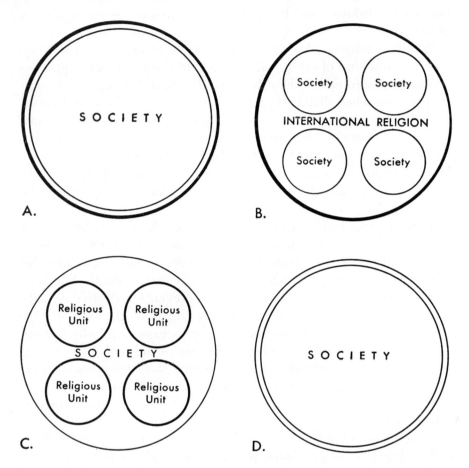

Fig. 15.1. Social (patriotic) and religious bonds. The light lines stand for the limits of social, national, or loyalty bonds; the dark ones for adherence to a common religion. A. The primitive condition. In nonliterate societies ties of religion tend to coincide with and reinforce the social bonds that hold members of a society together. The pattern so formed is structurally firmer than (B) or (C). B. Varying social units within a single, international religion. This represents the situation of those who adhere to a common faith but have differing political loyalties, as is true of French Catholics, American Catholics, Italian Catholics, Irish Catholics, and many others. C. Differing religions within a single social structure. A good example would include American Catholics, American Protestants, American Jews, and American Moslems. D. Double ties of loyalty. At present the Constitution prevents the United States from establishing a national religion. In times of crisis efforts are made to achieve the solidarity of A by doubling the patriotic bonds of loyalty that hold a national group together.

oaths and pledges of allegiance, more stringent investigations of the potentially disloyal, and by heightened demands for the exclusion of foreigners.

Primitive religion also acts to preserve a group's cohesion when it serves as a kind of safety valve to permit the escape of dangerous disintegrative forces, without harm to the social fabric. This is most clearly seen when dissatisfactions arise that are likely to be blamed on individuals, particularly chiefs. The dangers of rebellion against leaders or of withdrawal from a society are greatly diminished if dissatisfied persons are taught to believe and say: "Thy will be done, even to my own undoing." All societies are internally strengthened if their members are convinced that whatever happens is the will of God.

Since no social unit can exist without people, the withdrawal of any individual is a threat to the society as a whole. On this basis death represents the greatest of all forces of disintegration. No society remains indifferent to the consequences of death, but inasmuch as there is no physical means of preventing death's inroads, recourse to something supernatural is the only possible way to cushion or neutralize its impact. This helps to explain why the notion of another world in the hereafter, where the souls of the dead live on after the fashion of life on earth, is so very common. It amounts to saying that a deceased person, even when his body is no longer present, is still a spiritual member of his former society. There are tribes that go even further, by developing beliefs that at some future time the living will be reunited with the dead. Such beliefs function to guarantee that a society, like a perpetual belt, will never come to an end. By extending the continuity of a social group into the indefinite future death is "eliminated" as a threat to any society's perpetuation.

Social scientists of the future will have to deal with the problems involved in the growth of widespread international religions. It is obvious that they do not have the same functions as do religious beliefs in the world of primitive man. Apart from whatever other purposes they may serve, the supernatural practices of many tribes can be shown to be tailored to the needs of particular societies. Yet, except in a figurative sense, there is no single Christian, or Jewish, or Buddhist, or Moslem society. Members of each of these faiths reside in a large number of widely separated nations, with vastly different patterns of culture. Perhaps that is one reason why international religions put so much stress on moral or ethical principles that are supposedly applicable to all of mankind.

Religion may well be disruptive in a large, heterogeneous society that contains adherents to various faiths, but in primitive, relatively homogeneous communities, it acts as a strong, cohesive force. It strengthens the allegiance of individuals to their social unit, functions to overcome dissatisfactions arising in the realm of man's relations to his environment, smooths over many rough spots in man's dealings with his fellows, and helps to negate the unsettling effects of death. It is with the help of deeply ingrained religious beliefs that societies everywhere try to hold in line the hungry, poorly housed, badly clad, and sexually starved. Imaginatively speaking, societies prefer those who will tighten their belts but salute the flag or bow to the will of a deity to those who will give allegiance in these respects only if they have been well served in others. No matter where cultural anthropologists may look, they always find religious convictions employed in primitive societies to bolster weak points in patterns of culture.

B. A MINIMUM DEFINITION

Religion is such a vast and emotionally-laden subject that it may mean all sorts of different things to different people. Cultural anthropologists have found it so difficult to establish a satisfactory all-embracing definition that they have gone to the other extreme. In keeping with a suggestion originally proposed by E. B. Tylor, they have tended to work with a **minimum definition** that provides the least common denominator of elements to be found in all manifestations of religion. By reducing Tylor's proposal to its barest essentials we arrive at a minimum definition of religion as "a belief in the supernatural." Of itself the word "belief" implies an element of faith, a willingness to accept something without tangible demonstration or proof. To borrow an idea and a phrase from Wordsworth, religious, like "poetic faith," calls for "a willing suspension of disbelief." It should be realized that faith has strong emotional connotations, based on a sense of wonder or awe aroused by something mysterious. Earlier writers, not infrequently, referred to this aspect of emotionalism as a **religious thrill.**

When belief is applied to the supernatural, it signifies the willing acceptance of an order of things that cannot, so far as is known, be proved by logic nor grasped by man's senses or any extension thereof. When we describe something as supernatural, then, we mean that it lies beyond the reach of the sense organs and that it can never be made manifest to human taste, touch, smell, sight, or hearing, even with the aid of devices like powerful telescopes or sound amplifiers. To believe wholeheartedly in the existence of something that cannot and may never be grasped by one's senses forms the very core of religion and furnishes the foundation on which all religious systems are reared. Beliefs of this kind, which need have no biophysicochemical reality whatsoever, comprise the quintessence of algebraic mentality which can deal with abstract or symbolic concepts as readily as if they had objective reality. Emily Dickinson has accurately expressed this idea in her famous lines:

> "I never spoke with God,
>   Nor visited in Heaven;
> Yet certain am I of the spot
>   As if the chart were given."

Actually, no religion fails to go far beyond the two elements in the minimum definition, but every society builds its religious superstructure on the same least common denominators. Since supernatural constructs have no material existence and may differ widely from culture to culture, there is no way that a cultural anthropologist in the field can recognize, before they are pointed out to him, the objects to which a tribe ascribes religious significance. It may take a long time before people confide their beliefs to an investigator, and meanwhile he must be very circumspect lest he unintentionally damage or pollute something that may turn out to be holy in the minds of the natives. All animals which cannot readily handle symbolic values are incapable of dealing with the supernatural. For this reason it may be flatly said that only human beings can formulate religious beliefs.

C. THE CONCEPT OF MANA [2]

As a cultural anthropologist gains the confidence of tribespeople and begins to learn their innermost system of symbolic values, he

---

[2] The term mana was originally reported from the islands of the South Pacific that run from New Guinea to Fiji and was first employed, with very little variation from the way it is used here, in R. H. Codrington, *The Melanesians*, Oxford, 1891, chap.

comes to realize that they divide their world into **sacred** and **profane** categories. Certain objects, places, words, and people will be classed as sacred, whereas other externally identical items will be treated as secular or profane. The only difference will be one of native belief. An example from the Christian religion might deal with the distinction between a font of holy water and a similar basin of plain water. Through the use of none of his senses or scientific apparatus could an outsider, even if he were a specialist in qualitative chemistry, detect any difference in the two liquids, yet no true Christian would dream of using them indiscriminately.

The particular component of supernaturalism that distinguishes the sacred from the profane may be described as **mana.** Mana can best be understood as a powerful force, beyond the understanding, direct observation, or control of ordinary folk, that has an unlimited capacity for getting things done. Within itself mana is amoral and neutral in the sense that it is neither automatically good nor bad, and that it is indifferent as to whether its accomplishments are considered beneficial or harmful to individuals or societies. In this respect it is exactly like electricity, which cares not at all if it is used to kill a person or to run a refrigerator. Because of the belief that it can with equal facility do good or harm in the eyes of man, mana is always regarded as potentially dangerous. However, again like electricity, it is subject to a measure of control, and some people in every society learn to·handle it safely, usually through training but sometimes by inspiration. All others must avoid unauthorized contacts with mana in any form.

A splendid example of how the power of mana may work is to be found in the Old Testament.[3] Uzzah, a cart driver, was transporting the sacred Ark of the Covenant from one place to another. The road was rough, and at one point Uzzah reached out to steady the Ark with his hand, whereupon he was stricken dead. No matter how good his intentions may have been, Uzzah was not authorized to touch so mana-charged an object, and his impulsive action cost him his life. Yes, the power of mana can destroy as well as aid mankind,

---

12. Cultural anthropologists have found that in other primitive societies there are usually words that correspond more or less exactly to mana. Among those which are most commonly cited are: *manitou,* as used by American Indian speakers of Algonkian languages; *wakan* or *wakonda,* as it occurs in Siouan tongues; *baraka,* which is sometimes equated with holiness, as it is used by several Moslem groups in North Africa; and *orenda,* as rendered by speakers of Iroquois in North America.

[3] II Samuel 6:3-8.

and that is why efforts must be made to keep it under control. In order to safeguard the lay public, sacred things may be plainly marked with symbols that serve to identify them and to act as warnings, they may be kept hidden in secret places, or they may be subjected to **tabu,** which has the effect of keeping unqualified people at a safe distance. A tabu is a restraining order, a prohibition backed up by the threat of supernatural punishment for any violation.

A society may ascribe supernatural value to anything that seems to have an inexplicable capacity for getting successful results. This capacity is thought to be the kind of mysterious power called mana and may be variously assigned to a weapon with which a warrior has dispatched many enemies, to a stone that is believed to have brought rain, to an individual with a powerful personality or to one who has been outstandingly successful, to a person of high rank whose commands win obedience, to anything worn by a mighty personage, or to whatever has been in contact with something already thought to have been endowed with mana. For mana is transferable by contact or **contagion** and can be handed on by touch, association, or inheritance. The best-known illustration of the transfer of mana by contagion is the **laying on of hands.** In all such cases it is believed that the mana of a superior person flows on contact into an inferior individual (Fig. 15.2). In England in times past the ailment known as scrofula was called "the king's evil," and it was believed that a cure could be brought about if the ruler touched a sufferer. The concept of a national leader as a healer should be kept in mind when the reader comes to the section that follows. As a rule of thumb, it may be said that everything that is endowed with mana is sacred, all else is profane.

Many years ago scholars believed that the power of mana was just about identical with the life force, that is, with whatever it is that gives an organic thing its quality of being alive. Life force was said to animate an organism and to depart temporarily when a person dreamed or swooned and permanently whenever an organism died. Under the influence of E. B. Tylor, the animating life force was in most cases described in English as a **soul** or **spirit,** and it was said that this was what lived on, after the death of a once-alive organism, in a shadowy kind of hereafter. Beliefs of this sort were grouped together under the heading of **animism;** and since living things

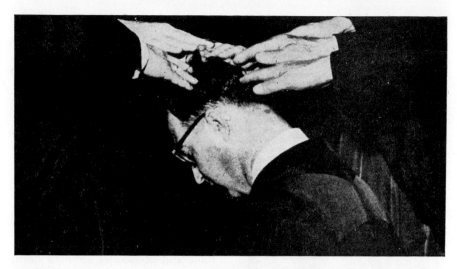

Fig. 15.2. The laying on of hands. Part of the consecration ceremonies for new ministers in many Christian sects involves the laying on of hands by officers who are already ordained.

were known to be either plants or animals, the term "animism" came to be subdivided into **botanical** and **zoological animism.**

Some time later, when field studies revealed countless examples of beliefs in supernatural power that could be lodged in nonliving objects such as those made of stone or metal, a new word was coined. For this entire category of belief Dr. Marett used the term **animatism.** For a while, there were some anthropologists who thought that animatism always preceded animism, but modern students have found so many examples of the two sets of beliefs existing side by side that they no longer regard the one as being prior or ancestral to the other.

D. PRIESTS, CHIEFS, AND GODS [4]

If the power of mana is too dangerous to be left uncontrolled, ways must be found of directing it into beneficial channels. This can be done only if some persons become qualified to deal with the super-natural and succeed in setting up techniques for getting it to work

---

[4] Primitive societies often exhibit a great deal of overlap between priests, chiefs, and gods. It seems hardly necessary to point out that "priest" is being used to denote any personage who is qualified to deal with the supernatural, and not with reference to a particular kind of Christian clergyman.

in a society's favor. Individuals who specialize in dealing with the world of the sacred are to be found in all societies and may be described, in general, as **priests**. Except in a limited number of tribes, priests are distinguished from laymen not only by their ability to deal with mana properly but also by the clothes they wear (Fig. 15.3), the tasks they perform, the objects they handle, the tabus

Fig. 15.3. A Witoto shaman. His costume and accessories serve to distinguish this individual from the ordinary Witoto men pictured in Figure 10.5. (Courtesy of Paul Fejos and the Bureau of American Ethnology.)

they observe, and the codes of conduct that they follow, with particular emphasis on food and sex habits. As their duties must bring them into close touch with things supernatural, all priests acquire an aura of sanctity and are themselves usually held to be charged with mana. The same applies to their costumes and to whatever they may use in the performance of their sacerdotal duties.

Members of nonliterate societies do not, as a rule, differentiate one kind of extremely great power from another. Tribal leaders or chiefs, with the exception of those who exert little or no authority, are regularly thought to have as much mana as priests. Their persons, garments, and accessories, together with their habitations and all their furnishings and belongings, are equally likely to be thought sacred and to be subject to tabu. To a commoner it makes little difference if the power to regulate, disrupt, or terminate his life is derived from a supernatural or a political source. Anyone who wields great authority over others will be looked upon with much the same awe and respect as a supernatural personage. The tendency to equate sacred and political power is particularly strong in societies where a chief really has priestly functions. Instances of this kind are far from rare. At Old Oraibi the village chief is automatically leader of the town's most important religious observance, the Soyal. Throughout the Pacific islands of Polynesia numerous chiefs serve as priests, and similar examples can be cited from any large area of the globe. Speaking broadly, it is only in recent times and in those restricted portions of the Euro-American world where a sharp distinction has been drawn between church and state that priests and chiefs have been entirely separated. Odd as it may seem to modern Americans, there are many people alive today who would find it difficult to understand how anyone could doubt the overlap of politics and religion.[5] In this connection it is interesting to note that Professor Horace M. Miner has independently written that the Koran, the sacred text of the Moslems, explicitly aims to achieve political unity through a common religion.[6]

Not only are chiefs frequently equated with priests, but they are sometimes, as has already been said, identified with **gods.** In minimum but basic terms, a god, in primitive society, may be defined as a local, supernatural personage, heavily endowed with mana. The tie between chiefs and gods seems to rest on the assumption that the soul of a person who once exerted great power while alive will retain his mana when he becomes a spirit in the other world. As it is to the advantage of the surviving members of the society to have their late chief's power exerted on their behalf, his soul is often called upon for help by his former subjects. For this important task, the dead chief's successor is commonly thought to be the best suited. Wherever such customs are practiced a succession is likely to be set up whereby a chief acts as a priest while alive and becomes converted to a god when he has died. These customs also help to explain why chiefs are so likely to be regarded as future gods that

[5] Even as late as the seventeenth century A.D., many religious sects in America functioned along political lines. For supporting facts see the fourth chapter, "Diversity of Religions," in L. B. Wright, *The Cultural Life of the American Colonies,* New York, 1957, pp. 72-97.

[6] H. M. Miner, *The Primitive City of Timbuctoo,* Princeton, 1953, p. 72.

Fig. 15.4. Emperor, high priest, and living god. Japan is far from a primitive nation, for it has one of the world's highest rates of literacy. Yet, before World War II, the Japanese were taught to reverence their emperor as a high priest and a living god. (International News Photos.)

they may be reverenced as divine even while they are still alive (Fig. 15.4).

E. GETTING IN TOUCH WITH THE WORLD OF THE SUPERNATURAL

Primitive man seldom regards his beliefs in the supernatural as luxury items, but is more likely to give them a practical value as something that can help his society to maintain itself. Hence, the mysterious world of the supernatural is not permitted to lie outside the sphere of ordinary existence, but is brought into the framework of life on earth. This is accomplished by the belief that some people, usually those who have been designated as priests, know how to get in touch with the other world. Communication may be established in either direction. Messages are sometimes sent from a social unit to the realm of the supernatural, but at other times the other world sends directives to the members of a living society. In either case it usually happens that priests, or other individuals endowed with mana, act as intermediaries between ordinary people and supernatural agencies.

Plain speech, often set in prescribed form to make a prayer, is the simplest and commonest way to send a message from this world. Prayers are generally addressed to a particular object or place where supernatural beings are thought to reside; they may be accompanied by required gestures or stances; and they may be uttered together with some device, such as striking a gong or bell, to attract the attention of the power for whom the message is intended. Songs may be substituted for spoken prayers, and they may be integrated with dances. Processions and dramas are sometimes little more than complex ways of sending messages to the other world.

Most prayers contain requests for guidance or help. There is implied a belief that supernatural agencies can, if they will, help living men and women to achieve what they most desire. So strong are such beliefs that it is frequently felt that people can get what they want if they act in conformity with the wishes of the supernatural. It thus becomes of the utmost necessity to interpret correctly whatever messages the other world may care to send to this one. Only by acting in accordance with expressed supernatural wishes can living people feel assured of getting supernatural backing for their deeds.

Once again do we see the importance of mana. It is mana that serves as the means of communication between the two worlds. Things that have mana are the most likely to convey messages from the supernatural, and people who have mana are best suited to act as interpreters.

All primitive efforts to determine the will of the supernatural are generally grouped together as **mantic "sciences,"** [7] that is, as "sciences" of prophecy, or efforts to find out in advance what kinds of behavior the gods expect of man and are willing to support. Such efforts may be grouped into two categories. In one case, which may be called **spontaneous,** the other world takes the initiative, and man needs only to know how to interpret aright whatever signs are sent; but at other times what may be called **directed messages** are sought, as when human beings deliberately set up test conditions and request the other world to make known its wishes in

---

[7] Closely related to the mantic "sciences" is **divination. A diviner** may try to discover the supernatural will, or else he may merely seek information, such as the whereabouts of a lost object, from the supernatural world.

some way. Spontaneous messages may take such forms as sudden claps of thunder, volcanic eruptions, unexpected dreams, uncontrolled body twitches, hiccoughs, or sneezes, strange behavior on the part of an animal, or the pattern of leaves left in the bottom of a cup of tea. Directed messages may be received when people deliberately seek visions, or when the organs or death throes of purposely slain animals are carefully observed, or if bones, twigs, or stones are tossed with the intent that the patterns into which the supernatural causes them to fall may determine what should be done (see Fig. 15.5).

Fig. 15.5. An African diviner. The individual shown is a member of the Bavenda tribe in Africa. He is believed to have the power of determining supernatural wishes by studying the patterns into which his divining bones fall when they are tossed. (Courtesy of the Museum of Anthropology, University of Michigan.)

Many children's games in our culture, like **counting-out rhymes** or "London Bridge," are thought to be relics of former primitive efforts to get directed messages from supernatural powers. Possibly, the tossing of coins or the cutting of cards, to which many literate people resort when faced with the need of making difficult decisions, are likewise "superstitions" or carry-overs of the primitive notion of getting a directed message from the supernatural world. In all such cases the underlying idea seems to be that man himself is not responsible for making a decision, but that he is acting in accordance with the expressed will of the gods. We shall encounter other possible elements of primitive religion when we discuss games and the fine arts.

F. SHAMANS AND CURING RITUALS; WITCHES
AND WITCHCRAFT

No society can possibly endure on earth if all its constituent members are suddenly removed by death or any other cause. True, deeply held beliefs in the continued existence of souls in another world may soften the impact of death, but never are convictions of this sort sufficient to make people completely indifferent to the effects of death. All societies, without exception, make an effort to keep death away from individuals as long as possible. In the primitive world these efforts are customarily made by **medicine men** or, as they are often but somewhat inaccurately called, **shamans.**

With the growth of scientific medicine in our country, we are taught to ascribe all diseases to known or knowable causes. Nonliterate men and women, knowing little or nothing of science, are very likely to attribute all sickness to supernatural agencies. So it is that their shamans are closely equated with priests and are supposed to know how to deal with mana-caused ailments.[8] Seldom, indeed, is any illness that befalls primitive man regarded as "natural." Most often, with the exceptions of ailments resulting from battle injuries or old age, the things that bring about death are thought to be of supernatural origin. Once in a while an act of indiscretion, such as the violation of a tabu, is regarded as the source of a sickness, but much more commonly a person is supposed to become ill because of **witchcraft.** Even accidental injuries are attributed in some societies to witchcraft. Either the accident was caused by a **witch,** or else the victim is himself a witch who suffered an accident as punishment for having previously engaged in antisocial activities.

A witch may be defined as an individual of any age and of either sex who uses the power of mana for antisocial purposes. Hence he causes sickness and death, makes crops fail, diminishes a game supply, or brings on foul weather. To appreciate why witchcraft is sometimes successful we must recall that in and of itself mana is neutral. The same power, as in an automobile en-

---

[8] The tie-up between priests and curers is still evident even in Christianity. A passage in the New Testament, James V:14, makes the connection perfectly clear. "Is any sick among you? Let him call for the elders of the church; and let them pray over him, anointing him with oil in the name of the Lord." The Bible is full of references to healing and healers.

gine, can be utilized for going forward or backward.[9] In medieval Europe, when Christianity was the dominant religion, it was widely believed that recital of the Lord's prayer was beneficial, but that evil would result when the Lord's prayer was recited backward. This illustrates the concept that mana can be manipulated either to strengthen a society or to weaken it. Whatever a witch does to harm a social unit, therefore, must be neutralized or overcome by one who uses mana for pro-social purposes.[10] This is the role of the shaman.

When it comes to causing sickness and death, witches are in many cases thought to have the power to send foreign, disease-causing substances into the body of a prospective victim. Where beliefs of this kind prevail, a shaman is often summoned to remove the offending objects from a patient. There then follows a sort of contest between the witch and the medicine man, and if the latter can mobilize more mana the patient recovers. Failures are blamed on the fact that the force of evil was too strong to have been overcome by the power of good.

It is always dangerous in cultural anthropology to derive a broad principle from instances observed in a single tribe, but some light may be shed on the topic under discussion by an episode that the writer witnessed among the Hopi Indians. On one occasion a man who was suffering stomach-aches summoned a shaman. In the author's presence the medicine man "extracted" from the patient's stomach a number of "poison arrows," after which the pains subsided. Some time later, attention was diplomatically called to the facts that the "poison arrows" had emerged dry and bloodless and that at no time had the skin of the stomach been broken. Far from arousing disbelief these facts had the opposite effect. "Aren't those medicine men wonderful?" asked the ex-patient. "Who else could take things out of a person's stomach without getting them wet and bloody and without breaking the skin?"

Questions are often asked about the sincerity of shamans who know that it is sleight-of-hand that makes it look as though they were extracting substances from a victim's body. Quite often, when

---

[9] Some religious people in our culture are inclined to believe that not all supernatural power is of the same sort. They prefer to think that forces of good emanate from such a source as the Christian God, whereas forces of evil come from the devil.

[10] Former writers on primitive religion were frequently in the habit of calling good or pro-social supernaturalistic activities **white magic,** while anti-social or bad activities were called **black magic.**

they are asked about such matters point-blank, medicine men reply in effect: "I don't know how it works, but you noticed that after I treated the sick person he got better." Since many of their patients do get better, it is not at all certain that every shaman is insincere.

Returning to the prevalence of witchcraft beliefs, there are at least two ways in which they may aid the cohesion of a society. Sometimes, when a group's culture forbids aggression, hatred of witches provides a socially-sanctioned outlet for aggressive tendencies. At other times, when disaster strikes, people do not blame their chiefs, their gods, or one another, but place the entire fault on witches. Nor are suspected witches invariably punished. There is often a widespread fear that witches will make things far worse if their victims show overt hostility toward them. Thanks to such beliefs, even witchcraft notions may serve to hold a society firmly together.

G. SCIENCE AND THE LAW OF CONTROLLED CAUSATION

Cultural progress is inevitably associated with an increase in a group's fund of knowledge. Primitive or nonliterate folk, by and large, have far less knowledge at their collective disposal than do the members of literate societies. This amounts to saying that primitive people are more ignorant than others. One must hasten to add, though, that ignorance is not to be confused with stupidity. Some men and women who are basically smart and quick to learn and apply new bits of information may be ignorant of many reputed facts, and others who are dull and slow to learn may have much factual knowledge.

Much of what literate folk know is organized under the heading of science. As it is to be interpreted in the present context, the essence of science is an understanding of tangible causes and their effects. A sophisticated society that has a great deal of knowledge in this respect has a choice of two ways of explaining phenomena, whereas a primitive group has only one. As an example, suppose a plot of ground which has yielded good crops year in and year out suddenly fails to grow anything although external conditions appear to be unchanged. Primitive farmers, if it is correct to assume that they lack all scientific knowledge of plant and soil diseases (yet wish to continue using the same spot), would have no choice but to regard the event as supernaturally caused and to resort for help to religious practices. A modern farmer, under the same circumstances, would have two courses of action. He might call on an agricultural specialist, or he might resort to religion. The difference is usually a matter of degree or proportion. Neither farmer is pledged to use one technique to the complete exclusion of the other. No primitive agriculturalist would expect to grow things, even if he relied heavily on supernatural assistance, without planting seeds at the right time, clearing the ground of weeds, and so forth. Nor would it be surprising if a literate farmer resorted to prayer or some other supernatural activity, in addition to calling for the help of an agronomist.

Within the limits of their knowledge and resources, people always try to gain their ends by using all the tangible means at their disposal, but if these prove to be inadequate, calls may be made for supernatural help. Rarely is one method used without a speck of the other. The more uncertain may be the satisfactory outcome of a difficult or dangerous situation, the more is it likely that a high proportion of religious elements will be combined with other efforts to get a happy solution.

Simple knowledge of cause and effect relationships may not in itself lead to greater reliance on science than on supernaturalism. What is much more likely to prove effective is based on **the law of controlled causation.** Whenever men are able to demonstrate that they can produce stated effects by manipulating their causes, the phenomena with which they deal move from the realm of religion to the realm of science. Thus, as more facts become scientifically known, the law of controlled causation covers ever more cases, and man's *reliance* on the supernatural shrinks. This is merely another way of saying that as the amount of knowledge in a society goes up, there is a proportionate decrease of its *dependence* on supernaturalism (Fig. 15.6). To test the validity of this hypothesis one has only to note that genuine *reliance* on the supernatural remains strongest in sophisticated societies in precisely those areas, like death, where the law of controlled causation cannot be said to operate.

Nor should an increase of church attendance be automatically equated with an increase of *reliance* on the supernatural. People may attend religious services for a variety of reasons. Within the last few years the United States has seen a great upswing of church memberships, but many professional religionists openly admit that they do not know the meaning of this trend. Of one thing, though, we may be certain. The great increase of worship in churches does not mean that Americans are going to abandon their faith in science for increased *reliance* on the supernatural to solve their problems.

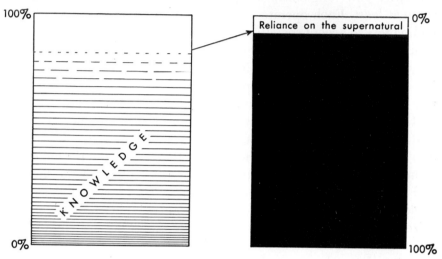

Fig. 15.6. Knowledge and reliance on the supernatural. As the percentage of a society's knowledge increases, a greater degree of controlled causation becomes possible and the group's reliance on the supernatural for the solution of problems decreases.

As Figure 15.6 suggests, religion does not remain static but stands in a dynamic relationship to the amount of a society's knowledge. As more and more items become known and brought into the range of controlled causation, there is less and less *reliance* on the supernatural. Hence, the explanation of a phenomenon might belong in the field of religion at one stage of a society's history, but might be classified under science at a later date. Many a tribe that used to dance for rain when water was scanty and depended only on the vagaries of nature has given up dancing for rain after wells were dug and ample water could be obtained by turning a faucet.

There are more than a few instances where scientists and religionists, operating from different premises, have reached surprisingly similar conclusions. A number of drugs, used by primitive medicine men because they were supposed to contain powerful spirits, have been used for nearly identical purposes by modern doctors because of their chemical properties.[11] Long before the germ theory of disease came to be widely accepted, shamans believed that sickness could be spread by contagion from one center of mana designed for evil to others.

For all their near approach to one another in certain contexts, scientists and religionists differ fundamentally on one important score at least. Each operates on a basis of faith, at least in so far as willingness to accept something without immediate tangible proof is concerned. But here is where the resemblance ends. A religionist may have unwavering faith in the supernatural and may not feel impelled to provide sensory proof or to change his position under any circumstances whatsoever. A scientist, on the contrary, feels that he must go on testing various hypotheses, and he has faith that pursuit of his methods will lead to an ever greater accumulation of knowledge, that all phenomena that are presently unknown to humans will some day be brought into the sphere of the known, and that when this happens more and more things will be made subject to the law of controlled causation.

Yet, one should not jump to the conclusion that science and religion must forever be in conflict. As was pointed out on page 183, biocultural trends cannot be assumed to move unfailingly in one direction. Moreover, human beings have an amazing ability to adjust to a diversity of ideas. Many an American citizen keeps varying concepts so compartmentalized that he can at the same time be a devout worshiper and a fine scientist.

SELECTED REFERENCES

Codrington, R. H., *The Melanesians: Studies in their Anthropology and Folklore.* Oxford, 1891.

Durkheim, E., *The Elementary Forms of the Religious Life.* Glencoe, Illinois, 1947.

Evans-Pritchard, E. E., *Witchcraft, Oracles, and Magic among the Azande.* Oxford, 1937.

Frazer, J. G., *The Golden Bough,* one volume edition. New York, 1941.

Goode, W. J., *Religion among the Primitives.* Glencoe, Illinois, 1951.

Howells, W. W., *The Heathens.* New York, 1948.

Lowie, R. H., *Primitive Religion.* New York, 1924.

------

[11] A belief prevails in some primitive societies that plants or other things in nature occasionally reveal their usefulness to man by something in their shape or color. Thus, bloodroot, whose sap is red, is supposedly a good remedy for blood diseases. Beliefs of this type have been categorized as **the doctrine of signatures.**

Malinowki, B., *Magic, Science, and Religion*. Glencoe, Illinois, 1948.

Mandelbaum, D. G., "Form, Variation, and Meaning of a Ceremony," in *Method and Perspective in Anthropology* (R. F. Spencer, ed.), pp. 60-102. Minneapolis, 1954.

Marett, R. R., *The Threshold of Religion*, rev. ed. New York, 1914.

Miner, H. M., *The Primitive City of Timbuctoo*. Princeton, 1953.

Radin, P., *Primitive Man as a Philosopher*. New York, 1927.

Titiev, M., "Shamans, Witches, and Chiefs among the Hopi," *Tomorrow,* Vol. 4, No. 3, 1956, pp. 51-56.

———, "Notes on Hopi Witchcraft," *Papers of the Michigan Academy of Science, Arts, and Letters,* Vol. 28, 1943, pp. 549-557.

CHAPTER 16

RELIGION (CALENDRICAL RITES) AND MAGIC (CRITICAL RITES)

A. THE SEARCH FOR A DISTINCTION

Many years ago cultural anthropologists became convinced that not all practices involving a belief in the supernatural were identical in character. To express the difference some activities were called **religious,** and others were termed **magical.** Soon, however, it became clear that no hard and fast distinction could be drawn between **religion** and **magic,** and at present a number of students of culture have become so convinced that there is no dividing line that they have given up the quest altogether.

One of the first bases of difference to have attracted the notice of scholars was the greater degree of compulsion that seemed to be involved in certain rituals. Religion, some scholars argued, leaves the ultimate decision for any action in the hands of a divinity, who may act or not as he sees fit. Truly religious behavior, in keeping with such arguments, never goes beyond supplication or the expression of a hope which a deity may or may not fulfill. Magic, so these same scholars used to say, compels supernatural agents to do man's bidding, provided only that magical formulae and practices are properly executed. Today it is realized that many **religionists** are as confident of getting results as are **magicians.** Still, it would be hard to deny that many magicians give the impression of being in control of supernatural forces, while most religionists express dependence on or submission to supernatural powers.

Efforts were also made in times past to separate religion from magic on the grounds that magic had no "church." The implication was that individual or private appeals to the supernatural were magical, whereas only group or social communications with the supernatural were truly religious. Before long it was pointed out that it was silly to call private prayer in one's own study or closet "magic," and similar prayer, publicly expressed, "religion." Examples of this kind tended to diminish the distinction between magic and religion, and that is one of the reasons why some scholars no longer try to differentiate between the two.

Yet, as one studies the range of supernatural beliefs and practices that exist throughout the world, the need for a distinction of some sort remains evident. As a fresh start it may be fruitful to divide all religious phenomena into two different categories—those that are **calendrical** and those that are **critical.** By "calendrical" are meant all practices based on a belief in the supernatural that are regularly performed at stated intervals, regardless of whether there is an immediate need for supernatural help. Calendrical rituals must be performed at a given time and can be scheduled recurrently long in advance. They are likely to be regarded as providing some sort of generalized benefit for everybody in a society. To an extent, therefore, calendrical performances always have a "church" and come closer to long-established concepts of religion than they do to those of magic.

Critical rites differ because they involve appeals for supernatural assistance to overcome a present difficulty. They cannot, because of their very nature, ordinarily be held at stated intervals, nor can they always be scheduled far ahead. Moreover, since it is unlikely, although not altogether impossible, that all the members of a society will be confronted with emergencies at one and the same moment of time, critical rites are less certain to have a "church," and so they conform to a limited extent to earlier definitions of magic. On some occasions, though, as in the event of a widespread drought, critical rites may be performed for the benefit of an entire group.

Lest this discussion should seem far-fetched to certain readers, illustrations will be given from Christianity. Christmas is a prime example of a calendrical rite. In the Euro-American world it always falls on December 25, and it is scheduled to be held whether or not any individual Christian feels the need that particular day for divine assistance. Personal prayer for the recovery of a sick child, however, seems to belong in another category and may well be called a critical rite. And when all Christians are asked to pray for peace if war threatens, we have an example of a critical ritual performed by a group of believers.

B. CEREMONIAL CALENDARS

Never should it be thought that calendrical rituals, because they are held without reference to the needs of the moment, are only of minor or secondary importance. Far from it. Customarily they are looked upon as strengthening the bonds of cohesion that unite all a society's members, or else as aiding an entire society's adjustment to its external surroundings. Ceremonies for increasing the food supply, augmenting raw materials, controlling the weather, and warding off natural catastrophes are universal and commonplace. It is in this sense that religious activities are most clearly definable as nonempirical means of attaining empirical ends.

No society waits until a serious crisis has actually arisen before it performs such group rituals as it considers beneficial to the whole social unit. In such cases the religious activities always take place at fixed times and are regulated by a **ceremonial calendar.** Even nonliterate people may have ways of keeping track of the year's progress. Simplest of all are means of watching each day's sunrise from one spot, following the sun's apparent north-south movements, and noting the solstices or turning points that occur annually around June 21 and December 21 in northern latitudes.[1] For about six months of each year, beginning on the twenty-first of June, the sun seems to rise a bit further south every morning, and for the remaining six months each sunrise appears to move to the north. Where the eastern horizon is irregular it appears to sunrise observ-

---

[1] In the southern hemisphere, or in other parts of the world, different calendrical points may be important. Onsets of rainy or dry seasons, equinoxes, seasonal floods, or other phenomena may be more crucial than the solstices. As it happens, cultural anthropologists know more about religions of the northern hemisphere, and few doubt that Judaism and Christianity arose among farming and herding folk who lived north of the equator.

ers watching from a given spot that the sun rises now from a bit of forest, now from a mountain peak, and so on (Fig. 16.1). In this way the coincidence of a sunrise with a particular landmark is used as a seasonal checkpoint and serves to indicate the time when a given calendrical rite is supposed to be held.

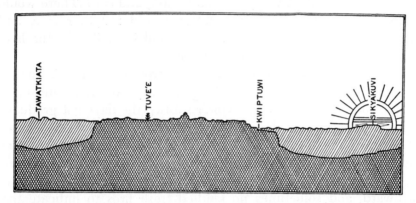

Fig. 16.1. Sunrise calendar at Oraibi. Sun watchers at Oraibi used to watch, from a given place, where the sun rose each day. In this way they kept track of the sun's seeming movements from north to south and south to north. Calendrical rituals were announced whenever the sun reached a designated spot on the eastern skyline.

Religious calendars are never limited solely to the recognition and celebration of the solstices. Observances that are celebrated at fixed times each year may be performed at any season, particularly when economic duties are slack, but only in well-integrated, actively functioning societies are annual ceremonies systematically held. Time and again have ethnologists found it to be true that when a tribe is neglecting its ceremonial calendar it is also giving up its old way of life. Failure to maintain regularly recurrent religious practices and failure to keep up a traditional pattern of culture are directly interconnected. Whether or not people are aware of it, it is their system of supernatural beliefs that gives their society much of its continuity, cohesion, and stability.

C. OFF WITH THE OLD, ON WITH THE NEW

Primitive farmers, realizing that the movements of the sun lie beyond their sphere of controlled causation, are greatly concerned lest a winter season should be so indefinitely extended that they would be unable to grow crops. Those who live north of the equator are most worried at the time of the winter solstice, when the rising sun reaches the southernmost point of its annual journey. Suppose the sun failed to reverse its course and start northward? That indeed would be a calamity. It would lead to perpetual winter with the sun so feeble that days would be short, dark, and cold. There would be no spring and summer, vegetation would fail to revive, and plant foods could not be grown. This would imperil alike the lives of grazing animals and of human beings.

Even today no scientific method of controlling the sun is known, so it is not surprising that primitive man had to resort to the supernatural. Noting that after the winter solstice the days got gradually longer and warmer as the power of the sun increased, he devised rituals to express his desires. Sometimes he twirled a disk-shaped object at midnight of December 21 to convey the idea that the sun ought to round the southernmost point of its yearly path and start northward, and sometimes he kindled fresh fires to indicate that the sun was to increase its light and heat. Each of these activities is based on the principle that cultural anthropologists describe as **mimetic magic.** Mimetic magic underlies any human activity that provokes similar behavior from the supernatural world. Thus, if a community wants wind, a mana-laden person may wave a fan; if a society desires rain, one of its officials might pour water on the ground.

Like any other activity involving mana, rituals based on mimetic magic may be performed either for individuals or groups, and for pro- or antisocial purposes. Most common of the hostile acts, usually done at one person's request, is the shaping of an image in the likeness of an enemy. If the effigy is caused to disintegrate, the enemy is supposed to waste away; if it is stuck with pins, he is supposed to suffer sharp pains from a disease like rheumatism. Those who have the power to make these images are usually regarded as witches. Such figures are most effective if their manufacture also accords with the principle of contagion. That is, they work best if they incorporate a bit of the enemy's body, such as his nail or hair clippings.

Beliefs of this kind help us to understand why so many people have special attitudes toward body parts and bodily excretions. Sometimes even urine and feces are carefully concealed lest they fall into the hands of a witch. This suggests the possibility of another link between religion and medicine, for toilets may result from beliefs in the supernatural as well as from a regard for sanitation and hygiene.

Best known of all calendrical observances involving the concept of mimetic magic are **New Fire Rites.** They generally occur at the time of the winter solstice, and, as the name implies, their central act consists of the kindling of a fresh blaze, in the hope of persuading the sun to grow brighter and warmer. Rituals of this kind benefit an entire society, and provide a sort of answer to Shelley's poetic question, "O, Wind, if Winter comes, can Spring be far behind?" It is interesting to note that both the Jewish festival of Hanukkah and the Christian celebration of Christmas, each of which falls in late December, involve symbolism suggestive of increased light and heat. At the same time, the implication that "dead" vegetation will soon "return to life" emphasizes the motive of death and rebirth.

Winter solstice rituals are always calendrical and, it should be kept in mind, they frequently call for the lighting of new fires. In such cases old fires are extinguished, fire hearths are cleaned out, and a fresh blaze is kindled. Sometimes a priest performs the office on behalf of an entire community, whereupon brands from the communal fire are carried home to ignite fires in individual houses.

Throughout the activities of the New Fire Rites there runs the idea that something old has ended and something new has begun. It is no accident that our New Year begins shortly after the winter season has reached its turning point. Various means may be used to express the same thing. They may range all the way from the making of new resolutions and the cancellation of old debts to thoroughgoing housecleaning, and even enactments of death followed by birth. The one concept that seems to be common to all these varied bits of behavior, as a sort of unifying thread, is the notion of starting afresh, of "turning over a new leaf."

Nearly as common as winter solstice ceremonies are **first-fruit rites,** which occur when a new crop is ready for harvesting. The central theme is always the same—man must express his obligation to the supernatural powers that sent him food, although the words "crop" and "fruit" may be used in such a figurative sense as to apply to fish, game, or edible insects as well as to all manner of agricultural products. In fact, one well-known interpretation of what is clearly a "first-fruit rite" deals with the first seasonal run of salmon.[2] First-fruit rites have been described as thank offerings, sacrifices to the gods, and ways of lifting tabus from the remainder of a crop, but no matter how they are interpreted they always conform to calendrical rituals that are designed for the good of a total society.

D. THE JOURNEY OF LIFE

Various primitive societies perform a series of critical rites almost with the same regularity as calendrical rituals. These are concerned with the welfare of individuals and with their relationships to their social units. About fifty years ago a student of human affairs, Van Gennep, made the astute observation that primitive peoples frequently regarded the life-cycle as a journey from one stage of existence to another. He noted that each individual normally passes through the phases of birth, puberty, marriage, and death. According to Van Gennep, these represent critical points which require supernatural help if a person is to make a safe and proper transition from one stage to the next. Van Gennep termed the appropriate religious practices **rites of passage**,[3] and in one guise or another they are likely to be found in any society.

In the light of information that has become available since Van Gennep's day, it is necessary to elaborate his stages. We shall keep his basic groundplan but in our treatment the four stages will represent birth and infancy, puberty and adolescence, maturity and marriage, old age and death. These cover the full life-cycle of every normal individual, and helpful religious rites are likely to be performed whenever a person is about to enter a new phase (Fig. 16.2A).

Birth and infancy are universally believed to be full of hazards for a mother and babe, and to some extent for other relatives and for the community at large. Fears of death in childbirth, of bloodshedding, of infant mortality, and of evil supernatural forces that may prey on weak or immature bodies are variously expressed. Protective countermeasures, designed to keep mother and child safely in the world of the living, are everywhere to be found. These devices may exhibit more concern over physical than supernatural dangers, or the other way round, but in most cases the means of

---

[2] E. Gunther, "An analysis of the First Salmon Ceremony," *American Anthropologist*, Vol. 28, 1926.

[3] A. Van Gennep, *Les Rites de Passage*, Paris, 1909.

protection will exhibit a blend of natural and religous elements. It is sometimes stated that primitive women give birth without much physical difficulty, but rarely can it be proved that they bear children any more easily than do women in nonprimitive societies. Cultural conventions may encourage loud outcries during labor or may insist on stoic silence, but the biological mechanisms of parturition are everywhere much alike.

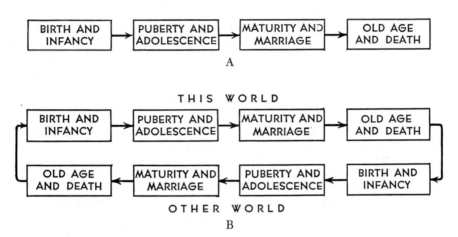

Fig. 16.2. The rites of passage. A. According to Van Gennep, every individual passes through four critical stages in his life cycle. To assure a safe passage, members of primitive societies customarily felt it necessary to hold rites whenever entrance to the next state, indicated by arrows, was being made. B. By combining existence on earth with life in the other world, death is "eliminated" as a final stage in this world. Not all primitive peoples believe that a disembodied soul passes through all of the four stages of life on earth, but there is wide acceptance of the idea that earthly death is followed by birth in the hereafter and that death in the other world is followed by birth on earth. Wherever such concepts prevail, the stages in the other world are the exact opposite of the stages in the world of the living.

Only a few exceptional societies attempt to treat the delivery and rearing of infants as natural phenomena that do not require supernatural help. Even so, the most scientific of obstetricians and pediatricians have something in common with primitive midwives and shamans, for all seek to make childbirth safe and to help a baby get through the dangerous period of infancy.

Nor do efforts to assist an infant stop when a successful confinement has been achieved. Many a youngster in the primitive world goes about wearing inanimate objects that are supposedly endowed with mana for attracting supernatural aid (**charms** or **talismans**), or for warding off supernatural powers of evil (**amulets**). It is felt that these will help a child even when it is out of the sight of its parents or guardians.

Of course, it is not always possible to draw clear lines between charms, talismans, and amulets, or between the attraction of good supernatural power and the repulsion of evil. Despite the dangers of overlap, charms are somewhat more commonly used to bring assistance, while amulets have a defensive connotation. Talismans partake of the nature of charms, but since they often include bits of sacred writing they do not occur technically in nonliterate societies. **Idols** are often included with other inanimate objects that are supposed to have mana. All of these are sometimes lumped together as **fetishes.** Idols are usually carved in three-dimensional form, and some of them are supposed to depict the appearance of the souls or spirits that they are thought to contain.

Psychologists and psychiatrists are agreed that the transition from infancy to the period of puberty and adolescence is critical and full of exceedingly hard problems. Primitive peoples long ago recognized the difficulties involved, and in countless ways they tried to get supernatural assistance. Formal rites of passage at this stage are much more likely to be designed for boys than for girls, who may simply be taught to resort periodically to menstrual lodges, out of the way of the rest of the community.[4] Quite often the masculine observances incorporate a **tribal initiation.** This is intended to teach a youth the lore of his group, so that he may be the better qualified to take his place as an adult member of his tribe. Sometimes the aspect of transition is dramatized in tribal initiation ceremonies by "killing" the initiate as a child and having him "reborn" as a man. Thus is symbolized the termination of one stage of an individual's existence and the start of a new one.

Unlike other aspects of the rites of passage, tribal initiation ceremonies may take place at a fixed time of the year. In such cases they apply to all who are eligible when the rites are scheduled to be held. On this score, tribal initiation rituals are unlike the ceremonies accompanying birth, marriage, and death, which apply to single individuals and events that cannot be determined in advance.

---

[4] Fear of menstrual blood is one of the most frequently encountered phenomena in primitive cultures.

Maturity and marriage represent a different set of problems. Foremost of these are the dangers, wherever virginity is demanded of a bride, of bloodletting, the needs of newlyweds to adjust to each other and their in-laws, reluctance to admit an outsider to intimacy with a group of consanguineous kin, fear that the married couple may fail to have offspring, and concern over a young pair's fitness to rear properly whatever children may be born to them. No sure method of guaranteeing the soundness of marriages is known anywhere, nor is there any assured solution to the many problems that are so likely to follow in the wake of a marriage. It is a realistic awareness of the difficulties involved that leads practically all societies to look upon weddings as critical transition points. There is on occasion a feeling that the principals might make the passage more safely if they had the benefit of supernatural help.[5] Only once in a while does a group completely dispense with religious activities at marriage, and rare are the societies that fail to allow divorce to serve as a kind of safety-valve for allowing the escape of tensions arising from marriages that have failed.

Not all peoples recognize old age as a distinct stage of existence,[6] but rites of passage that are concerned with death are among those that occur most regularly. Here is an inevitable source of recurring crises, for no social unit is complacent about losing members, yet none can prevent their loss. Some actions, such as the pinching of a patient's nostrils to keep his life force (soul) from departing, strike us as irrational; but others, including treatment with herbs, appear perfectly logical to us. If, despite all efforts, death takes place, religious rites may be performed to encourage the soul of the deceased to depart, without undue delay, for the other world. Often, too, steps involving supernatural practices are taken to make sure that the soul of the departed enjoys his existence in the afterlife.

Many people believe that the soul of a dead person can utilize

---

[5] Only a minority of the world's societies recognizes the validity of civil marriages. In the United States even people who are not deeply religious are likely to have church weddings or their equivalents.

[6] Societies which may not invoke the supernatural when old age is reached may sometimes recognize this phase politically. This is true of those groups which assign political power to a **council of elders.** Government conducted by such councils is not uncommon in the primitive world and is known as **gerontocracy.**

In a few instances there is sociocultural rather than political recognition of old age. A Japanese elder, particularly in rural areas, was expected to retire in his mid-fifties and to turn over the active management of his household affairs to his eldest son.

its mana more effectively because it is no longer confined to a material body. Since a society's dead, in broad terms, are the forebears of the living, a form of **generalized ancestor worship** comes into play. This is not the same thing as the particularized veneration of specific ancestors that used to prevail in China and other Far Eastern countries but, different though they are, the two systems of belief have a common base. In each case the dead are somehow kept within a society instead of being expelled from it.

Nevertheless, social groups incline strongly to have an ambivalent attitude toward their dead. On the one hand, they may love a dying individual and sincerely mourn his departure if he expires. On the other hand, they may also fear the spirit of a deceased person and may do all they can to speed its departure to the other world and to make sure that it does not return, unauthorized, to the world of the living.

Fear of a dead person's soul is one of the most recurrent themes of **mourning customs** in primitive societies. Corpses may be re-

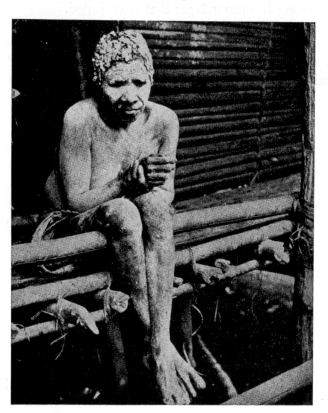

Fig. 16.3. Mourning in New Guinea. Among a number of New Guinea tribes a recent widow must daub herself with white clay. This has the effect of reversing her normal coloring, which is Negroid. (Courtesy of G. P. Putnam's Sons.)

moved through a specially made opening, other than the usual doors or windows, that is later sealed; returns from a burial may be made by circuitous paths in the hope that a spirit will be unable to follow the living; and the bereaved may adopt various disguises, such as painting black skins white, in order to conceal their identities (Fig. 16.3).

Throughout parts of Asia, particularly from India to the east and south, many communities are subject to **genna tabus.** There may be a variety of motives for the imposition of a genna tabu, but whenever one is proclaimed it has the effect of stopping all but the most vital of activities. Genna is most likely to be proclaimed whenever a mighty personage has died. The thinking behind it seems to run somewhat as follows: "If the powerful antisocial forces that caused the death of so great a person are still around, think of what they could do to you. Therefore, the more inconspicuous and inactive you are, the better." It is tempting to think that genna-like ideas are somehow at the bottom of the restrictions on activities that play so prominent a part in the Sabbath "blue-laws" of Judeo-Christian societies.

Another prominent feature of mourning customs is an effort to show that death has not seriously weakened the cohesion of a social group. Survivors are frequently called upon to make a show of great solidarity following a death. This is most readily done by having the kin of the deceased gather or feast together. It is a commonplace observation among us that one meets more of his remote relatives at a funeral than on any other occasion. So highly regarded are the supernatural practices associated with death that they are likely to be carried out even by persons who claim to be agnostic or atheistic.

E. O DEATH, WHERE IS THY STING?

All societies try to minimize the inroads of death. To help accomplish this end, one course is followed almost universally. It consists of developing myths that explain death as something trivial and quite unimportant. The effect that is sought is to assure people that death doesn't really matter. Among some tribes the origin of death is attributed to a lapse of memory; among others it is said to be the result of a trifling error of conduct. In all cases, it raises the possibility that death might have been avoided if only. . . . In terms of Christian beliefs, it amounts to saying: "If only Adam and Eve hadn't eaten the fruit of the forbidden tree."

Even more effective is the notion that life and death on earth are no more than parts of a continuous chain of existences (Fig. 16.2B). Thus, death can be "eliminated" if the idea gains acceptance that it is followed by birth in the other world and that death in the afterlife is followed by birth in this world. Where such beliefs are held, death is robbed of much of its sting. Instead of meaning that a deceased person is forever lost to his relatives and society in general, it means only that the departed has moved temporarily to another sphere and will ultimately be reborn in this world. Something of the same notion may be found in the words attributed to Christ: "I am the resurrection and the life. He that believeth in Me, though he were dead, yet shall he live."

As is shown in Figure 16.2B, life in the other world is the opposite or reverse of life on earth. This notion of reversal may be found in any body of supernatural practices, whether they be calendrical or critical. For example, some tribes believe that while it is daytime on earth, it is night in the other world (Fig. 16.4A); and that when it is summer here it is winter there (Fig. 16.4B). Consequently,

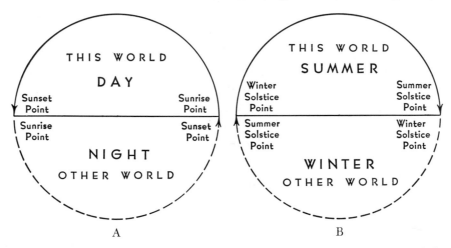

A   B

Fig. 16.4. The opposition of this world and the other world. A. The sun's daily journey. Primitive people have observed that the sun rises daily in the east and sets in the west. Many believe this to mean that during the night it travels elsewhere from west to east. Thus daytime on earth corresponds to nighttime in the other world. B. The sun's seasonal journey. By analogy with "A," the seasons are often reversed between the world of the living and the world of the dead.

those who represent the dead usually act in reverse fashion from the living. Many instances are known to cultural anthropologists of **clowns** who speak or act backward or by opposites. When they are hot, they complain of being cold; and where sacred dancers stamp with the right foot, they may stamp with the left. Unfortunately, it cannot always be proved that clowns who act by opposites are representatives of the dead, but a few cases are known where clowns and the dead are equated.

F. SUMMARY AND CONCLUSION

No society likes to think that it will soon be terminated. This leads it to take whatever practical measures it can to preserve its existence, but, if these give evidence of being insufficient, they are buttressed by resort to religious beliefs. These generally call for the setting up of a system of communication by means of which people on earth may send or receive messages meant to secure help or guidance from the supernatural world. Quite often the messages involve mana-laden objects, and their meanings are interpreted by priests, who serve as intermediaries between the lay members of a society and their gods.

A social unit may also seek supernatural help by the performance of ceremonies. These are of two kinds. Some occur at regular times, in conformity with a ceremonial calendar, regardless of whether or not any worshiper has a pressing problem when the time comes. Most common of the calendrical observances in primitive societies are New Fire Rites, which come in northern latitudes at the season of the winter solstice, around December 21. When the sun is observed at daybreak to have reversed its course and started northward, a feeling of starting afresh prevails, and there is likely to be either a dramatization of the end (death) of one era and the start (birth) of another, or the celebration of a new year.

First-fruit rites make up another common category of calendrical observances.

Critical rituals, which represent the second type, are performed primarily in times of need. They can, accordingly, seldom be scheduled far in advance. Those which are most widely found in primitive societies are the rites of passage. They are based on the notions that life is a journey from birth to death and that each stage of the trip creates a crisis for the individual and his society, a crisis

that has a better chance for a socially desirable outcome if supernatural help is obtained. Rituals which are designed to assist boys,
usually at puberty or early adolescence, to enter into manhood customarily take the form of tribal initiations, during which the initiate
learns the sacred lore of his tribe. Nor is it unusual to find that in
the course of the proceedings the candidate's childhood is "killed"
or brought to an end in one way or another and that he is "re-born"
as a man. Of all the rites of passage, only those pertaining to adolescence can be regularly planned ahead, for no one can predict, before a conception has taken place, when a child will be born, nor
does anyone know ahead of time when a person will get married
or die.

When religion is analyzed in terms of biocultural dynamics, it
becomes clear that one of its major purposes—the only one discussed here—is to strengthen the cohesion that binds the people of
a social unit to their group. Judged from this point of view, death is
the greatest of all threats to the continuation of any society, for it
constantly takes members away from a group. Several supernatural
factors combine to negate the social consequences of death. Myths
frequently dismiss death as a mere trifle, concepts of an afterlife
teach that souls or spirits of the dead continue to live on in another
world, and beliefs in rebirths, days of judgment, or reincarnation
make people feel that death is not final, that it may be followed by
a re-appearance on earth, and that it is no more than a passing
phase in a continuous round of existences.

Beliefs in the supernatural, on which all religious systems depend,
are possible only to creatures in possession of complete algebraic
mentalities. Except in this indirect way, religion, unlike man's interrelations with his environment or with his fellows, does not seem
to be a direct outgrowth of any aspect of biology. Nevertheless,
religious notions are exceedingly important for the maintenance of
any biocultural configuration. Perhaps that is why cultural anthropologists have never found a society which had failed to develop
a belief in the supernatural.

SELECTED REFERENCES

Boas, F., "Ethnology of the Kwakiutl," *Bulletin, Bureau of American
Ethnology,* Vol. 35, 1921.
Fewkes, J. W., "The New-Fire Ceremony at Walpi," *American Anthro-
pologist,* Vol. 2, No. 1, 1900.

Gunther, E., "An Analysis of the First Salmon Ceremony," *American Anthropologist,* Vol. 28, 1926.

Herskovits, M. J., and F. S., "An Outline of Dahomean Religious Belief," *Memoir, American Anthropological Association,* No. 41, 1933.

Mead, M., "The Mountain Arapesh," Vol. 2, "Supernaturalism," *Anthropological Papers, American Museum of Natural History,* Vol. 37, 1940, Part III.

Nadel, S. F., *Nupe Religion.* London, 1954.

Powdermaker, H., *Life in Lesu.* London, 1933.

Singer, C., *et al.,* eds., *A History of Technology,* Vol. I, Chap. 5. New York and London, 1954.

Titiev, M., "Old Oraibi," *Papers of the Peabody Museum of American Archaeology and Ethnology,* Cambridge, Vol. 22, No. 1, 1944, Part Two.

Tschopik, H. Jr., "The Aymara of Chucuito, Peru," *Anthropological Papers, American Museum of Natural History,* Vol. 44, 1951, Part II.

Van Gennep, A., *Les Rites de Passage.* Paris, 1909.

Whiting, J. W. M., *Becoming a Kwoma.* New Haven, 1941.

17

LANGUAGE AND THE

VERBAL ARTS[1]

A. LANGUAGE AND CULTURE

Among other things, this chapter is meant to drive home the lesson that a biocultural triangle does not encompass all the essential aspects of a society's way of living together. Foremost of the facets so far omitted is language. While it is widely held that each language consists of patterned and repetitive forms of behavior that are part and parcel of every society's way of life, linguistics has long been studied by itself and has developed many traditional approaches of its own, far removed from the customary concerns of cultural anthropologists. Consequently, anthropologically trained linguists are generally well aware of the cultural implications of their work, but many another student of language has but little concern with things cultural. The basic importance of human speech for the development and continuation of any pattern of culture need not be questioned. Symbolic values can best be expressed through linguistic utterances, and no better medium is known for teaching children to accept and follow a particular form of culture. When

[1] The material presented in this chapter has benefited greatly from a detailed and thoughtful criticism provided by my colleague, the linguistic specialist, Professor Kenneth L. Pike. Professor Pike is not, of course, responsible for any flaws that may have crept in.

they are put into words, abstractions and imaginary or non-sensory concepts of any kind acquire a sort of reality. Without the use of language, therefore, it would be practically impossible to teach the essentials of a system of supernatural beliefs. Neither Judaism nor Christianity could be taught without reference to words like faith, soul, God, and Heaven.

Every human society, it is worth repeating, has a language and a culture. The two are completely interdependent. Some scholars would go so far as to say that language and culture are one and the same, but for practical purposes it is better to admit their close ties but to treat them as separate. By definition, language deals only with forms of behavior that can be vocalized, but culture is also concerned with numerous activities, like motor habits, that may never be expressed in words nor accompanied by speech. There need be nothing verbal about tipping one's hat, yet it may be an important act of culture and may convey as subtle a symbolic meaning as any word.

That human beings who possess algebraic mentalities are the only animals capable of assigning symbolic and even arbitrary values to vocal utterances has already been pointed out (p. 97). But once man acquired that capacity he seems never to have improved on it. On the basis of their experiences with many societies and cultures, ethnologists find it impossible to rate entire languages as better or worse, or more or less effective. It does not follow that all vocabularies are at present equally serviceable for dealing with anything whatsoever. Specialized vocabularies, such as our own lists of words for scientific and technological things, are very well known. All that is meant is that each language is adjusted to the culture in which it is used and that new forms of speech can be borrowed or invented to keep pace with any changes of culture that may occur.

As far as is now known, all languages serve equally well as systems of communication among the members of a society who have learned to associate the same meanings with the same sounds. Never should it be overlooked that as a method of communication a language is of inestimable value only in the society where it is habitually used. Across cultural lines it may be quite worthless. So it is that a craftsman such as a potter could watch and understand the work of a maker of pottery from any part of the world, but he would not necessarily understand a word of any other artisan's speech.

Language is so integral to the formation and continuation of culture that a group of anthropological specialists devote themselves almost exclusively to its study. As is true of cultural anthropologists in general, anthropologically trained linguists most often deal with primitive peoples. Before modern methods of investigation were developed, the analysis and interpretation of nonliterate tongues were attempted by scholars who had been trained to deal with the written languages that make up the great Indo-European family. Some of these scholars engaged in field work, but they usually took along grammatical tables of declensions and conjugations based on their knowledge of Indo-European forms. Into these previously prepared diagrams they tried to force whatever native language they were studying, and anything that could not be fitted in was marked missing or deficient. None of the pioneer students of primitive speech was particularly interested in the fact that each culture has its own distinctive vocabulary and grammar and that its ways of expressing ideas may differ from the methods commonly found in Indo-European tongues. In the footsteps of men like Boas, Sapir, and Bloomfield, anthropologically trained linguists in the United States began to go into the field without preconceived ideas, and they were among the first who tried to understand and analyze native languages only in terms of what they actually heard and saw.

B. LINGUISTIC ANALYSES AND CLASSIFICATION [2]

Vocal utterances to which a social group may assign symbolic meanings cover a wide range of possibilities. Sounds that strike speakers of English as clicks, hisses, snorts, gulps, or whines may be just as conventional for speaking other languages as are the consonants and vowels familiar to us. The only requirements for what is called **articulate speech** are that each unit of sound to which values are to be attached must be distinct enough to be set apart from other sounds, that it must have a beginning and an end that can be reasonably well recognized, and that the meaningful sounds should be capable of a marked degree of repetition by all who speak the same language.

All languages consist of sounds whose production, orderly

---

[2] This section owes much to the treatment of language in Beals and Hoijer, *op. cit.*, Chapter 17.

arrangement, and combination serve to communicate definite meanings from a speaker to his listeners. Every tongue that is spoken uses only a fraction of all the vocal utterances that men can make. Each language, then, has a finite number of distinctive sounds to which its speakers attach meaning, and the smallest identifiable unit of significant or contrastive sound is called a **phoneme.** English examples are *th* in *something,* or *b* in *banker.* Phonemes rarely stand alone, but are combined with other minimum units of sound in fixed patterns, of which the smallest element that has meaning is called a **morpheme.** When an indivisible morpheme can stand by itself and carry the significance of a word, it is called *free.* Monosyllables in English are usually **free morphemes,** as in the case of words like *fish* or *book.* When a morpheme conveys no meaning as long as it is by itself, it is called *bound.* Examples of **bound morphemes** include the *ly* of *lovely,* and the *er* of *driver.*

Sounds that frequently recur in a language fall into characteristic sequences or patterns that may be quite rigid. Thus, in English, the *ng* of *clang* never begins a word, the *h* of *hollow* never ends one, and the sound *r* may follow initial *p* as in *pray,* but *p* can never follow initial *r.* Such speech arrangements are learned early in life, and adult speakers adjusted to one language find it very difficult to learn a different one. Both the production of sounds and their position in words or morphemes are equally fixed in each culture. This explains why people who habitually use a sound in one place, let us say initially, may have trouble in using virtually the same sound in a different position, let us say finally.

Besides studying sounds and their order of occurrence in morphemes or words, linguists are also concerned with their arrangement into meaningful phrases and sentences. Syntax or grammar is now the goal. Again, each language has a set of fixed rules. If word order is an important grammatical device it means one thing to say "dog bites man," and quite another to say "man bites dog." Pitch or intonation changes are equally effective for conveying different meanings, as we realize when we say, in level tones, "Oh, yes," or, with rising pitch, "Oh, yes?" Differences of accent also produce a variety of meanings. School children in recent years have teased their parents to say "What am I doing?" with the stress on a different word each time. When the unwary adult obliges with "Whát am I doing? What ám I doing? What am Í doing?" and "What am I dóing?" the child retorts, "Making a fool of yourself!"

Another example of the way in which meanings may be changed without any change of vocabulary or grammatical arrangement may be found in the old saying:

> The devil was ill,
>> The devil a monk would be;
> The devil got well,
>> The dévil a monk he'd be.

Here the entire meaning depends on matters of stress, pitch, intonation, rhythm, and the like. This bears out what cultural anthropologists have long known about speaking foreign languages. Again and again has it been found that one can make himself understood by imitating the cadence or rhythmic flow of a linguistic utterance, even if one's enunciation is poor or his knowledge of vocabulary and grammar is limited.

There are many ways of changing the meanings of words and sentences. Well known is phonetic modification, whereby, in English, *woman* is singular and *women* is plural. Also widely used is reduplication, so that when the Saramacca Bush-Negroes of Dutch Guiana say *hesi*, it means "to go fast," but when they say *hesihesi*, it means "speed." [3] Frequently employed, too, are the devices of adding prefixes, infixes (the addition of an element into the middle of a word), and suffixes. No language uses one method to the total exclusion of the others, and linguists are alert to describe all the ways in which speakers of a specific tongue achieve variations of meaning.

A number of goals are sought by anthropologically trained linguists. They are anxious to record accurately as many primitive languages as possible; they try to analyze the sounds, arrangements, and grammatical changes by which a variety of meanings may be communicated; they seek to show in how many details a language may reflect the environmental or cultural setting of its speakers; they attempt to demonstrate the historic changes brought about in a language by internal factors or external processes such as borrowing; and they are interested in fitting single tongues into larger and larger relationship units, such as speech families. This last approach is reminiscent of the efforts of taxonomists to group biological specimens into species, genera, and families.

Students of oral languages require first of all a means of noting

---

[3] This example is taken from M. J. Herskovits, *op. cit.*, p. 449.

down whatever sounds they hear in articulate speech. Only after a language has been recorded in writing can its component parts later be systematically analyzed and compared with other tongues that natives speak. Obviously, the English alphabet is not equipped to render accurately the many sounds that human beings can make with their vocal apparatus. Before linguistic analysis could proceed, therefore, it was necessary to develop an all-embracing system of notation by means of which any articulate utterance could be transcribed. Although present-day linguists can write down for later review and analysis just about every sound they hear, including all shades of inflexion and pronunciation, they are most interested in recording the significant elements that are classed as phonemes. A method of phonemic transcription was worked out several decades ago and, with some variations, it is still widely used by linguists.[4]

Those who habitually converse with one another form a **speech community,** but within the same speech community different usages may exist for infants and adults, men and women, occupational groups, residents of different parts of a large area, or those who are differently trained and educated. If these variations of speech, known as **dialects,** do not prevent all or most of the members of a society from understanding each other, the speakers of the various dialects may still be said to form a single speech community, and this is usually the case with primitive tribes. Only within large and heterogeneous social units is one likely to find speakers of dialects or languages that are not mutually intelligible.

A complete language, including its patterned use of phonemes, its ways of producing sounds, its vocabulary, and grammar, is so complex that it is unlikely to have been independently invented in its entirety more than once. Accordingly, when contemporary linguists find two separated peoples speaking closely similar or identical tongues, they feel justified in assuming that at some earlier period of their history the two were together, in touch or in close proximity. On the primitive level this kind of analysis has served to demonstrate that the Navaho and Apache, who now live in the southwestern United States, once resided close to the speakers of Northern Athabaskan tongues, who still live in northern Canada

---

[4] The system of phonetic or phonemic transcription most widely used was devised by the International Phonetic Association, and is reproduced in K. L. Pike, "Phonemics," *University of Michigan Publications in Linguistics,* Vol. III, Ann Arbor, 1947, p. 232. In this book Dr. Pike thoroughly discusses the techniques for rendering oral language in writing.

and Alaska. Similarly, even if every other fact about the Anglo-Saxon settlement of the United States were to be lost, linguists would infer from their speech resemblances that these colonists had once been in contact with other speakers of English. Simple linguistic analysis might or might not reveal which group had remained in its homeland and which had migrated to other regions, but an earlier connection between two social units speaking much the same language could be postulated beyond reasonable dispute. One complicating factor that makes all such hypotheses open to doubt is the possibility of diffusion. It is not inconceivable that a language could be spread from one group to another by travelers, traders, or military conquerors. The result would be two widely separated societies, who might never have lived near one another, using closely similar forms of speech.

A more refined approach to this sort of interpretation, staunchly proposed and defended in this country by Dr. Swadesh, goes by the name **glottochronology, or lexicostatistics**.[5] Among other objectives, this method attempts to provide the date when two related languages became separated. Every language consists of sounds, structure, and vocabulary; and it is the last that is best suited for lexicostatistics. Essential to the technique is the preparation of word lists in the languages to be compared. Lists of about two hundred items, lately cut in half by Dr. Swadesh in the interests of greater accuracy,[6] are recommended. Analysis of the lists rests on a number of assumptions, not all of which have been tested and accepted. It is assumed that some portions of a vocabulary, such as pronouns and words relating to numbers or to parts of the body, form a basic core and are slow or resistant to change. It is further assumed that whatever changes do take place in the basic core will occur at a regular or constant speed through time, and that basic cores will be modified at a similar rate in all languages. Hence, proponents of the method claim that if one knows the percentage of true cognates within the core vocabularies of any pair of related tongues, one can figure out the length of time that has elapsed since

[5] S. C. Gudschinsky, "The ABC's of Lexicostatistics (Glottochronology)," *Word*, Vol. 12, No. 2, 1956. This article gives an account, in simple language, of glottochronological techniques.

[6] M. Swadesh, "Towards Greater Accuracy in Lexicostatistical Dating," *International Journal of American Linguistics*, Vol. 21, 1955, pp. 121-137.

For a summary of what glottochronology has so far accomplished, see A. L. Kroeber, "Linguistic Time Depth Results So Far, and their Meaning," *International Journal of American Linguistics*, Vol. 21, 1955, pp. 91-104.

the two languages began to diverge. At present, a loss of roughly 15 or 20 percent of cognate forms is supposed to take place every thousand years. Simply stated, this means that the number of changes which can be shown to have taken place in a core vocabulary may be used as a measure of time. Even some of those who have faith in the validity of glottochronology are likely to recognize that such historic factors as migrations or conquests, which are agencies of diffusion, may wreak havoc with the satisfactory use of this technique. Just the same, they feel that lexicostatistics yields dates that can be linked with those of archeology and history, and they are of the opinion that this method may provide a means for connecting some peoples and cultures, hitherto unidentified but known from archeological remains, with certain groups that have actually been identified in history. As for its linguistic values, supporters of the glottochronological approach believe that this technique yields information about the time order in which various dialects were formed, and they think that such data can be correlated with known or suspected prehistoric migrations as well as with various aspects of cultural growth and change.

Not very long ago it used to be taken for granted that a person's thoughts dictated his choice of words. Now this sequence is being challenged. Indeed, some modern linguists are of the opinion that the opposite is true and that the words an individual customarily uses may direct his thoughts. The late Benjamin Whorf once stated flatly that a socially accepted pattern of word usage is often prior to certain culturally sanctioned forms of thinking and behavior.[7] Whorf's notion should be taken in conjunction with Professor Kluckhohn's assertion that the underlying conceptual images of each language make up a coherent though unconscious philosophy.[8] Stated somewhat differently, the idea has been proposed that our very vocabularies and grammars might well influence our outlooks on life, on our fellow men, and on the world about us. Paradoxically, we render our thoughts in words, but our words help to shape our thoughts.

Wonder is sometimes expressed because no international language, like Esperanto, has ever been a success. The failure is not due to any lack of knowledge or technical skill on the part of linguists.

[7] B. L. Whorf, "The Relation of Habitual Thought and Behavior to Language," *Language, Culture, and Personality* (L. Spier, *et al.*, eds.), Menasha, 1941, p. 75.
[8] C. Kluckhohn, *Mirror for Man*, New York, 1949, p. 111.

What is often overlooked is the patent fact that no language exists apart from some society and its culture. Every tongue, to a marked degree, reflects the cultural background of its speakers and gives an indication both of their universe and of how they interpret it. Thus, Eskimos are said to have a great number of words describing snow under varying conditions, and the Hopi insist on distinguishing light showers from heavy rains. Furthermore, they never confuse in speech still and running water. Not until there is a universal culture by which all the world lives is there much chance for a global language to succeed.

On the basis of recent estimates by Professor Harry Hoijer,[9] the most widespread family of languages is the Indo-European. It includes Germanic, Slavic, Romance, Greek, Indo-Iranian, and other languages and, taking all its branches together, it is spoken by about one billion inhabitants of Europe and Asia. Within these continents another 45 million folk or so speak languages of the Turkic, Mongolian, and Tungus families. Southern India has about 60 million speakers of Dravidian tongues, and East Asia has close to 600 million Sino-Tibetan speakers, of whom some 500 million or more use Chinese tongues. East Asia also includes approximately 25 million users of Korean and around 90 million speakers of Japanese.

Africa has relatively small numbers who speak historically important Semitic and Hamitic tongues, but there are about 50 million people each who speak Sudanic, just south of the Sahara, and Bantu, further south. The islands of the southern basin of the Pacific Ocean (Oceania) are dominated by tribes belonging to one large linguistic family called Malayo-Polynesian. These languages are used by nearly 50 million natives and include all the tongues of aborigines in this vast area, except those of the inhabitants of Australia and of New Guinea, whose native languages are extremely varied. In sharp contrast to the uniformity of the greater part of Oceania is the situation in the New World, which seems to show the greatest linguistic diversity on earth. Many linguistic scholars in the past, with the noteworthy exception of Edward Sapir and his followers, believed that a few million pre-Columbian American Indians spoke tongues pertaining to well over 80 distinct families, each of which was unrelated in any manner to the others, and none of

---

[9] Beals and Hoijer, op. cit., pp. 511-514. The figures cited are somewhat higher than those given by Professor Hoijer, to account for recent increases of population.

which had any connection with the languages of the Old World. Modern scholars are somewhat more conservative, but in view of the probable diversity of American Indian languages, cultural anthropologists may be forgiven if they smile a bit knowingly when people ask, "What is *the* Indian word for . . . ?"

C. FOLKLORE

Speech forms are widely used for communicating ideas from a speaker to his auditors, but they may also be used for arousing particular forms of behavior or reaction on the part of listeners. Most utterances in daily life are directed to some practical end, but it is perfectly possible to employ language for self-expression or else to convey or heighten emotions. Story-telling combines practical and emotional purposes, for it may be used to impart lessons at the same time that it arouses pleasure. Few primitive peoples look lightly upon story-telling. There may be restrictions on who is permitted to tell tales, as well as on the time, place, subject-matter, and listeners. Simple stories are told in what we would describe as prose and are subject to a minimum of restrictions. Anonymous tales that are well known and often repeated throughout a speech community make up its **folklore**.[10] Attempts have been made to distinguish various kinds of tales on the basis of their subject-matter, but it is impossible to make clearcut distinctions. As a general rule, stories may be classified as **myths** if they deal primarily with supernatural characters or events, and as **legends** when they are devoted to historic or supposedly historic happenings. There are so many narratives that blend the two characteristics that anthropologists have practically given up the effort to separate myths from legends.

Folklore is not without practical significance. It often mirrors a tribe's culture, past or present, and affords clues to migrations and contacts with other peoples. Many stories reassert the moral values of a society, and some tales are specifically used to provide instruction. Of world-wide distribution are narratives that seek to describe the origin and nature of the universe, to account for the characteristics of familiar animals and other aspects of the environment, to tell how a particular pattern of culture originated, to explain the

---

[10] Further information on this subject may be found in S. Thompson, *The Folktale*, New York, 1946.

beginnings of life and death, and to picture the other world and what goes on there. Two common features of folklore help to strengthen the solidarity of a society. Death, as has been previously noted, is dismissed as unimportant, arising from some trivial error; and the less favored are given opportunities to blow off steam, without harm to the social fabric, by laughing at stories in which the high and mighty suffer failure or discomfiture. People who find themselves occupying low statuses and those who believe that they have, through no fault of their own, been forced to undergo hardships or tribulations are much less likely to rebel against their society and its leaders if they hear that even the mightiest of personages sometimes suffer identical discomforts.

D. POETRY, PRAYER, AND SONG

Because each language imposes a rigid limitation on the number of vocal sounds to which meanings are attached and because each tongue likewise delimits the way in which sounds are to be combined, the order in which they must be stated, and the stress and intonation with which they are to be expressed, every prose utterance cannot fail but repeat some of its elements over and over again. Repetition of sounds provides a potential basis for alliteration, vowel harmony, and rhyme; and ordered recurrences of stress can be used to make rhythmic patterns. When these aspects of speech, singly or together, are deliberately emphasized, **poetry** results. Its use is found in all cultures, and it has been noted that it always increases the emotional impact of a statement on its hearers. Furthermore, both rhyme and rhythm, as they are employed in poetry, make remembrance and memorization easier on account of their repetitive qualities. All of these factors are basic to an understanding of why **prayer** so frequently resembles poetry. In addition, investigators have found that people commonly have a covert belief that a prayer formula which is supposed to have gained supernatural help in the past will lose its effectiveness if it is changed in any way at all. That is why the language of prayer is so much more conservative than everyday talk.

Very closely allied to poetry is vocal music, or **song.** In each instance the same anatomical mechanisms are employed. It is easy enough to say that song is poetry with the addition of melody, but

it is extremely hard to explain what melody is. Cultural conditioning, which may at times incorporate some seemingly arbitrary
values, plays so great a part in this context that what strikes some
people as a pleasant succession of sounds may appear to others as
harsh and disturbing. Nevertheless, the intimate relation of song to
poetry has been recognized at least for many centuries, and it has
been firmly established that in ancient times much poetry, both
secular and sacred, was meant to be sung.

Sacred singing as a means of putting human beings in touch
with supernatural powers is an accepted habit of many primitive
societies.[11] Cultural anthropologists know of numerous religious
practices wherein singing plays a fundamental part, and even in
modern services chanting and singing are outstanding features. As
any English dictionary shows, the very word "charm" is derived
from "carmen," which was originally a sacred incantation, and
cantors who sing holy songs in synagogues are important religious
officers among persons of Jewish faith.

The effectiveness of poetry and song as ways of communicating
ideas has been given prominence of late by those who advertise
their wares over the radio and television. Many a "blurb" nowadays
is delivered with rhyme or in the form of a song. Esthetically such
renditions may leave much to be desired, but their practical value
for making people remember advertised products can scarcely be
doubted.

Singing does not always have pleasant connotations in primitive
societies. It can be a very grim affair, packed with "social significance." This was the case among the Eskimo, who used to settle
disputes, often very serious ones, by resort to the custom of **song-
tieing.** An aggrieved Eskimo might challenge an opponent to a song
contest. In the presence of their fellows each contestant sang as
bitterly and satirically as he could about the other. He who received
the greater acclaim and applause from the audience became the
winner, and the loser was for the time being disgraced.[12]

Song contests as substitutes for other forms of aggressive conduct
are known in many societies. They may not conform exactly to
Eskimo song-tieing, but their general resemblance is usually easy to

---

[11] For an example see R. Underhill, *Singing for Power*, Berkeley, California, 1938.
[12] For further information on this topic consult K. Rasmussen, *Across Arctic America*, New York, 1927.

detect. In all cases they serve to release sociocultural tensions without resort to physical violence.

Somewhat related to the foregoing, but quite different in various details, is the custom of social singing among the Araucanians or Mapuche. It used to be the habit of these Indians to visit friendly chiefs from time to time. On these occasions young women, who usually held low status in Araucanian society, were permitted to express their pent-up grievances. Brides were particularly apt to be unhappy because of the strict enforcement of patrilocal residence in a tribe where several brothers might be living under the same roof as their father. Many a wife revealed her unhappiness under these conditions in her songs, and while she might be answered and even be told euphemistically to shut up, she was not subjected to punishment for anything she sang about. On the contrary, if some of her auditors felt that they could remedy her situation, they might take steps to make things better for her in the future.[13]

E. DRAMA

There is always a close connection among language, poetry, song, and **drama.** Regardless of specific forms and aims, which vary in every conceivable way, all dramas contain characters who usually wear costumes or have symbolic accessories and who take turns in a fixed order in saying, reciting, or singing something to be heard by an audience. The vocal utterances are generally accompanied by gestures or other movements of the body. Like all of the verbal arts, drama serves to arouse and heighten the emotions of those who watch and listen. Again, like folklore, it may be used effectively to drive home lessons that reflect a social unit's cultural beliefs and values. Drama has an added advantage in that it can also be used to give concrete expression to intangible abstractions. This can be done by having players act as representatives of such abstract things as lust or greed.

Religionists early realized the power of dramatic devices for instilling supernatural concepts. Virtually all societies use dramatic performances in conjunction with the practice of religion, and a high percentage of primitive rituals may be shown to be clever

---

[13] More details, and a number of typical songs, are given in M. Titiev, "Social Singing among the Mapuche," *Anthropological Papers, Museum of Anthropology, University of Michigan,* No. 2, Ann Arbor, 1949.

dramatizations of myths dealing with supernatural personages and events.

Accordingly, it is not by chance that one of the main streams of the modern English drama flowed out of sacred theatrical performances. As every student of the subject knows, parts of Christian services were often dramatized in the early medieval period. Some of these bits of drama were called **tropes** and were associated with Gregorian chants. They were extremely popular, a fact that is not surprising when one considers that the vast majority of the worshipers were nonliterate or illiterate and that the others were generally forbidden to read the Bible for themselves. As a consequence, the tropes or dramatized portions of the liturgy, during which the faithful could personally see enacted many of the things that they had been told, drew great throngs into the churches.

One of the most popular tropes of tenth-century Europe was called "Quem Quaeritis." It was performed at Easter, and its title, "Whom do ye seek?" was taken from the Gospel. Originally, "Quem Quaeritis" was sung as a choral addition to the procession with which the Mass began. Later, it was dramatized to portray the three Marys who came to the sepulcher seeking the body of the newly risen Christ. At the tomb they encounter an angel who addresses the title question to them, tells them that Christ has risen from the dead, and bids them to spread the news. As long as this trope was an integral portion of Christian worship, all the parts were played by churchmen, and the costumes and objects that were used to suggest scenery were always religious properties.

A number of scholars believe that the very popularity of the tropes so badly overcrowded the churches and so threatened to unbalance the remainder of the service that the authorities finally felt it necessary to ban the dramas from within the church. In this way an important segment of the English drama moved outdoors and step by step became altered from a performance controlled by religious leaders to a popular form of secular entertainment.

F. THE POWER OF WORDS AND NAMES

We, who have readily available so many forms of activity and entertainment, do not always grasp the full import of words and speech in primitive societies. To many peoples, even an ordinary conversation may be of prime significance, and it is most unusual to find that words are taken lightly. Statements that we would classify as empty gossip or mere yarning may be highly regarded and carefully analyzed. Unlike ourselves, many primitives pay considerable attention even to the remarks of known liars. If a bewildered anthropologist protests against such an attitude, he is likely to be told: "But he (or she) *said* it!"

Some observers feel that the value which many primitive men and women assign to words stems from their confusion of a word and the actual thing for which it stands.[14] Thus, if a thing is important, so too is its associated word. A number of students believe that in the primitive attitude toward speech we may have a covert forerunner of something known to all clinical psychologists and psychiatrists. They know very well how much a person may reveal about himself when he is encouraged to talk without restraint. Even downright lies are apt to have deep significance.

Once we learn to appreciate how much words mean to primitive people we can readily grasp why **orators** and **oratory** are so highly regarded. It is not everyone who can sway an audience. A great speaker, who can bend the thoughts and actions of his hearers to his will, is seldom regarded as an ordinary mortal. In many societies no man could hope to exert powerful leadership unless he were a good orator.

More important than ordinary words are **names**. In this connection it can be shown that names, too, are frequently regarded as much the same as the personages or things for which they stand. Accordingly, it follows that to get hold of a person's name is equivalent to getting hold of the person himself. That is why names are most unlikely to be freely bandied about, and that explains why married couples, in some primitive societies, wait for years before getting up courage to reveal their true names to one another. In the meantime, for purposes of convenience and identification, **nicknames** serve very well. Nicknames may be employed for a wide variety of purposes, but in a large number of cases they are used to enable a true name to be concealed.

---

[14] A fuller discussion of this topic may be found in B. Malinowski, "The Problem of Meaning in Primitive Languages," in C. K. Ogden and I. A. Richards, *The Meaning of Meaning*, New York, 1923, pp. 451-510.

For a penetrating analysis of some of Malinowski's linguistic material, see D. Lee, "Being and Value in Primitive Culture," *Journal of Philosophy*, Vol. 46, No. 13, 1949, pp. 401-415.

Names may also be used interchangeably with or else to stand for abstract or non-sensory concepts. Names of supernatural powers, especially gods, are carefully concealed lest they fall into unauthorized hands. "Thou shalt not take the name of the Lord, thy God, in vain" is a commandment of very wide distribution. And to make the names of one's gods known to an opponent is a treacherous act of the greatest magnitude. It is equivalent to turning one's deities over to an enemy.

Supernatural notions are not the only abstractions that can be made more concrete by being named. We sometimes overlook the fact that this same principle is operating among us whenever an officer says: "In the *name* of the law." The great power of words and names is not limited to primitive societies.

SELECTED REFERENCES

Bloomfield, L., *Language*. New York, 1933.

Child, C. G., *The Second Shepherd's Play, Everyman, and other Early Plays*. Cambridge, Massachusetts, 1910.

Greenberg, J. H., "Essays in Linguistics," *Viking Fund Publications,* No. 24, New York, 1957.

Gudschinsky, S. C., "The ABC's of Lexicostatistics (Glottochronology)," *Word,* Vol. 12, No. 2, 1956.

Hoijer, H., ed., "Language in Culture," *Memoir, American Anthropological Association,* No. 79, 1954.

Kluckhohn, C., "Myths and Rituals: A General Theory," *Harvard Theological Review,* Vol. 35, 1942.

Pike, K. L., "Phonemics," *University of Michigan Publications in Linguistics,* Vol. 3, Ann Arbor, 1947.

Rasmussen, K., *Across Arctic America*. New York, 1927.

Sapir, E., *Language*. New York, 1921.

Swadesh, M., "Towards Greater Accuracy in Lexicostatistical Dating," *International Journal of American Linguistics,* Vol. 21, 1955, pp. 121-137.

Thompson, S., "Advances in Folklore Studies," *Anthropology Today,* A. L. Kroeber, ed., pp. 587-596. Chicago, 1953.

———, *The Folk Tale*. New York, 1946.

Titiev, M., "Social Singing among the Mapuche," *Anthropological Papers, Museum of Anthropology, University of Michigan,* No. 2, Ann Arbor, 1949.

Underhill, R., *Singing for Power*. Berkeley, California, 1938.

Voegelin, C. F., and Harris, Z., "Linguistics in Ethnology," *Southwestern Journal of Anthropology,* Vol. 1, 1945, pp. 455-465.

Whorf, B. L., "Four Articles on Metalinguistics," *Foreign Service Institute, Department of State*, Washington, 1949.
————, "The Relation of Habitual Thought and Behavior to Language," in *Language, Culture, and Personality*, L. Spier, *et al.*, eds., pp. 75-93, Menasha, Wisconsin, 1941.

18

NONVERBAL ARTS AND GAMES

A. PRELIMINARY REMARKS

As far back as the Old Stone Age, craftsmen sometimes took pains to perfect an implement in ways that could not possibly improve its practical effectiveness. This tendency has continued into our own day and modern examples would include decorated chairs that are no more comfortable for sitting than plain ones, ornamental garments that add nothing to the wearer's "creature comforts," carved musical instruments that may not sound as well as their uncarved parallels, and pearl-handled revolvers that may or may not shoot straight. For want of a better way of explaining this phenomenon, originally expressed as symmetry, there are some scholars who refer to an esthetic urge or drive. Whether or not human beings actually possess such a drive toward art is still unsettled, but the fact remains that great numbers of people go to considerable lengths to embellish things for nonpractical purposes, or to look upon or purchase artistic products. Whatever their basic motives may turn out to be, such activities are customarily related to a pleasurable emotion. Either the workman takes delight in what he is doing, or the user enjoys the non-essential elements, or mere spectators find pleasure in the contemplation of something artistic. It is also possible, as our expression "art for art's sake" implies, to make esthetic objects that have no reference whatsoever to practical considerations. On the whole, though, primitive peoples are unlikely to separate art from utility. Anything capable of arousing emotion can be put to use, without exception, in the exercise of religion. If we bear this in mind, we do not wonder at finding so much painting, sculpture, music, rich ornamentation, and other expressions of the fine arts intimately associated with religious structures and services.

Many anthropologists believe that art arose out of man's handling of various substances in the course of toolmaking and the development of technology in general. Sometimes craftsmen liked to display their mastery of techniques by going beyond the boundaries of plain efficiency; in other cases, it can be shown, pleasing patterns emerged simply as offshoots of methods of manufacturing or through the use of differing kinds of materials. Considerations of this sort form the essence of a recent book on the subject by Dr. Gene Weltfish, who believes that art, especially elements of design, was born from industry.[1]

Be that as it may, anthropologists have long been intrigued by the place of fine arts in culture, and in recent years a great deal of attention has been focused on the relation of the artist to his society and culture. Answers are being sought to such questions as: Is artistic ability inevitably inherited or can it be brought into being, stimulated, and developed through cultural training? Does the impulse to make a work of art arise spontaneously, or does it have to be acquired? Is there an unlimited freedom of scope to artistic formulations, or is each artist forced to work within broad limits set by the nature of his medium and the cultural concepts of his society? None of these questions can be settled fully, and some cannot even be partially answered. This much is known. Primitives can and do distinguish what they consider good art from bad. They also recognize great differences in individual ability, and the vast bulk of their artistic output conforms in general to the established forms and techniques that prevail in their culture. Rare, indeed, is the individual genius who ranges far beyond the cultural boundaries of his group. It is well known that pottery designs from a given time and place are usually so standardized that they can be readily recognized by a student or expert, yet they often show individual characteristics. How a potter can introduce personal elements while staying within the limits of his society's conventions is a problem of the fine arts that has not yet been conclusively solved.

---

[1] G. Weltfish, *The Origins of Art*, Indianapolis and New York, 1953.

B. INSTRUMENTAL MUSIC

The productions of **instrumental music** come very close to the structured patterns of the verbal arts. Their aim is to produce particular sounds in a definite order and in accordance with a fixed arrangement of stresses, pitches, intonations, and rhythms. In each of these matters the conventional pattern may vary from group to group. Moreover, there is little to prevent a society from assigning to musical utterances, as it does to words, whatever emotional or other symbolic meanings it wishes, although one must not overlook the possibility that some kinds of music may arouse physiological responses that affect all of mankind rather than the members of one particular community. The performance of instrumental music is not only a universal human achievement, but also one that man does not share with any other animal.

As a rule, the meanings that are associated with musical compositions are likely to be culturally determined. Euro-American listeners learn to consider some forms of instrumental music as jolly and others as sad. We are also inclined to think of marching soldiers when we hear what we interpret to be a martial air and of brides when we listen to the strains of what we regard as a wedding march. As in the case of vocal utterances, however, no two social units need necessarily ascribe the same meanings to the same sounds. Hence, what one group regards as mournful another may interpret as gay.

The cultural implications of music are of particular concern to those anthropologists who are coming to be known as **ethnomusicologists.** They are, at present, few in number, largely because their specialty calls for a great deal of training in music as well as in anthropology. Their broad aims are to acquire an understanding and to present an interpretation of the totality of human music, without limitations of race, time, or geography. As anthropologists, too, they tend to look upon a musical production as only a single segment of culture, linked to other manifestations of a group's way of life.[2]

Conventionally, musical instruments have been classified according to whether they are intended to emphasize melody or rhythm, but it is also possible to describe and discuss them in terms of their

---

[2] W. Rhodes, "Toward a Definition of Ethnomusicology," *American Anthropologist,* Vol. 58, 1956, pp. 457-463.

structures, the ways they are played, or the materials of which they are made. A recent classification, based on methods of sound production, divides musical instruments into four groups: **idiophones,** such as bells and rattles, which make sounds by the vibration of the entire implement; **aerophones,** like flutes, clarinets, trumpets, and pan pipes (Fig. 18.1) that depend on a closed column of vibrating air; **membraphones,** all manner of drums, that utilize a vibrating membrane; and **chordophones,** including violins and guitars, that

Fig. 18.1. Playing the Panpipe. A South American Indian playing the Panpipe. Musical instruments of this type are classed as aerophones.

get their effects from the vibrations of strings.[3] Regardless of which methods of classification are used, data on instrumental music can always be employed to round out descriptions of culture patterns, to help delineate culture areas, to aid studies of invention and diffusion, and to provide factual materials that are useful in the consideration of topics like migration, culture history, and culture change.

People in primitive societies, unlike ourselves, seldom play instrumental music for its own sake. They are much more given to use it as an accompaniment for singing, processions, dances, or some other activity. Experience has shown that the emotional impact of many actions is greatly increased when they are combined with music produced by a variety of instruments.

C. PROCESSIONS AND DANCES

Nowadays, **processions,** except in the form of parades, or at funerals in some countries, play so trivial a part in our way of life that we are apt to overlook the importance they once had in Euro-American culture or that they still have in a number of primitive societies. In its simplest terms a procession need be no more than a movement of people along a fixed route, but not often is it as prosaic as that. Seldom does one find a procession which fails to have a specific purpose or which does not combine a number of the fine arts, such as painting, masking, costuming, or the making of music. To appreciate its significance as an artistic outlet we must try to picture the contrasting effect of a highly colorful procession on a folk whose daily lives unfold in rather colorless and even drab surroundings. Apparently people everywhere enjoy opportunities to escape from the humdrum round of their usual activities.

Like other renderings of the fine arts, processions are seldom regarded as ends in themselves. They may be held for a variety of purposes. It would be extremely difficult to try to give all the reasons for processions, but a partial list would include those that take place in conjunction with economic activities, for political purposes, in carrying out rites of passage, especially when death strikes, and as prayers or other ways of communicating with the supernatural world.

Processions that are somehow connected with religious observ-

---

[3] B. Nettl, *Music in Primitive Culture,* Cambridge, Mass., 1956, p. 90.

ances are among those that are best known to cultural anthropologists. In a majority of instances the marchers carry an idol or a supernatural image of some sort, and their route generally takes a circular or squarish form. These customs imply that such processions are designed to spread about mana, especially among those enclosed within the line of march, at the same time that they prevent evil supernatural forces from penetrating the charmed circle.

Processions of a religious nature are everyday features of primitive ceremonialism and were once exceedingly important to the practice of Christianity. Even the parochial Mass, so the Catholic Encyclopedia tells us,[4] used to open with a procession; and from the same source we learn that in times of crisis or emergency extraordinary processions may be held to ask for rain or fine weather, or else to avert storms, famine, plague, and war.

Closely allied to processions, instrumental music, religious practices, and esthetics in general is the art of **dancing.** In truth, it is not always easy to tell a procession from a dance. For instance, in some African tribes it used to be customary to render special treatment to a girl when she attained puberty. Her head was shaved, her body was anointed with medicinal oil, she was dressed in bark cloth, and she walked along carrying a model of a house as a sign that she was ready to become a housekeeper. From the nature of the performance most of us would call it a procession, but the natives described the rites as "dancing a girl into womanhood."[5]

In primitive societies, especially, there is very often a close connection also between dancing and the verbal arts. Dancing has been aptly described as "poetry in motion," and, like speech production, its essence consists of rhythmically controlled movements of the body or some of its parts. Furthermore, as modern choreographers know so well, dancing can also be used to tell a story. When it is combined with instrumental music, dancing has a powerful emotional effect on performers and spectators alike. It can induce trance, mass hypnotism, ecstacy, or frenzy (Fig. 18.2). Primitive religions make such great use of dancing that the terms *dance* and *rite* are often used synonymously. Early Christianity relied much on dancing, but in recent years a number of sects have frowned on the use of either instrumental music or dancing.

Dances may be performed as social festivities, to honor a deity

---

[4] *Catholic Encyclopedia*, Vol. II, p. 446.
[5] W. D. Hambly, *Tribal Dancing and Social Developments*, New York, 1927, p. 125.

or some abstract supernatural power, to win the pity of the other world, or as a way of asking for supernatural help. It is in the latter context that the renowned **Kachina dances** of the Pueblo Indians can best be understood. They are essentially religious performances,

Fig. 18.2. Dancing in a trance. On the islands of Malaya or Indonesia, as well as in other parts of the world, native dancers regularly become entranced. Here an entranced dancer on Bali is about to wound himself with a kris. Spectators often have to interfere to prevent a dancer from seriously injuring himself. (Courtesy Museum of Anthropology, University of Michigan.)

but they incorporate a great many esthetic and social elements. In the belief of the Hopi, a typical Pueblo tribe, a **Kachina** is a friendly spirit, capable of bringing rain and other benefits. Long ago, as several myths have it, the Kachinas were supposed to have lived on earth, but enemies later killed them off. To gain their spiritual

Fig. 18.3. Hopi Kachina dancer. The Jemez (Hümis) Kachina costume pictured is a favorite type for the Homegoing (Niman) dance, which ends the open season for Kachina performances in midsummer. However, this costume is not obligatory for the Homegoing dance. It may be worn, in addition to many other styles, on other occasions. (Courtesy of Frederick J. Dockstader.)

RED

YELLOW

TURQUOISE

GREEN

aid, Hopi men learned to impersonate the Kachinas and presently to represent them by dressing in elaborate costumes, gaily painted and including large, colorful masks that completely hide the face and head of the wearer and come to rest on his shoulders (Fig. 18.3). According to the Hopi, a man becomes a living god as soon as he dons a mask. Thereafter he is forbidden to speak lest his voice reveal his identity. In advance of a public performance the dancers resort to kivas to prepare their costumes, learn a newly composed cycle of songs, and practice the appropriate steps and gestures. On the scheduled day they appear in the village plaza to sing and dance, with intervals of rest interspersed, from daybreak to sunset. Throughout their afternoon appearances they bring gifts, usually prepared in advance by the kin of the recipients and most often consisting of carved and painted wooden **Kachina dolls** which help youngsters to learn the proper markings of an untold number of beneficial spirits. Occasionally, the dancers are accompanied by a drummer, or by performers who scrape an animal shoulder-blade (scapula) rhythmically against a notched stick that rests on an inverted gourd. Kachina dances are highly esteemed by participants and observers alike, both for their religious values and their artistic appeal. Only males may perform as Kachinas, but women on these occasions dress themselves and their children in their best clothes, fix elaborate meals, and keep open house throughout the day.

Kachina dances are regulated by the ceremonial calendar. In native theory there is an open season, running approximately from the first of January to the end of June, while the rest of the year makes up a closed season during which no masked (Kachina) dances may be held. All the Kachinas except one, *Masau*, who stands for the god of death and therefore does things by opposites, are supposed to be sleeping or resting throughout the closed season.

D. GRAPHIC AND PLASTIC ARTS

Under the heading of **graphic** and **plastic arts** one generally includes all manner of painting, engraving, carving, and sculpturing. These may follow realistic and representational styles, or else abstract or conventionalized ones. Many years ago, under the stimulus of work by A. C. Haddon,[6] it was thought that realism always preceded conventionalization. Since Haddon's day, Boas and others have

---

[6] A. C. Haddon, *Evolution in Art*, London, 1895.

shown that art styles seem on occasion to move in the reverse direction, and today matters of priority excite but little interest.

Whether it be a realistic portrayal or a geometric figure, a work of art is presently thought of in terms of its meaning, and this, in turn, is looked upon as a matter of cultural interpretation. Some works of art have significance only for their creators or for the restricted membership of a particular subculture, but more commonly an artistic expression conveys a similar meaning to all the people who make up a particular society. At the opposite extreme, it is to be doubted if any esthetic product has ever been created that has an identical meaning in all the cultures known to anthropologists. The swastika, for example, is very widely distributed throughout the world, but it is variously portrayed and interpreted in different places (see Fig. 18.4).

Much has been written about the supposed resemblances of primitive art to the art of children. Anthropologists are agreed that such analogies are misleading. Many a work of primitive art shows a mastery of techniques and an understanding of materials that are far from childish. Nor should we forget, if we are judging a piece of primitive art which was produced in a school or other institution, that an artist from any culture may appear crude if he is forced to work with unfamiliar tools and materials. Then, too, we must beware of criticizing something that the artist might have neither tried nor wanted to do in the first place. Almost from the time of their discovery, observers have noted that Upper Paleolithic cave paintings have many splendid portrayals of animals but practically no realistic representations of human beings. No contemporary critic knows whether the lack is due to the inability of Upper Paleolithic artists to picture the human figure or to a complete lack of interest in depicting human beings.

Like other expressions of esthetics, the products of the graphic and plastic arts are seldom created for their own sakes in primitive societies. Sometimes they double as house-posts, graveyard markers, headrests, cooking utensils, or containers.[7] These represent but a sprinkling of the practical purposes which works of art may serve. It should also be kept in mind that many cultural anthropologists agree that writing is somehow an outgrowth of pictorial art.

---

[7] A good deal of additional information on this topic may be secured from M. J. Herskovits, *Man and His Works*, New York, 1948, pp. 378-413.

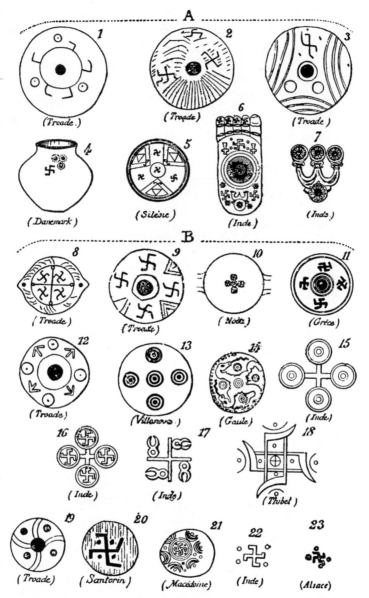

Fig. 18.4. Distribution of the swastika. The swastika is a very old and widely distributed element of design. It occurs in a great profusion of forms and is variously interpreted in different societies. (From Count d'Alviella, *The Migration of Symbols*, New York, 1956. Courtesy of University Books, Inc.)

To cite only a few of the best known examples of primitive art, we can mention the splendid ritual bronzes of the Shang period in ancient China, the carefully sculptured and painted wooden totem poles of the Indians who used to dwell along the northwest Pacific coast of the Americas, the awe-inspiring masks and shields of countless aboriginal tribes, the highly symbolic sand-paintings of the Navaho Indians, the subtle metal figures created by African dwellers in the neighborhood of the Bay of Benin, the exquisite textiles of aboriginal Peru, and the amazing religious architecture of the Mayas and Aztecs, to say nothing of the splendor of the buildings and stone sculptures at Angkor Wat in Cambodia or the remarkable Borobodur monument in Java (Fig. 18.5). Such a list is really incomplete, for it leaves out a host of equally important artistic creations in an incredibly broad assortment of media. For all their diversity these products are alike in that they give pleasure to their creators as well as to their users and countless observers.

E. PLAYING GAMES

Professor Kroeber has defined play as wasteful but pleasurable bodily activity.[8] By "wasteful" he means presumably that play is not directed to the satisfaction of any of the biological imperatives or other essential physical needs of mankind. He finds playfulness most fully developed among mammals, and he attributes to the rechanneling of play impulses a great many human actions that culminate in esthetic and intellectual products. Kroeber's viewpoint is very interesting and may explain why games and amusements are uni-

---

[8] A. L. Kroeber, *Anthropology*, New York, rev. ed., 1948, pp. 28-29.

Fig. 18.5. Examples of primitive arts. A. Navaho sand painting. A medicine man is teaching an apprentice how to make a sand painting by sprinkling grains of colored sand on a neutral background. Figures so constructed represent gods and cosmic symbols, part of the elaborate curing rites that comprise the essence of Navaho religion. B. Brazilian pottery vessel. This type of jar was used as a burial urn by Indians living at the mouth of the Amazon. In the original, the painted design is in several colors. C. Bronze head from Benin. West African tribes in the vicinity of Benin are famous for their skillful work in bronze. D. The Borobodur in Java. This splendid architectural monument is dedicated to Buddha, but it is highly respected by the Moslems of Java. (A. Courtesy of D. Clifford Bond. B. Courtesy of Clifford Evans and the Smithsonian Institution. C and D. Courtesy of the Museum of Anthropology, University of Michigan.)

B   C

versal features of all societies. Without exception, though, among human beings play is inevitably a biocultural rather than a biological activity. Bodies may perform all the requisite actions, but cultures determine how the bodies shall be used and what the rules of any game shall be.

Nor is play invariably wasteful. Youngsters everywhere like to mimic their elders, and many children's games serve to train them for adult tasks. Such games may be said to have important educational functions and to be practical rather than wasteful.

Anthropologists distinguish between **games of chance** and **games of skill.** Since their outcome is always a matter of luck, games of chance offer obvious opportunities for wagering and gambling. As with the question of his supposed esthetic urge, the nature of man's interest in gambling has never been settled. A novice in the study of cultural anthropology is usually amazed to discover how varied and widespread games of chance are in primitive societies. Card games, dice games, guessing games, and lotteries occur in a tremendous profusion of forms, and the stakes may be exceedingly high. In many tribes an excited player may gamble away not only valuable property, but even a beloved wife or child. Men have gambled themselves and their families into destitution and even slavery, yet no society seems to have profited from their misery and games of chance continue to be played throughout the world.

Various motives may exist for the playing of games of skill. A few such games are played for gambling, sheer amusement, or intellectual pleasure; others are little more than physical pastimes; many involve difficult competition and a determined effort to outdo one's rivals; some serve the avowed purposes of training exercises for war; and not a few have religious motivations. It is rather firmly held, on the basis of convincing proof, that many of the implements that are used in games of skill, particularly sticks and clubs, were originally weapons.

Games of skill testing intellectual prowess fall into classes closely resembling checkers or chess. These are allied to others, like backgammon, which combine skill with chance. In such games counters are moved across a board not according to individual decisions but as determined by throws of dice (Fig. 18.6). E. B. Tylor, late in the last century, found that such games had world-wide distribution, and his studies led him to conclude that their presence in

America gave evidence of diffusion from Asia,[9] but Kroeber has more recently cast doubt on Tylor's conclusion.[10]

Many games of skill, particularly those that we identify as **sports,** depend on the strenuous yet well controlled use of the body. Essentially, this requires what modern athletes call "good form." Once

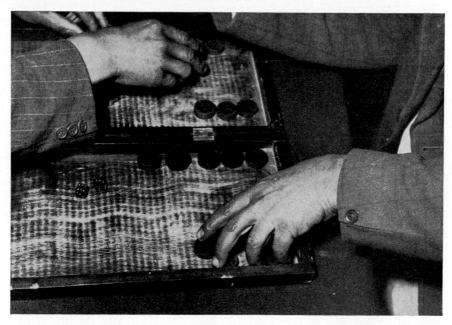

Fig. 18.6. Iranian (Persian) men playing backgammon. Known as *tric-trac,* this form of backgammon is very popular in Iran. It is usually played by men in coffee shops. (Courtesy of Three Lions.)

more do we meet the advantages of man's ability to look ahead and to anticipate future rewards for difficult actions that yield no compensation at the moment. All athletes are aware of the drudgery of practice periods during which good form is acquired, but few players dare rely on inherited talents to the extent of foregoing training sessions. As sports become more highly organized, the amount of effort devoted to preliminary training increases.

Wrestling, which depends on the skillful use of the body, is practically universal. So important an aspect of culture was it once con-

---

[9] Tylor's studies are conveniently summarized in A. L. Kroeber and T. T. Waterman, *Source Book in Anthropology,* New York, 1931, pp. 388-397.

[10] A. L. Kroeber, *Anthropology,* New York, rev. ed., 1948, p. 551.

sidered to be that, according to a story which is still current, the Olympic games originated from a divine wrestling match in which Zeus, the chief deity of the ancient Greeks, overcame Chronos, the god of time. Races of all kinds are also very common. Many of them are simple running races, but among several tribes of Indians the contestants also kick a stone or a stick as they run.

Archeologists have uncovered a vast number of ball courts (Fig. 18.7). Their evidence makes it clear that ball games of many kinds

Fig. 18.7. A Maya ball court. The ancient Maya Indians played an important game on a court. Not all the details are known, but it is thought that scores were made by passing a ball through a loop such as the one shown on the wall at the right. (Courtesy of Southwest Museum.)

had a wide distribution in times past, and many contemporary people continue to hold such contests regularly. Among these one of the best known examples is hockey *(chueca)*, as played by the Araucanian Indians of Chile. This tribe was among the last big ones in the New World to be pacified by Caucasoids, and until a few decades ago its entire culture was geared to war. As long as active fighting prevailed, the Araucanians frankly looked upon hockey as a training exercise for war and the terms for hockey player and warrior were used interchangeably, but since their pacification the natives play chiefly for sport and wagering. The game resembles field hockey as played by teams of women in Euro-American countries, but it is a rough and tumble masculine sport among the

Araucanians. It calls for speed, stamina, daring, and good coordination, qualities whose usefulness in war is self-evident.[11]

In trying to understand the world-wide prevalence of games, it is possible to analyze some of their functions in terms of biocultural dynamics. All games increase the solidarity of a group by providing socially sanctioned outlets for aggression. We must remember that all those who indulge in games of chance are forever trying to win over others, and even when we play intellectual games like checkers or chess we speak of trying to beat an opponent. Whether we watch or play games of bodily skill, we identify ourselves with one social unit, usually our own, and do our best to make it triumph over a group of other folk.

F. SUPERNATURALISM IN GAMES

Stewart Culin, an outstanding specialist in the study of games, has unequivocally stated that many games which appear on the surface to be played only for gain, exercise, or amusement are also performed as sacred rites for pleasing the gods. They may be played in the hope of winning general approval from the supernatural world or else for such specific purposes as driving away evil, averting sickness, bringing rain, and aiding the reproduction of plants, animals, and human beings.[12] Games have undergone so many changes and reinterpretations in historic times that a modern reader may doubt the truth of Culin's analysis, although everyone rather vaguely associates superstition with gamblers and athletes. Many of us find it hard to believe that innocent-looking games or processions involving hoops and poles very often go back to a period when these objects stood for the female and male sex organs, respectively, and when their use symbolized sexual relations as a prayer for fertility.

The clearest links between the playing of games and religious practices seem to depend on the element of the unknown. When we are at a loss to understand why something unexpected happens in sports or gambling we are apt to attribute it to "luck," but primitive peoples more often assign such events to supernatural forces. From this standpoint it is simple to see why all games of chance should have religious implications. The connection with games of

[11] M. Titiev, "Araucanian Culture in Transition," *Occasional Contributions from the Museum of Anthropology*, No. 15, Ann Arbor, 1951.

[12] S. Culin, "Games of the North American Indians," *Annual Report, Bureau of American Ethnology*, No. 24, Washington, 1907.

skill may be less clear until we realize that in them, too, the outcome is never known in advance, and wherever controlled causation does not apply, recourse may be had to the supernatural.

Games of chance are closely related to ordeals in so far as the
winner is supposedly determined by some extrahuman or supernatural agency. That is why difficult decisions may be left to the
throw of dice, the cutting of cards, the toss of a coin, or a similar
activity. Counting out procedures, if truly left to chance, belong in
the same category. It seems unnecessary to repeat that literate individuals who indulge in such practices may have no awareness of
the supernatural implications of what they are doing and may even
resent any interpretation along religious lines. Not everyone in our
culture is willing to equate belief in luck with faith in the supernatural.

Many a primitive personage prays long and earnestly for supernatural guidance before he draws lots or makes a decision in what
looks to us like a childish game of "Button, button, who's got the
button?" Also, it is reported that some of the Sioux-speaking tribes
long ago had a **ghost gamble,** the purpose of which was to play for
the effects of a recently deceased individual. The goods were placed
into a number of piles, marked peach stones were used as counters,
and the living pitted their luck against a player who impersonated
the deceased. If a man were fortunate he might thus win cheaply
some of the dead person's belongings. All proceeds went to the
heirs of the deceased.

Games of skill likewise show frequent religious motivations. A
swift runner who carries water may not only triumph over others,
but may also, on the basis of mimetic magic, represent an automatic prayer for rain to come quickly. Similarly, several North
American Indian tribes used to play a type of hockey or shinny in
which the ball was stuffed with seeds. The idea was that if the ball
were quickly burst and the seeds widely scattered, the gods would
send early and bountiful harvests. Throughout many parts of the
world, too, games organized like a tug-of-war are used to induce
supernatural powers to send favors such as sunshine in the direction
indicated by the winners.

Some games associated with religion may be calendrical while
others are critical. Of the calendrical games the most widely distributed consists of assorted ways of making **string figures,** or what
we call cat's cradle. Not all peoples who go in for elaborate designs

with string limit themselves to playing at the same seasons of the year, nor do they all offer identical explanations for similar designs or for the game itself, but it is not uncommon to find a calendrical or seasonal implication. Some Eskimo groups make string figures primarily late in the summer, in order to enmesh and detain the sun; but certain New Guinea tribes play cat's cradle in the growing season, in order to make their yams grow (Fig. 18.8).

Funeral games, on the other hand, must always, from their very nature, be played only in times of crisis. They need not, though, always be limited to a single purpose. In some cases their main intent seems to be to speed the spirit of the deceased to the other world, where he belongs. In other cases, the chief purpose appears to be to free the survivors from the fear that they might be stricken by the same evil power that caused one of their members to die. Feelings of relief, joy, or pleasure may thus enter into the performance of funeral games.

Those who strive for victory in games very commonly seek super-

Fig. 18.8. Cat's cradle in New Guinea. Cat's cradle is played almost universally. While it may have had religious connotations in the past, it has often degenerated into a simple game for children. (From H. I. Hogbin, *Peoples of the Southwest Pacific*, New York, 1945-1946. Courtesy Asia Press, Inc.)

natural additions to their skill. Everything from a favorite garment to a lucky coin or a rabbit's foot may be used to supplement one's own ability. Paraphernalia that are thought to be full of mana because they were used with success in the past may be used to the exclusion of all similar items. Sporting circles are full of talk about "lucky bats," "lucky shoes," "lucky racquets," "lucky fishing-rods," and so forth. Many players also resort to bits of private ritual, such as always repeating a set formula in a crisis or always touching second base with the left foot on the way in from the field.

It is difficult for us to realize how seriously many groups take their games. The Cherokee Indians of North Carolina and elsewhere used to play a tough lacrosse game in which teams from various towns competed.[13] Contrary to our practice of resting players in seclusion on the eve of an important contest, the Cherokee players remained awake all night. They were subjected to painful ordeals, and they participated in highly important rituals (Fig. 18.9), designed to gain supernatural support which would help them to victory on the morrow.

---

[13] J. Mooney, "The Cherokee Ball Play," *American Anthropologist*, Vol. 3, No. 2, 1890.

Fig. 18.9. Cherokee ball game. The players are shown around the fire at the right. Their rackets are being blessed by the drummer, priest, and women. The game was a very serious affair, and it was felt that supernatural support was needed for victory. (Courtesy of the Bureau of American Ethnology.)

The wholehearted reliance which primitive peoples may put on supernatural decisions as expressed in the results of games should not be minimized. Early in September of 1906, the Hopi pueblo of Old Oraibi found itself so badly divided over many questions, including the acceptance of "white" schooling, that it was agreed to separate the two factions permanently. To decide which faction should leave its traditional home, the Indians traced a line on the ground, and the sides faced each other, with the understanding that those who were pushed across would be the losers and would have to leave. In the ensuing "push-fest" the conservatives who opposed the new schools lost, whereupon their leader yielded to his fate and led his followers to a vacant site where they founded the village of Hotevilla.[14] Here were about four hundred individuals who, with their ancestors, had lived at Oraibi for centuries, but who left their old homes without further argument because their gods had made known their wills through the outcome of a game.

SELECTED REFERENCES

Adam, L., *Primitive Art,* rev. ed. London and Baltimore, 1954.

Boas, F., *Primitive Art.* Oslo, 1929.

Breuil, H., *Four Hundred Centuries of Cave Art.* New York, 1950.

Chard, C. S., "Distribution and Significance of Ball Courts in the Southwest," *Papers of the Excavators' Club,* Vol. I, No. 2, Cambridge, Mass., 1940.

Culin, S., "Games of the North American Indians," *Bureau of American Ethnology, Annual Report,* No. 24, Washington, D. C., 1907.

Derringer, D., *The Alphabet.* New York, 1948.

Haddon, K., *Artists in String: Their Regional Distribution and Social Significance.* New York, 1930.

Hambly, W. D., *Tribal Dancing and Social Developments.* New York, 1927.

Herzog, G., "Research in Primitive and Folk Music in the United States," *American Council of Learned Societies, Bulletin,* No. 24, 1936, pp. 1-97.

Kurath, G. P., "A New Method of Choreographic Notation," *American Anthropologist,* Vol. 52, No. 1, 1950, pp. 120-123.

Linton, R., and Wingert, P. S., *Arts of the South Seas.* New York, 1946.

Mooney, J., "The Cherokee Ball Play," *American Anthropologist,* Vol. 3, No. 2, 1890.

---

[14] M. Titiev, "Old Oraibi: A Study of the Hopi Indians of Third Mesa," *Papers of the Peabody Museum of American Archaeology and Ethnology,* Harvard University, Cambridge, Vol. 22, No. 1, 1944, p. 86ff.

Nettl, B., *Music in Primitive Culture*. Cambridge, Mass., 1956.

Newcomb, F. J., *et al.*, "A Study of Navajo Symbolism," *Papers of the Peabody Museum of American Archaeology and Ethnology*, Vol. 32, No. 3, Cambridge, Mass., 1956.

Rhodes, W., "Toward a Definition of Ethnomusicology," *American Anthropologist*, Vol. 58, 1956.

CHAPTER **19**

THREE REPRESENTATIVE

PATTERNS OF CULTURE

A. BY WAY OF INTRODUCTION

Up to this point we have been primarily concerned with setting forth the principles of cultural anthropology. Only occasionally, and for the sake of example, have allusions been made to the specific customs found in particular societies. It seems highly appropriate, therefore, that we should now depict the ways of life of a few folk in reasonably complete thumbnail sketches.

The two primitive groups to be described were not chosen at random. The Tikopians are Oceanic Negroids, island-dwellers in the South Pacific; the Hopi are American Indian Mongoloids who live in a semidesert portion of Arizona, where water of any kind is scarce. Racially, geographically, linguistically, and culturally, no two people could be more different. Yet, each is an equally proper representative of *Homo sapiens,* and some of their ways are surprisingly alike. This is what makes the study of cultural anthropology such a fascinating pursuit. In the exercise of our profession we are always on the watch for the internal universals of human behavior that so often underlie the external diversities of man's conduct. Our task is not merely to ferret out the universals but also to interpret them as well as we can.

It will be noted that the present tense is used throughout our descriptions, even though the works on which they are based were published years ago. This is done only for the sake of convenience and is not meant to suggest that the peoples in question have remained unchanged. Cultural anthropologists know full well that processes of change operate constantly on all patterns of culture, sometimes without being detected and sometimes in clear view. Since our major purpose in this chapter is not to trace or discuss culture change but only to summarize ways of life as they appeared at one moment of time, we shall write in the present without further apology.

Studies of primitive customs would have only limited value if they failed to provide clues for a better understanding of our own mores. Examples from American culture have occasionally been given in the earlier portions of this book. They were, on the whole, introduced to show that many basic principles of human conduct apply to Euro-American society just as well as to the world of primitive man. It is in the belief that we can gain a wider and better understanding of ourselves through a study of primitive cultures that a sketch of life in the United States is included in this chapter.

In order to tie together the accounts of specific cultures with the more general propositions scattered throughout the book, cross-references in parentheses have been provided. To avoid a great deal of repetition, page references have been inserted only in the summary of Tikopian culture, but their use may serve as a model for the sketches that follow.

B. LAND, LABOR, AND DAILY LIFE ON TIKOPIA [1]

Tikopia is a small island, roughly elliptical in shape, running about three miles from northeast to southwest and approximately one and a half miles in the other direction. Spatially, it lies within the area of Melanesia, although the customs of its 1281 inhabitants brand them as part of a Polynesian fringe.[2] For a small island Tikopia has

---

[1] Sections "B" and "C" are based on Raymond Firth, *We, the Tikopia,* American Book Company, New York, 1936. Permission to summarize Professor Firth's volume was graciously given by the author and publisher.

Professor Firth lived on Tikopia as a participant-observer for a full year beginning in July, 1928. He quickly learned to speak the native language and thereafter worked directly, without using an interpreter.

[2] Melanesia conventionally refers to the islands that range from New Guinea to Fiji. Polynesia lies further east in the South Pacific and includes the territory within the approximate triangle formed by Hawaii in the north, New Zealand in the southwest, and Easter Island to the southeast.

a varied terrain, including a reef, but no lagoon, coastal beaches, woodlands, plains, a swamp, a fresh-water lake, and fairly rugged cliffs. At first impression it appears heavily wooded, with small and infrequent patches of cultivated land in the vicinity of scattered villages, but closer familiarity reveals that much of what seems to be wasteland is privately owned and carefully utilized. Very little of the island's resources is wasted, and the inhabitants pride themselves on the beauty and bounty of their homeland.

The people of Tikopia live primarily on vegetable foods, some of which grow wild and some of which are deliberately cultivated. Taro makes up the principal crop, but coconuts, breadfruit, yams, and bananas are also grown or gathered. **Betel nut,** a mild narcotic that stains the saliva red, is universally chewed by adults, and **kava** is drunk or offered to the gods during religious observances. Vegetal products are supplemented with fish, and fresh water is obtained from springs.

Theoretically, all land and drinking water are owned by four chiefs, each of whom dwells near a spring and represents or controls the ancestral spirits who are thought to be the true owners of the island (p. 339). The natives believe that the living and the dead are very much interested in one another's doings (p. 360). In practice, there is a close link between land holdings and places of residence. Every cluster of huts is recognized as a village entity and with each there goes a name and fixed boundaries. Food-bearing lands are privately owned, but not much fuss is made over trespass if permission is sought beforehand or if a transgressor later tells a proprietor what he has done. Should an owner desire to prevent intrusions on his property he may declare his land tabu to all others. Customarily, a man's holdings are inherited by his sons; a female eats from her father's land before marriage and from her husband's thereafter.

Foods are by no means the only products that the natives get by interacting with their environment. Some fields are regularly set aside for the growing of first-fruit offerings (p. 355). Houses, built low to minimize the effects of gales, are made principally of local woods and sago palm (p. 228). Furnishings are scant, consisting primarily of mats made of plaited coconut leaves, and people sleep under bark-cloth covers on pandanus bed mats (p. 230). Although the temperature is fairly equable and quite high, averaging between 80 and 85 degrees Fahrenheit, the humidity is great and some periods of coolness are known. Everyday garments consist of waist-bands or kilts of bark cloth for men and skirts of the same material for women. Adults of both sexes like to wear as much calico, which has been given religious significance (p. 237), as they can get. Youngsters run about naked.

Tikopians awaken soon after sunrise every morning and straggle to the beach, where they bathe and make their toilets. Each sex goes to a different spot, but men and women remain in full view of one another and trust to cultural blindness (p. 242) to preserve their modesty. Within each house a smoldering fire is blown into flame, but breakfast is eaten informally and usually consists of cold left-overs. People then go to work, farming, gardening, gathering food, fishing, beating out bark cloth, or caring for infants. Tasks are often combined with a bit of fun, and in the afternoon everyone returns to prepare for the big meal of the day. For this, both sexes share the responsibility. Normally, the inhabitants of each house-hold fix and eat their food by themselves. Cooking is done in ovens, which are generally located in separate structures (p. 232), close by each dwelling. After eating, people chew betel and relax before turning to various arts and crafts. Late in the day those who wish drift to informal assembly points on the beach, where older folk chat and gossip (p. 380) while younger ones, especially if they are unmarried, play games, wrestle, dance (Fig. 19.1), or make love. Many songs are composed and sung, most of which are timely and soon forgotten, but some of which are taken up and so frequently repeated that they become traditional. Everyone retires at will; there is no fixed bedtime.

As is to be expected, there is some sexual dichotomy (p. 240), but it is not greatly marked on Tikopia, for cooperation is more impor-tant than separation. Besides bearing children and looking after households, females make bark cloth, plait mats, perform dyeing operations, help to grow or gather vegetal foods, and fish by hand along the reef. Men do the heavier farming tasks, climb coconut trees, work at carpentry, make all manner of cordage, serve as tattooers, conduct the major rituals, and fish in the open sea from outrigger canoes.

Respect and avoidance are important mechanisms of social con-trol and make up an elaborate code of etiquette. Chiefs expect a great show of respect, all married women are supposed to be treated respectfully, restraint marks the reciprocal behavior of all cousins,

A

B

Fig. 19.1. Tikopians dancing. Dancing is an important activity on Tikopia. Women dance in one style (A), and men in another (B). (Courtesy of R. Firth and American Book Company.)

personal body contact is generally avoided, and an individual's head, particularly that of a chief or parent, is never to be carelessly touched. So it is that the populace is ranked and differentiated, even though there is ample food for all, everyone dresses and lives alike on the surface, and matters of wealth, except for land containing coconut palms, are of little moment.

C. TIKOPIAN KINSHIP AND SOCIORELIGIOUS BEHAVIOR

Kinship plays an extremely important part in Tikopian social organization. Many aspects of the aboriginal religion are based on recognition of the fact that a kinship system continues to operate, even beyond the life spans of particular individuals (p. 193). Each term employed may be regarded as a guide to a particular way of behaving (p. 274), and children are taught how to address and act toward their various relatives. All natives of the island share a sense of kinship, and only those who come from elsewhere are considered to be true strangers (p. 287). At the same time, not every inhabitant of Tikopia is regarded equally. Place of residence, age, sex, and social status (p. 248), as well as the ties of "blood" or marriage, all make a great difference. Roughly speaking, the long axis of the island divides Tikopia into rival districts between which there is a great deal of distrust, competition, and slander, although the members of one unit are free to marry into the other.

Space and kinship are complexly interwoven on Tikopia (p. 284). Large units of kin comprise **kainanga,** which may be equated with patrilineal clans (p. 266). These are political and religious (p. 267), in the sense that only the members of a *kainanga* may attend the rites performed by their leader; and the status of a group depends on the importance of the gods with which it is affiliated. In turn, each *kainanga* is subdivided into a number of *paito,* or households, whose inmates are determined by the combined workings of patrilineal descent and patrilocal residence (p. 280). That is to say, each child finds itself born into a *paito* that contains as a nucleus his father's father, his father, and his father's brothers. All the females in the household would be either unwed or women who had moved in at marriage. Throughout their lives all men are expected to retain an interest in the women who once resided in their natal households. Each residence group has a headman, who speaks for it whenever necessary.

Strong links of kinship unite the males in every household, but on Tikopia, as elsewhere, relationship ties established involuntarily at birth are balanced by other links (p. 289). Much is made of the affinal connections that develop at marriage (p. 272). Although kin reckoning is entirely unilateral through males, the existence of the nuclear family is fully recognized (p. 271). Furthermore, an infant is taught to show especially high regard for his mother's brother (p. 416). On his part, a man will always befriend and help his sister's child. Very warm bonds also develop between a youngster and its grandparents. The formal relations of those in alternate generations are much less severe than the ones that prevail among those of successive generations (pp. 284-285).

A number of complicated ceremonies attend the birth of an infant (p. 356). Family size is usually restricted by the performance of *coitus interruptus,* and infanticide is sometimes practiced at a father's discretion. When a child reaches the age of three, its mother pierces its earlobes and nasal septum, usually a rather painless operation. Some years later, another milestone is passed when a boy, and once in a while a girl, is taken on his first fishing expedition by torchlight. This event is signalized by the wearing of a distinctive garment.

Adolescents of both sexes often band together for work or play. There is some resistance to parental authority, but there is no adolescent rebellion against established social practices. Children grow up in a permissive atmosphere and are even allowed to imitate sexual relations without much reproof. The onset of menstruation is not marked in any way, and among these people menstruants are neither isolated nor regarded as dangerous.[3]

Somewhere between the ages of nine and fourteen, but not directly connected with the attainment of puberty, a few boys at a time are put through a tribal initiation (p. 358). The principal feature consists of an operation on the foreskin of the penis, involving a cut that is a **superincision** rather than a circumcision. The whole affair is entrusted to a boy's mother's brothers, one of whom performs the superincision. Each youngster is smeared with turmeric and oil and dressed in a new waistband by his female relatives. The rites are said to have had a supernatural origin, but very little of a religious nature accompanies their performance. Instead,

---

[3] This is by no means typical of primitive societies.

there is a great deal of feasting and gift exchanging. Failure to go through the rites makes a young man subject to teasing and taunting.

Not much serious attention is paid to premarital sexual experience, but virginity is known and a man who happens to marry a virgin is very proud of the fact. Despite the general absence of shame or punishment for youthful sexual intercourse, an unmarried girl who bears a bastard is sometimes regarded with contempt. Tikopians have no preferential marriages, and polygyny is common, but the levirate is not practiced (p. 273 and 359). Females usually want the security of marriage but males are less eager to settle down. A lover who makes a girl pregnant is expected to marry his partner, and elopements of sweethearts are not unknown. Most often, however, men capture their wives, sometimes by prearrangement, and sometimes by actual abduction (p. 274).[4] As a rule, feasts and amicable exchanges of gifts between the households and kinsfolk involved follow soon after a capture. Within a short time after a marriage, too, a groom is expected to accompany his bride on a visit to her parents at her natal household (p. 280).

If a new wife so resents a captor that she violently rejects his initial advances, his kinsmen may hold her by force until her husband enjoys her. Women are expected to remain true to their mates, but infidelities on the part of men are lightly treated. There is no formal mechanism of divorce, but separations for various reasons do take place (p. 359).

Death removes a person to the supernatural realm, but it does not end his contacts with the world of the living (pp. 359-360). When someone dies, it is customary to light two ovens, which means that the pair of households which the deceased most frequented show their sympathy by serving feasts. Corpses are wrapped in mats or plain lengths of bark cloth, and burial takes place either within the confines of a house or in a designated sector just outside. Some houses have their floor space partitioned for use by males or females, or for other purposes. In such houses one portion may remain unoccupied except at funerals. Important spirits of the dead may be commemorated by special mats, and people are reluctant to abandon a

---

[4] It is often extremely difficult for an anthropologist to ascertain the true facts of a custom that may be described as "wife-capture." On the island of Bali, Dr. Margaret Mead tells us (*And Keep Your Powder Dry*, New York, 1942, p. 42), no one but a neurotic would "abduct" a bride without first having obtained her consent.

house in which some of their ancestors are buried. Personal grief is often expressed by the bereaved, but some purely formal wailing is also prescribed.

On the whole the island of Tikopia is quite isolated, and the abundance of its resources is sufficient to keep the inhabitants from wanting to leave. Nevertheless, objects of metal, obtainable only from outside sources, are greatly coveted, and other aspects of acculturation, notably Christian teachings, are known (p. 197). As far back as 1928 Firth found that many young men tried to stow away on ships, but their purpose was not to escape but to acquire heightened prestige so that their status would rise when they returned.

D. MATERIAL CULTURE AND SOCIAL ORGANIZATION OF THE HOPI INDIANS [5]

Perched picturesquely on the flat tops of a trio of mesas in a semi-arid portion of northeastern Arizona are the nine traditional pueblos whose inhabitants comprise the core of the Hopi Indian tribe. As one approaches from the east, the only feasible way in the old days, he comes successively to First, Second, and Third Mesa. Atop the Third Mesa is to be found the ancient village of Oraibi, until September of 1906 the largest of the Hopi towns and unofficially known as the capital of Hopiland. In reality, the Oraibi chief never exerted political authority over the other pueblos, and each village is jealous of its autonomy.

In 1934 there were in all about 3000 Hopi Indians, but an exact count has never been made. The native language is a form of Shoshonean, a tongue that belongs to the Uto-Aztecan family, which was spoken here and there from Utah to Mexico City. Despite their lack of political unity and numerous local variations of custom, all the Hopi speak one language and share a way of life that is typified by the inhabitants of Oraibi.

Every pueblo is divided into a number of exogamous, matrilineal clans, from one of which town chiefs are regularly drawn, and each of which has the privilege of farming on a particular bit of land. Theoretically, a village chief owns all the land associated with his

---

[5] Sections "D" and "E" are summaries of material taken, by permission, from Mischa Titiev, "Old Oraibi: A Study of the Hopi Indians of Third Mesa," *Papers of the Peabody Museum of American Archaeology and Ethnology*, Vol. 22, No. 1, Cambridge, Mass., 1944.

A

B

Fig. 19.2. Views of Oraibi. A. A general view of the Hopi Indian pueblo of Oraibi. It is the oldest continuously-occupied village in the United States. B. The oldest inhabitant of Oraibi in 1934. He was about 100 years old. He is dressed in winter underwear, which used to be worn as summer clothing. He is eating half a watermelon for lunch, and his spindle rests beside him. Despite his age, he was weaving a woolen rug, and he retained his interest in ceremonies.

pueblo, but in practice every clan knows where its holdings lie and hardly ever does a chief interfere with long-established customs of land use. Hopi men are diligent and expert dry farmers, and whenever they get sufficient rain they raise good crops of maize, beans, and squash. In addition, they grow a variety of such fruits as watermelon, peaches, and apricots, and they supplement these foods with meat from flocks of sheep or with rabbits killed by hunting. Since land is owned by clans and clans are matrilineal, a man is expected to farm for his mother or sister while he is unwed and for his wife after marriage.

In summertime men like to arise before daybreak so that they may finish their field work before the afternoon heat begins. They usually breakfast at home and take for lunch a few loaves of **piki,** a paper-thin bread, made from a cornmeal batter, that is quickly baked on a hot stone. *Piki* is customarily eaten with a liquid, perhaps plain water or the juice of a fruit. The big meal of a day is taken toward evening.

Men who herd sheep usually do so with partners. Each partner herds for two days and spends the intervening night at a sheep camp.

Hopi pueblos are built in terraced style of local stone and adobe mud. Structures are ordinarily two or three stories high, but each home, consisting essentially of a main room and a supplementary storage chamber, is privately held within the over-all ownership of a clan. A man may do the major work of building or repairing a house, but when he is through, the home belongs to his wife and her clan.

Both sexes have many duties. Women cook and run their households, carry water, nurse and rear children, tend small vegetable gardens, weave plaques and baskets of dried rabbitbrush, and occasionally make pottery. Men do the heavy work of farming and house-building, herd sheep, conduct most of the rituals, weave blankets and garments of all sorts, and make moccasins. Neither sex can get along well without the help of the other.

In addition to being matrilineal, these Indians are also matrilocal. This means that a man moves into his spouse's house when he marries and that his children belong to his wife's clan. The core of each household, accordingly, consists of an elderly woman and her spouse, together with their married daughters and the daughters' daughters and unwed sons. Nevertheless, each married man, though he moves in from the outside, is called "father" by his offspring, so that the nuclear family is adequately recognized even though the kinship system is rigorously unilateral. Warm affection often prevails between mates and between fathers and their offspring, and it is not unusual for a man to stick with his family even if it means opposition to his clan. The friendliness of a father and his children is certainly aided by the Hopi convention that all discipline should be carried out by a mother's brother.

Apart from its household mates, a child, especially a boy, forms its warmest and dearest ties with its father's sisters (ikya'am).[6] Indeed, there is reason to believe that at one time a Hopi boy was expected to marry his father's sister's daughter, a custom that is consonant with one form of cross-cousin marriage.

A married woman is so firmly rooted in her natal household that a divorce is of relatively slight importance. Her father, unmarried brothers, brothers-in-law, or sons can always be relied upon to look after her material needs, and she always has a roof over her head. As for a man, if his wife asks him to leave, he is free to marry again, or he can go back to his mother's or sister's (that is, his natal) household. Under such conditions it is small wonder that there is a high divorce rate and that Hopi monogamy is very brittle indeed.

Everyone sleeps on sheepskins stretched out on the floor or ground. Small children lie close by their mothers, but adolescents sleep further apart, and young men are free to roam about at will. Very often such youths call during the night on unmarried girls, and if they are favorably received, they indulge in sexual intercourse. This custom is known as dumaiya. It is found in all Hopi towns and is not uncommonly a preliminary to a wedding. Discovery of lovers is seldom taken seriously, and the bearing of a premarital bastard scarcely affects a girl's chances of marriage. Both boys and girls apparently grow tired of love affairs and eventually marry and settle down.

Nuptial ceremonies are long-drawn-out affairs, culminating in an act of union symbolized by the mingling or knotting of the couple's hair in a single washbasin. During the preliminaries a bride lives at her groom's house and prepares much of the food for his household

---

[6] In the Hopi language *ikya'am* means either "my father's sisters" or "women of my father's clan." Each infant belongs to its mother's clan, but is known as a child of its father's clan. It is named shortly after birth by its father's clanswomen, who name it in some fashion suggestive of their clan. Thus the child of a Sand clansman might be named by its father's womenfolk "Shifting Sand."

while her wedding outfit is being made. When the rites are concluded, the young wife proceeds to her permanent residence in her mother's house, and there later in the day her husband joins her.

Puberty receives no official recognition for either sex, and a menstruant continues to carry out all her customary obligations.

When a person dies, he is buried the same day by a kinsman, and only those who were present at the time of death are expected to weep. Spirits of the dead, except for witches, are supposed to travel quickly to the other world, *Maski,* where they live a shadowy replica of life on earth. Witches make a slow and painful journey to *Maski* and are burned in ovens to emerge as beetles.

The word *Hopi* means peaceful, and these people are nonaggressive and strongly Apollonian in most of their behavior. They are prone, however, to much bickering and gossiping. Furthermore, their pueblos are so compact that privacy is virtually impossible to attain, and everyone's actions are subject to endless discussion. Yet, each Hopi is brought up to be a strong individualist, all decisions are left to the person most concerned regardless of sex or age, chiefs exert very little authority, and there are no agencies to enforce compliance with traditional mores or to punish those who refuse to conform. Under such a system of extreme *laissez faire* the native communities are always potentially disintegrative, and in each town the culture pattern must somehow achieve harmony to prevent collapse. Much of the cohesion that is so necessary for the maintenance of the Hopi way of life comes from religion, to which we now turn.

E. HOPI CEREMONIALISM

In every pueblo the populace is organized into a number of secret societies, each of which is responsible for the conduct of a single ceremony. A particular clan is said to own each ceremony, but this only means that it has charge of some of the requisite sacred paraphernalia and that it has the added duty of supplying the ceremony's leader or chief. Even here the principle of *laissez faire* continues to operate, for should a headman refuse to perform his rites, no one could force him to do so. On the other hand, since lesser officials and ordinary participants are drawn from anywhere in the village, the ceremonies cannot help but pull together a number of people from various clans. In this way, participation in religious affairs, which is an important test of good Hopi citizenship, helps to weld together the inhabitants of each village.[7]

All important Hopi observances tend to be calendrical. Some may occur at any time within a given season, but others must be held at a precise time. A very small number of tribally significant rituals are held in houses, but an overwhelming majority of rites take place in kivas. These are underground chambers, roughly rectangular in shape, that can be entered only by climbing down a ladder. Each kiva has a slightly raised platform behind the ladder's base, regarded as a minor area for occasional spectators, and a lower main area in front of the ladder, where the important parts of an observance always take place.

Kiva rites vary from ceremony to ceremony, but they generally include the rearing of a temporary altar, brought piecemeal into the kiva at the proper time, the smoking of native tobacco, praying, singing to the accompaniment of shell or gourd rattles, and the manufacture of prayer-offerings that are later deposited at appropriate shrines. Sometimes, too, a man and a woman dress in costume to represent a cult's hero and heroine, dancing takes place, and medicine is brewed.

As a rule, it is relatively simple to join any secret society. All one has to do is to locate a member of the group in question, give him a handful of sacred cornmeal, and ask him to serve as one's sponsor during initiation. Another way of getting in is to stumble, by accident or design, into a place where an esoteric ritual is in progress. Whenever someone does this, the Hopi feel that the only safe way to guarantee that the intruder will not reveal what he has seen or heard is to force him to enter the society whose privacy he has violated. Customs of this sort are known to cultural anthropologists as **initiation by trespass.** Among the Hopi, participation in the proceedings of any society, whether or not one has been forcibly initiated, is completely optional.

By far the greater share of the religious activities falls to the men, although both sexes begin their careers in the same way. Ceremonial life starts when a father and mother select ceremonial parents who will put a child of eight or so into the Kachina society. The Kachina cult is open to all of the appropriate age, but parents decide

---

[7] It should not be forgotten that another tie arises from the fact that Hopi clans are exogamous. This forces each person to get a mate from an outside group and thus to establish affinal bonds and some cooperation with a clan other than his own.

if a child is to join the simple Kachina group, whose initiation procedure includes a whipping, or the more elaborate Powamu society, whose observances include admission to the Kachina cult and whose initiates are not whipped. Thereafter boys may dance as the masked figures known as Kachinas, but girls may not. In fact, unless a female happens to be called upon to act as a cultus heroine, her later ceremonial life is limited to membership in one or more of the women's societies, named Marau, Oaqöl, and Lakon.

When a boy reaches adolescence, at an age of twelve to fifteen, he may join either of two Flute societies and he may also enter the Snake or the Antelope fraternity. Several years later, whether or not he has already married, a young man is expected to go through a tribal initiation by joining any one of four concurrently held observances. After that, his ceremonial career reaches a climax when he goes into the winter solstice, or Soyal society, whose leader at Oraibi is the village chief.

In addition to the formal, calendrical rituals just mentioned, the Hopi have an indeterminate number of critical rites that are held in case of emergency. Most of these are performed by shamans or medicine men and are designed to render a field fertile, to counteract witchcraft, or to cure a sick person.

The most fundamental concept of Hopi religion is a belief in the continuity of life after death. The Hopi have many myths which purport to tell how, in the beginning, all of mankind emerged from under the ground through a hole known as the *sipapu*. It is through the self-same *sipapu* that the spirits of the dead pass into the other world. There they live much as they did on earth, but on some occasions they may revisit their former homes in the shape of clouds or Kachinas. It is in this way that the spirits of the dead may bring rain and other benefits to those who are still alive.

The Hopi keep careful track of the sun's apparent movements by having officials designated as **Sun Watchers** observe each day's sunrise from one spot. Long ago they noted that the sun each day comes up in the east and goes down in the west, and they believe that this is possible only because the sun journeys underground from west to east while it is dark on earth. Hence, daytime among the living is nighttime among the dead and vice versa. By analogy, too, winter in this world corresponds to summer in the other world, and in all regards death is looked on as the reverse of life. Yet, as day and night follow each other and as the seasons are regularly repeated, so does death follow life and life follow death. On the basis of such beliefs, the Hopi feel assured that their society and its culture will endure forever.

F. SOCIETY AND TECHNOLOGY IN THE UNITED STATES [8]

All anthropologists who have attempted to analyze contemporary life in America have been struck by the historic influences exerted by the mingling of numerous cultural elements, originally brought into this country by various immigrants, and by the part played in the past by our frontier. As several writers have pointed out, the American frontier, unlike European frontiers, was not a barrier to movement but an invitation to get away from cramped quarters or confining customs. It seems safe to assume that the mingling of many different traits of culture, which is really diffusion in action, has done much to enrich and variegate our lives and that the nature of our frontier has had a great deal to do with making us admire mobility, rugged individuality, and independence.

As American culture matured, however, an over-all stamp of sameness developed in most areas. We hear so much talk about sectionalism and the formation of subcultures that it is easy for us to forget that there is such a thing as an American and a national way of life. Practically all of us who have traveled abroad have had the experience of being recognized as Americans even when we were not aware of having done or said anything to betray our nationality.

Perhaps on account of their diverse origins and backgrounds, Americans in unfamiliar places, even within their own country, are likely to feel ill at ease unless they can establish a common bond with those around them. In conversation with strangers, many Americans strive desperately, and sometimes pathetically, to find a bit of shared experience. Did they come from the same home town or state? Did they happen to graduate from the same college?

---

[8] Sections "F" and "G" are not based on any particular book. Students who wish more data on how American anthropologists view life in the United States are advised to read C. Kluckhohn, *Mirror for Man*, New York, 1949, Chapter 9; and M. Mead, *And Keep Your Powder Dry*, New York, 1942. An interesting analysis of Americans, made by an English anthropologist, may be found in G. Gorer, *The American People: A Study in National Character*, New York, 1947.

Much that will be said about culture in the United States applies to other Euro-American nations whose ways of life are generally comparable to those of the United States of America.

Are they members of the same Greek-letter society or fraternal order? These are the kinds of questions that Americans perpetually
ask one another, no matter what their motives and no matter what
part of the country they come from.

Nowhere does the need for balancing sectional differences within
an over-all national framework stand out more clearly than in a
consideration of the distinctions between rural and urban conditions. While the countryside has made little change, comparatively
speaking, in the natural environment, the city has almost completely altered its original physical setting. Urban dwellers live almost entirely within a man-made environment, and so much has the
landscape been modified that city folk can neither raise their own
food nor secure at first hand the raw materials needed for the erec-
tion of buildings and the manufacture of garments, utensils, and
similar products. Willy-nilly, each city's population must depend for
vital supplies on rural sources beyond city limits, and the larger
the city the bigger will be the district required to service it.

Because of the greater density of urban populations, the amount
of their total knowledge is much greater than can be found within
a rural area of comparable size. This means that a higher degree of
specialization must exist in the cities and that some country residents will be drawn cityward whenever they require the services of
specialists or desire to learn a specialty. Some specialists will inevitably concentrate on arts and entertainments, which will exert another magnetic pull toward the city. Others will make improvements
in housing and various material traits, which will prove attractive
to Americans whose cultural values stress physical comforts, body
cleanliness, and the use of devices that conserve time and human
muscular energy. City dwellers, cut off from direct contact with the
natural environment, must purchase raw materials and vital necessities, so that a pattern of exchanging work for money has to be
formed. The accumulation of money is a compelling motive of
American culture, and rural folk who want to increase their dollar
earnings find themselves attracted to large cities.

America's population trend toward urbanization cannot be understood only as an aspect of material culture. Enormous changes of
social organization have always accompanied the technological advances made or enjoyed by city dwellers. To ensure and facilitate
the necessary cooperation without which hordes of specialists cannot possibly exist, each city devotes much effort to social legislation,

making rules to protect the property which specialists produce and trying to strike a balance between the cost of goods and the wages of workers. City life provides more possibilities than rural residence for social mobility, and one of the strongest cultural motivations in America is the desire of parents to have their offspring do better than themselves. Coupled with this attitude is the lack of compulsion for children to take up the same occupations as their elders. If youngsters are to advance beyond their parents, they must be encouraged to follow pursuits that hold forth the promise of greater prestige, larger money rewards, or both. Cities offer better opportunities of this nature than do rural communities, where most people are farmers and a child has little alternative but to follow in the footsteps of the parent of his sex.

One of the most telling social effects of a city environment has been the decreasing reliance on kin (despite some effort to maintain ties of relationships), and the corresponding increase of dependence on strangers. This becomes most noteworthy after an individual has begun to go to school; thereafter, he will receive less and less of his education and training from kindred. He will also depend on non-relatives to prepare his food, make his garments, protect his property, punish his transgressions, provide him with transportation, and afford him the pleasures of recreation. Residence in an urban setting rarely makes possible a concentration of kinfolk in one place and, regardless of our folk sayings about blood being thicker than water, a distant relative who is seldom seen plays little effective part in an American's life. Whether in a primitive tribe or in an American city, nearness of residence provides a potential substitute for ties of kinship. A person who lives in the country, or a native in a non-literate community, rarely has dealings with strangers, whereas an adult city dweller spends much of his waking time in their presence.

The intimate connection of technology with social affairs was brought home to the writer with startling clarity in the off-hand remark of a friend. "We worry about solving our present difficulties," he said, "and we haven't even settled the social problems of the cotton gin." If this statement is carefully studied, it reveals a train of ideas that runs something as follows. The cotton gin was invented just prior to 1800. Before that time the difficulties of clearing seeds out of cotton were so great that it was pointless to raise vast crops and, consequently, there was little need of great numbers of farm-hands. With the invention of the cotton gin, the conditions were reversed. Seeds could be quickly picked out, profits grew with the size of a yield, and there was a persistent demand for cheap labor. To meet this demand Negro slaves were imported, and it is a historic fact that virtually all American Negroes are descended from ancestors who were brought to the United States between the time of the cotton gin's invention and the beginning of the Civil War. In so far as race problems in this country concern Negroes, they may in this fashion be traced back to the cotton gin. This shows what grave social consequences may result from the introduction of a single, helpful technological item.

Although many vital aspects of interpersonal relations in the United States are directly connected with matters of urbanization and technology, there are other features of social organization that are only indirectly concerned with material culture. One of the most important of these pertains to the status of women. American males who realize that they have neglected females, because of the pressure of business or for any other reason, are likely to feel ashamed and guilty and to make acts of atonement from time to time. Nor has the granting of equal rights to women failed to produce its crop of problems. Some of them are not unrelated to technological advances. Due to the large number of wonderful inventions that have so greatly reduced the need for an outlay of human muscular strength and energy, women are able to do nearly anything non-biological that men can do, and a high percentage of our labor force is now feminine (Fig. 19.3). As a result, our educational system fluctuates between training girls for business careers or for motherhood and domestic tasks.

Equalization of women's status is directly interwoven with a change in American values. Only a few generations ago an American woman was not expected to have a career outside the home or to receive much formal schooling. In keeping with this situation, high value was attached to being a good mother and housekeeper. Women took pride in keeping their children neat and their houses spic and span, and got much pleasure from being praised for their efforts. Nowadays, mechanical implements are capable of taking so much drudgery out of a housewife's duties that she can have extra time for outside work.[9] It is considered old-fashioned for a woman

---

[9] Reliance on servants may have been equally or even more helpfully effective in reducing a housewife's duties in times past, but mechanical appliances are much more readily available to all classes of American society than servants ever were.

Fig. 19.3. American women at work. In the United States a high percentage of the work force is feminine. To the extent that they work outside, American women cannot devote themselves to their homes, husbands, and children. (Courtesy of General Electric Company.)

to have no interests outside her home and family. Social rewards go to those who play the most active parts in education and community affairs or who demonstrate the greatest skill in business or politics. After all, it is hardly to be expected that a young woman with a Ph.D. degree in astrophysics will regard keeping her children neat as her chief mission in life. With the highest honors being won in activities outside the home, American women cannot be blamed for refusing to restrict their talents to the lowly valued tasks of keeping house and children spotlessly clean.

As has already been indicated, the citizens of the United States, like the members of any other large and far-flung national unit, do not comprise a homogeneous society. What complicates the situation in America is the inconsistent way in which differences from an assumed norm may be used either to reward or punish. Yet, there is no absolute standard of behavior which can guarantee freedom from social displeasure to all who conform. In upper-class circles around Boston, a person who speaks English with Italian intonations might well be looked down upon, but one who speaks with an English accent might be admired. But in any class of Middle West society, fun may be poked at anyone who affects English mannerisms of speech.

We are equally inconsistent in regard to biological differences of race. Caucasoids who have one-sixteenth Negro blood may try to hide the fact, but those with the same amount of Indian blood may brag about it. Again, where a small percentage of Indian blood may be esteemed, a half-breed may be stigmatized. A similar lack of uniformity prevails in our attitudes toward religion. America is a Protestant Christian country, but in some districts Baptists are greatly respected and in others they are not.

Lack of consistent cultural values may lead to very tragic consequences. Throughout most aspects of American life there runs a current of emphasis on speed. "Time is of the essence," the lawyers say, and our children are frequently admonished to hurry up and not to waste time. Industrialists build automobiles capable of going faster and faster, and communities compete in building roads suitable for greater speeds. Yet, overtly, we are reluctant to admit that high speeds are responsible for so many traffic fatalities. Recently, a bright young woman who had survived the crash of a speeding car that had killed some of her companions was asked by a judge why she had consented to go on what was sure to be a wild ride. "I like speed," she replied simply. No doubt the judge was so shocked that he failed to give the young woman credit for being honestly consistent.

Another outstanding problem of American society, related to the lack of fixed standards, is the rapidity with which cultural values change. A social subgroup which has adjusted itself to one set of cultural values is disorganized and bewildered during any period of transition. Children of immigrants, who reject the ideas of right and wrong that their parents brought from a foreign country, are apt to feel uneasy until they have absorbed the values of American culture. Much the same applies to the native-born. When Professor and Mrs. Lynd studied Muncie, Indiana, during the boom years of the mid-1920's, they found the populace firmly believing in the traditonal American values of rewards for hard work, the difficulty of keeping a good man down, the notion that anyone who really wanted work could find a job, and the idea that it was a disgrace to take government relief money. About ten years later, when the Lynds came back to Muncie in a time of economic depression, they found the populace upset and in a state of transition.[10] They were in the process of being forced to give up their old system of values, but they were not yet ready to accept a new set of principles. So, the Lynds found such incongruities as people standing in line to cash government checks on which their lives depended, yet cursing the government for sponsoring the very work projects for which they were being paid.

G. AMERICAN RELIGION AND SCIENCE

Every student of modern American culture is struck by the lack of reliance on religion. Even where the number of steady churchgoers is high, the tendency is to attribute the fact to various causes, but not to a deeprooted conviction that help can be obtained from the supernatural. Unquestionably, a good part of the reason for this situation lies in the high development of science. Where controlled causation by human beings can be demonstrated, there is not much need to seek supernatural assistance. With few exceptions, scientists rather than priests, are called upon for help when people fall ill, crops fail, animals sicken, or mentalities break down. True reliance on religion is most manifest in fields like international tensions where scientists are, at present, most helpless. Until recent years, man had little prospect of regulating the weather, and prayers for relief from bad conditions were his only recourse. Today the picture in America is changing. Science is still uncertain about methods of producing rain or sunshine, but one does not have to be very bold to predict that in the near future the regulation of rainfall will move into the sphere of controlled causation, and when it does, man's reliance on the supernatural will decrease still further. A preview of this situation has already been given. Tribes in the southwestern United States, whose men formerly prayed and danced for rain, no longer hold these ceremonies now that they can get ample water by turning a faucet. Emotional and other satisfactions may continue to be sought from religious exercises, but in practical matters the rise of scientific knowledge will unfailingly result in a shrinking reliance on supernaturalism.

---

[10] R. S. and H. M. Lynd, *Middletown in Transition*, New York, 1937.

There is likewise a strong possibility that the lack of deep religiosity in the United States is related to the fact that no national religion exists in our country. Apparently, religious systems are most powerful when they are directly associated with particular social structures. In America all of the prevailing nation-wide religions were originally developed elsewhere and were tailored to conform to societies entirely different from our own. Only bits of these imported systems seem applicable to us.

American faith in science is coupled with a belief in the power of reason. In most areas of behavior we reject mysticism of any kind and make a veritable cult of being rational, according to our cherished principles of logic. Furthermore, since we like to moralize and to judge everything as good or bad, we have tended to combine this characteristic with our belief in rationality by making the assumption that whatever is reasonable is good and whatever is unreasonable is bad. On this basis we assume that people who are well-informed and reasonable are good. We are surprised and pained if a well-educated person turns out to be a scoundrel or a thief.

Education in America holds an ambivalent position. On the one hand, especially since the Russian advances into space, we worship science, technology, and material things; but on the other hand, we are likely to be suspicious of ideas as such. In fact, many Americans regard thinkers as loafers and condemn contemplation as a waste of time. Yet, one of America's greatest and most original contributions to the rest of the world has come from the realm of ideas. This is our emphasis on the importance of the common man. Not only is this idea the very cornerstone of our own democracy, but its influence has not yet run its full course in other areas of the globe.

H. COMPARISONS AND CONTRASTS

As we project American culture against the background of primitive ways of life, certain resemblances and differences immediately stand out. Sometimes our culture seems clearly superior to that of non-literates, but at other times comparison reveals unsuspected weaknesses in our sociocultural structure. When flaws show up, they cannot be remedied by a simple return to primitive conditions. Defects brought out by comparative analysis should be regarded only as diagnostic. They serve to show social scientists where remedial action is necessary, but they do not of themselves suggest what that action should be.

Americans, like all other members of *Homo sapiens,* must develop satisfactory interrelationships with their physical setting. We are, however, expanding our use of natural resources so rapidly that we are in far greater danger than is any primitive group of exhausting what nature can provide. Then, again, our infinitely larger population and our tendency to concentrate in big cities impose great strains on the few who must provide the many with the necessities of life. So far, constantly more effective ways of manipulating the environment and greatly improved means of communication have enabled us to keep going, but it is obvious that our way of dealing with our setting creates some difficult problems.

Our interpersonal relations, too, are vastly different from those found in primitive societies. We do not segment our social structure into such unilateral groups as clans, nor do we tolerate so high a degree of premarital sexual license. Yet, though we reckon kindred bilaterally, we seldom expect direct help either from our mother's side or our father's. Instead of dealing regularly with relatives, we find ourselves driven to deal with strangers.

Children, as well as older people and housewives, are differently evaluated in the United States, particularly in its large cities, than they are in the primitive world. Whereas primitive parents often regard their offspring as economic assets, not a few American parents look upon their youngsters as economic liabilities. No realist can deny that among us offspring are often unwanted, neglected, or rejected, even by legally married couples. Many social scientists realize that this is partly so because potential parents do not always care to assume the responsibility as well as the expense of rearing youngsters who will yield little in return. Fathers and mothers may even bring up and train children in such a way as to show that they fully expect them to shift for themselves as soon as they can marry and move away from home. Ironically, we may go so far as to poke fun at those who remain too long tied to parental apron strings. Among the tribal groups studied the phenomenon of unwanted, dismissed, or rejected children is unknown. Even where infanticide is practiced on occasion, the children who are allowed to live are given loving attention.

As for premarital sexual freedom, not enough is yet known about the part it plays in personality formation. There are some grounds for believing, though, that the greater lack of restraint and adult disapproval that prevails in numerous tribes, is correlated with a

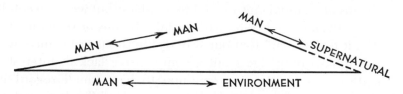

Fig. 19.4. The American way of life. The biocultural configuration that pre-vails in the United States appears unsymmetrical and disjointed. We seem to have over-elaborated man's dealings with his environment, at the expense of man's relations with man and, particularly, of man's interplay with the super-natural.

decrease of adolescent revolt against parental authority and society in general.

It is in the field of religion that some of the greatest differences exist. Like all primitive people we, too, have calendrical and critical rites. Sometimes they appear related to our ways of life, and some-times they do not. To many Americans, supernatural practices lie outside their social structures, not within them. Above all, we lack anything corresponding to a tribal initiation. As Americans, we do not feel sufficiently integrated to make up a single, perpetually in-teracting society, and we would feel at a loss to know what it was into which we were expected to initiate young people. If it were a case of training them to follow in the footsteps of their parents or to play particular roles in society, that would be another matter. But we do not expect children to live like their parents; we have neither fixed roles nor unchanging social statuses, and we would find it hard to see what supernaturalism has to do with such matters in any event.

Compared to primitive ways of life our culture seems to be terribly segmented and disjointed, particularly when it comes to supernatu-ralism. In a primitive society it is easy to see the connections of all three sides of a biocultural triangle. We do not think it peculiar that the Tikopians should pray for good weather when they plan to go to sea, while the Hopi pray for rain to aid their crops. Yet, who among us knows the relationship of our religions to economic pur-suits?

Americans have up to now given an undue amount of attention to that side of a biocultural configuration that depends on man's dealings with his environment. We have an excellent record in solving problems of material culture and technology, but we are woefully weak when it comes to dealing with social relations or religion. Consequently, it may be said that our way of life is out of balance, with an over-emphasis on gadgets but a comparative lack of interest in other matters. As long as we continue to have small regard for intellectual pursuits, we shall find it extremely difficult to put together a coherent pattern of culture that gives security to all concerned.

SELECTED REFERENCES

Firth, R., *We, the Tikopia*. New York, 1936.

Gorer, G., *The American People: A Study in National Character*. New York, 1947.

Keesing, F. M., "Culture Change," *Stanford Anthropological Series*, No. 1, Stanford and London, 1953.

Kluckhohn, C., *Mirror for Man*, Chapter 9. New York, 1949.

Lynd, R. S., and H. M., *Middletown in Transition*. New York, 1937.

Mead, M., *And Keep Your Powder Dry*. New York, 1942.

Murdock, G. P., *Our Primitive Contemporaries*. New York, 1934.

Service, E. R., *A Profile of Primitive Culture*. New York, 1958.

Thompson L., and Joseph, A., *The Hopi Way*. Lawrence, Kansas, 1944.

Titiev, M., "Old Oraibi: A Study of the Hopi Indians of Third Mesa," *Papers of the Peabody Museum of American Archaeology and Ethnology*, Vol. 22, No. 1, Cambridge, Mass., 1944.

Warner, W. L., *American Life: Dream and Reality*. Chicago, 1953.

CHAPTER 20

SOME NEW APPROACHES;

SUMMARY AND CONCLUSION

A. PREAMBLE

Until about thirty years ago, anthropologists in America were neither expected nor trained to concern themselves with large, literate societies, including their own. It then dawned upon some scholars that ethnologists working with nonliterate tribes had developed techniques that might successfully be applied wherever groups of human beings habitually lived together. First in the field was Dr. Robert Lynd, who, with his wife, Helen, and a small staff, undertook an intensive study of the city of Muncie, Indiana, in 1924. Professionally, Dr. Lynd was classed as a sociologist, but his methods combined features of sociology with cultural anthropology. The Lynds resided in the community under observation, participated in its life, conducted interviews, distributed questionnaires, analyzed newspapers, and examined census data. Throughout their stay they tried to maintain the same objectivity that a cultural anthropologist seeks to achieve while he is living with a primitive tribe. When the results were published,[1] they created a furor that soon led others to enter the promising new field which the late Clark Wissler called, "the social anthropology of contemporary life." Within a period of

---

[1] R. S. and H. M. Lynd, *Middletown: A Study of Contemporary American Culture,* New York, 1929.

431

about three decades, a great number of books have been published on various phases of life in contemporary America.

Only a few years after the appearance of *Middletown,* a very interesting group of studies was being sponsored at Harvard University. Dr. Elton Mayo, who had worked at the Fatigue Institute in England during World War I and who had become convinced of the biocultural nature of weariness, organized a research project that was carried out at the Hawthorne plant of the Western Electric Company, near Chicago. The investigations were conducted jointly by representatives of the firm and members of the Harvard School of Business Administration. One of their immediate objectives was to study the output of six girls who assembled telephone relays in a small room. Production increased as physical improvements were made in working conditions. Toward the end of the period of experimentation the working conditions were returned to the original level, yet there was no attendant drop in the number of relays assembled. Analysis showed that the girls had been organized into a team, whose pride in their work continued to make them exert themselves even when they were no longer pampered with physical comforts.[2] Other studies have supported the conclusion that working teams are sociocultural units, with integrated and cohesive elements and systems of values, such as exist in any society.

Dr. Mayo also exerted much influence on the career of W. Lloyd Warner, who had recently returned to Harvard from a long ethnological sojourn among Australian aborigines. Professor Warner was led to apply anthropological techniques to American society. With a large staff to assist him, he undertook an exhaustive study of a typical New England community in Massachusetts. The results were published in a number of volumes under the general title of "The Yankee City Series," after Professor Warner had transferred to the University of Chicago. They represent the most intensive analysis ever made of an American city and its patterns of culture. It is impossible to single out the most important contribution resulting from this project, but one of its most telling consequences was the convincing proof that social classes really exist in America, despite assertions of democracy and the belief that all men are equal. Warner and his associates found six classes in Yankee City, two

---

[2] This experiment was fully described in F. Roethlisberger and W. J. Dickson, *Management and the Worker,* Boston, 1934. It had a profound effect on labor-management relations in many industries.

Lower, two Middle, and two Upper. These were clearcut in terms of occupation, place of residence, degree of prestige, and membership in clubs and other associations. No one factor was all-important as a determinant of one's class. Doctors, for example, ranged from Lower Middle to Upper Upper, but the negative fact that money in and of itself was not decisive for membership in a social class was thoroughly demonstrated and came as a shock to some social scientists.

Since the early 1930's a great many cultural anthropologists have devoted themselves to investigations of American and other literate communities. Some have worked alone but most have worked with colleagues from other disciplines. Some have reported on an entire city; others have devoted themselves to subgroups; and some have continued to deal with organizations of workers. Out of their combined efforts has emerged a more accurate picture of America's social organization and a better grasp than had previously existed of its patterns of culture. A large number of fine studies are now available, too many to review here.[3]

Under the leadership of Professor Robert Redfield, of the University of Chicago, considerable interest has been aroused in the ways of life that are to be found in what he terms **folk societies.** These are neither primitive, as that word is customarily defined, nor are they "advanced." They resemble most nearly those communities which are sometimes labeled "peasant societies." An understanding of how they operate and change should be obtained by anyone who professes to deal with the whole species of *Homo sapiens*.

B. HUMAN ENGINEERING

Soon after the application of ethnological techniques to nonprimitive societies had been demonstrated, cultural anthropology was drawn into the arena of practical affairs. During the 1930's the Commissioner of Indian Affairs, Mr. John Collier, began to rely increasingly on anthropologists to help him revise the workings of his Bureau. Somewhat belatedly, this established a rough parallel to the British program of providing training in anthropology for co-

---

[3] Only two works will be cited, but they contain many references to other studies. See C. Kluckhohn, *Mirror for Man*, New York, 1949, Chapter 9, and W. L. Warner, *American Life: Dream and Reality*, Chicago, 1953. For further sources, see the Selected References at the end of this chapter.

lonial administrators. By the time that the United States entered World War II late in 1941, a good number of anthropologists had had some experience in dealing with practical problems as they applied to primitive peoples. Within the United States cultural anthropologists were called upon, particularly by the War Relocation Authority, to help with programs that concerned the removal of Japanese inhabitants from the Pacific coast and the administration of various relocation centers.[4] When American forces, during the Asiatic phases of the war, were brought into contact with strange tribes in remote places, it did not take long to discover that among the Americans who were most likely to have had previous experience in the regions concerned were a handful of ethnologists. Their knowledge of these spots and their experience with natives and native patterns of culture were widely drawn upon by several government agencies.

At about the same time that these activities were going on, other anthropologists continued to apply their knowledge to civilian affairs, particularly in the field of industrial relations. Spearheaded by Dr. Eliot D. Chapple, much was done to supplement and expand the findings that had been made at the Hawthorne plant, and Chapple's scheme of analyzing social situations by determining which person initiates action whenever there is contact among individuals was made part of the conceptual framework.[5] Dr. Chapple states that his basic assumption for an understanding of human relations in industry is that attitudes, emotional reactions, and productivity are functions of the interactional situation, which represents an interplay of personality and culture. Improvements are made either by putting people with personality problems into different interactional systems or else by changing some aspect of the culture pattern within which a person works. Dr. Chapple's approach is based on his awareness that workers in a large industrial plant form a sociocultural unit with its own system of values, coupled with the knowledge that changes in one segment of a biocultural configuration are likely to bring about alterations in the other parts. He thus finds it possible to introduce material innovations, such as modifying a layout, with the intention of causing subtle changes in an indi-

---

[4] For an important work on this subject, see A. H. Leighton, *The Governing of Men*, Princeton, 1946.

[5] A good summary and review of anthropological techniques for studying industrial relations is to be found in E. D. Chapple, "Applied Anthropology in Industry," *Anthropology Today* (A. L. Kroeber, ed.), Chicago, 1953, pp. 819-831. Dr. Chapple uses a machine, the Interaction Chronograph, which provides accurate statistical data.

vidual's personal relations, usually without the subject's knowing what has happened.

Another group of anthropologists, more directly under Professor Warner's leadership, has entered the field of industrial relations, chiefly in the Chicago area. They do not use Dr. Chapple's methods but they also base their work on anthropological concepts of social and cultural structure. Much of what they do is related to psychological techniques of interviewing and counseling. Large industrial concerns have found the services of various kinds of applied anthropologists to be so valuable that members of this branch of the profession earn higher salaries than their academic colleagues.

Other cultural anthropologists have recently been advocating the improvement of living conditions among various groups of aborigines who are still to be found in the New World. They call their program **action anthropology,** and their principal leader is Professor Sol Tax, of the University of Chicago. **Action anthropologists** are concerned with such problems as the betterment of prevailing conditions on reservations, in terms of what the natives themselves want.

C. A BACKWARD GLANCE AT THE SCIENCE OF MAN

Throughout the last century an impressive amount of work has been done in all branches of anthropology. When a massive stockpile of knowledge had been accumulated, an unfailing law of cultural growth went into effect and an increasing number of specialists arose. Much is to be gained from such a development, for specialists always refine existing techniques and learn to use them in ways that bring to light previously unsuspected facts and that make possible fresh interpretations of data and the formulation and testing of new hypotheses and theories. Counterbalancing the advantages is the great danger of disintegration resulting from the threatened separation of parts that were once found together. As is true of so many other sciences, anthropology is faced with the possibility of fragmentation or dismemberment. Already there are archeologists and ethnologists who know little of each other's work and physical anthropologists who cannot understand an essay on primitive linguistics. This book seeks, among other things, to demonstrate that all segments of the science of man belong together and contribute to a total understanding of the human species and its cultural behavior.

No matter from which direction one chooses to approach the study of anthropology, it soon becomes apparent that the thing called culture cannot exist without mankind. No other animal can develop it, live by it, or maintain its existence by transmitting it through education from one generation to another. It is true that for purposes of certain theoretical analyses one can separate culture from its carriers, but this does not apply to the study of its beginnings. There is no means of understanding how culture arose without taking into account the ways in which the biology of *Homosapiens* differs from that of other animals who ade devoid of culture. And since man did not come by his body suddenly, it becomes necessary to examine the process of evolution by means of which the human figure acquired its unique characteristics. Most of the biological material in this text has been included with a view to clarifying the steps by which man came to have a distinctive body, one capable of devising and continuing culture. Once that stage was reached, we find mankind dividing into a number of stocks and races, every one of which is equally capable of symbolic cultural behavior. As far as is known, *Homo sapiens,* in spite of its diversity of forms, is truly a single species within which interbreeding may take place without biologically harmful consequences.

Having brought the story of man to the point where culture begins, we next took up the record of cultural progress through time. Archeologists have been able to prove that after a painfully slow start in the Old Stone Age, there was a gradual speeding up of new developments in the Middle Stone Age, followed by rapid acceleration, which became the rule throughout the Metal Ages and has continued into our own day. Not until cultural progress had matured over many millennia did it reach a stage where it could provide mankind with an alternative to biological behavior. As cultural devices became more and more fitted for coping with life, man came to rely on them increasingly, sometimes to supplement his biology and, occasionally, to take its place. Just the same, man has had to continue obeying the biological imperatives. There have been times when men took pride in claiming that they had triumphed over their physical bodies and animal natures, but the facts reveal that such claims must be understood to have been figurative. What seems to be the case is that human beings everywhere have chosen to convert biological activities to biocultural processes. This they have done by introducing symbolic cultural values which call for the